Cruel and Unusual

ALSO BY MARK CRISPIN MILLER

Boxed In: The Culture of TV
Seeing Through Movies (ed.)
The Bush Dyslexicon: Observations on a National Disorder

Cruel and

BUSH/CHENEY'S NEW WORLD ORDER

Unusual

Mark Crispin Miller

W. W. NORTON & COMPANY

NEW YORK · LONDON

First published as a Norton paperback 2005

For information about permission to reproduce selections from this book,
write to Permissions, W. W. Norton & Company, Inc., 500 Fifth Avenue,
New York, NY 10110

Manufacturing by Quebecor World, Fairfield

Book design by Chris Welch

Production manager: Anna Oler

Library of Congress Cataloging-in-Publication Data

Miller, Mark Crispin.
Cruel and unusual : Bush/Cheney's new world order /
Mark Crispin Miller.—1st ed.
p. cm.
Includes bibliographical references.
ISBN 0-393-05917-0 (cloth)
1. United States—Politics and government—2001– 2. Bush, George W.
(George Walker), 1946– —Political and social views. 3. Cheney, Richard B.—
Political and social views. 4. Political culture—United States. 5. Democracy—
United States. 6. Conservatism—United States. 7. United States. Constitution.
8. Mass media—Political aspects—United States. 9. Talk shows—Political
aspects—United States. I. Title.
E902.M55 2004
973.931—dc22   2004002574

ISBN 0-393-32678-0 pbk.

W. W. Norton & Company, Inc.
500 Fifth Avenue, New York, N.Y. 10110
www.wwnorton.com

W. W. Norton & Company Ltd.
Castle House, 75/76 Wells Street, London W1T 3QT

1 2 3 4 5 6 7 8 9 0

For Lou and Billy

Contents

Acknowledgments

A full account of the Bush regime's betrayal of America's ideals would fill several volumes, and would no doubt require a lot more legal expertise than I possess. To make the partial case that I have made was challenging enough; and I would certainly have found the task impossible if many people had not aided me.

My editor, Starling Lawrence, was exemplary: unfailingly supportive of this project, tolerant of my perfectionism, and a master stylist, ever capable of strengthening a sentence or an argument. His assistant, Morgen Van Vorst, as courteous as she is competent, is a delight to work with. I want especially to thank Emma Parry, my peerless agent, who, while handling all the necessary business with aplomb, always sees to it that I do my best; and I am grateful also to her colleague, Byrd Leavell, who is as able as they come and a true pal.

My research assistant, Danielle Holke, has been extraordinarily helpful—ever accurate, resourceful, sensible, and prompt as she contended with my hundreds of inquiries, some of them a little sketchy. Maia Cowan, proprietor of failureisimpossible.com, also showed great kindness and astuteness in answering scores of queries that I could not bring myself to add to Danielle's burden; Maia also was an edifying reader. My dear friend Stef Cannon was another who took time on my behalf, giving me not only further information but also the benefit of her lucid editorial judgment (and sharp eye: Stef spotted the revealing photograph that's on the cover of this book). Matt Roush came through at the eleventh hour, at considerable inconvenience to himself. And my good buddy Josh Ozersky was a life-saver. I was also aided greatly by Mark Karlin of BuzzFlash.com, Bob Fertik of democrats.com, Bob Somerby of The Daily Howler, Jerry Politex of BushWatch, William Rivers Pitt at truthout.com, the guys at DemocraticUnderground.com, Ms. X at media whoresonline.com, Tom Englehardt at www.TomDispatch.com, and Alice Cherbonnier of the *Baltimore Chronicle*. Don Hazen of AlterNet provided me with indispensable assistance. I also owe a special debt to David Clennon.

Through two online threads devoted to discussions of *The Bush Dyslexicon* (one on Salon's Table Talk, the other on the People's Forum), I have made dozens of good friends who know their way around the cyberuniverse, and who have never failed to help when I have asked my pesky questions. Although I thank them all, I have the space here to name just a few: Denis Wright, Doug Watt, Chuck Lawhorn, P. Glass, mbroglio, didius falco, Mrs. P, Doxieone, DKNJ, dsduryea, ShannyFan, Aleta S., Zan, Brad, seas, S. Todd, Elaine Supkis, and Phoenix Woman.

A lot of off-line friends have also been, as ever, generous with their time and knowledge. I thank Robert W. McChesney, Jim Naureckas and Janine Jackson of Fairness and Accuracy in Reporting (FAIR), Charles Sheehan-Miles of Veterans for Common Sense, Todd Gitlin, Theresa Aiello, Roses Prichard, Marilyn Young, Mark Gery, William Benzon, Morgan Pillsbury, Chip Berlet, Sidney Blumenthal, Ken Sawyer, and Joe Conason. Karla Hale and Archer Irby have enabled me to weather the peculiar crisis of this book's completion, and Doris Friedman has enlightened me immensely. I am especially grateful to my friend Ted Magder, chair of the Department of Culture and Communication at New York University, and also thank my other excellent colleagues there.

While writing *Cruel and Unusual*, I have been doing a stage show on the danger of Bush/Cheney. As it has influenced this book, I want to thank Antonio Soddu, without whose inventiveness and drive there would have been no show; Marc Posnock and Steve Kraftsow, with Antonio the original producers; my costar Steve Cuiffo; and Caryn Cline. I owe a special debt of gratitude to Gregory Keller, my director and my guru in the world of theater. I am particularly grateful to Jim Nicola, Lynn Moffat, Linda Chapman, and Tom Pearson at the New York Theater Workshop, where I have had the privilege of performing.

For their close readings of the manuscript and for their wise advice, I want to thank my dear old friends Ross Posnock, Rochelle Gurstein, and Jackson Lears. I also warmly thank my parents, Jordan and Anita Miller, for their editorial guidance and spiritual support, and my brothers, Bruce and Eric. And once again, I thank my wise and often silent mentor, Fritz von Spüchen.

Finally, I can only start to thank the matchless Amy Smiley, my dear wife and closest friend, lately serving as the best of editors. Such sweetness, subtle humor, high intelligence, and analytic penetration would make quite a brilliant combination under any circumstances. In times like these, to know her and live with her is a blessing that cannot be overestimated.

Preface to the
Paperback Edition

Today in the United States, the highest crimes are somehow less offensive than it is to talk about them publicly. A president "elected" by judicial fiat; "preemptive war" put over by official lies; tax dollars used to fund religious groups that proselytize; "free speech" confined to "First Amendment zones"; vital covert operations blown deliberately to punish disagreement with the White House; foreign nationals arrested without charges and indefinitely jailed; untold thousands tortured by U.S. troops and contractors, or sent to other nations to be tortured; Americans searched and arrested, conversations bugged and transactions monitored without a warrant; seemingly independent journalists paid surreptitiously to spout the party line; and so on. All such doings are profoundly un-American. If George Washington or Thomas Jefferson—or Andrew Jackson, Abe Lincoln, Teddy Roosevelt, Harry Truman, or Dwight Eisenhower—were to come back here today and take a look around, he wouldn't recognize the place.

The great Americans of yesteryear would speak out readily against Bush/Cheney's manifold betrayal of America's ideals; not to do so would be un-American. But such patriotic candor would be loudly booed in this new nation under Bush, where all the old republican ideas now sound courageously subversive, or heretical. "To announce that there must be no criticism of the President, or that we should stand by the President, right or wrong, is not only unpatriotic and servile, but is

morally treasonable to the American republic." If Teddy Roosevelt were
to say that now on Fox or on the air with Michael Savage, he would be
accused of treason. Of course, there have been moments of such noisy
public paranoia throughout this nation's history; but never have we had
a government so criminal, nor has it ever seemed so dangerous to challenge
those in power. Bush's partisans are outraged not, say, by the regime's gross
mistreatment of our soldiers and our veterans, or the grand annulment of
our civil liberties, but by anyone who dares to bring such subjects up.

This dark conundrum is particularly glaring on the right, and has
intensified since mid-2003, when the occupation of Iraq stopped making cheery news on the home front. However, the refusal to acknowledge
Bush & Co.'s fascistic drive—that impulse to assail the regime's critics
rather than its crimes—is *not* apparent only on "the right," i.e., inside
the Bizarro Universe of Fox News Channel and the House of Representatives. Nor did that impulse start to thunder only after 9/11, but was
apparent from the start of Bush's reign. "The liberal media" has turned a
blind eye to Bush/Cheney's un-American activities right from the get-go,
as I have sought to demonstrate both in this book and in *The Bush
Dyslexicon*, which appeared in the summer of 2001.

So it was no surprise that both books met with brickbats from "the
liberal media." The *Washington Post*'s reviewer, for example, found *The
Bush Dyslexicon* self-evidently off the wall. He objected hotly to my readings of the president's impromptu oratory, judging them both unpersuasive and without "interpretative charity": "There is no gaffe that cannot
be interpreted to show Bush's woeful 'uninterestedness,' 'callousness,'
'ignorance,' 'inability to reason,' 'incoherence'—or his 'absolute unfit-
ness' to be president." If that weren't bad enough, "Miller's jeremiad also
extends to the media," whose honesty and fearlessness, like Bush's learning, sensitivity, eloquence, and wisdom, are somehow beyond question.

> The transparent awfulness of the Bush candidacy went unscruti-
> nized, Miller argues, because—"subtly guided by propagandists of
> the right"—the television media showed itself to be "fatally dyslexic
> when it comes to doping out the very spectacle that it presents." In
> conjunction with the actions of the "sedentary putschists of the

Supreme Court," the GOP and the major media forced Bush on us. *The Bush Dyslexicon* demonstrates that left-wing media criticism can be every bit as cartoonish as that from the right.

Such broadsides only reconfirm the argument that they purport to crush, as they do not tell us why, or how, the argument is wrong. Bush *was* installed precisely as that passage says, however sneeringly one might rephrase it. Thus "the liberal media" often struggles to dismiss the truth, relying not on observation, evidence, and logic, but on a fuming rhetoric of debunkment: mere scornful paraphrase irately sprinkled with outrageous-seeming snippets of the text.* So did the *New York Times Book Review* dismiss *Cruel and Unusual* in a dyspeptic screed entitled "The New Pamphleteers," which labored to impugn "a slew" of recent books on Bush—both pro and con—by casting them as equally uncouth and ill-informed. Having started by decrying Ann Coulter's Nazi repartee, the reviewer cast his unforgiving gaze across the moral universe: "Coulter's style of attack politics, while still far ahead of the pack in the violence of its language, is no longer confined to the right," he asserted, then turned to *Cruel and Unusual*, which he thus hastily dispatched:

> Miller, who teaches media studies at New York University, dangles the possibility that the Bush-Cheney team took no action on intelligence warnings in the months leading up to 9/11 because it "chose to let those horrors happen for its own political advantage." Bush Republicans, Miller writes, are "genuine subversives"; "more than the Islamists," their aim "is to undo the framers' work, and force an alien form of government on the United States."

The aim here was to make this book sound like a piece of North Korean propaganda, or a communiqué from Shining Path guerrillas. Such is the effect of being defined as Ann Coulter's leftist counterpart. The reviewer then added to that charge of rollicking maliciousness by implying that this book deals chiefly with the Bush regime's collusion in the terrorist attacks on 9/11. It was a misleading suggestion, as the book

---

*Or snippets nowhere in the text. The word "uninterestedness" is a neologism absent from *The Bush Dyslexicon*.

merely touches on that issue in a brief aside, and with a carefulness not evident in the quotation.* Because the simmering controversy over 9/11 seldom has been mentioned by the U.S. media, it tends to seem far-fetched to those Americans not tracking it. Therefore, to imply that 9/11 is my chief concern is to locate this book somewhere beyond the far horizon, where strange, pale folks disport themselves forever on the grassy knoll. With the reader thus invited to keep smirking, the review seeks to finish off my argument with this blunt paraphrase—which is quite accurate, albeit over-simple, and obscured by the sarcastic context: "Bush Republicans, Miller writes, are 'genuine subversives'; 'more than the Islamists,' their aim 'is to undo the framers' work, and force an alien form of government on the United States.'"

The purpose of *Cruel and Unusual* was indeed to make that case, which I believe it does, without hyperbole and with abundant evidence. The *Times* failed to mention my supporting evidence, or the evidence presented by the several other books that the reviewer likewise damned, ostensibly for their "ugliness of language and unpersuasive fury": Lewis Lapham's *Gag Rule*, David Brock's *The Republican Noise Machine*, Arianna Huffington's *Fanatics and Fools*, Nicholas von Hoffman's *Hoax*,

---

*The section quoted deals not with the theory of Bush/Cheney's terrorist collusion, but with the simple question as to why the White House "took no preventive steps whatever prior to 9/11, even though they had been clearly and repeatedly forewarned throughout the summer of 2001." Here then is the offending clause in its full context: "It is quite possible, of course, that Bush/Cheney chose to let those horrors happen for its own political advantage—a chilling theory for which there is abundant evidence. But if they had no such dark motive, their inaction at that moment would be wholly typical, as they have always been impervious to warnings in the public interest" (p. 48).

Thus the regime's possible complicity in 9/11 was no wild invention of my own, but the subject of some careful studies, including Nafeez Mossadeq Ahmed's *The War on Freedom* (Joshua Tree, CA: Tree of Life Publications, 2002) and David Griffin's *The New Pearl Harbor* (Adlestrop, UK: Arris Books, 2004). Also highly edifying is the 9/11 timeline, managed by Paul Thompson of the Center for Cooperative Research (http://www.cooperativeresearch.org/project.jsp?project=911_project). My aside is but a nod to such impressive works—which, of course, the mainstream does not recognize, preferring to regard such troubling research as a sign of paranoid delusion.

T. D. Allman's *Rogue State*, and Michael Moore's *Stupid White Men*.*
Despite their ideological diversity and sound documentation, the *Times*
identifies these writings—"shoddily researched and poorly argued"—
with the univocal propaganda diatribe of Ann Coulter and such other
little Foxes as John Gibson, Bill O'Reilly, and Sean Hannity. It is a dismissive tactic not peculiar to that one review, of course, and not peculiar
to the *New York Times*. Such glib equation is a venerable means of bol-
stering the status quo, however unacceptable, against the threat of any
serious critique. It offers not enlightenment but comfort, by evoking a
fictitious "middle ground" in which all stolid citizens can huddle and
attempt to feel serene, despite that hard rain coming down on everyone.

Thus does the U.S. press today—or "liberal media"—routinely shirk
its constitutional duty to the people, by turning a blind eye to the ever-
growing threat of Christo-fascist domination here and elsewhere. To har-
rumph at all unpleasant truths and turn away with that convenient cry,
"A plague on both your houses!" is not to show due journalistic caution
but to abdicate responsibility, and, tacitly, to counsel silence. Through
such quietism does the Fourth Estate, with few exceptions, now play a
constabulary role throughout the reign of Bush & Co., engaging in a
daily exercise of pseudo-centrist crowd control: "Move along, everybody!" it keeps telling us. "There's nothing here to see!" This is, in effect,
collaboration; for the civic wrongs committed by the Christo-fascist
right today are *not* apparent "on both sides," any more than "both sides"
were equally at fault in Hitler's Europe, or in Stalin's empire, or on the
slave ships and plantations of America before the Civil War, or in Spain
or Rome under the Inquisition.

Where the center has not held, there is no virtue in centrism, nor does
it make sense to counsel "even-handedness," discretion, caution, or any
other such evasive pose. This book describes a mortal threat to our
democracy, and to the welfare of the world—and it deals only with the
evidence available before Election Day 2004. Since *Cruel and Unusual*
first appeared, the theocratic movement has made giant strides on every

---

*The review includes some passing words of praise for John W. Dean's *Worse Than
Watergate* and Eric Alterman's *What Liberal Media?*

front. U.S. troops inflict religious torture on their Muslim prisoners (who may or may not have committed crimes), and do so with the blessings of the government. Darwin's theory is belittled or suppressed throughout our schools, and even Hollywood dares not make documentaries that may appear to contradict creationism. Congress baldly violates the Constitution and the doctrine of states' rights—and even "family values"—in its relentless efforts to cut off the judicial branch, or fill it with blunt theocrats, so that it will not thwart the movement's plans. And there is copious evidence, much of it on the public record, that this last election was—yes—rigged, through a well-planned national campaign to cut the Kerry vote, and hype the Bush vote, by any and all means, in states from coast to coast.

So many and so brazen are the crimes of this regime that it can easily seem quite impossible even to keep track of them, much less investigate them, then somehow prosecute them. And yet the place for most of us to start is not with this or that particular misdeed, but with the recognition that our rights have been repealed, our national heritage disgraced, and that we Americans no longer live in a democracy. We do, however, have the right to see that that's the case, and the obligation, as Americans, to change it.

—Mark Crispin Miller
New York, 2005

Introduction

"The beginning of the words of his mouth is foolishness: and the end of his talk is mischievous madness."

—ECCLESIASTES 10:13

O n Independence Day of 2001, back when it was still permissible—indeed, obligatory—to mock the president's substandard English, Bush visited the Jefferson Memorial, ostensibly to venerate the Father of American Democracy. "What does the Fourth mean to you, Mr. President?" a reporter asked him. "Well," he replied, "it's an unimaginable honor to be the president during the Fourth of July in this country." He continued:

> It means what these words say, for starters: the great "inalienable rights" of our country. We're blessed with such values in America. And I—it's—I'm a proud man to be the nation based upon such wonderful values.
>
> I can't tell you what it's like to be in Europe, for example, to be talking about the greatness of America. But the true greatness of America are the people.

At the time, it seemed to be a typical "Bushism"—just one more flight of gibberish from the president, who, we knew by then, would often say the darnedest things off-script. To his detractors, such slips were comic proof of his stupidity. To Bush's true believers, on the other hand, and to those middling folks still hoping that he might be who he said he was, the presidential bloopers were endearing signs of folksy unpretentiousness.

Both notions are mistaken. As I have argued in *The Bush Dyslexicon*, the presidential tongue goes haywire mainly when it's forced to tackle subjects that Bush finds boring or offensive. He just can't fake it when it comes to talking peace ("I will use our military as a last resort, and our first resort"), or education ("We want results in every single classroom so that one single child is left behind!"), or nation-building ("It'll take time to restore chaos and order" in Iraq), or unemployment ("One of the problems we have is that enough people can't find work in America"), or conservation ("We need an energy bill that encourages consumption"), or relief for those oppressed abroad ("We're freeing women and children from incredible impression!"), or caring for the needy here at home ("The goals for this country are a compassionate American for every single citizen").

On the other hand, Bush has no trouble talking tough: "We're not into nation-building. We're focused on justice. And we're going to get justice." "The evil ones think they can hide. They think they can run." "There are no shades of gray. Either you're with the United States of America or you're against the United States of America." "Bring 'em on." Trying to discuss domestic issues or extol the arts of peace, the president can't help but lurch and stumble often, as his heart is just not in it; but, generally, the thought of war or vengeance limbers up his tongue, working on his system like a good stiff drink. When extemporizing as a *punisher*, in short, the man has always been coherent, first as a candidate and then as president.*

Now that we have had the Bush regime installed despite the will of the electorate, and as we face Bush/Cheney's run for "reelection" after 9/11, we should take especial notice that the president cannot speak standard English when he tries to talk about American democracy. His effort at the Jefferson Memorial was not just laughable but inadvertently revealing, as it betrayed Bush/Cheney's animus against our democratic institutions and their contempt for our inalienable rights. Conversely,

---

*He can also hold his own when talking politics or baseball; and on the subject of his property in Texas, Bush is always clear, and sometimes even eloquent. Only through the formulas of evangelistic oratory can this president speak comprehensibly about compassion, love, etc.

Bush has always spoken clearly when the subject is his one-man rule. "I'm the commander," he told Bob Woodward in the summer of 2002.

> See, I don't need to explain—I do not need to explain why I say things. That's the interesting thing about being the president. Maybe somebody needs to explain to me why they say something, but I don't feel like I owe anybody an explanation.

Concerning the decision to invade Iraq, on December 13, 2002, Bush said to Barbara Walters, "There's only one person who is responsible for making that decision, and that's me." And on New Year's Eve a few weeks later, Bush answered a reporter's question (about "the possibility of war looming in Iraq") with this rebuke:

> You said we're headed to war in Iraq. I don't know why you say that. I hope we're not headed to war in Iraq. I'm the person who gets to decide, not you.

More than merely egotistical, such utterances betray Bush/Cheney's autocratic view of Bush's power. "There's only one person responsible for making that decision, and that's me." According to the U.S. Constitution (Article I, Section 8), the Senate, not the president, is "responsible for making that decision," and Bush's claim that "I do not need to explain why I say things" would be more appropriate if he were not the president of the United States but the emperor of China, or the founder of his own religion.* Bush appears to have been driven slightly mad, or madder, by his exalted status after 9/11, as, until that fatal day, he had not often postured with the orb and scepter (not in public, anyway).

Although somewhat more subdued in his first year, however, this president has had the wrong idea for quite some time. According to his friends, Bush took to politics because, he said, God wanted him to throw his halo in the ring. And on the day before he was inaugurated, he said this: "In 24 hours I have the highest honor, and that's to become the commander in chief of the greatest nation in the world." That would have been true, perhaps, if we were living under martial law; but as the

---

*Such grandiosity provoked no comment from Bob Woodward or Barbara Walters.

Constitution has it (Article II, Section 2), the president is *not* commander in chief *of the nation*, but only of the nation's armed forces, and not unless the nation is at war.

In short, this Bush, despite his team's incessant propaganda and inordinate secretiveness, has always been an open book—and it is not a book that any of the Constitution's framers would have found appealing. When Bush *has* spoken more or less coherently about "democracy," it is because the system he describes is no more democratic than the regimes in Zimbabwe, Pakistan, or Cuba:

> That's the great thing about a democracy: occasionally there is a chance for the voters to express their belief or disbelief. I guess that chance will be coming down the road one of these days.

That "the voters" have "a chance," now and then, "to express their belief or disbelief" is a feature of dictatorships, which do "occasionally" hold plebiscites so as ostensibly to let the populace say "yea" or "nay" (and, somehow, it's always "yay!"). The same despotic bias is no less apparent in the second sentence, which folksily implies that we just *might* have such a "chance"—i.e., election—maybe not on the appointed day but . . . later, when all "evildoers" are gone and "the homeland" is at last secure.

The current crisis is more serious than Bush's wish to broaden his authority. Many presidents have craved more power. Our unprecedented problem is that Bush & Co.* is intent not just on fortifying the presidency, as did, say, FDR. The regime's goal is to abort American democracy and to impose on the United States another kind of government entirely. The regime, in other words, is *not* conservative, but one that every true conservative should find repugnant. Not being conservative, moreover, Bush & Co. is finally inexplicable in standard leftist terms, as an order driven purely by material or economic motives. It is indeed

---

*Throughout this book, I use "Bush & Co." as a singular, and "Bush/Cheney" as a plural noun.

imperialistic, but its imperialism is not rational, like Rome's or Britain's; for Bush/Cheney's mission is not only antidemocratic *and* antirepublican, but fundamentally apocalyptic, and so it poses a grave threat not just to this republic, but to peoples everywhere and to the entire planet.

It is to define that threat that I write once again about this president. "Sometimes that's where you want your opponent, half asleep," Bush told a supportive crowd in Arkansas, just before the midterm races in 2002. There he was quite right, as he often is when talking politics. We should take him at his word and finally wake up to the fact that his regime is un-American—as the framers would have recognized at once. In 1799, amid the crisis over the Alien and Sedition Acts, James Madison made the following observation, which he offered up as one of two "momentous truths"* that must be "deeply engraven on the American mind":

> That *the fetters imposed on liberty at home have ever been forged out of the weapons provided for defence against real, pretended, or imaginary dangers from abroad.*

History would often reconfirm the wisdom of that truth—sometimes catastrophically. Long after 1799, a very different sort of politician echoed Madison's sage warning, albeit in a spirit not of democratic admonition but of nihilistic cynicism. Sweating in his cell at Nuremberg on the evening of April 18, 1946, Hermann Goering made this point about the masses, whether their government be democratic or authoritarian:

> Voice or no voice, the people can always be brought to do the bidding of the leaders. All you have to do is tell them they are being attacked and denounce the pacifists for lack of patriotism and exposing the country to danger. It works the same way in any country.

Thus has Bush & Co. become all-powerful since 9/11, exploiting that convenient horror to speed their domination of the federal government

---

*For Madison's other "truth," concerning the threat posed to democracy by standing armies, see p. 17. Both appear in his anonymous essay "Political Reflections," published in the *Aurora General Advertiser* on February 23, 1799.

in every branch, and to intimidate the press into respectful silence.* Under such a threat, all those who really love this country are obliged to resurrect the legacy of Jefferson and Madison, so that this antidemocratic counter-thrust does not prevail. To return to those republican ideals, we must, of course, remember them—a task that sometimes feels intolerably lonely in the culture of TV, especially now that the United States is ruled by one extremist party. Opposed to the republican ideal that drove our founding revolution, Bush/Cheney would prefer that we forget about it, and so it is our patriotic obligation to emancipate this nation from them, by whatever means the Constitution will allow.

*On October 27, 2003, Senator Robert C. Byrd (D-W.V.) quoted Goering's statement in an excoriating Senate speech that likened Bush & Co.'s political success to the collective self-delusion satirized in the fairy tale "The Emperor's New Clothes." The speech was mentioned only in a few newspaper editorials—and not a single U.S. news outlet reported that the eldest member of the U.S. Senate compared Bush/Cheney's use of 9/11 to the propaganda practice of the Nazis.

Cruel and Unusual

Nations reel and stagger on their way; they make hideous mistakes; they commit frightful wrongs; they do great and beautiful things. And shall we not best guide humanity by telling the truth about all this, so far as the truth is ascertainable?

—W. E. B. DUBOIS, 1935

CHAPTER 1

"The bright constellation which has gone before us"

The U.S. Constitution is today unknown in the United States, although we still claim to regard it with a certain reverence. By this I do not mean that only legal scholars and historians, and a few militia members, know what's in the document, while "the average person" doesn't have a clue because he hasn't done the reading. Although it is certainly the case that most Americans don't know our Constitution, this ignorance is not a consequence of insufficient study. Back in Andrew Jackson's time, Americans in general were thoroughly familiar with the Constitution, but not, Tocqueville observed, because they were more bookish in those days. Ask him about Europe, Tocqueville wrote, and the American will "probably display much presumption and very foolish pride," and air "those crude and vague notions which are so useful to the ignorant all over the world." He added:

> But if you question him respecting his own country, the cloud that dimmed his intelligence will immediately disperse; his language will become as pure and precise as his thoughts. He will inform you what his rights are and by what means he exercises them; he will be able to point out the customs which obtain in the political world. You will find that he is well acquainted with the rules of the administration, and that he is familiar with the mechanism of the laws.

It was not by reading that such able democrats learned how to rule themselves. "The citizen of the United States does not acquire his practical science and his positive notions from books," wrote Tocqueville, who observed a kind of self-instruction far more thrilling and effective than mere study:

> The American learns to know the laws by participating in the act of legislation; and he takes a lesson in the forms of government from governing. The great work of society is forever going on before his eyes and, as it were, under his hands.

Americans have long since lost that civic aptitude. Here in the culture of TV, where all you need to do is shop, or dream of shopping, and where labor is increasingly a push-this-key routine, there is as little call for us to govern as there is for us to make our children's clothes or churn the butter. Of course, despite so vast a change, Americans still ought to know their rights, "the rules of the administration" and "the mechanism of the laws"—knowledge that could also be conveyed, albeit abstractly, in our schools, if they would try to do that job. And yet the nation's classrooms, by and large, don't bother much with civics. Even in well-funded schools, private or taxpayer-supported, the general study of our history and government is comfortably vague and cheery, as if a robust intellectual introduction to American democracy might be a little *too* illuminating for the students' parents, the community, the Board of Education, the governor, state legislature, textbook publishers, pressure groups, and all the other interests that weigh in on what Americans should know. Because of such widespread political correctness, especially rampant in this endless time of war, it is difficult even for those teachers who are so inclined to plumb the Constitution thoroughly, because the history of that document concerns the democratic use of power, a subject that seems to make some good Americans uneasy.

Such robust education would raise questions too complex, and issues too disquieting, for the sort of superficial overview and tacit reassurance that most U.S. high schools use to tranquilize their student bodies. It isn't just that many teachers, having been ill-taught themselves, are not prepared for vigorous debate about American democracy. Civic education serves little purpose in a nation of consumers, as Americans in general are several worlds away from that republican democracy whose citizens—i.e., those enfranchised—took part daily in "the great work of society." Such civic work is almost inconceivable today, for U.S. politics is nothing but a spectacle with which we have no more connection than we do with any other fiction or nonfiction on TV. Most of us have been completely depoliticized in ways that would have horrified Samuel Adams and James Madison, although it's fine with, say, John Ashcroft and Ralph Reed. To bring this up, to make this clear, would ask a lot of any good American, who naturally prefers to be amused, encouraged, awed, or otherwise distracted from the sense of helplessness and boredom that afflict so many of us living day to day in this once promising, now nominal democracy. Better, maybe, not even to think about the Constitution than to be reminded of what we, the people, do *not* have—and *cannot* buy—today.

And so the Constitution is unknown in the United States, and not just by the folks at home who read *People* and *Parade* and watch TV, but also—or, perhaps, especially—by the privileged ones who write for *People* and *Parade* and make the TV shows, the news included. It is unknown, with a few exceptions, by the editors and writers of our major daily newspapers; unknown, with a few exceptions, by the U.S. professoriate and other "knowledge workers" who comprise America's intelligentsia; unknown, with very few exceptions, by the politicians in our states' and nation's capitals and by the members of the U.S. military. Indeed, although the Constitution has ostensibly empowered them, those currently managing the U.S. government seem wholly unfamiliar with it; or, perhaps, they know it all too well and therefore work around it—or against it—while the rest of us read *People* or the *New York Times*, or listen to Rush Limbaugh or *All Things Considered*.

In claiming that our national charter is unknown in the United States, I do not mean to say that Americans know absolutely nothing of the document. Certain of our fellow citizens are experts on specific constitutional issues; and so there are large blocs of activists that do know this or that bit of the Constitution very well and are adept at arguing it their way.

Take the Second Amendment: "A well regulated militia, being necessary to the security of a free state, the right of the people to keep and bear arms, shall not be infringed." Does this odd quadripartite sentence mean that there should be no standing army, but an orderly militia whose members must be free to "keep and bear" the arms that the defense of liberty and property requires? Or does it simply mean that each and every U.S. citizen is free to stockpile his own arsenal of Glocks, Magnums, Uzis, Stinger missiles, and any other weapon he would like to have on hand or hidden in his coat? This question has long absorbed the energies of several million citizens on either side of the debate.

Such commitment is exemplary; and yet so tight a focus on one passage in the text does not require, or entail, a proper knowledge of the Constitution—by which I mean a full awareness of its *purpose*, which is finally not at all unclear. Of course, the text is full of ambiguities, owing largely to the document's great age. A governmental charter crafted during the Enlightenment must sometimes seem quite unrelated to postmodern life, whose many innovations—multinational corporations, biotechnology, cybersex, "smart wars," touch-screen voting, cable news—would have left the framers gaping. Nor is the Constitution's meaning always plain, the text often requiring, as James Madison advised, that we also study the deliberations of its authors. But it is possible to know the Constitution without need of scholarly assistance, just as it is possible to know the Sermon on the Mount without a doctorate in theology or a personal relationship with Jesus. While there is much to argue over in our Constitution (as there has been from the start), there is no rational argument against its basic purpose: to maintain the power and freedom of the people through a system that will not enable despotism or degenerate into a tyranny of the majority. Only such a system, Thomas Jefferson believed, would honor the progressive course of history: "The republican is the only form of government which is not eternally at open or secret war with the rights of mankind," he wrote in 1790.

It was to make that purpose unmistakable that Jefferson prevailed upon his peers to amplify the Constitution with a bill of rights, whose absence was his main objection to the document composed in Philadelphia. In a letter to James Madison dated December 20, 1787, Jefferson praised much in the new charter, then turned to "what I do not like":

> First the omission of a bill of rights providing clearly and without the aid of sophisms for freedom of religion, freedom of the press, protection against standing armies, restriction against monopolies, the eternal & unremitting force of the habeas corpus laws, and trials by jury in all matters of fact triable by the laws of the land & not by the law of nations.

Here, "without the aid of sophisms," was a short list of the rights that Jefferson regarded as essential to republican democracy—wherever it might thrive: "Let me add that a bill of rights is what the people are entitled to against every government on earth, general or particular, & what no just government should refuse, or rest on inferences."

Aware that such rights must be forever reasserted, Jefferson remained untiring in his effort to articulate that vision, as he did with especial brilliance in his first inaugural address in 1801. There he elaborated on the points he had made to Madison, with a stirring overview of the American ideal:

> Equal and exact justice to all men, of whatever state or persuasion, religious or political; peace, commerce, and honest friendship with all nations, entangling alliances with none; the support of the State governments in all their rights, as the most competent administrations for our domestic concerns and the surest bulwarks against antirepublican tendencies; the preservation of the General Government in all its constitutional vigor, as the sheet anchor of our peace at home and safety abroad.

Before returning to those crucial freedoms that had finally been incorporated in the Bill of Rights some twelve years earlier, the president reemphasized the value of the fundamental democratic process, whereby government authority might always be legitimized and always changed without recourse to violence or fraud:

> a jealous care of the right of election by the people—a mild and safe corrective of abuses which are lopped by the sword of revolu-

tion where peaceable remedies are unprovided; absolute acquiescence in the decision of the majority, the vital principle of
republics, from which is no appeal but to force, the vital principle
and immediate parent of despotism . . .

From there the president went on to note those basic rights that, in his
view, "the people are entitled to against every government on earth":
freedom of religion, "a well-disciplined militia," trial by jury, habeas corpus,* freedom of the press. "These principles form the bright constellation which has gone before us," he concluded,

> and guided our steps through an age of revolution and reformation.
> They should be the creed of our political faith, the text of civic
> instruction, the touchstone to try the services of those we trust; and
> should we wander from them in moments of error or alarm, let us
> hasten to retrace our steps and regain the road which alone leads to
> peace, liberty, and safety.

Today there is an aching poignancy to Jefferson's forgotten words, now
that the "constellation" of those basic democratic principles has disappeared behind the sudden darkness cast by Bush & Co.'s illegitimate
dominion. Under the chief executive who now purports to be in charge,
America has bolted from the path cleared by the Founders, promiscuously violating every tenet of the "creed" that finally guided Thomas Jefferson and his associates. Most dangerous is this regime's overt hostility
to fundamental democratic practice. Empowered not at the polls but by
judicial fiat, Bush & Co. has nothing but contempt for "the right of election by the people," which they have worked consistently to undermine
in the United States, through mob violence, bureaucratic fraud, impetuous gerrymandering, co-optation of the media, and—a major innova-

*Habeas corpus is a judicial writ to a prison official, mandating that a given
arrestee be brought before the court to ensure that the arrestee's imprisonment is not
illegal. In *Harris v. Nelson* (1969), the Supreme Court deemed habeas corpus "the fundamental instrument for safeguarding individual freedom against arbitrary and lawless state action."

tion—fake electoral "reform" devised to have the people voting on com-puterized machines that can be hacked with ease and leave no paper trail—machines built, programmed, and maintained by firms owned and controlled by ultraright Republicans. Such machines are, as of this writing, now set up in nearly thirty states, ready for Bush/Cheney's "re-election." (See p. 276.)*

Bush & Co. is no less scornful of electorates abroad, attacking allied governments that have responded to their own constituents (France, Germany, Belgium, et al., which Donald Rumsfeld calls "Old Europe"; Spain and Turkey, when their respective governments responded to the people's views), while praising those regimes that disregard the will of their own citizens so as to toe the White House line (Britain; Poland, Bulgaria, Romania, et al., which Rumsfeld calls "New Europe"; Spain and Turkey, when their respective governments ignored the people's views). As Nixon's people did in Chile in 1973, Bush/Cheney have been actively soliciting the ouster of the democratically elected president of Venezuela, funneling a million dollars to the anti-Chavez "opposition" in 2002 alone; and on April 30, 2004, the regime terminated the first dem-ocratic presidency in the history of Haiti, abruptly muscling Jean-Bertrand Aristide into surrender of his mandate and a permanent sojourn abroad. And even as Team Bush subverts democracy at home and spurns it all throughout the West, they baldly occupy Iraq—blocking its self-govern-ment, plundering its resources, shutting down its press, demolishing its infrastructure, killing thousands of civilians and torturing and raping thousands more—and call it "liberation." Here, there, and everywhere, Bush/Cheney work relentlessly to undercut "the vital principle of republics"—"absolute acquiescence in the decision of the majority"—elevating always the same few (i.e., themselves) over all the rest of us.

---

*There is strong evidence that such machines were used in the 2002 midterm elec-tions to put the Senate in the hands of the Republicans. Gross irregularities marked a number of state races—especially in Georgia, where Saxby Chambliss pulled what seemed to be a stunning upset by defeating Senator Max Cleland, the very popular incumbent. Pollsters generally were flummoxed by the unexpected Democratic losses nationwide. See Farhad Manjoo, "Will the Election Be Hacked?" *Salon*, 2/9/04 (http://archive.salon.com/tech/feature/2004/02/09/voting_machines/index_np.html).

Looking at the United States today, and at Iraq, and at Camp X-Ray in Guantánamo, the Founders of American republican democracy would see the Bush regime as militantly antidemocratic *and* antirepublican; it is likely that they would not even see Bush/Cheney as American (*or* British, for that matter), but as a horse of an entirely different color.

The preemptive war against Iraq has been another blunt betrayal of the Jeffersonian ideal, as the promise of "peace, commerce, and honest friendship with all nations" has been supplanted by that Manichaean threat, "You're either with us or against us." Endless war is Bush & Co.'s specialty. It surely is significant that, early in the "war on terror," Donald Rumsfeld publicly used Hitler's *Blitzkrieg* as a paradigm for U.S. military strategy.* Nor was he incorrect to do so. After all, that robust means of international expansion fully suits the regime's long-term plans, as

---

*Rumsfeld has been heavily influenced by *Shock and Awe: Achieving Rapid Dominance*, a study by Harlan K. Ullman and James P. Wade, which the Pentagon published in 1996. The strategy of "shock and awe," the authors write, is "aimed at influencing the will, perception, and understanding of an adversary rather than simply destroying military capability." The Nazi *Blitzkrieg* strategy is one example that its authors cite approvingly (while the bombing of Hiroshima and Nagasaki is another). In an interview with Jim Lehrer on February 4, 2002, Rumsfeld casually invoked the Nazi paradigm in expounding on the "transformation" that he had in mind for U.S. forces:

> When the Germans transformed their armed forces into the *Blitzkrieg*, they transformed only about 5 or 10 percent of their force. Everything else was the same, but they transformed the way they used it, the connectivity between aircraft and forces on the ground, the concentration of it in a specific portion of the line, and it—one would not want to transform 100 percent of your forces. You only need to transform a portion. (*The NewsHour with Jim Lehrer*, PBS, 2/4/02.)

(As it happened, the need for such a strategy against Iraq was largely obviated by the deal struck, very early in the war, between Maher Sufyan, commander of the Republican Guard, and the U.S. military. Sufyan agreed to have his troops stand down if the United States would fly him and his family somewhere safe. First reported by *Le Monde* on April 15, 2003, this arrangement—*saafqa* in Arabic—made news throughout the world but went largely unreported in this country. See Michael Young, "Will the Mideast Buy the Roadmap?" *Slate*, 5/27/03. Unless it was a case of mere corruption, Sufyan's move suggests the possibility that U.S. forces took Baghdad so easily not because of the invader's military brilliance but because it was the Ba'athist strategy to draw our soldiers into an impossible guerrilla war.)

spelled out clearly in "Rebuilding America's Defenses," an imperial proposal published in September of 2000 by the Project for the New American Century (PNAC), a group of hawkish visionaries close to Cheney, Rumsfeld, et al. As that document makes clear, the regime's purpose is eternal domination of the globe by the United States: "to maintain American military preeminence, to secure American geopolitical leadership, and to preserve the American peace." For a pithier expression of that impulse, I quote Michael Ledeen, the leading architect of neoconservative military strategy (and a major player in the Iran/Contra affair): "Every ten years or so, the United States needs to pick up some small crappy little country and throw it against the wall, just to show the world we mean business." Some might regard that line as vintage Uncle Sam, and yet it would have been offensive to the framers, who expected the republic not to bully other nations but to inspire them as a paradigm of revolutionary virtue: "It will be worthy of a free, enlightened, and at no distant period, a great nation, to give to mankind the magnanimous and too novel example of a people always guided by an exalted justice and benevolence," as George Washington observed in his farewell address.

Thus they would not have been surprised to see how radically Bush/Cheney have infringed our freedoms, using the emergency of "terrorism"—a crisis they themselves have aggravated—to repeal the Bill of Rights. Under the USA Patriot Act, this government has unilaterally *suspended* "the eternal & unremitting force of the habeas corpus laws," keeping U.S. citizens and foreign nationals alike locked up in solitary confinement, without lawyers, without charges, possibly forever (or "until the war on terrorism ends," as the regime sometimes puts it).* All of this was well established long before the shocking revelations about Abu Ghraib, which only made this regime's penal barbarism clear for all the world to see.

The right to trial by jury has likewise been limited by Bush & Co.,

*On January 12, 2004, the Supreme Court rejected an appeal that challenged the regime's secret detentions after 9/11. "Of the nearly 1,000 people arrested, the government eventually released the names of 129 against whom it brought criminal charges," reported Linda Greenhouse in "Justices Allow Policy of Silence on 9/11 Detainees," *New York Times*, 1/13/04.

which now has countless suspects locked up in a global U.S. gulag, awaiting trial—if there should ever be a trial—not by a jury of their peers but by a military tribunal. Over six hundred of these vanished men (a few were boys, penned up for months) are foreign "detainees" incarcerated at Camp Delta in Guantánamo Bay, "the world's worst prison," as one journalist has called it. Prisoners are often beaten, tightly chained for hours, fed on nauseating scraps, and otherwise tortured physically and psychologically—the Muslims most devout among them forced to watch prostitutes caress themselves, and all the detainees tormented with disinformation and incessant threats. (There is also a death chamber in the compound, so that anyone found guilty can be executed quickly, right nearby, if that's what President Bush decides.) The White House dismissed as "without merit" the concerns publicized by Amnesty International—whose representatives were not allowed to see the camp. Indeed, no human rights groups have been let in to look around, although the International Red Cross, concerned about the number of attempted suicides among the men—thirty-five as of December 1, 2003, according to the agency—did gain entry to the camp and then, uncharacteristically, released a public statement on the poor conditions there.* And as those foreigners have hung in legal limbo, so have three Americans been held, lawyerless and incommunicado, in U.S. military custody: Jose Padilla, Yasser Hamdi, and Ali Saleh Kahlah al-Marri, each kept in isolation merely on the say-so of the president and/or his deputies.† Meanwhile,

---

*Worldwide, according to reporter Louise Christian, "at least 15,000 people are being held without trial under the justification of the 'war on terrorism'. They include more than 3,000 detained in Iraq after the war, of whom at least 1,000 are still in detention; an estimated further 1,000 to 3,000 detained at Bagram airbase in Afghanistan; and an unkown number being held on the British territory of Diego Garcia." Christian reports that "Bagram is a CIA interrogation centre," where the inmates are subjected to "the regular practice of sensory deprivation and sleep starvation, as well as incidents of throwing prisoners against walls while hooded." "Guantanamo Bay: A Global Experiment in Inhumanity," *Guardian* (UK), 1/10/04.

†Padilla, a Chicago gang member who had converted to Islam, was accused of planning to set off a so-called dirty bomb in the United States; Hamdi was captured on the field of battle in Afghanistan; and al-Marri stands accused, by someone, of being a sleeper agent. All three have been held in solitary confinement in U.S. Naval

thousands of Iraqi innocents, disappeared into a web of secret U.S. prisons, were being subjected to a kind of treatment not sufficiently unlike the prior treatment of Iraqi prisoners by Saddam Hussein.

John Ashcroft has also scorned the rights of several hundred other people in this country, zealously betraying Jefferson's ideal of "equal and exact justice to all men, of whatever state or persuasion, religious or political." On June 2, 2003, Glenn A. Fine, inspector general of the Department of Justice, came out with a scathing survey of the Ashcroft "sweeps" after 9/11, which led to the imprisonment of 762 people—all Muslim immigrants, all held at length in grim conditions, and not one ever charged with terrorism or related crimes. As *New York Times* reporter Adam Liptak put it, Fine's judgment was that Ashcroft had replaced "ordinary rules" with "no rules or perverse ones," and thereby perpetrated a gigantic violation of the constitutional right to due process.* Despite their innocence, the detainees were often brutally mistreated, Fine reported. Those held at the Metropolitan Detention Center in Brooklyn suffered " 'lockdown' for at least 23 hours per day [with

---

brigs. "Bush Names 3rd Enemy Combatant," *Chicago Times*, 6/24/03. In January 2004, the Supreme Court agreed to address the constitutionality of the government's indefinite detainment of U.S.-born "enemy combatants."

*Ashcroft also helped to make the U.S. prisons in Iraq infernal places. "The man who directed the reopening of the Abu Ghraib prison . . . and trained the guards there" is one Lane McCotter, who, in 1997, was forced out as director of the Utah Department of Corrections after a schizophrenic inmate had been shackled naked to a chair for 16 hours. The prisoner died from his ordeal. McCotter later joined the private sector, as an executive with Management & Training Corporation (MTC), the nation's third-largest for-profit prison company. MTC's prison in Santa Fe was cited by the state and federal government for unsafe conditions and insufficient medical care, and one of the corporation's Texas prisons is in federal court, having been sued by an inmate who was raped repeatedly and treated as a slave by other prisoners, despite his numerous requests for help from the authorities.

McCotter was selected by John Ashcroft for a U.S. team sent over to Iraq "to rebuild the country's criminal justice system." Fox Butterfield, "The Struggle for Iraq: Prisoners; Mistreatment of Prisoners Is Called Routine in U.S.," *New York Times*, 5/8/04.

two bright lights on in each cell 24 hours a day]; escort procedures that
included a 'four-man hold' with handcuffs, leg irons, and heavy chains
any time the detainees were moved outside their cells; and a limit of one
legal telephone call per week and one social call per month." Many were
prevented from contacting lawyers, and some were slammed against the
wall and otherwise abused by prison guards (mistreatment that was
caught on tape). As Nat Hentoff has argued, Ashcroft's conduct then,
and since, makes clear that he is unfit for his office; and yet the (evidently) unimpeachable attorney general merely shrugged off Fine's
report, offering "no apologies" for his illegal raids.

The ordeal of those "detainees," and the attorney general's inquisitorial
zeal, ought to worry all Americans. For Bush & Co. has clearly set its sights
not just on certain swarthy foreigners but on the very principle of civil
rights. In opposition to the Jeffersonian ideal, which always places individual liberty above the caprice of the state, this regime has radically
expanded its surveillance of the people, allowing its police much broader
latitude to tap your phone(s), and letting them review your health records,
library withdrawals, and book purchases and read your e-mail and survey
your Internet transactions and, in fact, detain you if the cops think you
look like you might be a terrorist, or be helping one, or be thinking about
helping one. So glaring are the Patriot Act's infringements on the Bill of
Rights that it would not have been approved by Congress if our legislators
had been given time to read it, and if Vice President Cheney had not
threatened to tar all would-be dissenters as al Qaeda tools.

    And yet the rigors of that act would seem quite "liberal" by compari-
son with the successor legislation, which, starting in the fall of 2003, was
pitched directly to the people, or some of us, by the irrepressible attorney general. Under Section 501 of "Patriot II," as it's been called, the
government is free to *disappear* you if any "terrorist" intent might be
"inferred from conduct." Even if you break no laws, in other words, you
could be "legally" abducted from your home, or from the street, and
forced before a secret military tribunal—without any prior notice and
with no word to your family or your lawyer or the press. Under this bill
(which, as of this writing, is still under congressional consideration), any

violation of the law, whether federal or state, could earn you the status of an "enemy combatant," which would permit the government to annul your citizenship. And under Section 102, the state would have the freedom to define particular acts of information gathering as espionage—"pursuit of covert intelligence for a foreign power." Thus any inconvenient news reporting would be classed as "terrorism," and so prosecuted.*

This is nothing like the form of government invented by our Founders, but a system with its roots in certain alien imaginations. So obvious and permanent a state of military rule would surely have revolted *all* the authors of the Constitution, who were not unanimous on many subjects, but none of whom admired the Spartan model. Their consensus was expressed with vehemence by James Madison, when he noted that "*there never was a people whose liberties long survived a standing army.*" This animus against a formal military establishment induced them to approve the Second Amendment. It was, in the words of Elbridge Gerry of Massachusetts, "to prevent the establishment of a standing army, the bane of liberty," that the Founders deemed *the people* a militia, whose members, Pennsylvanian Tench Coxe noted, must be duly armed to "form a powerful check upon the regular troops." Bush/Cheney's stand on gun control is hardly based on that republican concern, as they have done far more than any prior administration to

---

*There has been much popular resistance to the first Patriot Act, which, by March 2004, had been formally condemned by three states and 270 U.S. cities, towns, and counties, all passing ordinances against Bush/Cheney's "anti-terror" legislation. Reflecting this mass disapproval, on July 23, 2003, the House voted, 309 to 118, to deny funding for the Justice Department's "sneak and peak" investigations—covert searches authorized by the Patriot Act, but now forbidden by a skittish Congress. For an up-to-date tally of ordinances against the Patriot Act, see the Web site for the Bill of Rights Defense Committee, http://bordc.org/OtherLocalEfforts.htm.

Such resistance to Bush/Cheney's self-empowerment, however, did not prevent Congress from approving, in December of 2003, an expansion of the Patriot Act. According to *Wired News*, the act now permits "the FBI to subpoena business documents and transactions from a broader range of businesses—everything from libraries to travel agencies to eBay—without first seeking approval from a judge." "Congress Expands FBI Spying Power," *Wired News*, 11/24/03 (http://www.wired.com/news/politics/0,1283,61341,00.html).

turn the U.S. military into a domestic weapon for the government and
its one ruling party. That plan has thus far been advanced invisibly,
through an incremental rollback of states' rights; the use of strong-arm
tactics in the legislative process, at both state and national levels; and a
vast bureaucratic rearrangement of the federal government, intended to
endow the Pentagon with broad new powers here at home.

On October 1, 2002, the U.S. Northern Command, or NORTH-
COM—the first regional unified command to have this country as its
sphere of operations—started up at Peterson Air Force Base in Colorado.
(It will eventually move to new headquarters in the nation's capital.)
Tasked with the provision of "military assistance to civil authorities,
including consequence management operations," NORTHCOM further jeopardizes the already weakened Posse Comitatus Act of 1878
(which Bush/Cheney have been working to repeal). That act, based on
the bitter experiences of both sides in the Civil War, forbids the use of
federal soldiers to police American civilians. And as NORTHCOM now
entangles the Department of Defense in national law enforcement, the
new Department of Homeland Security (DHS) is also likely to confuse
the foreign and domestic fronts. DHS—itself an outgrowth of "Garden
Plot," a "civil disturbance plan" long ago established in the Pentagon—
includes, among its scores of erstwhile separate entities, the Federal
Emergency Management Agency (FEMA), which is responsible for taking charge in catastrophic national crises.

Under Patriot II, the U.S. federal government, as well as certain areas
of the state governments, would fall under the exclusive jurisdiction of a
directorate of giant agencies: John Ashcroft's Department of Justice,
Bush/Cheney's Office of Homeland Security, and, in direct partnership
with FEMA, NORTHCOM, a subsidiary of Donald Rumsfeld's Pentagon. Thus is the regime prepared to formalize what would in essence
be a theocratic/military takeover of the government, both national and
local.

Even now, without the passage of the second Patriot Act, DHS is well
beyond the purview of the people—a circumstance especially unfortunate, as there is ample evidence of gross ineptitude throughout the
agency, which seems to be far less equipped to keep us safe from further

terrorist attacks than it is to snoop on the affairs of innocent Americans and hapless immigrants. DHS is, as the ACLU has put it, "100% secret and 0% accountable." Not only is that agency well shielded, by a number of directives, from the Freedom of Information Act, but its workers have no whistle-blowers' protections, because Bush & Co. would not allow DHS employees to be unionized. Leaking information from the agency has been declared a special criminal offense.

We cannot look inside DHS. On the other hand, those inside the agency can look into our business anytime they want, and use the state's entire intelligence bureaucracy to do so. Homeland Security is authorized to order, without explanation, intelligence reports from the FBI, CIA, and U.S. state and local governments. Thus it would be a very easy matter for that agency to blur the difference between terror and dissent, and use its resources to spy on dissident domestic groups, as happened with the CoIntelPro operation in the sixties and seventies—and as is happening again with other law enforcement agencies at state and local levels, where mere protests of Bush/Cheney's "antiterrorism" policy are cast as "terrorist events" themselves, and stigmatized accordingly.* Thus DHS itself poses a grave threat of national *in*security. "If the government is allowed to operate in secrecy," noted Senator Robert Byrd on July 8, 2003, "then the people's liberties easily can be lost."

---

*After the police attacked a peaceful demonstration at the Port of Oakland in the spring of 2003, it came out that their overzealousness had been encouraged beforehand by officials at the California Anti-Terrorism Information Center (CATIC), which had been gathering information on all dissidents from the first day of its operations after 9/11. CATIC's bulletin of April 2 had hinted strongly that the demonstrators mght riot and "shut down" the port. The lack of any evidence for such a claim seemed not to have inhibited CATIC analysts from warning the police to take tough measures. Indeed, the center has no need for evidence at all, according to its spokesman, Mike Van Winkle of the state Justice Department: "You can make an easy kind of a link that, if you have a protest group protesting a war where the cause that's being fought against is international terrorism, you might have terrorism at that [protest]. . . . *You can almost argue that a protest against that is a terrorist act* (emphasis added)." "State Monitored War Protestors," *Oakland Tribune*, 5/18/03.

This case is an excellent example of the danger posed by state surveillance of legitimate dissent. It is worth noting that CATIC works closely with federal authorities, considering itself "a hub" of official antiterrorist activity.

• • •

In this new model, the states would no longer serve even theoretically as our "surest bulwarks against anti-republican tendencies," as Jefferson put it two centuries ago. Rather than encourage such waywardness, Bush & Co. has sued those states whose laws would contradict the rightist creed, and have otherwise used federal means to turn state legislatures into simple echo chambers of the national party. (It was, of course, a different matter back when "states' rights" meant resistance to desegregation.) Because his own religious scruples were offended by the "right to die" law passed in Oregon, John Ashcroft brought suit to block physicians from administering lethal drugs to ailing patients who had asked to be allowed to die. (Oregon is the only state that allowed assisted suicide— a measure that, since 1994, the state's voters have approved not once but twice.) In California, Ashcroft's Justice Department prosecuted, and convicted, Ed Rosenthal for growing marijuana for medicinal use: a practice backed by the state's voters (under Proposition 215) *and* by the city of Oakland. California's attorney general had acknowledged the legality of Rosenthal's endeavor, but the grower was found guilty—a crime for which he could have ended up serving eighty-five years in federal prison. The local judge saw things differently, however, and sentenced Rosenthal to pay a $1,000 fine and spend one day in jail. The Justice Department announced plans to appeal the Rosenthal ruling.*

---

*Californian Tommy Chong was not so lucky. On the basis of an obscure statute, on October 3, 2003, Chong was convicted of selling drug paraphernalia across state lines (his company, Chong Glass and Nice Dreams, made pipes and bongs). The comedian was sentenced to nine months in federal prison, payment of a $20,000 fine, and forfeiture of $100,000 of the company's profits. (Chong Glass is out of business.) That heavy sentence was intended as a punishment not for the crime per se, but for Chong's stoned-out film persona: "The defendant has become wealthy throughout his entertainment career through glamorizing the illegal distribution and use of marijuana," wrote Assistant U.S. District Attorney May Houghton, in a special pleading filed before Chong's sentencing. "Feature films that he made with his longtime partner Cheech Marin, such as 'Up in Smoke,' trivialize law enforcement efforts to combat drug trafficking and use." "He's Taking One Big Hit; Chong, who built a career on drug-based humor, begins serving a nine-month term for selling drug paraphernalia," *Los Angeles Times*, 10/10/03.

Aside from its vindictiveness, the case was notable for its irrelevant expense. At a

California seems to be especially offensive to Bush/Cheney, whose satraps have frequently reversed its judges and thrown out its laws. In November of 2002, the Rehnquist Court reversed the decision of a California federal appeals court that had allowed a Guatemalan man, fearful of ill treatment in his home country, to remain in the United States. (It was up to the Bush administration, not the courts, to make that call, the Supremes said.) In June, the Court voided a state law that had been upheld by the Ninth Circuit and that would have made it easier for Holocaust survivors to collect on their insurance policies. (*That* the Supreme Court declared unconstitutional: improper meddling by the state in U.S. foreign policy.) But Bush & Co. has been most diligent in trying to get around the state's exemplary, and popular, antipollution laws: "California's environmental protection laws, among the toughest in the nation, are being challenged frequently as the Bush administration acts to blunt regulations viewed as inconsistent with national policy," reported the *Los Angeles Times* on September 14, 2003.

> The administration has weighed in on matters ranging from offshore oil drilling to air pollution to toxic waste cleanups, outraging state officials and environmentalists, who warn that the actions threaten to undermine the role California has played as a laboratory for innovative environmental solutions intended to improve the quality of people's lives.

So contrary had California been that Bush & Co. engineered regime change there, the White House using its resources to make Arnold Schwarzenegger governor. There was a specific motive for that step. In the spring of 2001, Enron and its giant colleagues in the U.S. energy cartel were fearful of a costly retribution. Having gouged $9 billion from the state, the cartel now faced the likelihood of having to return the money because of California's Civil Code provision 17200, the "Unfair Business Practices Act." (California Lieutenant Governor Cruz Busta-

___

time when the United States is under constant threat by able foreign terrorists, Bush & Co. used 1,200 federal, state, and local authorities to nail Tommy Chong. Deroy Murdock, "What Are They Smoking?" *National Review Online*, 10/28/03 (http://www.nationalreview.com/murdock/murdock200310280851.asp).

mante, who had filed suit for reimbursement, had solid proof.) The cartel wanted an alternative: to plead guilty to conspiracy and then pay two cents on the dollar. Such a settlement would be impossible, however, with Gray Davis at the helm—and so the robber barons decided to recall him, first asking Schwarzenegger to become the governor. Allegedly with the approval of the White House, the Terminator met with Enron CEO Ken Lay (and junk-bond magnate Michael Milken) at L.A.'s Peninsula Hotel on May 17, 2001, and soon agreed to beat Gray Davis for them. And the rest is history.*

Bush/Cheney have been meddling far more crudely in the politics of Texas, through Representative Tom DeLay, their top congressional cohort (who calls himself "the Hammer"). By law, the state of Texas must redraw its congressional districts once a decade, when the census cycle is complete. As such redistricting had duly taken place in 2000, the next round could not take place until 2010—a moment seven years too late for Bush & Co., who wanted Texas locked up *now*. DeLay therefore arranged to have the state's Republicans declare a premature redistricting by party fiat, and not, certainly, because minorities down there were getting shafted at the polls: on the contrary. Their purpose, as the *Washington Post* put it, was "to wipe out moderate and white Democrats from the Texas congressional delegation." Do Texans, asked the *Post*, "really want a state with a white party and a minority party?" The means were as improper as the goal. "Mid-decade redistricting—absent a voting rights lawsuit—has been virtually unprecedented for the last century and

*Buried history. The story, based on Enron's own internal memos, was broken by BBC reporter Greg Palast on October 3, 2003—four days prior to the election. It made no national news, the media preferring the less complicated subject of Schwarzenegger's long history of sexual assault. Although that story too had its importance, the mainstream coverage played it down, and even took some shots at the *Los Angeles Times* for *its* aggressive coverage of the candidate's simian sexual behavior. Typically, the very same reporters, and performers, who defended the Republican, and smeared his victims, had been loud and livid critics of such sexual predation when Bill Clinton was alleged to have engaged in it, or something like it. (See pp. 215ff.) Greg Palast, "Arnold Unplugged," 10/3/03 (http://www.gregpalast.com/detail.cjm?artif=283). The Enron memos are available online at the Web site of the Foundation for Taxpayer and Consumer Rights (www.ConsumerWatchdog.org).

entirely unprecedented since the mid-1950s, in Texas and every other state in the union," Joshua Marshall wrote in May of 2003. Moreover, DeLay used federal PAC funds to buy the Texas legislature for the GOP—an innovation of extraordinary crassness.* So egregious was that power grab that Texas's Democratic legislators fled the state in protest, to prevent a quorum in the Texas senate. (That effort of resistance ultimately failed.)

In their campaign for national dominion, Bush & Co. have not refrained from using force, or threatening it, to have their way. Here again Bush/Cheney stand out in stark contrast to Jefferson, who posited, as an ideal of our republican democracy, "the preservation of the General Government in all its constitutional vigor, as the sheet anchor of our peace at home and safety abroad." When the Texas Democrats took off for parts unknown (they ended up in Oklahoma), "[Texas Speaker Tom] Craddick and DeLay wanted the errant legislators arrested and returned to the House to force a vote on the bill," the *Houston Chronicle* reported. Aside from ordering state troopers to round up the fugitives, the Hammer also used the Department of Homeland Security, in an attempt to track the airplane of former Texas Speaker Pete Laney. (This was a violation of the law.)

Bush & Co.'s House enforcers also used such tactics in the nation's Capitol. On July 18, 2003, Representative Bill Thomas, chair of the House Ways and Means Committee, sicced the Capitol police on his

---

*"The effort was coordinated by Jim Colyrando, a former colleague of Karl Rove. Colyrando did more than write checks on the account of DeLay's Texans for a Republican Majority political action committee (TRMPAC). Colyrando and his staff carefully selected Republican candidates, provided each one of them a cut of the $1.5 million, plus, as the *Washington Post* reported, $35,000 in political research, $52,000 in phone banks, $12,600 in direct mail, $27,000 to a Washington polling firm, and $27,600 to the fund-raising operation run by DeLay's daughter, Danielle Ferra. (Ferra also was paid $3,300 herself.) In a word, a campaign was provided for each Republican candidate funded by DeLay's Texas PAC." Lou Dubose, "Texas Crude: Racial politics hits another low in redistricting fight," *LA Weekly*, 6/6/03.

Democratic colleagues, who, to protest his Soviet-style chairmanship, had walked out of the proceedings, refusing to vote on the pending bill, and holed up in the committee's library. That call to the police—which had been approved by Tom DeLay—was not just gratuitous but flagrantly illegal. The senators and representatives, our Constitution tells us,

> shall in all cases, except treason, felony and breach of the peace, be privileged from arrest during their attendance at the session of their respective Houses, and in going to and returning from the same; and for any speech or debate in either House, they shall not be questioned in any other place. (Article I, Section 6)

When the dissidents were not dragged back into the room, the explosive Thomas called the vote out of sheer spite, and had the bill passed only by the GOP majority.

The Democrats were outraged. Representative Nancy Pelosi (D-CA) proposed a resolution to protest that extraordinary breach of law and protocol. Her colleagues spoke out forcefully during the House debate. "My friends, this is how tyranny begins," said Representative Lloyd Doggett (D-TX). "It is our responsibility to stand against a police state, to stand in favor of open dialogue rather than to permit a bill to pass with only the votes of one party, and move toward a one-party state." "I never thought, as a member of Congress, that I would be threatened with arrest in the library of the Ways and Means Committee," said Representative John Lewis (D-GA). The resolution was defeated by the House Republican majority. Six days later, Thomas tearfully apologized, calling his tough tactics "just plain stupid." Some Democrats were half-placated by his tears—which, however, did not address the crucial issue of due legislative process. Although Thomas's despotic measure certainly was aberrant for the U.S. House of Representatives, such bald oppression had hardly been, nor is it now, unusual for this regime.*

---

*The congressional Republicans have also used some slyer methods to subvert the opposition. In February 2004, it was reported that two GOP staffers for the Senate Judiciary Committee had illegally downloaded thousands of the Democrats' internal memoranda. "The memos were leaked to conservative outlets like *The Washington Times*, *The Wall Street Journal* editorial page, and columnist Robert Novak; they were

In the eyes of Bush & Co., *all* unfriendly protest—which is to say, all protest—is a subversive menace, driven either by unpatriotic malice or, at best, an ignorant sympathy with evil foreigners. Those brave few who have dared to contradict or criticize Bush/Cheney publicly have, for the most part, been discredited by smears. Jesse Jackson's advocacy of a statewide vote recount in Florida was halted by the revelations that he had a love child. J. H. Hatfield's troublesome biography of Bush, with its details on the latter's odd stretch of community service back in 1972 (reportedly a punishment for coke possession), was canceled by the publisher and universally reviled when it came out that Hatfield had himself done time in prison.

Scott Ritter, the blunt ex-Marine whose lucid and relentless case against Bush/Cheney's *casus belli*—i.e., that there were tons of weapons of mass destruction (WMDs) still hidden in Iraq—was broadly vilified, and finally halted by a charge, or hint, of an attempted sex crime. UNMOVIC, the second inspection team sent by the United Nations, against Bush/Cheney's wishes, to determine whether such weaponry was in Iraq or not, was sullied (on U.S. talk radio, at least) by the salacious news that Harvey John "Jack" McGeorge, a member of the team, was active in Black Rose, a pansexualist sadomasochist society in Washington.* After he appeared on *Hardball* to attest to the improper handling of George W. Bush's personnel file at the Texas Air National Guard (the governor's men discarded several compromising documents), Bill Burkett had his private medical information leaked to the press (and was denied a hearing to protest a sudden large reduction in his veterans' dis-

also allegedly used to prepare some of President George W. Bush's judicial nominees for confirmation hearings." Matt Bivens, "The Daily Outrage," *The Nation*, 2/13/04, http://www.thenation.com/outrage/index.mhtml?pid=1258.

*So eager was Paul Wolfowitz to undermine Hans Blix, UNMOVIC's chief inspector, that he asked the CIA to look into the diplomat's background, in hopes of finding something compromising that the regime could then publicize, and thereby get the whole inspection mission canceled. This would have made it easier for Bush & Co. to hit Iraq with a preemptive strike. A former official at the State Department told the *Washington Post* that Wolfowitz "hit the ceiling" when the CIA came up with nothing. "Skirmish on Iraq Inspections; Wolfowitz has CIA probe UN Diplomat in Charge," *Washington Post*, 4/15/02.

ability payment). Freelancer Jason Leopold's dogged exposés of the connections between Enron and Thomas White, then-secretary of the army,
were stopped cold by the insinuation, floated from on high (and first
publicized by rightist pundit Bob Novak), that the journalist had actually forged the documents that he had used to prove his case. Other uncooperative reporters have been punished by the White House: Dana
Milbank of the *Washington Post*, blackballed for suggesting, most politely,
that the president seems often not to tell the truth; veteran reporter Helen
Thomas, banished from the White House for asking pointed questions
at press conferences. And those ex-insiders who have dared to tell uncom-
fortable truths about the Bush regime—Paul O'Neill, and the relentless
Richard Clarke—have been defamed as viciously as any Democrat.

The most egregious shot of all, however—and the most criminal—
was the outing of CIA agent Valerie Plame to punish her husband,
Joseph Wilson, a State Department stalwart who had dared to publicize
the truth about Iraq's alleged attempt to buy uranium from Niger. Pointedly refuting one of Bush & Co.'s major fabrications, Wilson's op-ed
piece in the *New York Times* enraged Bush/Cheney, whose operatives
were quick to blow Plame's cover (by leaking it to Bob Novak), in order
both to punish Wilson and to "send a message" that such public statements of the truth are not allowed.

Clearly, such revenge meant more to Bush & Co. than did U.S.
national security. Plame's exposure put her foreign contacts, and perhaps
herself, in jeopardy—and meant a major setback in the "war on terrorism," because it had been her covert job to track the sales of just the sort
of unconventional weapons that might indeed be used against us, some
day, by some terrorist. Her husband's fame and honesty, however, were
apparently so galling to Bush/Cheney as to justify her premature retirement. (Bush—who was alleged to have said, "I want to get to the bottom of this"—for weeks resisted the appointment of an independent
counsel, finally permitting it seventy-four days after Novak's column had
appeared.*)

---

*By contrast, as Josh Micah Marshall notes, it took Bush/Cheney just *one* day to
announce that it was mounting an investigation into former Treasury Secretary Paul
O'Neill's tell-all appearance on *60 Minutes*, which allegedly entailed improper use of

Most of Bush & Co.'s opponents are not bold individuals but ordinary Americans in ever-growing numbers. The regime began to limit their free speech rights prior to 9/11, when it quietly revised the First Amendment, wiping out our freedoms of assembly and speech through the establishment of special little areas where public protest is *allowed* whenever Bush or Cheney is in town. Devised back in the Reagan years, when they were imposed primarily on certain college campuses, these "free speech zones," or "First Amendment zones," are now a common feature of the landscape fashioned for us by Bush & Co., who first used this imperial gimmick in the summer of 2000 at the GOP convention in, of all places, Philadelphia. The citizens who came there to protest the ticket found themselves restricted to a fenced-in First Amendment zone in FDR Park, across and down the street from the convention center. (Any group intent on demonstrating elsewhere had to get a permit, and it was very hard to get one.)

The dictatorial thrust of that decree was clear to those who tried to exercise their rights. "If that's the zone where the First Amendment applies in Philadelphia," one activist remarked, "that means de facto that in the rest of the city, the First Amendment doesn't apply, and we think that's outrageous." In fact, this nation was itself the first and greatest First Amendment zone in history; and yet, in city after city, Americans protesting Bush have been restricted to some tiny area so distant from the action that the president can't know they're there, nor does the press, which is, of course, the tactic's purpose. At the same time, Bush supporters, and people with no visible opinion, are free to gather anywhere they choose, since their loud cheers and upbeat signs do so much to improve the picture for the White House spinners and network news.*

---

secret documents. See Marshall's Web log for 1/12/04 (http://www.talkingpoints memo.com/archives/week_2004_01_11.html#002404).

  *It isn't clear that there's a difference, as I will argue here. One anecdote might help to dramatize the problem. On March 14, 2003, a week before the reinvasion of Iraq, Robert Jerelski, protesting near the UN building, was assaulted by an ABC technician who did not want him and his rude placard—"STOP BUSH"—screwing up the 5:00 P.M. live shot of Eyewitness News reporter Joe Torres. Shoved into a metal barricade, Jerelski sustained injuries requiring emergency treatment at the NYU Medical Center, and later sued the network. The incident was caught on tape. Jerelski's civil suits

Bush/Cheney's government has cracked down ever harder on dissent, especially since 9/11, which marked the start of a new chapter in the history of U.S. "crowd control." At first it was primarily the Secret Service, using local cops as White House troops, that often used sheer force to get protesters out of public view. From the fall of 2002, those dissidents refusing to convey their placards off into the proper zone were busted in St. Louis, Kalamazoo, Evansville, Neville Island, Pennsylvania, and Columbia, South Carolina, on the orders of the Secret Service, whose agents also had the cops force demonstrators into zones in Houston, Albuquerque, Trenton, Washington, D.C., and Richmond, Virginia. (In September of 2003, the ACLU filed suit against the Secret Service.) And yet the use of force seems meant not just to quiet the streets but to make clear that the regime loathes public protest (unless, of course, it's in Iran). In Phoenix, on September 27, 2002, mounted cops in riot gear charged suddenly into a peaceful crowd of protesters and arrested seven people, including a legal observer for the ACLU. ("She was taking a picture, and I don't think they liked that," said another ACLU officer at the site.) On April 7, 2003, police in Oakland "fired lead-shot-filled bean bags, wooden dowels and 'stinger grenades' spewing rubber bullets at crowds blocking the gates to two shippers with Iraq war-related government contracts," according to the *Alameda Times-Star.* The assault on the nonviolent protest injured thirty-one Americans, including nine longshoremen who were mere bystanders. (Such "nonlethal ammunition" leaves gaping bloody welts the size of golf balls.) In Manhattan the same day, the New York Police Department preemptively arrested scores of demonstrators standing quietly on Madison Avenue, across from the Manhattan office of the Carlyle Group, a major holding company that owns a number of defense contractors (and that at the time employed the president's father as a liaison to the Saudi elite).* Those arrested

---

against the network and his individual assailant are now before the Supreme Court of New York County. Interviews with Robert Jerelski, 10/7/03, and Raymond Rauges, his attorney, 4/6/04.

*Two lawyers present at the demonstration "told the [Village] Voice that a swarm of helmeted police—so many as to seem to outnumber the protesters—abruptly surrounded the group of supporters. Spurning the participants and lawyers, who said the

spent the day in jail and were not allowed to call their lawyers, and many were subjected to interrogation as to their political beliefs. (After those arrested filed a lawsuit, all either had their charges dropped or were acquitted.)

However bloody and gratuitous, such actions soon seemed mild in retrospect, as Bush & Co., in late autumn of 2003, turned up the heat to Third World levels, or rather brought it back to where it was in, say, "Hooverville" in 1932, but now enhanced with certain of the latest military tactics used to put down restive "terrorists" in Baghdad and Tikrit. In Miami during the third week of November, a massive paramilitary force came down with extraordinary violence on those attempting to protest the summit meeting of the Free Trade Area of the Americas (FTAA), the latest step in the ongoing "globalization" of the Western Hemisphere. "Police violence outside of trade summits is not new," Naomi Klein reported, "but what was striking about Miami was how divorced the security response was from anything resembling an actual threat." The turnout was meager and demoralized, as the planning for the protest had been thwarted by police for weeks. Nevertheless, the summit failed—not because of the protestors, but because the people of Bolivia, Brazil, and Argentina had made it clear to their respective governments that they would tolerate no further deference to "free trade"; and so the delegations from those countries would not ratify the pact, thereby handing the United States and its partners an unusual defeat.

Bush & Co. showed greater power out in the streets, where hapless demonstrators of all ages, although wholly peaceable, were treated like invading aliens. "The forces fired indiscriminately into crowds of unarmed protesters," reported Jeremy Scahill of Pacifica Radio's "Democracy Now!"

> Scores of people were hit with skin-piercing rubber bullets; thousands were gassed with an array of chemicals. On several occasions, police fired loud concussion grenades into the crowds. Police

crowd was willing to disperse, police reportedly would not let anyone leave and arrested approximately 80 people, ranging from teens to seniors." "Activists Push Back at NYPD," *Village Voice*, 7/8/03.

shocked people with [stun guns]. Demonstrators were shot in the back as they retreated. One young guy's apparent crime was holding his fingers in a peace sign in front of the troops. They shot him multiple times, including once in the stomach at point blank range.

"Our goal was to drown you out," one Miami-Dade police officer told Klein.

Small, peaceful demonstrations were attacked with extreme force; organizations were infiltrated by undercover officers who then used stun guns on activists; busses filled with union members were prevented from joining permitted marches; dozens of young faces were smashed into concrete and beaten bloody with batons; human rights activists had guns pointed at their heads at military-style checkpoints.

Bentley Killmon, seventy-one, a former airline pilot (and policeman's son) who was there to protest with the Alliance for Retired Americans, saw plenty more, and got the same treatment himself. Trying to get back to their buses, his group was waylaid by Miami cops:

They were pointing their guns at us. I guess they had those rubber pellets in them, but I didn't know, I was just incredibly frightened. Some of the people with us got down on their knees, and as I got down on my knees, I was briskly pushed to the ground. It felt like I had a foot to my back knocking me down. Everyone in our group was knocked to the ground and handcuffed. I had my hands cuffed behind my back for 7½ hours. My father was in the Norfolk City Police Department for many years. Until Thursday, I respected the badge. I respected the job the police had to do. But I no longer respect the badge. Not in Miami. Not after what I saw. Not after what happened to me and others.

His view was shared by many others, including members of the AFL-CIO, who vowed to sue Miami for their treatment. "As the story comes out, over the next few hours and days and weeks," said Ron Judd, an AFL-CIO regional director, "the public is going to learn what we saw on the street, that the police provoked these exchanges and went way out of their way to increase the magnitude of their response." (In fact the story never did go national.)

Although carried out by local personnel, the action in Miami was a federal initiative: the $8.5 million that it cost came straight out of the president's $87 billion budget for the "war on terror" in Iraq. And as the crackdown on U.S. dissent intensified, it broadened to include the resources of federal entities beyond the Secret Service. Also in late November of 2003, the *New York Times* reported that the FBI had started broad surveillance of antiwar activities, including an advisement urging local law enforcement officers around the nation to alert the bureau's "counterterrorism squads" if anything "suspicious" should occur at demonstrations. This initiative suggested a revival of J. Edgar Hoover's CoIntelPro, which eventually provoked strong legislative curbs on FBI surveillance of American dissidents—curbs that were removed by the attorney general after 9/11. Here was another move against the Bill of Rights. "As a matter of principle, it has a very serious chilling effect on peaceful demonstration," Herman Schwartz, a law professor at American University, told the *New York Times.* "If you go around telling people, 'We're going to ferret out information on demonstrations,' that deters people. People don't want their names and pictures in F.B.I. files." That chill was deepened as the bureau went beyond liaising with municipal police and started visiting activists in their own homes, to question them about their plans, their views, their patriotism.*

The framers surely would have been appalled by the very notion of a federal police force like the FBI, which worried constitutional purists when it swiftly rose to prominence and power after World War I. And, as we have seen, the framers did not want a standing army, which they knew to be a great potential instrument of government repression. It would therefore trouble them to know that Bush & Co. has also brought

---

*For other instances of federal surveillance or harassment, see Edward Wenk, Jr., "Threats to Democracy at Code-Red Level," *Seattle Post-Intelligencer,* 12/31/03; Robert Block and Gary Fields, "Is Military Creeping into Domestic Law Enforcement?" *Wall Street Journal,* 3/9/04; Michelle Goldberg, "Outlawing Dissent," *Salon,* 2/11/04, http://archive.salon.com/news/feature/2004/02/11/cointelpro.

the U.S. military into their ambitious program for the federal suppression of dissent.

"We must start thinking differently," observed General Ralph E. Eberhardt, commander of the new U.S. Northern Command, in late November of 2003. Whereas the intelligence agencies and military had, prior to 9/11, been focused on "the away game," they now must focus on "the home game"—i.e., our civilian polity, which has been reconceived as the domestic front in the U.S. "war on terror." As reported by William Arkin in the *Los Angeles Times*, Eberhardt commented that while "we are not going to be out there spying on people," NORTH-COM will "get information from those who do." By this the general meant the Counterintelligence Field Activity (CIFA), a Pentagon department founded after 9/11 to protect Defense Department personnel and "critical infrastructure" from espionage by foreign evildoers. In August of 2003, however, Secretary Rumsfeld broadened CIFA's mandate to maintain "a domestic law enforcement database that includes information related to potential terrorist threats directed against the Department of Defense." CIFA also has "a domestic 'data mining' mission: figuring out a way to process massive sets of public records, intercepted communications, credit card accounts, etc., to find 'actionable intelligence,' " Arkin wrote. "Though the military is just getting its systems in place," he concluded, "there can be no other conclusion: Domestic surveillance is back."*

---

*The regime is also using litigation to suppress dissent. In April of 2002, two Greenpeace activists boarded a vessel carrying mahogany that had been harvested illegally in Brazil and that was being shipped to the United States, in violation of the Convention on International Trade in Endangered Species—"the CITES Treaty"— which the U.S. government had signed in 1973. To alert the agents of the U.S. Fish & Wildlife Service that a criminal act was underway, the activists unfurled a banner: "President Bush: Stop Illegal Logging."

The activists, who openly declared themselves as Greenpeace members, were arrested and served time for their trespass. In July of 2003, however, the Department of Justice indicted Greenpeace for the actions of those individuals, charging that the organization had violated an obscure maritime law drafted in 1871 and never used throughout the twentieth century. (That law, U.S. Code 18, section 2279, was meant to end the piratical practice of "sailor mongering"—snatching or seducing sailors from their ships, so as to sell them to the crews of other vessels.)

Intended to shut Greenpeace down entirely, this tactic marked the first time that

While thus tracking and harassing those Americans who exercise their rights, the regime has also found an innovative way to balk, or ground, the most committed ones, thereby denying the basic right to freedom of assembly. On the basis of no law passed by the Congress, after 9/11 Bush & Co. quietly compiled a "no-fly" list that keeps perhaps—the exact number is unknown—a thousand citizens from flying on commercial airliners. The subject listed finds out, at the airport, that the airline has a mark on his/her name, signifying that the subject is an "aviation hazard," not allowed to board that flight or any other. A longer list includes the names of travelers who can board their planes, but only after undergoing a thorough search and inquisition. Those known to have been listed, by and large, are not of Arabic descent or otherwise hypothetically connected to Islamism or the Middle East, but mostly antiwar activists, Green Party organizers, and other harmless persons. (Oddly, David Nelson, son of Ozzie and Harriet, is on the longer list.) When people listed ask how they might clear their names, they're told that there's no way it can be done—an experience of hidden government authority that would appear to be quite foreign to us, its peculiar chill more reminiscent of Franz Kafka than Mark Twain, or Flannery O'Connor, or Bob Dylan.

Bush/Cheney justify such un-American activities, or most of them— preemptive war, denial of free speech, suspension of the writ of habeas corpus, the drive for global domination, etc.—by saying that "everything has changed" since 9/11, the threat of global terrorism now requiring us to ditch the childish fancies of U.S. democracy and let the White House take command. In other words, to be a good American, concerned about the rights of *all*, and loath to bend the knee to anyone in power, is not to be a good American, according to the Bush regime. As John Ashcroft said to those impertinent congressmen concerned about the Bill of Rights after 9/11:

---

an entire organization had been prosecuted for the civil disobedience of certain of its members. John Passacantando, "Civil Disobedience on Trial," TomPaine.common sense, 12/2/03 (http://www.tompaine.com/feature2.cfm/ID/9522).

To those who scare peace-loving people with phantoms of lost liberty, my message is this: Your tactics could only aid terrorists, for
they erode our national unity and diminish our resolve. They give
ammunition to America's enemies and pause to America's friends.
They encourage people of good will to remain silent in the face
of evil.

Far from being "patriotic," that outright threat was thoroughly anti-
American; but, no less important, it was also thoroughly untrue,
reasserting, as it did, the premise that Bush/Cheney have been driven by
a militant concern about the welfare of the people. While it has dili-
gently worried and harassed the public in the name of public safety, the
regime has done little to protect Americans from further terrorist attack.
They have, of course, provided many seemingly protective *gestures*, each
one calculated less to head off an attack than to goose up mass anxiety,
which, as Madison (and others) have observed, helps make people more
compliant. Such dubious symbolic "reassurances" include the omnipresent and Teutonic-sounding "Department of Homeland Security," its
random color-coded terror bulletins, and now and then a press conference called dramatically by the attorney general to tell the world about
a "big" arrest. There are also many pairs of soldiers, dressed in camou-
flage and hefting semiautomatic weapons, solemnly protecting places
like Penn Station and the Golden Gate Bridge. It isn't clear how such
patrols might halt a nuclear explosion on a cargo ship, or the bombing
of a petrochemical facility—possibilities just as likely at this moment as
they were on the day that "everything" putatively "changed" forever.

An administration genuinely interested in keeping people safe from a
repeat of 9/11 surely would have tried to figure out how 9/11 happened
in the first place. This regime's response has been to work as hard as
possible *against* such necessary discovery. They have been so diligent to
keep the truth hushed up that you would think they must be hiding
something.

For the past century, our major national calamities have been followed by commissions of inquiry. The morning after the *Titanic* sank,
soon after the Japanese bombed Pearl Harbor, the day John F. Kennedy

was shot, and less than two hours after the destruction of the *Challenger*, the government planned commisions to determine what went wrong. It took three months for the White House to respond to 9/11—and it was not to get an independent inquest going but to keep the Democrats from starting one. In January 2002, Cheney made repeated phone calls to Tom Daschle, then the Senate Majority Leader, who intended to initiate congressional hearings on the failure of U.S. intelligence before 9/11. Cheney advised Daschle *not* to call for a more sweeping public inquest—or else the Democrats would be depicted as al Qaeda sympathizers. Soon Bush himself met privately with Daschle, to hammer home the point; and so the Democrats sat back for months.*

Meanwhile, the White House acquiesced in the congressional hearings, since that inquiry (which began in February) was closed to public view and limited to the apparent failures of the CIA and FBI, both those clannish agencies being quite unlikely to tell Congress much of anything.† At the regime's urging, such major issues as homeland security, aviation safety, and immigration policy were taboo subjects. As restricted as it was, however, even that investigation was too nosy for Bush/Cheney, who from the start held back key documents—so zealously that the committee's Democrats grew hardened in their call for a commission with a broader mandate and an ample budget of its own. In June, that call became bipartisan, as those bereaved by 9/11—a tireless corps of widows, widowers, grieving children, grieving parents—started to persuade the public also to demand some answers. Still the White House worked behind the scenes to sabotage all efforts to establish a commission. For months Bush/Cheney lobbied Congress *not* to vote for it; and

*Ditto for the U.S. media. Bush/Cheney's efforts to prevent an independent inquest were reported in a wee item in the *Washington Times* on January 30, 2002, and soon thereafter by the Copley News Service and the *Congressional Quarterly.* The mainstream media did not report on the regime's obstructive moves until the summer, when public lobbying by the relatives of people killed on 9/11 forced the issue, briefly, out into the light of day.

†At one point, the FBI began investigating every member of the Joint Select Committee, ostensibly to find the source(s) of allegedly illegal leaks. "Major Battle Brewing over Leaks in Senate," *Christian Science Monitor,* 8/29/02.

once it passed the Senate on September 23, on a vote of 90 to 8, they managed to delay it more by pushing for a final version of the bill that would ensure no revelation whatsoever. Bush/Cheney insisted on a deadline of one year, limited subpoena power, the right to name the body's chair, and full authority to publish only some—or none—of the commission's ultimate report. The budget was a meager $3 million: $50 million had been dedicated to the *Challenger* commission, while the Whitewater investigation cost upward of $40 million.

All this happened *after* Bush & Co. had announced, on June 6, that it would *support* the legislation. (That news of an ostensibly new openness was itself timed so that no one would notice it, June 6 also being the day that FBI agent Colleen Rowley, lately famous as a whistleblower, testified in Congress.) While thus pretending to cooperate, Bush/Cheney worked intently to abort the inquiry or render it completely ineffectual.

In late October, Democratic legislators, by accepting several of Bush/Cheney's terms, worked out a compromise with Representative Porter Goss, chair of the House Intelligence Committee (and an ex-spook chummy with the White House). After Goss agreed, and the Democrats had held a jubilant press conference on the deal, Goss got a call from Cheney telling him to "keep negotiating." Representative Tim Roemer, Democrat of Indiana, noted rightly that "the White House is trying to pull the carpet over the independent commission, and do the slow roll and kill it."

The truth of that description became clearer still when, on November 14—nine days after the GOP's apparent surge of wins in the midterm elections—congressional Republicans unveiled a version of the new Homeland Security Bill that simply *left out* the agreed-upon provision for an independent inquest. Democrats at once decried that sneaky move, and forcefully enough so that the White House restored the stipulation by that evening—although the victory came at a further price, Bush/Cheney having wangled a few choice concessions from the Democrats. The president now *would* appoint the chair of the commission, and it would take a vote of six of the ten commissioners (five

Republicans, five Democrats) to issue a subpoena. The Democrats did manage to extend the schedule for the inquiry—from just one year to eighteen months.

And yet the commission still was not quite compromised enough to suit Bush/Cheney. Two weeks later, the president abandoned all pretense at any interest in a real investigation by assigning the chairmanship to Henry Kissinger, all-time champion dirty trickster. Although it was successful as a gesture of contempt, and certainly deserves some recognition as the most perverse appointment in our history, the effort failed: the chair-select was not about to publicize the client list of Kissinger Associates, as he would have been required to do if he had accepted the position. (Saddam Hussein had once been a client.)* Soon thereafter, the Joint Select Committee—Congress's inquiry into the catastrophe—submitted its nine-hundred-page report on 9/11; and Bush/Cheney promptly classified it, withholding all of it for months, and then, on July 24, releasing it with much blacked out.

Especially controversial was a missing twenty-eight-page chapter, allegedly detailing the Saudi government's failure to combat Islamist terrorism. That story was big news. Although it hinted that Bush/Cheney might be covering for their Saudi friends, the real effect was to help Bush/Cheney cover for themselves. (The Saudis angrily denied the rumors and insisted that the entire chapter be released at once.) The hoo-ha over that one missing chapter helped distract attention from the regime's constant and extensive interference with the legislators: a record of

---

*On June 4, 1989, twenty-three members of the US/Iraq Business Forum, a powerful pro-Ba'athist lobbying group headquartered in Washington, D.C., took a trip to Baghdad to discuss a number of commercial partnerships with Saddam Hussein. The delegation included prominent representatives of Amoco, Mobil, Occidental Petroleum, Xerox, Westinghouse, General Motors, and Bell Textron, among other corporations; included in the group as well was Alan Stoga, a specialist in debt restructuring and a senior associate of Henry Kissinger's consulting firm. "The Iraqis specifically invited Stoga to come," said Marshal Wiley, the Forum's founder, "because their biggest problem at this time was obtaining credit to finance their reconstruction programs." Kenneth R. Timmerman, *The Death Lobby: How the West Armed Iraq* (Boston: Houghton Mifflin, 1991), p. 349.

stonewalling that *was* allowed in the released report, in an afterword pro-
saically entitled "Access Limitations Encountered by the Joint Inquiry."*

And so that seeming exposé about the missing chapter had itself
served to help the White House hide a lot *more* information from the
public. First of all, there was considerably more material withheld from
Congress than that bit about the Saudis; and it came out that the White
House had found numerous ways to keep a world of data from the legislators in the first place. The congressional investigators were forbidden
to see any of the contents of the President's Daily Brief (PDB); and "CIA
personnel were not allowed to be interviewed regarding the simple
process by which the PDB is prepared." Nor could the Joint Select Committee interview George Tenet, director of the CIA, or read a series of
reports, drafted by the CIA's Counter-Terrorism Center, "regarding the
strengths and weaknesses of the CIA's liaison relationships with a variety
of foreign governments." The congressional investigators asked to see the
budget requests submitted by U.S. intelligence agencies over the years,
but the White House would not let them. They tried to learn how U.S.
covert action programs had been set up to fight al Qaeda, but the
National Security Council (NSC) held back all the pertinent documents. For that matter, "access to most information that involved NSC-
level discussions was blocked . . . by the White House." Having been
informed by the FBI that "two of the hijackers had numerous contacts
with a long time FBI counterterrorism informant," the Joint Select
Committee asked to interview the latter, to resolve some ambiguities in
his reporting and evaluate the bureau's use of his services. "The FBI, supported by the Attorney General and the Administration, refused to make
the informant available for an interview or to serve a Congressional dep-

---

*While those redacted twenty-eight pages came up everywhere, and often more
than once—on CBS, ABC, NBC, CNBC, and Fox, on NPR and PBS, in the *New
York Times*, *Washington Post*, *Chicago Tribune*, and *USA Today*, by the news services of
Copley, Cox, Knight Ridder, and Gannett, in *Time* and *Newsweek*, and so on—the
damning afterword about Bush/Cheney's systematic noncooperation was noted by
Marie Cocco in a New York *Newsday* column (August 7, 2003), which also ran in the
Akron Beacon Journal, the Albany *Times-Union*, and the *Tallahassee Democrat*.

osition notice and subpoena on the informant, whose whereabouts were known to the FBI at the time."

All such tactics served not just to shut out Congress, but, primarily, to further handicap the 9/11 commission, whose mandate was to build on what the Joint Select Committee could dig up. When the commission started work in January 2003, the Joint Select Committee's findings had been classified, and would stay classified for six more months; and even after certain parts of the report had been made public, some would be capriciously *reclassified* by a certain White House "working group." And as if all that were not enough to slow the inquest to a crawl, the White House also classified the *transcripts of the Joint Select Committee's hearings.* (As a Commission member, Representative Roemer found that he was not allowed to see the transcripts, even though he had himself served on the Joint Select Committee.) Any documents requested from that heavily guarded cache had to be "reviewed" first by White House lawyers, just in case the contents might be "privileged."

Such bureaucratic interference ate up seven months of the commission's precious time,* and the inquiry continued to find roadblocks at every turn. As Slade Gorton, former senator from Washington, complained at one point, it took months for some of the commission members even to get security clearances from the FBI and CIA. Papers would take ages to appear, or never did appear: the Pentagon and NORAD—

---

*Although it did not meet until February 11, 2003, the commission's clock had started ticking on November 27, 2002: the day Bush signed the bill approving the inquiry, which was set to run for eighteen months, until May 27, 2004. Thus had the commission already lost three months by the time its members first sat down together.

While their overall purpose clearly was to keep the lid on the details of 9/11, Bush/Cheney also had a more specific reason to delay releasing the congressional report. As Commissioner Max Cleland noted, the White House, eager for a war against Iraq, did not want it known that the report had found no links between al Qaeda and Saddam Hussein. "The reason this report was delayed for so long—deliberately opposed at first, then slow-walked after it was created—is that the administration wanted to get the war in Iraq in and over . . . before [it] came out," the senator observed in late July. "Had this report come out in January like it should have done, we would have known these things before the war in Iraq, which would not have suited the administration." "No Iraq Link to Al-Qaida," UPI, 7/23/03.

North American Aerospace Defense Command—were especially unre-
sponsive to commission queries; and the White House claimed at times
that some requested documents "were missing or did not exist." Interviews were likewise blocked, or otherwise policed. Until Bush reversed
himself about the matter in late March of 2004, the commission could
not question Condoleezza Rice, but "were forced to submit written
questions to a deputy." Those witnesses who did appear, moreover, were
not made to answer under oath, so that they were not legally obliged to
tell the truth. And even if witnesses were inclined to shed some light on
things, the urge was likely to be killed by the unfriendly presence of
some higher-up from their department sent to monitor their testimony.
"The commission feels unanimously that it's some intimidation to have
somebody sitting behind you all the time who you either work with or
works with your agency," said Chairman Thomas Kean six months into
the inquiry.* Such tactics, on top of the commission's meager budget and
tight schedule, finally made a proper inquiry all but impossible.

On every homeland front, Bush/Cheney either have done nothing, or
too little, as they have always acted not to keep the people safe but
to enrich their donors, gratify their base, and augment their own
power.

In April of 2003, Senator Ernest Hollings (D-SC) tried to dedicate $1
billion to improving port security by adding an amendment to a bill for
covering the costs—$79 billion—of the invasion of Iraq. The GOP-
dominated Senate turned it down. And so authorities are now inspect-
ing somewhere between 1 percent and 2 percent of all incoming ships.
Neither has the regime done anything to improve security at the nation's

---

*Kean's complaint about the White House using "minders" to inhibit witness
testimony got just one day of modest coverage in some twelve American newspapers, mostly local. By contrast, when the Iraqi government tried to influence the
global news by having Ba'athist agents present at all interviews and broadcasts by
foreign journalists, the U.S. press reported *that* repressive use of "minders" often
and indignantly.

nuclear and petrochemical facilities, any one of which would make an excellent terrorist target. There was the Chemical Security Act, a strong bill drafted by Senator Jon Corzine (D-NJ), requiring that those companies work up response plans for such sabotage, submit them to the Environmental Protection Agency (EPA) and DHS for official review, and spend the money necessary to design inherently safer technologies. The bill also set firm standards for security measures. It was too much for the industries concerned, which instead supported (and had helped to write) the Chemical Facilities Security Act, submitted by Senator James Inhofe (R-OK). This bill stipulates that no response plans need to be submitted to the government; that the companies must take "security measures to reduce the vulnerability of the chemical source"—but sets no standards for such measures; and that the EPA will be prohibited from "fieldwork"—i.e., checking out the companies' "improvements."

Bush & Co. seeks to dominate the skies, investing billions in "National Missile Defense" (NMD) as if it were an antiterrorist program (and as if it worked). Bush & Co. also wants to keep the planet under full surveillance. "We need an illuminator, throwing into relief all the pictures and activities on the earth's surface," said one of Rumsfeld's people in October of 2003. To that end, Congress has agreed to spend $100 million on "space-based radar" (SBR), while the Pentagon, under its "NextView" program, has granted $530 million to promote the manufacture of a hot new satellite with unprecedented imaging capacity. The navy has invested $4 million in a fleet of mighty blimps, able to spot enemy activity through heavy clouds.

Here on the ground, meanwhile, Bush hasn't spent a nickel on improving truck security, as countless rigs pull into the nation's cities every day and night. In New York, the Port Authority police are able to check only certain of the *smaller* trucks approaching the congested Lincoln Tunnel. The work is tedious, and so the force is undermanned. "A lot of people didn't sign on to check trucks," said the captain of the Lincoln Tunnel detail in the spring of 2003. "It's tough on them."

And yet our cities may still be less dangerous than air travel in America today, which is evidently just as risky as it ever was. Although

Bush/Cheney did increase the number of airport security personnel by
nearly seventy thousand, the quality of those new hires is dubious, as
Bush & Co. would not permit that federal workforce to be unionized.
Thus the job had less appeal for people adequately trained, and, more
important, management is not obliged to heed workers' complaints
about poor training, too long hours, ill-functioning equipment, and
other hazards to the public welfare.*

Certainly airport security has not improved perceptibly. (Nor has
train security, which Bush & Co. ignored until al Qaeda's bloody strike
at Spanish trains in March 2004.) An interim report by the Government
Accounting Office, published two years after 9/11, revealed that the
office's investigators had no trouble sneaking box cutters and other lethal
items past all those guards and onto planes. "Guns and knives are still
getting through. It's very depressing," a congressional source told *Airport
Security Report.*

Every day, some 950,000 passengers fly into and out of New York's
airports on planes loaded with uninspected cargo. In September of 2003,
as Congress debated the first Homeland Security spending bill, Democrats proposed to include a ban on the use of passenger planes for ship-
ping such blind items, but the GOP, at the urging of the airline industry,
rejected the proposal. Instead, the bill would halt that daily risk, eventually, by throwing lots of money at it: $85 million to research and develop,
then procure, high-tech devices for screening air freight. Whereas a ban
could save innumerable lives, in other words, the slower and iffier alternative would benefit some corporate donor, and so the issue was, as
usual, decided by Bush/Cheney to the detriment of public safety.

As the regime has ignored such deadly possibilities as a car-bombed

*Bush/Cheney's cosmetic measures do not take account of the pervasive problem
of corruption among federal agents, whose laxness and venality have seriously weakened the security apparatus at some airports, notwithstanding all the tough talk after
9/11. Diane Kleiman, a U.S. Customs agent at John F. Kennedy Airport (and formerly a Queens prosecutor), witnessed gross malfeasance of all kinds among her colleagues, but when she reported it, she was threatened and harassed and ultimately
fired. See Craig Horowitz, "An Inconvenient Woman," *New York Magazine,* 6/2/03.

oil refinery, a nuclear explosive hidden in a truck or ship, or another spate of skyjackings, its reckless foreign and economic policies have only made these dangers that much more potentially destructive. Before 9/11, Bush/Cheney were, to say the least, indifferent to the global threat of weapons proliferation, which has always meant enormous wealth for some. In July of 2001, Bush & Co. opposed a UN-backed nonbinding small-arms treaty that would have tracked arms sales and prohibited foreign arms sales to nongovernmental groups like, say, al Qaeda or the Shining Path.* In its annual budget for 2001, moreover, Bush & Co. proposed extensive cuts in U.S. programs that had done much to help the Russians clean up their old nuclear facilities, significantly tightening the security at those crumbling, leaky sites.† And now the global weapons trade increased by such unthinking moves has been expanded and diversified immeasurably by Bush & Co.'s erratic, devastating "war on terrorism." A world thus gruesomely destabilized is one in which it's

---

*John Bolton, U.S. delegate to the UN conference, invoked the Second Amendment as the reason why the regime could not back the treaty. While this explanation surely gratified the National Rifle Association, a power to be reckoned with by any national politician, Bush/Cheney's motives had to do with more than constitutional rights and rural voters. According to the International Action Network on Small Arms (IANSA), "The real reason the accord won't work is because the major small-arms producers and buyers oppose it. The United States—the world's largest exporter of small arms, accounting for about $1.3 billion of the $4 billion total sold worldwide— joins with Russia and China against the pact. So do their top customers in Africa, Asia, and Latin America." "U.S. Panders to Gun Lobby on Small-Arms Treaty," IANSA press release, 07/11/01. The treaty was backed by Oxfam and Amnesty International as well as IANSA.

†"The International Materials Protection Control & Accounting Program (IMPC&A), which puts in place security measures at Russia's more than 100 nuclear sites, now faces reductions of nearly $40 million. The Nuclear Cities Initiative, which works to combat 'brain drain' by creating civilian jobs for nuclear workers in the closed nuclear cities, was cut by $20 million. The Initiative for Proliferation Prevention faces cuts of only $2 million, but the cuts will affect Russian programs most severely, hindering the project's efforts to couple displaced weapons scientists with private companies doing research in their region." Fiona Morgan, "A Dangerous Step Backwards," *Salon*, 5/16/01 (www.salon.com/politics/feature/2001/05/16/loose_nukes/).

easier than ever to get hold of killing agents of all kinds—the very situation that, the regime told us endlessly, a war against Iraq would certainly prevent. "On balance, we are not safer," said nonproliferation expert Henry Krepon, on the second anniversary of the terrorist attacks. The broader new availability of nuclear materials, poison gas, and bio-weapons represents a great leap backward. "We are actually less safe than we were before the war on terror was waged after 9/11."

And, finally, the impact of Bush/Cheney's economic policies has made it practically impossible for local governments to reach the proper point of readiness for further terrorist assault. According to Jamie Metzl of the Council on Foreign Relations,

> [T]he United States remains dangerously ill prepared to handle a
> catastrophic attack. On average, fire departments across the coun-
> try have only enough radios to equip half the firefighters on a shift,
> and breathing apparatuses for only one-third. Only 10 percent of
> fire departments in the United States have the personnel and equip-
> ment to respond to a building collapse. Police departments in cities
> across the country do not have the protective gear to safely secure
> a site following an attack with weapons of mass destruction (WMD).

In most states, public laboratories "still lack basic equipment and expertise to adequately respond to a chemical or biological attack, and 75 percent of state labs report being overwhelmed by too many testing requests." Most cities also lack "the necessary equipment to determine what kind of hazardous materials emergency responders may be facing." Although Bush/Cheney spend our money with imperial lavishness—a tax-and-spend extravagance that would have staggered Roosevelt, or Kennedy, or LBJ—there are no revenues for such essential preparations. The grants bestowed by Homeland Security go only for training and equipment, which has left municipalities nationwide without the funds to pay a workforce. "It is great to have money to train and equip people, but if you don't have the people to train and equip it's really not all that helpful," testified Mayor Thomas Ambrosino of Revere, at a Massachusetts State House hearing on the lack of funds afflicting many cities' efforts. "Money for salaries and overtime is what is essential at this point."

Because of Bush/Cheney's priorities, in short, we the people are all sitting ducks, and no amount of wishful thinking or upbeat propaganda can improve our chances.

Bush & Co. is keenly sensitive to public needs, but only insofar as they provide good opportunities for hammering at the *message* that "Bush cares." Surely every politician takes advantage of emergency conditions, using them as the dramatic backdrop for a jut-jawed pose of fatherly concern, a solemn offer of immediate assistance, and, usually, a promise of some new protective measures. Team Bush, however, takes the cynicism of such histrionics to a whole new level, as the heroic pose itself is all they care about. If Bush offers aid, there is no guarantee that anyone will ever see it (unless a major industry has asked for it). The fact that President Bush showed up to have his picture taken seems to him to be support enough.

Bush/Cheney's tendency to milk catastrophe for its theatrical effects has long been obvious to those who have been harmed directly by it. The 9/11 rescue workers, for example, learned of it firsthand, some months after the president's boffo bit of martial cheerleading at Ground Zero on 9/14.* "President Bush, you are either with us or against us. You can't have it both ways," said Harold Schaitberger, general president of the International Association of Firefighters, on August 15, 2002, after Bush had slashed the funding to improve the radios used by firefighters. "Don't lionize our fallen brothers in one breath and then stab us in the back." Seasoned U.S. soldiers in Iraq feel likewise about Bush's routine teary invocations of "our troops," and his now-and-then upbeat appearances in their vicinity. "It's too bad Mr. Bush didn't add us to his holiday agenda. The men said the same, but you'll never read that in the paper," wrote an army nurse in late November 2003, following the pres-

*Bush stood tall amid the rubble, with a small group of exhausted rescue workers. "The people who did this will hear from us soon!" he shouted through his bullhorn, and the crowd erupted in a grateful fury. The scene played beautifully on television. (The next day, speaking with reporters at Camp David, Bush referred back to Ground Zero as "the construction site.")

ident's meticulously staged Thanksgiving visit to a (preselected) group of soldiers at Baghdad International Airport.

> Mr. President would rather lift fake turkeys for photo ops, it seems. Maybe because my patients wouldn't make very pleasant photos . . . most don't look all that great, and the ones with facial wounds and external fixation devices look downright scary. And a heck of a lot of them can't talk, anyway, and some never will talk again. Well, this is probably more than you want to know, but there's no spin on this one. It's pure carnage.*

There is no doubt that a corrosive cynicism drives the president's ongoing propaganda effort. ("Thanks for serving as a prop," he joked sarcastically to Democratic Senator Paul Sarbanes, who was one of several legislators standing mutely at the president's back while Bush performed for the reporters.) And yet Bush & Co.'s inordinate overemphasis on "spin" expresses more than an elite's contempt for the manipulable masses. The regime's obsessive use of propaganda trickery also bespeaks a buccaneering scorn for the constraints that mere reality must finally place on the imperial imagination. They *do* believe that they can spin it *all*—yes, even the "pure carnage" in Iraq—not just because they think that we, the people, are all suckers, but, fundamentally, because they are themselves unable to believe that they cannot do anything they want to do. They lie as wildly as they do because they are forever lying to themselves; and they must keep up the self-deception, or be confronted by the fact of their infallibility. The virtue they most value, therefore, is *intransigence*. Hence Bush's constant self-description as "determined," "focused," and "resolved," as if he were an entity as fixed and imperturbable as his own statue. This simple doctrine of the iron mind is Bush's managerial

---

*This clear perception of the giant gap beween Bush/Cheney's words and deeds is widespread in the U.S. military: "In recent months, President Bush and the Republican-controlled Congress have missed no opportunity to heap richly deserved praise on the military. But talk is cheap—and getting cheaper by the day, judging from the nickel-and-dime treatment the troops are getting lately." Thus the *Army Times* began a cogent editorial—"Nothing but Lip Service"—in its issue for June 30, 2003.

credo. "A president has got to be the calcium in the backbone," he told
Bob Woodward in August of 2002. "If I weaken, the whole team weak-
ens. If I'm doubtful, I can assure you there will be a lot of doubt."

Of all our presidents, this Bush is certainly the only one who would
thus cast himself as a hard mineral with a primitive cohesive function.
His metaphor suggests not worldly leadership of either the civilian *or* the
military kind, for heads of thriving states and winning armies must alike
be capable of improvising, innovating, changing course as circumstances
change. They have to think. On the other hand, Bush sees himself not
as a mind, nor even as one part of a collective mind atop the government, but only as an ossifying agent, rather like cement or starch. In his
command there is no flexibility, no openness, only fear of weakness—
which the president apparently associates with thought itself: "If I'm
doubtful, I can assure you there will be a lot of doubt." In Bush's moral
universe, *doubt* is the bad opposite of godly *zeal*. The latter he must endlessly and vividly—and, necessarily, unthinkingly—exude, as the inspir-
ing figurehead of a crusade. *Doubt*, on the other hand, he must avoid as
if it were the plague. To raise questions, study every option, call on
expertise outside the leader's inner circle, would be a sign of insufficient
faith. Bush regards it as perhaps his greatest virtue that he has his mind
made up and tightly closed. "I believe what I believe is right," as he put
it to a pack of unbelieving journalists in Rome in the summer of 2001.

His presidency is, in short, a radical faith-based initiative—and in
that way is also opposite the Jeffersonian ideal. *Learning* was not just the
greatest passion of the sage of Monticello, but, in his view, a mass
endeavor vital to democracy and crucial to the progress of humanity. He
desired it for the people as whole-heartedly as he pursued it on his own:
"No other foundation can be devised, for the preservation of freedom
and happiness." Bush/Cheney, on the other hand, do not believe in anybody learning anything: not the people, whom they prefer to keep completely in the dark; and not themselves, as they believe they know it all
already. Certainly the people still can learn, despite the vast impediments
thrown up by this regime, but the regime itself just does not want to
know, and therefore has learned—can learn, will learn—nothing.

This disability, and Bush/Cheney's absolute indifference to the public good, may help explain why they took no preventive steps whatever prior to 9/11, even though they had been clearly and repeatedly forewarned throughout the summer of 2001 (see pp. 221–22). It is quite possible, of course, that Bush/Cheney *chose* to let those horrors happen for its own political advantage—a chilling theory for which there is abundant evidence. But if they had no such dark motive, their inaction at that moment would be wholly typical, as they have always been impervious to warnings in the public interest. Alerted, by both the CIA and the State Department, that they had made no plans for a postwar Iraq, Bush/Cheney simply blew off the alert. Likewise, they were deaf to frequent warnings from their only ally. "The British regularly raised their concerns about how much planning was going on to secure the country after Saddam, but the issue was largely ignored," reported the *Observer*. ("One of the things that did not work out between us was a properly agreed strategy," the British ambassador to Washington, Sir Christopher Meyer, observed dryly in November of 2003.)* Bush & Co.'s indifference came at a terrific cost, still being paid in blood day after day.

The situation is just as dire on the home front. Bush/Cheney's FEMA just said no when Governor Gray Davis asked the president for funds to clear the combustible deadwood getting ever hotter throughout southern California. Beyond noting that it had already spent some $40 million on the governor's forest problem (Davis had requested $430 million), "FEMA added, in its own words, the thought that its job is to help clean up after emergencies, not try to prevent them," reported Richard Reeves. The fires that all of California could see coming finally cost over $2 billion and killed twenty-two people. Governor Davis wrote to Bush in April. The fires struck in October.

In May, Dr. Stanley B. Prusiner, winner of the 1997 Nobel Prize in Medicine, tried to get a meeting with Ann Veneman, Bush/Cheney's sec-

*The United States was also warned by the Iraqi National Accord (INA), an opposition group of ex-Ba'athist exiles and army dissidents, that organized resistance was in the works. "Militias are being established," INA head Ayad Allawi told the U.S. administrators in Baghdad, to no avail. "US Warned of Consequences If It Does Not Clamp Down on New Militias," *Financial Times*, 4/26/03.

retary of agriculture, to warn her of a looming danger to the nation's food supply. A case of mad cow disease had broken out in Canada, and so Prusiner, discoverer of the disease's etiology, wanted Veneman to have all U.S. cattle tested for the illness. (Only 10 percent were being tested then.) Veneman would not see the neurologist. He later met Karl Rove, who set up a meeting. "I went to tell her that what happened in Canada was going to happen in the United States," Prusiner said. "I told her it was just a matter of time." The meeting was a failure. "Ms. Veneman's response (he said she did not share his sense of urgency) left him frustrated," reported the *New York Times* on Christmas Day of 2003—the same day that mad cow disease was first reported to have broken out in the United States. (It came from Canada, just as the neurologist had warned.)*

In part, such unresponsiveness betrays the regime's tendency to stiff the enemy whenever possible: Davis was a Democrat, as were most Californians—so what would be the *point* of doing anything for them? The same partisan calculus dictates the weird inequities in Bush & Co.'s antiterrorism budget, which gives New York and California ("blue states") far *less* aid per capita than Utah and Wyoming ("red states"). Rather than prevent the fires from devastating southern California, Bush & Co. exploited them to further free the hand of corporate lumber (through the "Healthy Forests Initiative"); and instead of trying to halt mad cow disease, Bush/Cheney wanted to protect the beef cartel from any news about mad cow disease, an epidemic looming on the near horizon now for years, as several experts have observed.

Such interests rule this White House, and yet the economistic argument alone does not account for the peculiar zest with which

---

*Bush & Co.'s Department of Agriculture would not expand its testing for mad cow disease until mid-March of 2004—by which time over fifty countries had banned imports of U.S. beef. A Kansas beef company had offered to test its own cattle voluntarily, to boost consumer confidence, and California legislators were at work on a new bill requiring that all beef in the state be tested. "The USDA initially rejected the two proposals and even threatened to prosecute unauthorized mad cow testing under a 1915 law." "U.S. expands testing for mad cow disease," *Chicago Tribune*, 3/16/04.

Bush/Cheney have ignored repeated warnings of all kinds. Those trying to alert Bush/Cheney to protect the people have roused only the regime's contempt, as all such rational concern strikes these intrepid swaggerers as wimpy, priggish, *soft*. "If there's a kind of a hand-wringing attitude going on when times are tough, I don't like it," Bush told Woodward. Of course, this is in part a matter of political theatrics, as Bush does better when he gets to strut and thump his chest amid the ruins than he would have looked campaigning, or agreeing, to forestall the big disaster in the first place. However, the Machiavellian argument is also insufficient, as it begs the question, *Why* does Bush do best as an avenging he-man, turning up belatedly to call for foreign blood? The fact is that such bully posturing works best for Bush and for his deputies because they *like* that role, whereas they *hate* those who would only mess with Texas, urging this or that precautionary measure, the need for which is never obvious to the extremists at the top. Hence Cheney's infamous antienvironmentalist sneer before 9/11: "Conservation may be a sign of personal virtue, but it is not a sufficient basis for a sound, comprehensive energy policy." Bush spoke similarly in response to his own EPA's analysis of global warming, which the agency confirmed as a deadly side effect of international industrial activity: "I read the report by the bureaucracy." In Bush's universe, that was somewhat like saying, "I read the report by al Qaeda."

Clearly, Bush/Cheney are not bothered by apocalyptic prospects, in part because they are unable to imagine them—or, concerning those catastrophes that have already taken place, unable even to perceive them. This president is deaf and blind to evidence, however harrowing, of past atrocities. In July of 2003, for example, Bush started his brief trip to Africa in Senegal, with a look inside the Slave House on Goree Island. After having toured that gloomy prison (where Africans were kept chained up for weeks, or months, before the Middle Passage), the president said this at the airport near Dakar:

> I had the opportunity to go out to Goree Island and talk about
> what slavery meant to America. It's very interesting when you think
> about it, the slaves who left here to go to America, because of their

steadfast and their religion and their belief in freedom, helped change America.

America is what it is today because of what went on in the past.*

Apparently, Bush did not know, or want to know, that "the slaves who left here to go to America" were hauled across the sea against their will. In fact, he even seemed to be suggesting that those Africans dispersed *because* they were enslaved in Africa, and so "left here to go to America," where they'd be free. And, indeed, those Africans, Bush claimed, helped make this a free country, by bringing with them "their belief in freedom," which evidently might have been unknown here if the slaves had not imported it. (America would also have no "steadfast" if the Africans had not brought in their own; and, of course, they also came with "their religion," as we can clearly see today, there being so many animist congregations in the United States.)

It is remarkable that any U.S. president would know so little about slavery in America, and it is astonishing that Bush could make so blithe a statement on the subject *right after having toured a slavery museum.* That establishment's whole point is to commemorate the fate of millions of West Africans who were kept warehoused there, and thence shipped off to the Americas for sale, each one passing through a "Door of No Return," which makes it very clear that they would never see their homes again. Unless he had his eyes closed during the tour, Bush must simply have refused to take the lesson in, such education striking him as pointless, all wrong, unacceptable.†

*The president continued: "Yet when I looked out over the sea, it reminded me that we've always got to keep history in mind. And one of the things that we've always got to know about America is that we love freedom, that we love people to be free, that freedom is God's gift to each and every individual. That's what we believe in our country."

†A few months earlier, Bush had toured Auschwitz. Afterward, he asked the guide one question: "Do people challenge the accuracy of what you present?" That odd query may have been inspired somehow by Holocaust revisionism; or, as journalist David Neiwert argues, it may actually have been an oblique effort by the president to reconfirm his case against Saddam Hussein. (Posted on Orcinus on 6/1/03, at

Bush & Co.'s refusal to acknowledge the dark strains and chapters in our national past pervades the regime's powerful hostility toward the sixties and seventies, when it was suddenly permissible to talk about our national misdeeds. The regime feels itself deeply insulted by that noisy, painful, gorgeous interregnum, when there emerged, for all to see, some truths that Bush & Co. will not take in; and so the regime has been struggling to *repeal* what happened then. That era taught that it is un-American, and quite impossible, to pacify an entire foreign population through the use of force: Bush/Cheney have ignored that warning, so we are back in Vietnam, only this time in the deserts of Arabia. That era taught that it is un-American, and quite impossible, for a democracy to answer mass dissent through antidemocratic means, whether in Birmingham or Baghdad, Miami or Fallujah, Oakland or Tikrit: Bush/Cheney have ignored that warning, shooting protestors with rubber bullets or live rounds, and throwing them in jail, and otherwise abusing them, and thereby only broadening the resistance to their own dominion. That era taught that democratic politics must function openly and by the rules, and not use private forces, dirty tricks, and secret funds: Bush/Cheney have ignored that warning, routinely using Richard Nixon's smear technique and other stealthy methods, while also rehabil-

———

www.dneiwert.blogspot.com/2003_06_01_dneiwert_archive.html-62k.) At the time, Bush & Co. was going all out to liken the Iraqi dictator's atrocities to Hitler's. The stop at Auschwitz was a part of that campaign, as Bush made clear in his speech afterward (which implicitly attacked the French and Germans for their failure to resist the evil in both cases). Hence those who "challenge the accuracy" of Holocaust survivors' memories would be comparable, in Bush's mind, to those who were then "challeng[ing] the accuracy" of Bush & Co.'s claims about the threat posed by Saddam Hussein. For all the vileness of the Ba'ath regime, that linkage was absurd, at once exaggerating the Iraqi danger and trivializing and exploiting the annihilation of the European Jews. In short, whether Bush himself was skeptical about the evidence at Auschwitz, or merely using the death camp as propaganda for his own preemptive war, his question was another sign of an extraordinary obtuseness. "Witness to Auschwitz Evil, Bush Draws a Lesson," *New York Times*, 6/1/03.

itating all the perpetrators of Iran/contra,* and otherwise displaying an imperial disdain for U.S. and international law.

The era of "the counterculture" was, in short, a moment perfectly congruent with the spirit of our Declaration of Independence and the Bill of Rights, and that is why Bush/Cheney so detest it, and keep attacking it, forever overstressing the long hair and the hash pipes and the loud profanities on campus. To say only that Bush/Cheney hate American democracy, however, merely names the animus without explaining it. The peculiar vitriol of today's Republicans arises not from ideology or class interests alone, but has a deeper source, to be examined later. For now, it is enough just to identify the force that we, the people, are now up against. Although he ran as the un-Clinton (another lie, as we shall see), Bush is in fact the anti-Jefferson, his movement now intent on cancellation of the Bill of Rights, radical abridgement of the Constitution, and a betrayal of the Revolution that was waged so that we might be free to rule ourselves, to hear the truth, to speak our minds, and to seek our happiness.

How did this happen? How could we, as a nation, have so thoroughly devolved, going from George Washington to George W. Bush? For the framers, many factors were crucial to the maintenance of American democracy: freedom of expression, habeas corpus, separation of powers, the disentanglement of church and state—and civic virtue, which impels the people to defend democracy against whatever enemy would threaten it. As we have seen, our basic rights are now at risk. Their fate, and ours, depends on an immediate revival of the only institution left among us to enable the survival of our system: the U.S. press.

---

*John Poindexter, Otto Reich, Elliott Abrams, and John Negroponte are all working for the government again, while Michael Ledeen, as noted earlier, now enjoys resurgent influence. Bush & Co.'s attempt to make Henry Kissinger the chairman of the 9/11 commission was a remarkably broad case of such rightist rehabilitation.

CHAPTER 2

What We Don't Know

That all this could have happened here, and life, apparently, could go on as usual, suggests that the U.S. Constitution is unknown in the United States—not just generally unread, but its key tenets and essential vision largely absent from the public consciousness. And this is *not* to say that most Americans have spurned the great republican ideal that permeates the founding document of their own nation. It is, rather, that the Constitution's import has been minimized or buried, as if driven underground, so that the very credo of American democracy sounds slightly off the wall, or even dangerous. Those who cling to its ideals—and they are, still, the national majority—perceive no general reconfirmation of their vision, which is the vision of our Constitution. Although we often hear that noble document invoked as if it were a patriotic totem, like Old Glory or (as some believe) the Ten Commandments, never is its still-revolutionary vision reaffirmed in public, unless in opposition to Iran or Cuba or some other obviously closed society. Indeed, our Constitution's dearest and most revolutionary declarations are shrugged off or belittled or distorted when they do happen to come up in public. Those who are, in fact, this country's most devoted patriots often tend to feel isolated and eccentric, that consensus going unreflected in the bright commercial propaganda picture of America sold daily, inescapably, to all of us and to the world at large.

To set things right when they're so deeply wrong would necessarily mean thinking revolutionary thoughts again, but even that will be impossible for most of us as long as the essential vision of our Constitution goes largely unconfirmed, and even unacknowledged, by the very institution that is most obliged to nurture it. By this I do not mean the nation's schools, which, as noted earlier, have for the most part shied away from just the sort of honest, thorough civic education that the preservation of our system would require (and that Jefferson established at the University of Virginia). Certainly our schools have been remiss and must do more to ready our young people for political participation. But even that improvement can't take place until another basic institution has fulfilled *its* civic obligation, for there can be no democratic institutional reform, educational or otherwise, until the issue has been brought to our attention, and the problem studied openly and all our options fully put before us, by the press.

It is because the U.S. press has largely shirked its all-important constitutional duty that we strong believers in American democracy now feel like exiles in this country. Major public crimes and glaring improprieties take place out in the light of day—a presidential race subverted, the investigations into 9/11 stonewalled by the White House, preemptive war promoted with transparent lies or bald delusions—and yet the U.S. press has mainly gone about its business, hemming and harrumphing as if such corruption were quite normal. The press abroad, meanwhile, *has* covered such enormities, so that the people of Canada, Japan, France, India, Germany, and Britain (among other nations) actually know more about what's happening here, and more about what's happening abroad at U.S. hands, than most Americans could ever know from watching U.S. network news *and* cable news *and* reading each day's paper. Many good reporters are still out there, but they seem to have a hard time getting space above the fold, or much time before the camera, with the sort of story that every good American would want to know and needs to know. Thus we come to feel as if there's something wrong with *us*, as we begin to doubt the evidence of our own senses and even half-forget our rights, the law, and the great democratic vision that inspired this nation and that we had believed in all our lives.

The Unknown First Amendment

We have come to see the First Amendment as a sort of constitutional sanctuary set up mainly for the brash *producers* of "free speech." Thus sheltered, individual Americans can vent their views, talk dirty, call each other names, etc., while groups of citizens are free to congregate outdoors and make a lot of racket (if they can find a First Amendment zone to do it in). And while such amateurs are free to rant and ramble to their hearts' content—it is *their right* to do so—cultural professionals of every kind are also free to write their novels and TV shows, sing their songs, direct their movies and commercials, rap their raps, and do their in-your-face performance art. The commercial giants that vend such products, and use them to vend other products, are likewise free to make their pitch and make the sale, no matter how offensive some Americans may find the CD or the movie or the show. And so, according to this view, the First Amendment is entirely *democratic*, as it protects your average noisy guy no less than it protects Time Warner, Bertelsmann, and General Electric. All being free to "speak," we are all free.

Certainly, all such expression must, in a democracy, be well defended from state censorship or wrathful mobs, because if any sort of content can be blotted out at someone's whim, all expression, finally, will be prey to censorship. But the purpose of the First Amendment is not just to keep performers on the job, or newspapers above the libel laws, or media corporations in the black, or art museums abuzz. Free expression cannot serve to keep *us* free unless it ultimately tells *us* what *we* need to know, so that *we* can dictate how the government is run and not vice versa. In short, the First Amendment is far more than just a license to offend. Shock value, so commonplace today, was a tactic unknown to the framers. They did not craft the Bill of Rights with Howard Stern in mind, or full frontal nudity, or Karen Finley, or Ann Coulter, or Lil' Kim. Nor did they value freedom of the press because it might one day make Rupert Murdoch very rich and boost GE's stock price. The press was to be free for purely civic reasons: to help the people keep track of

the government's performance, and to enable broad and vigorous debate
about it and thereby stay in charge of this republic.

This was the framers' goal in singling out the press—the only private
institution thus included—for special constitutional protection. That
the press must serve as an impediment to tyranny, by the state or
by an ignorant majority, is a point on which the first Republicans
were adamant and unambiguous. "[T]o the press alone," wrote Madison, "checkered as it is with abuses, the world is indebted for all the triumphs which have been gained by reason and humanity over error and
oppression." Madison was zealous in defense of an unfettered press—he
wanted all newspapers mailed for free—and he was not alone in that
commitment.* "If a nation expects to be both ignorant and free, in a
state of civilization, it expects what never was and never will be," wrote
Jefferson, who also made this famous observation: "Were it left to me to
decide whether we should have a government without newspapers, or
newspapers without a government, I should not hesitate a moment to
prefer the latter." Even in his final years, much scarred by journalistic
calumny in his two presidential contests, Jefferson remained devout in
his commitment to the freedom of the press: "The only security of all is
in a free press," he wrote to Lafayette in 1823. "The force of public opinion cannot be resisted when permitted freely to be expressed. The agitation it produces must be submitted to. It is necessary, to keep the
waters pure."

This view, which was self-evident to those early republicans who
championed freedom of the press, strikes Bush & Co. as preposterous.
"I don't believe you have a check-and-balance function," Andrew Card
has told reporters, and Bush himself has scoffed at the idea that news

*The framers also intended copyright to serve an edifying public purpose. "The
Congress shall have Power," the Constitution states, "To promote the Progress of Science and useful Arts, by securing *for limited Times* to Authors and Inventors the exclusive Right to their respective Writings and Discoveries" (Article I, Section 8; emphasis
added). The purpose of that text was to prevent perpetual ownership of intellectual
property—a precautionary measure that the media cartel has long since obviated. Since
the passage of the Sonny Bono Copyright Term Extension Act (CTEA) in 1998, copyright remains in private—i.e., corporate—hands for decades. (See note on p. 313.)

outlets "represent what the people think." What makes that deeply cynical idea so dangerous is not just that the president and all his men believe in it, but that the Fourth Estate has also bought it. Jefferson's belief in "a free press," in other words, is now regarded as eccentric by the U.S. press itself.

At a symposium on September 4, 2001, CNN's Judy Woodruff voiced annoyance when John Moyers, editor of the noncommercial Web magazine *Tompaine.commonsense*, suggested that reporters must do more than just repeat the public statements of Republicans and Democrats, and actually "go out into the country" to investigate the actual effects of federal policy. Using Bush's education policy as an example, Moyers noted that although both parties hailed extensive testing, teachers were themselves reporting serious problems with the testing system, which they found to be both unreliable and costly. There must be "a broad public discussion" of this issue, Moyers argued, and the press, of course, would have to take the lead. Woodruff found that view absurd. "You know, we can argue all day about the role of the press," she said,

> but I think most of us would agree the role of the press is to cover what's going on rather than to get out front ourselves with solutions. I mean, the way the press generally works in this country is to cover what the two main political parties and other opinion leaders are saying, rather than be the opinion leaders ourselves.

That claim would have stunned James Madison, but it was the obvious consensus of the panel, which included NBC's David Gregory and the *New York Times*'s Richard Berke as well as the unhappy Moyers (and, perhaps for "balance," a GOP consultant).* It is also clearly the consen-

---

*Earlier in her career, when she was NBC's White House correspondent (and NBC was not yet owned by GE), Woodruff had a somewhat bolder conception of her craft. Toward the end of her autobiography, published in 1982, she strongly recommends more airtime for the news: "Expanding the time devoted to news-gathering and broadcasting can only improve the quality of TV news coverage. Increasingly in our daily coverage we'll be challenging newspapers in such areas as long, in-depth stories, behind-the-scenes reports, and so-called 'think pieces' on current issues, in addition to the live coverage we already do better. More news programming will also mean more

sus of "the liberal media," whose personnel routinely kowtow to the very powers they should be dissecting for the public good. Woodruff was unfortunately right about "the way the press generally works in this country"—except for her suggestion that the coverage is nonpartisan, giving equal time and treatment to "the main political parties." In fact, the way the press generally works in this country is to smear or ridicule dissenting arguments, however valid or important, and this, of course, has generally meant deferring to the White House and the GOP, while challenging and often jeering at the Democrats—although their dissidence is often imperceptible—and anybody else who might resist the party line.

Bush & Co.'s Drive to War

Such authoritarian bias has disastrous consequences, as Jefferson and Madison well understood. The first republicans could not have foreseen the national dominion of commercial television, the extraordinary power of corporate advertisers, the disappearance of "the press" into a giant multinational cartel of entertainment companies, the cult of journalistic "objectivity," or the right's political hegemony in the United States. Surely democratic politics has always tended toward simplistic bits, with all our presidents in one way or another "packaged" to their best advantage. U.S. democratic politics today, however, seems finally to have bottomed out. Whereas it formerly required a major element of popular participation, it is today a one-way process so spectacular, deceptive, and irrational as no longer to be democratic *or* political. With such a strong disorienting force at the disposal of the White House and the Pentagon, our journalists are more than ever obligated to report the truth, and yet, it seems, they are less than ever free, or qualified, to do so.

---

opportunities to do follow-up stories, and less opportunities for politicians to manipulate their television news coverage by playing on our deadlines." Woodruff's gradual shift from that idealistic view of telejournalism to the quasi-stenographic kind she advocates, and practices, today reveals a lot about "the way the press generally works in this country," and the way it has worked since the seventies. Judy Woodruff, with Kathleen Maxa, *This Is Judy Woodruff at the White House* (Reading, Mass.: Addison-Wesley, 1982), p. 218.

We are living with—and many of us dying from—the consequences of this situation, which amounts to rule by propaganda, with the press not questioning but merely servicing the White House. Take the U.S. rush to occupy Iraq: a goal that Bush & Co. had been pursuing privately since January 1998, when Rumsfeld, Perle, Woolsey, Wolfowitz, and other Busheviks-to-be* wrote the then-president a letter urging him "to turn your Administration's attention to implementing a strategy for removing Saddam's regime from power." (The group also lobbied Congress.) Clinton having turned them down, they waited and, once placed in power, started planning for the reinvasion of Iraq. This project picked up steam on 9/11, after which the White House started dropping hints of a dark Ba'athist hand behind the terrorist attacks. It was not until September of 2002, however, that the White House propaganda drive for war began with all the proper sound and fury. "From a marketing point of view, you don't introduce new products in August," Andrew Card, Bush's chief of staff, serenely told the *New York Times* at summer's end.

And so, on September 7, after many months of groundwork, Team Bush kicked off their autumn war drive with a blitz of allegations that Saddam Hussein was close to nuclear capability. It started at Camp David, at a joint press conference with Bush and Tony Blair, who noted that "the threat from Saddam Hussein and weapons of mass destruction—chemical, biological, potentially nuclear weapons capability—that threat is *real*." Blair continued:

> We only need to look at the report from the International Atomic Energy Agency this morning, showing what has been going on at the former nuclear weapon sites to realize that.

Bush then reemphasized Blair's evidence:

> BUSH: We just heard the prime minister talk about the new report. I would remind you that when the inspectors first went into Iraq

---

*The letter's other signatories were Elliott Abrams, Richard L. Armitage, William J. Bennett, Jeffrey Bergner, John Bolton, Paula Dobriansky, Francis Fukuyama, Robert Kagan, Zalmay Khalilzad, William Kristol, Peter W. Rodman, William Schneider Jr., Vin Weber, and Robert B. Zoellick.

and were denied—finally denied access, a report came out of the Atomic—the IAEA, that they were six months away from developing a weapon. I don't know what more evidence we need.

BLAIR: Absolutely right. And what we know from what has been going on there for a long period of time is not just the chemical, biological weapons capability. But we know that they were trying to develop nuclear weapons capability. And the importance of this morning's report, is that it yet again shows that there is a *real issue* that has to be tackled here.

Apparently referring to the new report, the prime minister added, "And I mean I was just reading coming over here the catalog of attempts by Iraq to conceal its weapons of mass destruction, not to tell the truth about it over—not just over a period of months, but over a period of years."

The next day, as the news of Blair and Bush's joint concern was still reverberating, the *Sunday New York Times* ran a front-page article by star reporters Judith Miller and Michael R. Gordon ("U.S. Says Hussein Intensifies Quest for A-Bomb Parts") asserting that "[i]n the last 14 months, Iraq has sought to buy thousands of specially designed aluminum tubes, which American officials believe were intended as components of centrifuges to enrich uranium." And once he had the bomb, Saddam Hussein would threaten to deploy his other heinous goods:

"The jewel in the crown is nuclear," a senior administration official said. "The closer he gets to a nuclear capability, the more credible is his threat to use chemical or biological weapons. Nuclear weapons are his hole card."

To that problem there was only one solution:

"The question is not, why now?" the official added, referring to a potential military campaign to oust Mr. Hussein. "The question is why waiting is better. The closer Saddam Hussein gets to a nuclear weapon, the harder he will be to deal with."

That same day on NBC, Dick Cheney was on *Meet the Press*, promoting war against Iraq because of what had happened to the United States on 9/11:

> If you start with that as background, then you deal with Saddam Hussein and his 11 years, now, since 1991, since the end of the war, his refusal to comply with the U.N. Security Council resolutions. If you look at the extent to which he has aggressively sought to acquire chemical, biological and nuclear weapons, over the years, the fact that he has previously used them—he used chemical weapons both against the Kurds and against the Iranians during the 1980s—the fact that he has twice invaded his neighbors. He's launched ballistic missiles against four of his neighbors over the years. There's a pattern and a track record there that one has to be concerned about.

Although they demonstrated no connection whatsoever, Cheney's urgent sentence fragments served the purpose of *suggesting* a close link, which then led him to invoke that morning's *Times* and the imaginary possibility of an Iraqi A-bomb. Russert was a helpful interlocutor.

CHENEY: He now is trying, through his illicit procurement network, to acquire the equipment he needs to be able to enrich uranium to make the bombs.

RUSSERT: Aluminum tubes.

CHENEY: Specifically aluminum tubes. There's a story in the *New York Times* this morning—this is—I don't—and I want to attribute the *Times*.* I don't want to talk about, obviously, specific intelligence sources, but it's now public that, in fact, he has been seeking to acquire, and we have been able to intercept and prevent him from acquiring through this particular channel, the kinds of tubes that are necessary to build a centrifuge. And the centrifuge is

*Cheney's brief fit of unclarity suggests that *he* may well have been the "senior administration official" quoted in the *Times*.

required to take low-grade uranium and enhance it into highly
enriched uranium, which is what you have to have in order to build
a bomb.

The vice president went on at length about the need for war, with
Russert drinking in his every word.

Meanwhile, other White House wheels were spinning on TV that
day: "We don't want the smoking gun to be a mushroom cloud," said
Condoleezza Rice on CNN's *Late Edition.* "Imagine a September 11
with weapons of mass destruction. It's not 3,000—it's tens of thousands
of innocent men, women and children," said Donald Rumsfeld on
CBS's *Face the Nation.* And on *Fox News Sunday,* Colin Powell tried to
make it clear to all the world that Bush would do whatever he might
have to do to keep us safe from the Iraqi bomb. "The president will
retain all of his authority and options to act in a way that may be appropriate for us to act unilaterally to defend ourselves [*sic*]," said the secretary of state. This more or less recalled, and reconfirmed, what Bush had
said the day before: "There's all kinds of ways to change regimes."

Thus Bush/Cheney's war drive started well, with every player "on
message" loud and clear and the reporters suitably receptive. There was
one minor problem, but it was not allowed to resonate and therefore disappeared. "The new report" that Blair and Bush had used to document
their charge was fiction. "A spokeswoman at IAEA headquarters said yesterday that the agency has issued no new report. She said the newspaper
accounts referred to commercially available images the agency made
available [*sic*] in July in a presentation that elicited little media interest,"
reported Karen DeYoung in the *Washington Post.*

> "We didn't want to make a big deal of it, because we have no idea
> whether it means anything," spokeswoman Melissa Fleming said of
> the photos. "Construction of a building is one thing. Restarting a
> nuclear program is another."
>
> "We have a lot of commercial satellite imagery" indicating "that
> there has been construction at sites that were formerly nuclear,"
> Fleming said. "But what that means, we don't know." She said the

agency issued a news release late Friday to "make it clear there is nothing new."

This could have been embarrassing, of course, but as the U.S. press ignored it there was no harm done: DeYoung's revelation turned up in the twenty-first paragraph of her story ("Bush, Blair Decry Hussein; Iraqi Threat Is Real, They Say"), and the only other U.S. news outlets to mention it were United Press International and the Associated Press. It also came up briefly, quite early Sunday morning, on CNN, when correspondent Kelly Wallace had the following exchange with anchor Fredricka Whitfield, just after a short press conference with Colin Powell:

WHITFIELD: Kelly, when Prime Minister Blair addressed reporters that there was a new report that underscores his support and the need to go after Saddam Hussein, is there, indeed, a new report?

WALLACE: A lot of confusion about this, Fredricka. No, there is not any new report. At least the understanding of what British Prime Minister Tony Blair happened to be referring to, a *New York Times* article over the past few days in which the International Atomic Energy Agency had new satellite photographs showing there might be some buildup at possible nuclear facilities. Well, a spokesman for the agency says that these are not new photos, that the agency has been looking and doing satellite photography of Iraq over the past two years and it has no new evidence to show that there is any new development when it comes to the nuclear weapons program.

So U.S. officials say they believe that's what the prime minister was referring to and they say when the president commented, he didn't comment specifically on this. But the president was commenting on how—when weapons inspectors first got inside Iraq back in 1991, before they got inside the country the thinking was that Saddam Hussein was about three to five years away from having a nuclear weapon. Well, after the inspectors got inside the country, U.S. officials said they discovered that he was probably six

months away from having a nuclear weapon. So that was what they
say the president was referring to.

A little confusion there. The bottom line, no new report according to U.S. officials. Fredricka?

WHITFIELD: All right, a lot of confusion, but you've straightened
it out for us. Thanks a lot.

Thus Whitfield and Wallace worked together to erase a moment of
"confusion"—a euphemism that itself erased the fact that our president
had plucked a "new report" out of thin air (or out of Tony Blair's
ambiguous reference to the IAEA "report . . . this morning"). Wallace
did not straighten it out for us, unless "straighten out" means "make
unclear." Rather, she aborted a potential controversy by calmly nattering
about it, her tone and stance as reassuring as her utterance was incomprehensible. While her explanation straightened nothing out, however,
it was illuminating, as it demonstrated clearly how the mainstream press
conceives of "journalism" in the Age of Woodruff.

Suddenly, a little hole had opened in the massive propaganda tapestry
that Bush & Co. had just unveiled. But instead of peering in to try, on
our behalf, to see behind the curtain, Kelly Wallace sewed the peephole
shut, as if she were not with the Fourth Estate but working in the White
House spin machine. She did so, moreover, not by dispelling the "confusion," but merely by invoking her own institutional relationship with
Bush/Cheney's professional explainers: "So that was what *they say* the
president was referring to." It was apparently irrelevant that what "they"
said to Wallace made no sense at all, or that she herself was just as baffled by it as any viewer. All that mattered was that "they*" had said it to
her*, so that she could say it to the audience, whose members could then
feel that all was well, since "they" had told her something—anything—
and she accepted it, as did Fredricka and, by implication, CNN.

The Press Carries the Ball

Here, staring us all right in the face, was a discrepancy between Bush/
Cheney's story and the truth, and the reporter/anchor, rather than pur-

sue the truth (i.e., that there was no "new report," hence no new evidence of nuclear construction in Iraq), went with Bush/Cheney's story. Throughout the buildup to the war, and even afterward, the press would often go beyond merely deflecting inconvenient facts, to the straight suppression of whatever news the U.S. government—the Pentagon and White House—told them not to cover. Such deference gave Bush/Cheney's tales a hard, bright gloss of unimpeachability, just as in any closed society, like Brezhnev's Soviet Union (or Saddam Hussein's Iraq). Nothing that might contradict or even complicate the "message" of the presidential visuals could make its way inside the frame of U.S. coverage.

Such press collusion was the norm even before the kickoff of the autumn war drive. On August 21, speaking from his ranch in Crawford, Texas, with the secretary of defense beside him and a multitude of journalists before him, Bush said this: "I say it in my speeches, which you fortunately don't have to cover, that I'm a patient man." Rumsfeld chuckled. The president continued:

> And when I say I'm a patient man, I mean I'm a patient man, and that we will look at all options, and we will consider all technologies available to us and diplomacy and intelligence.

Tens of millions of Americans read, heard, or saw Bush's repetitious self-description as "a patient man" (a riff remarkable for its impatient tone), as it was noted in the *New York Times*, the *Los Angeles Times*, *Time*, *USA Today*, and *Slate*; broadcast on NBC, CBS, and NPR; and aired repeatedly on Fox, CNN, and CNBC. Such broad exposure helped drive home the point, inside the United States, that the president would not act hastily, or without extensive prior consultation with the Congress, with the people, and with our allies abroad. He made the same point on September 5, in Louisville: "I'm a patient man. And I've got tools—we've got tools at our disposal." And on October 16, during a White House photo op with Ariel Sharon, Bush once more noted his own patience and again elaborated on his willingness to work for peace. "You said you expected the United Nations to act in days or weeks on the Iraq resolutions," asked one journalist. "How much longer [do you intend] to wait? And why aren't you losing patience?" The president replied,

"Because I'm a patient man." He laughed; the reporters laughed. He paused, then said, "My mother and wife think it's hysterical when I say that, of course." The reporters laughed again. And Bush went on:

> Let's see. Because it takes a while to get things done in the U.N., I guess is the answer. I mean, we will—I've made the commitment to go to the U.N. I've asked the U.N. to act. We have got to deal with members of the Security Council. There are differing opinions on members [*sic*] of the Security Council, and we've got to work hard to reach a consensus, a resolution that will, on the one hand, do everything it can to disarm Saddam Hussein and also has got the capacity for there to be consequences should he not disarm. And therefore, we're working closely with the Perm[anent] Five as well as others on the Security Council to reach this resolution.
>
> I am a patient man.

Such hymns to patience helped to reconfirm the view, then prevalent inside this country, that the righteous, feisty Bush was—even in the face of still more damning news about Iraqi treachery—*holding off* and *doing everything he could* to go that extra mile for peace, or at least to win the world's approval of a U.S. strike, and only *then* to go to war. As that was all Americans could know about the situation, none could be expected to think otherwise: a mass assumption that would surely have been shaken if the public knew that Bush, right in the middle of the White House patience drive, had *already begun* the war against Iraq. On September 5—the very day that Bush, in Louisville, described the scrupulous prewar "discussion" he would soon be holding with both parties, and the people of the United States, and the United Nations, as well as representatives of Britain, Canada, Russia, China, France—a large Iraqi air base in the country's west was pummeled by one hundred jets, American and British. This was not just another skirmish of the sort that had been going on consistently since 1991, but represented a great escalation in the U.S.-led hostilities.

> Meanwhile, Iraq's main air base near its border with Jordan was bombed by US and British jets yesterday. About 100 aircraft took part in the operation against the air defence command post at Iraq's

H-3 airbase, 240 miles to the west of Baghdad, using precision-guided munitions.

The Pentagon said the raid—the largest air operation against Iraq since Operation Desert Fox in 1998—was launched in "response to recent Iraqi hostile acts against coalition aircraft monitoring the southern no-fly zone." Military sources indicated the RAF was involved.

That report, from the *Scotsman*, was one of many that appeared throughout the world. On the other hand, the story went unmentioned in this country (except for a brief meditation of my own that was posted by *Salon* on 9/11, dealing with the U.S. press's total failure to report the air assault). No U.S. print reporter brought it up, nor did any U.S. tele-journalist, or U.S. radio reporter, while the people of Great Britain and Australia knew about it. All *we* knew, on the other hand, was what Bush told us time and time again, and what he told us, time and time again, was false.

Shooting Down Scott Ritter

The U.S. press permitted no one, however qualified, to contradict Bush/Cheney's version of the truth. This became especially obvious in their treatment of Scott Ritter, who, from Day One of the White House propaganda drive, did everything he could to slow the juggernaut. A veteran of Operation Desert Storm (and a Republican), Ritter had been the most dedicated and aggressive member of the United Nations Special Commission on Iraq (UNSCOM), which searched Iraq for unconventional weaponry from 1991 to 1998. So diligent was Ritter, who called himself the team's "attack dog," that the Ba'athists finally asked for his expulsion, deeming him an agent of the CIA. (Some spooks *had* been let into the inspection team, which gave Saddam Hussein a reason to distrust the operation. Because it compromised the mission, Ritter had objected strongly to that stealthy use of spies.) He now attempted to defuse the crisis just as the Bush regime was starting its hard sell.

On September 8—the day the *New York Times* warned of the Ba'athist

"Quest for A-Bomb Parts," and Bush's men (and Ms. Rice) were all on
TV, talking World War III—Scott Ritter was in Baghdad, urging the
Iraqis to wise up and stop providing Bush & Co. with pretexts for a U.S.
reinvasion. Speaking to the Iraqi parliament, Ritter set the context for
that warning with a frank portrayal of Bush/Cheney's eagerness for war,
and their imperial tendency to act alone:

> My country seems to be on the verge of making a historical mis-
> take, one that will forever change the political dynamic which has
> governed the world since the end of the Second World War:
> namely, the foundation of international law that set forth a United
> Nations charter, which calls for the peaceful resolution of problems
> between nations. My government has set forth on a policy of uni-
> lateral intervention that runs contrary to the letter and intent of the
> United Nations charter.

Ritter continued, "The truth of the matter is that Iraq is not a sponsor
of the kind of terror perpetrated against the United States on September
11, and in fact is active in suppressing the sort of fundamentalist extremism that characterizes those who attacked the United States on that hor-
rible day." Although quite obvious to the Iraqis, their government's
hostility to Islamism was unknown in the United States. Iraq must therefore take extraordinary steps to demonstrate its harmlessness to the
United States or else face war again, and soon, said Ritter.

Unequivocally he told the Iraqi National Assembly that they had no
choice but to accept unlimited UN inspection. "Iraq must submit itself
immediately to unconditional and unfettered resumption of the UN
weapons inspections." Only through that measure, he explained, "could
Iraq eliminate the remaining doubts of Americans, which the fearmon-
gers are manipulating." He also urged them to extend their sympathy to
the victims of the terrorist attacks on 9/11, and thereby "make it clear to
the world that, although they are a Muslim country, Iraq in no way
sponsors such terrorist activity." Finally, he advised Iraq to give up its
hard line on Israel and accept a negotiated settlement in that region. "It
is time that you stopped being more Palestinian than the Palestinians."
Such straight talk, and from the erstwhile Lion of UNSCOM, earned

Ritter several waves of thunderous denunciation from the horde of Ba'athists sitting there before him.

For that same speech Ritter was slammed as well by the American press—especially the telejournalists (at first), and especially on CNN. They started to impugn him right away, and with a mounting vehemence that suggests a tacit partnership between the network and the White House, whose war drive could have run into some trouble if that meddlesome Marine weren't taken out.

"Is Scott Ritter disloyal?" *CNN Sunday Morning* host Miles O'Brien asked Clifford May, former director of communications for the Republican National Committee and now the president of the Foundation for Defense of Democracies, a neocon "antiterrorist" think tank.* "I don't think Scott Ritter is disloyal," May began magnanimously. "I think he's tremendously misguided. He has become an apologist for and a defender of Saddam Hussein." Thus Ritter was a Ba'athist stooge, if not an agent, May hinted, more in sorrow than in anger. "I just think Scott Ritter is tremendously, tremendously misguided. I'm not against dissension. We should all welcome dissension and welcome a real big debate on this thing. We need that kind of thing. But I don't understand why Scott Ritter has decided to defend Saddam Hussein as he has."

That view of Ritter as Saddam Hussein's "defender" and "apologist" was then obliterated, briefly, by the man himself, whom O'Brien interviewed by satellite. (He was still in Baghdad.) Ritter answered every question fully, clearly, and persuasively. How could he be so sure that the Iraqis weren't engaged in building weapons of mass destruction? What *was* certain, Ritter answered, was Bush's failure to provide a shred of evidence that Saddam Hussein possessed such weapons *or* had plans to build any. By 1998, when UNSCOM left Iraq, they could "ascertain a 95% level of disarmament that included all of the production equipment and means of production used by Iraq to produce these weapons." He continued:

---

*"Our founding members and distinguished advisors," the foundation's Web site tells us, "are Steve Forbes, Jack Kemp, Jeane Kirkpatrick, Frank Lautenberg, Newt Gingrich and James Woolsey." The Web site is at www.defenddemocracy.org.

So if Iraq has weapons today, like President Bush says, clearly they would have had to reconstitute this capability since December 1998, and this is something that the Bush administration needs to make a better case for, especially before we talk about going to war.

But how did Ritter know this? He hadn't toured any suspected sites on this trip, had he? All the more reason to send in an inspection team, said Ritter, who added that he had proposed a "mechanism" to ensure that, this time, there would be no espionage.

Let's keep in mind that the reason why inspectors are out of Iraq isn't because Iraq kicked them out, but rather they were ordered out by the United States after the United States manipulated the inspection process to create a confrontation that led to Operation Desert Fox* and then used intelligence information gathered by inspectors to target Iraqi government sites including the security of Saddam Hussein. . . .

So it's going to take a lot to convince Iraqis that they should once again trust inspectors, but frankly, they have no choice.

But hadn't the inspection team been thwarted by Iraq at every turn? "No, absolutely false," Ritter replied, explaining in detail that the inspection team had been working wholly unimpeded until 1998. They were obstructed only when they, or the spies among them, tried to penetrate Iraq's most sensitive locations: "intelligence facilities, security facilities, Saddam Hussein's palaces"—sites that "had nothing whatsoever to do with weapons of mass destruction." So while there ultimately was obstruction, it "had little, if anything, to do with actual disarmament."

---

*Operation Desert Fox, begun on December 16, 1998, was a four-day series of air strikes on Iraqi targets. U.S. and British forces fired cruise missiles at a broad range of Ba'athist sites. Officially, the operation was punishment for Iraq's ongoing refusal to submit to UN resolutions and for alleged interference with the UNSCOM inspectors. As Ritter and others have argued, however, those were mere pretexts for a calculated blow at Saddam Hussein's regime, as the targets were not all military, some being crucial to Saddam Hussein's security. Ritter's point was that Saddam Hussein was uncooperative not because he had something to hide, but because he had good reason to distrust the UN team.

Knowing nothing of the subject, while Ritter clearly knew it cold, O'Brien then made the only move he could, which was merely to *repeat* the fundamental premise of Bush/Cheney's propaganda. It was as if he felt a sudden need to reconfirm that CNN, and he himself, believed the president, no matter what:

> O'BRIEN: Let me ask you this, though, Mr. Ritter, it seems that sometimes we avoid seeing the forest for the trees here. Is there any doubt in your mind, taking aside what you've seen firsthand or heard from the Iraqis, is there any doubt in your mind that Saddam Hussein would love to get a hold of nuclear weapons?

> RITTER: Well, I think, you know, we have to be careful about, you know, trying to compare what Saddam Hussein and his regime were trying to do in the past with the current situation today. Saddam Hussein is a man who is very interested in the continued survival of Saddam Hussein, and I believe he recognizes that any effort by himself or his government to reacquire any aspect of weapons of mass destruction, let alone nuclear weapons, would be the equivalent of taking a suicide pill.

> It would invite the immediate harsh response of the international community and would result in his ultimate demise. So yes, I truly believe that Saddam Hussein today is not seeking to acquire, not only a nuclear weapon, but weapons of mass destruction of any kind.

Thus Ritter made an argument—a reasonable argument, and one that had already been confirmed by history (and one that history would reconfirm): Saddam Hussein cares most of all about Saddam Hussein. In response to Ritter's reasonable point, O'Brien left the realm of reason altogether, launching himself up into the wild blue yonder of the paranoid subjunctive, where the White House has been operating since Bush/Cheney were inaugurated.

> O'BRIEN: I guess the concern is, though, that we're perhaps in an era where—which invites the necessity of a preemptive strike [*sic*], and that perhaps the only smoking gun evidence we'll ever see here in the West of nuclear weapons [*sic*], weapons of mass destruction,

might well be a mushroom cloud.* The stakes are pretty high, aren't they Mr. Ritter? Isn't it time to act differently perhaps?

RITTER: No, I agree the stakes are very high, and that's why it's imperative that the United States acts in accordance with its obligations under international law. We are a signatory of the United Nations charter and in doing so, we've undertaken to respect international law, especially in regards to, you know, issues pertaining to war. If the United States shreds international law, rips up the United Nations charter and intervenes against Iraq unilaterally, we will be redefining the entire way the world chooses to deal with situations of this sort.

In other words, the real doomsday threat lay not in some potential nuclear program, but in the very sort of unilateral preemptive war that Bush & Co. was planning:

RITTER: You know, what will then stop India and Pakistan from going to war? What will stop China from intervening in Taiwan? There will be no guarantees. There will be no mechanism. We will be unleashing, you know, chaos. This is a bigger fear than any hypothetical concept of an Iraqi mushroom cloud exploding anywhere in the world.

O'BRIEN: All right—

RITTER: This is a reality. An Iraqi nuclear weapon, at this point in time, is sheer speculation.

Ritter's logic was impeccable, his knowledge unimpeachable, and so the only way to end the interview correctly was to smear him as a traitor:

O'BRIEN: Mr. Ritter, the satellites are about to go out, but I've got to ask you before we get away, I'm sure you've heard the criticism that this—you are perhaps acting in a disloyal manner toward the United States. How do you respond?

---

*This was O'Brien's garbled effort to repeat a White House talking point: Condoleezza Rice said the same thing, albeit more clearly, that same day, as we have seen (p. 64).

The former Marine was ready for that pitch, and hit the ball out of the park:

> RITTER: Well, I think I made it very clear that I'm acting as a fervent patriot who loves my country. As an American citizen, I have an obligation to speak out when I feel my government is acting in a manner, which is inconsistent with the—with the principles of our founding fathers.
>
> We have a Constitution, which says we will abide by the rule of law. We are signatories of the United Nations charter. Therefore, we are to be, you know, to adhere ourselves to the United Nations charter, and I see my government drifting decisively away from this. So, I feel I have no other choice as an American citizen than to stand up and speak out. It's the most patriotic thing I can do.

So impressive a dissenter—as physically imposing as he was articulate—clearly threatened Bush & Co.'s propaganda, and so Ritter was, from that point on, the object of attacks far less restrained than Clifford May's. First, the network pointedly impugned his credibility, if not his sanity, through the medium of Eason Jordan, "chief news executive" at CNN. Appearing shortly after Ritter (and for no clear reason), Jordan was interviewed by anchor Catherine Callaway: "This morning, I'm sure you heard Scott Ritter on our air, as Miles interviewed him, saying that he believes that there's really no threat of nuclear weapons of any type, according to him. What is your reaction to his comments this morning?"

> JORDAN: Well, Scott Ritter's chameleon-like behavior has really bewildered a lot of people around the world, in the United States, in Iraq—I thought it was interesting; we asked the Iraqi government for permission to televise live Scott Ritter's remarks, but they were so skittish about these remarks, they refused to let us provide a live transmission of what he had to say. And so, in Washington, in Baghdad, I think people are equally stunned, really, as to his position on these matters.

Having charged collusion between Ritter and the Ba'athists (because the latter were unwilling to permit a live transmission of the speech), the

CNN executive officially declared the balky expert an unperson: "U.S. officials no longer give Scott Ritter much credibility."*

CNN's problem, and Bush/Cheney's, was as daunting as it was unusual. There could be no refuting Ritter on the evidence (or lack thereof), and there was no tidy way to shut him up. Therefore, they would have to smear him a lot harder, to drown out his convincing voice and weighty image. CNN got started bright and early the next day. "So what do you make of what Scott Ritter says, a former U.N. weapons inspector, yesterday from Baghdad?" Paula Zahn asked Senator Richard Shelby, a Bush/Cheney stalwart. "He says Iraq poses no threat to the U.S." "Well, I was troubled by what he said," Shelby answered, looking grave indeed.

> I have met Scott Ritter before and I think he's an idealist. I think he wants to believe that everybody's good and the world's going to be safe. But I don't believe there's any real credence to his statements.
>
> It looks to me like that [sic] he's over there courting Saddam Hussein at the wrong time at the wrong place.

Then Ritter reappeared from Baghdad, after being thus dubiously introduced by the firm, blonde Zahn:

> The report from the International Institute for Strategic Studies confirming Saddam's enduring interest in developing weapons of mass

---

*Ritter was surprised by Jordan's comments. Before his trip to Baghdad, he had contacted the executive to report his plans and offered to do interviews on CNN. Jordan was excited at the prospect, Ritter claims, and thanked him for the heads-up. Nothing in his attitude suggested that he doubted Ritter's credibility or thought the ex-Marine "chameleon-like." In a private meeting at the network's Atlanta headquarters on September 17, Ritter asked Jordan to back up his on-air comments. Jordan could come up with nothing to support them. E-mail exchanges with Scott Ritter, 11/9/03.

The fact is that Jordan's institutional loyalties lay firmly with the Pentagon—as he himself revealed a month into the war. Appearing on CNN's *Reliable Sources* on April 20, he reported having gone to the Department of Defense to get approval for the network's list of likely military analysts: "I went to the Pentagon myself several times before the war started and met with important people there and said, for instance: 'At CNN, here are the generals we're thinking of retaining to advise us on the air and off about the war.' And we got a big thumbs-up on all of them. That was important."

destruction, that comes a day after former United Nations weapons inspector Scott Ritter insisted Iraq is not a threat to the U.S.

He told the Iraqi parliament the country is on the verge of making an historical mistake by trying to remove Saddam Hussein.

It was a damning setup, and yet Ritter once more blew the frame apart. Zahn started by invoking "the whole range of Bush administration officials," who, the day before, had claimed that Saddam Hussein was "trying to buy thousands of aluminum pipes that could be used in the manufacture of a centrifuge and ultimately used to manufacture [nuclear] weapons."

RITTER: What an absurd statement. Thousands of aluminum pipes, and we're going to go to war over thousands of aluminum pipes? Even the [I]ISS report that you cite says that if Iraq was trying to do uranium enrichment, it would take them many years before they could do it. This is patently ridiculous. These are aluminum pipes coming in for civilian use. They are not being transferred to a covert nuclear processing plant or any covert nuclear activity whatsoever.*

But the best way to figure this out is to send the weapons inspectors in. If they, if the United States, has this evidence that Iraq has these pipes—why not, heck, give me the data? I'll come to Iraq, hunt it down and we'll bring it to a close. That would save us going to war, killing thousands of people and destroying our reputation in the international community.

We cannot go to war because Vice President Cheney's worried about some aluminum pipes. This is ridiculous.

*Ritter slightly overstated his case here. "In later interviews and writing," he explains, "I modified that [point] to say the tubes were used for artillery rockets (which turned out to be correct). In any event, I knew from my time as an inspector that the Iraqis used maraging steel and filament-wound carbon fiber to make their centrifuge tubes—not aluminum. And if they were using aluminum, this represented a totally new design, something that was illogical in the extreme." A few months later, Mohamed ElBaradei, head of the International Atomic Energy Agency, confirmed Ritter's conclusion. E-mail from Scott Ritter, 11/11/03.

Zahn asked Ritter *why* he was "so convinced" that those pipes were harmless, "when so many other people out there are absolutely convinced" that they were not. Ritter was merciless:

> What makes them convinced? What evidence do they have? We're talking about going to war here, Paula. War. War kills people. War destroys things. War is something that's going to put the lives of American service members at risk and if we go to war along the lines that Bush is talking about, destroy our reputation in the international community.
>
> So frankly speaking, I'm going to need a hell of a lot more than some aluminum tubes before I'm convinced there's a case for war. The bottom line is in 1998 the International Atomic Energy Agency said that Iraq had no nuclear weapons capability, none whatsoever, zero.
>
> So how suddenly are they now an emerging nuclear threat? We'd better have a heck of a lot more to go on than some aluminum pipes.

Zahn then brought up the report by "the only independent voice in this whole argument, and that is the International Institute for Strategic Studies." She read from its conclusion: "War sanctions and inspections have reversed and retarded but not eliminated Iraq's nuclear, biological and chemical weapons and long range missile capabilities, nor removed Baghdad's enduring interest in developing these capabilities." Ritter went to town:

> Paula, what do we have here? Rhetoric? Where's the facts? "Enduring interest in weapons capability"? What does that mean? What evidence do they cite for this "enduring interest"? You know, ballistic missiles, they say he has twelve. What, did they grow? Where are they? They didn't have twelve when I was a weapons inspector.
>
> Chemical weapons? Biological weapons? They talk about bulk agent in terms of Iraq's biological weapons program. What bulk agent? Where did they make it? Bulk agent has a three-year lifetime in terms of storage in ideal conditions. The last time Iraq was known to have produced bulk agent was in 1990. That stuff, even

if they held onto it, is no longer viable. So to have bulk agent today, Iraq would have had to reconstitute a manufacturing base in biological weapons. Where is it?

This report is absurd. It has zero factual basis. It's all rhetoric. It's all speculative and, frankly speaking, it's meaningless without, you know—with the sad exception that hawks in the Bush administration are going to point to this as justification for war.

We need a heck of a lot more than this if we're going to talk about sending our forces off to fight in a war in Iraq.

Challenged to explain why more inspectors would succeed where others, she said, hadn't, Ritter once again explained that the CIA had used the inspection team "as a Trojan horse to insert intelligence collection capabilities to go after Saddam Hussein," and that this was why Iraq had ceased cooperating. He then corrected Zahn's mistaken view of the first team's effectiveness:

You know, *I* know that inspections *did* work. We achieved a 90 to 95 percent level of verified, absolutely certain accountability for Iraq's weapons program, including all the factories and associated production equipment. This is why I'm just amazed when I hear reports coming from the IISS that Iraq suddenly has the capability. Where did it come from? Did they suddenly grow factories?

You build factories, not in a basement, not in a mountain cave, but it's a modern industrial capability. Where did it come from? Where are the facilities? Where are the weapons? I'm tired of speculation. I won't support a war in which the Marines that I used to associate with are going to go off and fight and maybe get killed. It's just not worth it.

As there was no arguing with Ritter, the stubborn anchor was reduced to saying, in effect, "Oh, yeah? Well, *Daddy* says you're *wrong!*" "The former head of the CIA, James Woolsey, says you're very far off the beam on this one!" she blurted out, then introduced what Senator Shelby "had to say about you earlier this morning." The somber Alabamian reappeared, making his fantastic charge that Ritter was "courting Saddam Hussein." Zahn asked Ritter what he made of that "perception."

RITTER: Well, Senator Shelby, with all due respect: Back off, buddy. I'm an American citizen, doing the right thing for the United States of America. I'm not "courting Saddam Hussein" *or* the Iraqi people—I'm courting the American public. I'm trying to win over public opinion by asking the American people, "Before you sit back and allow your government to go to war against Iraq, make sure they have the facts on the table to back this war up."

Right now the government has provided nothing but rhetorically laced speculation. And I'm in here in Baghdad trying to facilitate the return of weapons inspectors to keep your service members from going to a war that doesn't need to be fought.

Senator Shelby and everybody else, you want to debate Iraq, let's do it face-to-face in front of a TV camera, where we can put the facts on the table—and I guarantee you this, I'll win that debate.

Having bid Ritter a strained adieu, Zahn quickly turned to Gary Saymore, director of studies at the International Institute of Strategic Studies in London—"the only independent voice in this whole argument," the anchor had asserted. Saymore had written the report that Ritter had just scorned. Zahn brought up the aluminum pipes: "Scott Ritter just said on the air that it's ridiculous to think that those pipes would have anything but a civilian use. Your response to his statement?" "Well," Saymore replied,

> U.S. and other Western governments have a very good understanding of the technical design for the gas centrifuges that the Iraqis were trying to build prior to 1991. And those centrifuges included high-strength aluminum tubes with particular dimensions and specifications.
>
> So if the U.S. government has information that Iraq was trying to buy those particular type[s] of tubes, in terms of the physical dimensions and the particular specifications of the type of material, then I think that's a pretty strong tip-off that the Iraqis are seeking to revive their nuclear weapons program. There aren't really other civilian uses for tubes of that precise dimension and type.

In other words, the pipes were bound for nuclear use because the U.S. government said so. That, it turned out, was the extent of Saymore's argument, which he tried gamely to dress up with many windy polysyllables ("in terms of the physical dimensions and the particular specifications of the type of material"), as if trying to pass a final without having done the reading.

Meanwhile, someone, somewhere, had decided that the network better toughen up and put this Ritter character away. Only such a diktat could explain what happened next, when Kyra Phillips interviewed the man in Baghdad. Now the network's tone abruptly hardened, as Ritter was subjected to contemptuous belittlement and base ad hominem insinuations. Although much honored as a television journalist,* Phillips acted less like an American reporter than a government inquisitor, intent on slandering "the only independent voice in this whole argument."

> PHILLIPS: Now, Scott, you say the U.S. is serving up rhetoric and not facts when it comes to an attack on Iraq, yet we have a president of the United States saying that Saddam Hussein harbors weapons of mass destruction, and he has the intent of using them. Are you saying that you, as a private citizen now, have better intelligence than the president of the United States and his staff?

> RITTER: I'm saying that I'm willing to put some facts on the table and back it up with sound analysis. You know, let's not be fooled here, OK? This wouldn't be the first time a president of the United States has lied to the American public to facilitate a war. Think back to the Gulf of Tonkin Resolution and how we got entangled in Vietnam. I believe the same thing is happening right now.

> If President Bush has a case to be made, if this administration has a case to be made for war against Iraq, then by God, they better start making it. I'm tired of hearing the rhetoric of war. I'm tired of watching American troops deploy for war. I'm tired of seeing the world reject the stance that America takes, because there are no

---

*According to her Web page at cnn.com, "Phillips has won four Emmy awards, two Edward R. Murrow awards for investigative reporting, and in 1997, the Associated Press named her Reporter of the Year. Additionally, she has won numerous Golden Microphones and other honors. Phillips' investigation into how a convicted murderer could purchase personal information about children triggered national legislation and earned her the Bill Stout Memorial Award for enterprise reporting."

facts right now to back up anything the administration says in regards to Iraq. I'm concerned about Iraq's weapons programs. I've always been concerned. That's why I'm encouraging the Iraqis to allow return, unconditional return, of U.N. weapons inspectors and giving them unfettered access.

I wish the United States would start talking about getting weapons inspectors back to work in Iraq and less about sending Marines into Iraq.

PHILLIPS: Scott, are you saying you trust Saddam Hussein and what he has to say?

RITTER: Kindly do not put words in my mouth.

PHILLIPS: I'm asking you a question. I'm simply asking you a question.

RITTER: I trust my own experience. Well, you did ask me a question, but I'm telling you the answer: I trust myself. I trust what I have experienced. I trust what I have seen with my own eyes. At this point in time, I do not have any information based upon my more than 10 years' experience, on-the-ground experience, dealing with Iraq that backs up anything the Bush administration has been saying about Iraq.

So if they have new information, and they claim they do, put it on the table, show it to the American people, but don't just sit here and feed the American people rhetoric, speculative rhetoric. We need facts before we will support sending our troops off to fight and perhaps die in a war.

PHILLIPS: But I think the facts do remain, Saddam has used these type of weapons against the Kurdish people. I mean, plain and simple, we've seen that, Scott.

RITTER: Yes, who cares? 1988, these weapons were used.

PHILLIPS: So you are saying they are all gone?

[*Crosstalk*]

RITTER: . . . clearly said Saddam can't have these weapons.

PHILLIPS: So you are saying he used it one time, he thought they were not effective, and now they are all gone.

RITTER: Excuse me, ma'am, listen to what I'm saying. I said that the United Nations special commission from 1991 to 1998 operated inside Iraq and destroyed the factories used to produce weapons that were used against the Kurds. If Iraq was to have weapons today, they would need to reconstitute this manufacturing base since December 1998 when inspectors left.

And until which time the Bush administration shows this is the case, that in fact Iraq reacquired chemical weapons, don't you or anybody else point back to the sins of 1998 [*sic*], which I admit are egregious and I wish they hadn't occurred, but you cannot point to 1998—or 1988—and claim that just because Iraq used weapons then, they have weapons now. That is not justification for war today.

PHILLIPS: Scott, who paid for your trip to Iraq?

RITTER: I paid for my trip to Iraq. If you would like to check the bill or check my bank account, you are welcome to.

PHILLIPS: While I have you on air, I don't think I can check anything. I'm hoping we can take your word for it.

I have another question to ask you, too. President Clinton even came on "Larry King Live" and said he regrets not doing anything about Osama bin Laden. We got to take a look at what happened.

Are you saying that you won't regret not doing anything about Saddam Hussein?

RITTER: Excuse me. I went to war against Saddam Hussein in 1991. I spent seven years of my life in this country hunting down weapons of mass destruction. I believe I have done a lot about Saddam Hussein. The international community said that we must get rid of Saddam Hussein's weapons, and I dedicated a good portion my adult life to doing just that.

You are asking me, am I regretting not going after Saddam Hussein and removing him from power. You show me where an inter-

84 Mark Crispin Miller

national law that says we or any other nation has the right [to] do this. You show me where Saddam Hussein can be substantiated as a threat against the United States and I'll go to war again. I'm not going to sit back idly and let anyone threaten the United States.

But at this point in time, no one made a case based upon fact that Saddam Hussein or his government is a threat to the United States worthy of war.

PHILLIPS: So right now, you do not believe that Saddam Hussein has any type of weapons of mass destruction, and you believe that Saddam Hussein will not use weapons of mass destruction against the United States or anybody else for that matter?

RITTER: Please, don't try and put words in my mouth. I believe that we have not completed the disarmament task in Iraq. I believe that we have outstanding requirements in 1998 and won't be allowed to fulfill our mission, so I resigned and protested.

He then ran through his history as an activist since 1998, and spoke again about the need for more inspections, reemphasizing the importance of the stakes: "Do not take war lightly. I don't."

PHILLIPS: Do you believe that if weapons inspectors do go into Iraq, that indeed they will have full access to all areas within Iraq?

RITTER: That's the prerogative of the Iraqi government. I believe the international community has made it quite clear that Iraq must allow the unconditional return of weapons inspectors and grant them unfettered access. Indeed, this is the message that I gave the Iraqi parliament yesterday, to Iraqi Foreign Minister Naji Sabri last night, to Iraqi Vice President Taha Yassine Ramadan this morning. I haven't deviated from anything the international community has said. I made it clear, Iraq has no choice. Let the inspectors in, or else face destruction. So it's their choice. If they let inspectors in, it is up to Iraq to comply with international—you know, the will of the international community.

With that, the interview was over, and Ritter—whose arguments were all ignored, as if he were on trial and Kyra Phillips was the prosecutor—had been depicted as an enemy of the state.

The next morning, Zahn interviewed Richard Butler, who had been in charge of UNSCOM and was therefore Ritter's boss back in the nineties. It was Butler, Ritter claimed, who had let the CIA infiltrate the inspection team, which had the dismal consequence of sudden Ba'athist noncooperation, a crisis that was then used to withdraw the UN team entirely and start another U.S. military action—"Operation Desert Fox"—at the end of 1998. Ritter had very publicly resigned over Butler's acquiescence in the U.S. plan, and the two men had been clashing just as publicly, and bitterly, since early 1999. Although Ritter had abundant evidence to back his claims—which were independently confirmed and heavily reported by the *New York Times*, the *Washington Post*, *Time*, NBC, and other mainstream outlets—Butler has consistently denied them all, insisting that the CIA did *not* infiltrate UNSCOM.

Interviewing Butler, who spoke from Sydney, Zahn appeared not to know any of this background; or, if she did, she suppressed it all, so as to further the portrayal of Ritter as a big loose cannon, if not altogether nuts. By way of introducing Butler, she said only this:

> Even as the Bush administration says it has evidence that Iraq has weapons of mass destruction, that nation's foreign minister says the burden of proof is on the U.S. to back up its claim. Well, yesterday on our show, Scott Ritter, former U.N. weapons inspector, insisted Iraq is no threat. Ritter also took a swipe at his old boss, the former U.N. chief weapons inspector, Richard Butler. Butler disagrees with Ritter, and believes history has shown that Iraq plays a shell game with its weapons, making the inspections ineffective.

She then replayed a moment from her recent interview with Ritter, who, with his usual bluntness, wrote off Richard Butler. ("Richard Butler knows for darned sure that the Iraqis were not moving weapons from his weapons inspectors. . . . So let's not bring up Richard Butler. Frankly speaking, he has no credibility on this issue.") The Australian responded:

> Now, his advice to me then, on the basis of good evidence which I knew, was that Iraq continued to retain illegal weapons. He resigned. A few months later, he crossed the road and for some reason—I don't know why, I'm not a psychoanalyst—but he crossed the road and started to tell the world that there were no such weapons.

So, I put it to you this way: Either he was misleading me when he worked for me, or he began to mislead the world's public later. Now, I know which one it is. He was misleading me—he was *not* misleading *me*, rather—he was—he is now misleading the world's public. And I find that sad, wrong and, frankly, a touch dangerous.

ZAHN: What do you think is his motivation if your charge is in fact accurate here?

BUTLER: I said—I don't know. I can't—I don't know why he has decided to do this. I know what the facts are. I find it incredible to hear some of the things he is saying, when he knows what the facts were then and are today. I don't know why he is doing this. As I said, I am not a psychoanalyst. I don't know.

Intent only on securing that defamatory bite, Zahn told the audience nothing of the pertinent background, nor did she question *Butler's* credibility, but presented as a solid diagnosis his dark hint that Ritter was insane, and doing something "wrong" and "dangerous."

Meanwhile, Ritter was being likewise stigmatized by other members of the cable trust. On *The Big Story*, Fox News Channel's aptly titled evening program hosted by John Gibson, Ritter, on September 12, was vilified for merely questioning Bush & Co.'s allegations. To promote his interview, Fox's David Asman came onto the show and spoke to Gibson about Ritter's motives. "Is he sticking up for Saddam Hussein and against the interests of the United States," yelled Gibson, "or, in fact, why is he saying Saddam Hussein doesn't have these things that for years he said he did have, and that the U.S. has no right or reason to go to war?" Although incoherent, that query prompted Asman to the following response:

That is the million-dollar question, or maybe the $80,000 question, because he did admit that that interview that he took $80,000 [*sic*], a cut from a movie which was funded by an Iraqi-American businessman with very close ties to Saddam Hussein's government.

But, you know, $80,000, is that enough to sell out your country?

I don't think so. Is he—a former Marine, we should mention—is he traitor material? He doesn't seem to be. Is he nuts? Who knows?

Gibson likened Ritter to Jane Fonda. Asman concurred:

That's right. There was a lot of Jane Fonda business in his speech to the Iraqi parliament. He admits that Saddam Hussein is a dictator, that in order to be a member of parliament, you have to be willing to sell your son and daughter to Saddam Hussein. Still, he was willing to speak in front of the Iraqi parliament, a kangaroo court, in order to condemn the United States. It didn't make sense.

Also, you wonder who Scott Ritter trusts. You know, we're supposed to believe that he is telling the truth, that Butler and even President Bush are lying. We asked him specifically about who he trusts in this whole debate about Iraq.

Fox then aired this clip:

RITTER: I believe that the United States government, the Bush administration, is deliberately distorting the record in regards to Iraq's weapons of mass destruction. And I have trouble believing what they're saying. I don't believe—it's not that I believe what Saddam Hussein is doing, it's not that I say I believe Saddam Hussein more.

I just don't trust, based upon my extensive experience, what's coming forward from the Bush administration.

ASMAN: There you are.

GIBSON: David Asman, interviewing Scott Ritter today. Great job!

Asman's interview, which ran the following night, was a true marvel of authoritarian irrationality, the eager telejournalist consistently ignoring, or mishearing, Ritter's lucid statements, using them to draw wild, warlike inferences that seemed, in Asman's mind, to prove that Bush was right and war was just.

ASMAN: So you think Saddam Hussein still has these chemical weapons capabilities?

RITTER: No. I said Saddam Hussein has the *potential* of having chemical weapons capability. We haven't completely confirmed the final disposition of these capabilities, and they must be of concern. But to say that Saddam Hussein retains chemical weapons—there's a big difference between weapons and capability.

ASMAN: You're talking about delivering the arsenal he has.

RITTER: I'm saying Saddam Hussein has the *capability*, inside Iraq today—Iraq has the *capability* to *convert aspects* of its civilian infrastructure to *reconstitute* chemical weapons. Six months is not an unreasonable time. I said it then and I'm saying it now.

ASMAN: So he might still have all of those barrels of evil stuff, the biochemical weapons?

RITTER: It's not a matter of "still have." He might have been able to make those weapons in the intervening time.

ASMAN: Right, and chances are he has those weapons but he doesn't have the power to deliver them?

RITTER: No. First of all, I never said he *has* them, and I'm *not* saying *chances are* he has them: I'm saying there's a possibility he could reconstitute this capability, and that's why we have to have inspectors in place.

You can't go from the fact [that] we can't confirm the final disposition of important elements of his program—which is the case—to suddenly giving Saddam Hussein massive strike capability that threatens the United States of America. You can't make that leap.

It is something you have to be concerned about. But the problem with what Bush is doing today is that he's made that leap, void of any intelligence information to substantiate that.

ASMAN: But it's not void of actions, Mr. Ritter. It is particularly in light of what happened on September 11, 2001, and the fear that there are evil people out there, some of whom may have consorted with Saddam Hussein in the past, that would get together and use some of these chemical weapons, if they're in Iraq, on U.S. citizens.

RITTER: But this is a purely hypothetical situation! Show me where is the link.

ASMAN: September 11, 2001, was not hypothetical, nothing hypothetical at all.

RITTER: Don't disgrace the death of those 3,000 people by bringing Iraq into the equation.

ASMAN: We know there are people out there willing to do the dirty deed and we also know Saddam Hussein has had contacts with these people in the past.

RITTER: No, you don't know that.

ASMAN: We know from Czech intelligence. Czech intelligence says that an Iraqi met with Mohammed Atta twice.

RITTER: What does the CIA and FBI say?

ASMAN: The FBI and CIA say the situation is not clear but Czech intelligence says it is. And why it is [*sic*] that the only person, only Arab leader, that Osama bin Laden likes and approves of and speaks highly of is Saddam Hussein? Why?

RITTER: That's an absurdity, David. Osama bin Laden in 1991 was offering his services to confront Saddam Hussein. Osama bin Laden has issued fatwas against Saddam Hussein.

ASMAN: We talked to representatives of Al Qaeda here in 1998 shortly after the bombings of those embassies in Africa. The only Arab leader—I spoke to them personally—the only Arab leader they were willing to praise, not to condemn, was Saddam Hussein. Why?

RITTER: Well, I'm just telling you that the fact of the matter is the Iraqi government—and I'm not an apologist for the Iraqi government, Saddam Hussein is the most brutal dictator I can think of today and from my lips to God's ear, I wish he was dead—but the fact of the matter is Iraq is a secular dictatorship that has struggled against Islamic fundamentalists for 30 years.

ASMAN: Exactly. So why is it that Saddam Hussein [*sic*] supports this secular individual?

RITTER: Well, first of all, I don't think that case has been made.

ASMAN: It's been made not only by Osama bin Laden himself but by representatives of Al Qaeda to me personally on air. We've got the tape. I can show it to you.

RITTER: I'm not disputing that.

ASMAN: You were disputing it.

RITTER: I'm not disputing that people have sat before you and said these things. I'm disputing that Al Qaeda is somehow in allegiance with Saddam Hussein.

ASMAN: Why shouldn't they be? They both want the destruction of the United States. You don't think they do? You don't think Osama bin Laden and Saddam Hussein want the destruction of the United States?

RITTER: Let's keep Osama bin Laden out of this equation because I'm not linking them.

ASMAN: He's directly a part of it! That's the point, Scott: the fact that Osama bin Laden has had, or is suspected to have had, contacts—well, just a suspicion, when thousands of American lives are at risk [*sic*]. Isn't a suspicion alone enough to really act upon?

That surreal exchange went on for half an hour, and while it may read like black comedy today, in the perfervid atmosphere of Bush & Co.'s alarmist drive, it came across as normal even if it seemed absurd, because the U.S. press at large was either tuning Ritter out or playing the story much like Fox—i.e., the way the White House wanted it. On September 13, the day that Fox broadcast its interview, Paula Zahn came back at Ritter in the confrontational mode of Kyra Phillips:

Let me talk to you about the transition some people have accused you of making. They said you went to Iraq, to Baghdad, in July of 2000 to produce a documentary film that you said would de-

demonize Iraq. An Iraqi-American, according to the "Weekly Standard," who is openly sympathetic with the regime in Baghdad, bankrolled this to the tune of some $400,000.

People out there are accusing you of drinking Saddam Hussein's Kool-Aid.

The interview continued in that vein, with Zahn either hinting at nefarious connections ("Who paid for your last trip to Baghdad?") or spouting old disinformation as if Ritter had not already rebutted it, and more than once. It ended thus:

ZAHN: Isn't it enough—and we've just got 10 seconds left—that [Saddam Hussein] has already violated 16 U.N. resolutions?

RITTER: Inspectors aren't in Iraq today, but not because Saddam kicked them out, but because the United States ordered them out in 1998. Keep that in mind.

ZAHN: That actually was as a result of U.N. negotiations.

RITTER: Negative. That was the result of Richard Butler unilaterally withdrawing from a system of inspection mechanisms.

ZAHN: But you—Kofi Annan was involved in all of that. But we don't have—

RITTER: No, Kofi Annan . . .

ZAHN: We don't have a lot of—well, look, we don't have—

RITTER: Study the chronology, that's all I'm saying.

[*Crosstalk*]

ZAHN: . . . the debate, the chronology of the U.N. and how it involved getting inspectors out.

RITTER: Well, it's important.

ZAHN: We're going to have to leave it there this morning. Scott Ritter, thanks for joining us. Appreciate it.

After such mistreatment by the network, and with the stakes so high for everyone, Ritter paid a visit to CNN's Atlanta headquarters on September 17, on his way to give a talk at Georgia State University. He wanted very much to set the record straight, and to that end met with the network's Executive Board and several dozen other senior figures there, including the top anchors. At Eason Jordan's urging, the reporters grilled Ritter at some length, and, as ever, got clear and thorough answers supported with hard facts and, in some cases, documents. At the session's end, Walter Isaacson, at that time the network's CEO, praised Ritter's openness and balance, and said that, while he himself might disagree with aspects of Ritter's general viewpoint (he was not more specific), he acknowledged him as a legitimate source of data that the network ought to use.

From there, Ritter went down to a studio to do another interview, this time with Arthel Neville, host of *TalkBack Live*. Of all his interviews on CNN, this one was easily the nastiest:

NEVILLE: Why did you meet with the Iraqi government?

RITTER: So I could be here today to get the message out to the American people. I have been saying the same thing for four years.

NEVILLE: So what did you say to them, Scott?

RITTER: First of all, it was my initiation. And I told them: "Allow the unconditional return of inspectors, give them unfettered access, or your nation will be destroyed." End of story.

NEVILLE [*skeptical*]: So that is why they are saying "yes" today?

RITTER: I am not giving myself any credit. You asked me what I said to them. I just told you what I said to them.

NEVILLE: So—and you paid for it out of your own pocket.

RITTER: Out of my own money.

NEVILLE: What about your friend, your Iraqi-American friend?

RITTER: First of all, let's put the—he is an American citizen.* And

---

*This refers to Shakir al-Khafaji, a Detroit businessman who helped fund the production of *In Shifting Sands*, Ritter's documentary about Iraq's disarmament status.

you do an insult to every American citizen of an ethnic origin when you call him—

NEVILLE: By saying Iraqi-American?

RITTER:—call him an American of Iraqi origin.

NEVILLE: So I shouldn't call someone African-American, Japanese-American?

RITTER: I am saying that, in these times, in post–September 11, let's focus on the fact that he is a law-abiding American citizen.

NEVILLE: I understand that. And calling him an Iraqi-American doesn't imply that he's not.

RITTER: But you said Iraqi.

NEVILLE: Iraqi-American, African-American.

RITTER: Whatever. I am telling you he is an American citizen and he has, in the past, provided funding so that I can get the message out to the American people. If you got a problem with me, come after the message. Don't come after him.

NEVILLE: I'm not talking about him. I'm asking—

RITTER: You just raised him.

NEVILLE: Yes, because I want to know what amount of money he gave you. Who is he? Why does he have an interest?

RITTER: That's none of your damn business. That's between me

He also facilitated Ritter's trip to Baghdad in September of 2002, which included an address to the Iraqi National Assembly. Of course, that trip was controversial in this country, where it, and Ritter's friendship with al-Khafaji, were invoked as signs of treason. Ritter sees no reason to apologize. "The trip to Baghdad," he says, "was a viable effort to avert a war which did not need to be fought (and indeed led to Iraq opening the door for the return of inspectors five days later). Shakir's role in facilitating both of these efforts is that of a patriotic American who loves his country. He should be applauded, not denigrated." E-mail from Scott Ritter, 11/5/03.

and the United States government. I don't violate American law. He is an American citizen, a private citizen.

NEVILLE: Who has family—does he have family in Iraq still?

RITTER: Yes, he does. What's your point?

NEVILLE: Point made.

RITTER: Point made?

NEVILLE: I have an e-mail I want to share with everybody right now. And that is coming from Rob in Colorado: "Scott Ritter is a traitor to the U.S. An American citizen never has the right to go into what is ostensibly enemy territory and speak out against the U.S. government and its president."

RITTER: I ask him to go back. First of all, calling me a traitor? Twelve years of service in the Marine Corps—I have gone to war for my country. I've put my life on the line for my country. I went to Iraq for seven years, where I again did the service of my country by getting rid of weapons of mass destruction. I have two classified commendations from the director of CIA for work I've done in support of the national defense. Call me a traitor? I think not. Back off, anybody who goes down there.

You can disagree with me, but I would say that you are also disagreeing with Theodore Roosevelt, who says that any American who blindly agrees to everything that comes out of the president's mouth is not only wrong and servile, but unpatriotic, that you have a patriotic responsibility as an American citizen to speak out against the president, especially if you think he is doing something wrong.

NEVILLE: We've got to take a break. Scott Ritter will be here when we return.

Despite the incoming, Ritter smoothly answered several pertinent questions from the audience, and then his time was up. "And now," Neville announced, "we'll hear the other side. Ritter has an army of critics who have called him everything from 'irrelevant' to a 'traitor.' " With that, she brought on the aptly named Max Boot of the *Weekly Standard* editorial page for some further jabs at Ritter, in the latter's absence. A frank proponent of U.S. imperial dominion overseas, Boot proceeded to charge, like so many others, that Ritter had flip-flopped ominously on the issue of Iraq's dangerousness. Boot's case was weak,* and yet *his* comments were respectfully received by Arthel Neville.

Thus the U.S. press impugned the testimony, and dismissed the expertise, of the only person qualified to contradict Bush/Cheney's propaganda drive for war. Ritter was done in not only by the cable operations, nor only by TV—the broadcast networks having tuned him out entirely. The drive to silence him *began* on CNN and Fox, but picked up plenty of momentum in the weeks to come when the nation's leading national newspapers started piling on. On October 21, the *Washington Post* weighed in with a hatchet job by Richard Leiby, "Fighting Words: Scott Ritter Says Iraq Is 'Not a Threat.' But His Critics See a Loose Cannon." And on November 24, the *New York Times Magazine* ran "Scott

---

*"Well, I'm puzzled by Scott Ritter's statements. There is an old Scott Ritter and a new Scott Ritter, and personally, I like the old one better.

"After he came back from Iraq in 1998 and quit the U.N. inspections program in disgust, what he said at the time was that Iraq was winning its bid to regain its prohibited weapons. He said, even today, Iraq is not nearly disarmed. This is what he said in 1998, and he quit, because the U.N. weapons inspection program, which he now advocates, was not getting the job done in 1998.

"Today, on this show, what I hear him say is something very different. He is saying, A, there is no real hard evidence that Iraq has weapons of mass destruction, and, B, if it does have weapons of mass destruction, the U.N. weapons inspections program will ferret that out. But why on earth would we believe either of those statements, when in the past, Scott Ritter has said Iraq does have weapons of mass destruction? And, in fact, there is overwhelming evidence from other sources that indicate that's the case."

As Ritter pointed out repeatedly, there was no contradiction between his positions in 1998 and in 2002. The question in the latter case was whether the United States had grounds for an invasion—or any right to wage a unilateral preemptive war. That apocalyptic option was never one that Ritter had in mind, even when he quit UNSCOM in August of 1998. Indeed, the only people advocating that extreme position at the time were Bush & Co., whose agitation for another war against Iraq had already started in late January of that year.

Ritter's Iraq Complex," a long, snide profile by Barry Bearak, which included this by-now predictable assessment:

> This is typical of Ritter. Even when admitting he is wrong, he is insisting he is right. His self-image requires it, for more than a life story, he has a personal mythology. Ritter, 41, loves the telling of it, which he does exceptionally well. In each chapter, he is the courageous man of principle, a stout-hearted citizen up against the dimwitted, the wicked and the power-mad.

That Bearak could mockingly cast civic dedication as neurotic grandiosity, despite the rigor and precision of Scott Ritter's arguments, and that the *Times* could run so sweeping a reproof, despite the issue's gravity, is further evidence of an enormous abdication of responsibility by the mainstream press in the United States. While Bearak's psychologizing sheds little light on Ritter, it may shed just a little light on Bearak, whose animus against the patriot would seem to indicate a certain guilty anger at the very thought of a "courageous man of principle, a stout-hearted citizen up against the dimwitted, the wicked and the power-mad." That anyone would dare to do exactly what the press ought to be doing, and do it in the face of constant slander by the powers that be, which is the way our press was meant to operate, would have to be quite galling to successful journalists, who, by and large, got where they are today by shirking their civic duty. Ritter's shabby treatment by the mainstream press was a betrayal of the First Amendment and a grave disservice to the American people.

Scott Ritter, it turns out, was 100 percent right: Bush/Cheney had no evidence for their contentions and therefore no good reason to invade Iraq. Ritter's scorn for all those half-baked claims was wholly justified, there evidently having been *no* Ba'athist arsenals of gas or germs, *no* secret stockpiles of plutonium, *no* active efforts to procure such stuff, and *no* plans even to start building the facilities for making or warehousing it. Saddam Hussein was bluffing, so as to stand tall in the eyes of Arabs everywhere. To have taken any of the lethal steps that were imputed to him would have been, as Ritter said, an act of suicide. And, notwithstanding all the U.S. propaganda, the Iraqi tyrant was not mad or even unpredictable, but, as Ritter noted, monstrously self-interested and therefore quite unlikely to do anything that might abort his rule. (He never used his poison gas on any stronger power, but on the Kurds and the Iranians.) Nor, as Ritter also argued, would Saddam Hussein, a secular pan-Arabist and eager murderer of many Islamists, ever have considered arming any of the latter faction, whose members would be just as likely to have used such weapons on himself as on the House of Saud, or on Americans, or on "the Jews." Thus did Ritter, in his efforts to prevent a war, shoot down Bush & Co.'s two main reasons for another "operation," which could only end up "killing thousands of people and destroying our reputation in the international community." Ritter warned that this would happen, and it has.*

While the prescient Ritter was dismissed as a subversive flake, the press hailed the opposing views of men who knew far less than he did and who were obviously not thinking straight, as their hearts and minds belonged to Daddy. History, however, has been far less kind to them. Clifford May, who charged that Ritter was "tremendously misguided," spent months before the war asserting that "the path to democracy in Iraq could be far smoother than many observers have indicated," as the *St. Louis Post-Dispatch* reported on August 9, 2002. "It'll be hard the next day," May conceded.

---

*With such a record of correct assessments, Ritter ought to have become a well-known talking head and frequent source for mainstream journalists, especially after he was vindicated by U.S. weapons inspector David Kay, who, on January 28, 2004, told Congress that, having scoured Iraq for WMDs, his team too had come up empty.

To its credit, CNN had Ritter on that day, to comment on Kay's findings for Wolf Blitzer. (He had also appeared on CNN on January 8.) Beyond that there was nothing in the mainstream press. As of this writing, Ritter has gone unmentioned in the *New York Times* and *Washington Post*, nor has he appeared on any other national TV show, network or cable. (The rightist press, meanwhile, continued to impugn him, as when the *New York Post* referred to "former arms-inspector-turned-Saddam-apologist Scott Ritter," "French for Bribery," *New York Post*, 1/31/04.) Nor does Ritter's name appear in Bob Woodward's ostensibly exhaustive history of Bush/Cheney's drive to war, *Plan of Attack* (New York: Simon & Schuster, 2004). Although he has continued to speak out loud and clear in lesser forums, this most reliable of experts has in effect been disappeared throughout the national media.

But can you get a transition to democracy, are there a lot of Iraqis
who would like to help make the transition, could you transform
Iraq into a productive society, an example for the rest of the
region—I think the answer to all these questions is yes.

James Woolsey, who, according to Paula Zahn, deemed Ritter "very far off
the beam," was, for many months before the war, a public optimist as
wrong as he was tireless. Having warned repeatedly that Saddam Hussein
was spending heavily on nuclear and chemical weapons, and that the
Ba'athists and Islamists would make common cause against us, or already
had, the ex-director of the CIA assured us of a quick and easy military victory (he predicted that the Turks would help us out), and that a "massive
demonstration of American power against the instruments of power of the
Iraqi state" would no doubt silence the world's Arab masses (or, as he put
it, "will have a very bracing effect on quieting the Arab street down"). He
also reckoned that our troops would be esteemed as saviors in the streets
of Baghdad, "just as we have become very popular in the streets of Kabul."

And Max Boot, who was so "puzzled" and distressed by Ritter's putatively schizoid viewpoint on Iraq, offered up this otherworldly game
plan in October of 2001:

> Once Afghanistan has been dealt with, the US should turn its
> attention to Iraq. It will probably not be possible to remove Hus-
> sein quickly without a US invasion and occupation—though it will
> hardly require half a million men, since Hussein's army is much
> diminished since the Gulf War, and the US will probably have
> plenty of help from Iraqis, once they trust that it intends to finish
> the job this time. Once Hussein is deposed, an American-led, inter-
> national regency in Baghdad, to go along with the one in Kabul,
> should be imposed.

That the news machine embraced such fantasists, while casting the
informed and sober Ritter as a madman, stinking drunk on "Saddam
Hussein's Kool-Aid," was but one of countless indications that the credo
of the U.S. press today is *not* the First Amendment, but rather "Ignorance Is Strength." The drive to neutralize Scott Ritter finally climaxed
in a murky but effective charge of something like attempted pedophilia,

stealthily "exposed" in January of 2003. That slander was, to say the least, gratuitous, inasmuch as Ritter had already been defamed aplenty by our journalists, who have become about as dissidence-averse as Soviet reporters used to be. While helping to discredit him, therefore, they also acquiesced as Bush & Co. intensified its propaganda drive, circulating whopper after whopper.

Father Knows Best

In Cincinnati on October 7, 2002, speaking to a wide-eyed audience of true believers bused in for the spectacle, Bush charged that Saddam Hussein's regime "possesses and produces chemical and biological weapons," "is seeking nuclear weapons," is "rebuilding facilities that it had used to produce chemical and biological weapons," and "is exploring ways of using [unmanned aerial vehicles] for missions targeting the United States" (aircraft that "could be used to disperse chemical and biological weapons across broad areas"). Bush hammered at the nonexistent partnership between al Qaeda and the Ba'ath ("We know that Iraq and al Qaeda have had high-level contacts that go back a decade"), and intimated frequently, and artfully, that Saddam Hussein was somehow closely linked to 9/11:

> Saddam Hussein also has experience in using chemical weapons. He has ordered chemical attacks on Iran, and on more than forty villages in his own country. These actions killed or injured at least 20,000 people, more than six times the number of people who died in the attacks of September the 11th.

Contending with this threat, Bush said, was "crucial to winning the war on terror." And Bush asserted that the Ba'ath had tried to thwart UNSCOM at every turn: "The UN inspection program was met with systematic deception. The Iraqi regime bugged hotel rooms and offices of inspectors to find where they were going next"—a charge that, through a neat reversal, utterly erased the fact that UNSCOM had been used by *us* to spy on *them*. (It was assumed, but never proved, that the Ba'athists "bugged hotel rooms and offices.")

Although Bush invoked "clear evidence of peril," his speech presented none, implying that his claims alone *were* "evidence." Every statement that he made was either dubious or demonstrably untrue, and yet the press was largely deferential. The frankly rightist media were blatant in their exultation at how strong an argument the president had made. "Case Closed," proclaimed an item in the *National Review;* "Case Closed," wrote John Podhoretz in the *New York Post,* which added this Orwellian subhead: "With Facts, the President Soberly Faces down Fear."

Such far-right praise was tacitly confirmed by the non-far-rightist mainstream media, which, with very few exceptions, only paraphrased the speech, or analyzed the president's "tone," or speculated as to how the speech might be *perceived* by the Great Audience. Although some journalists did hazard the suggestion that the speech "said nothing new," it was only journalists serving other countries, and U.S. dissidents in cyberspace, who did what Jefferson and Madison believed the press should do.

The big shots of the U.S. Fourth Estate, and of telejournalism in particular, were careful *not* to criticize the speech or bring on anyone who might, aside from the occasional guarded Democrat. On NBC's *Today Show* on October 8, the talking head of choice was Richard Butler, who told Katie Couric and Matt Lauer that Bush had delivered "an outstanding speech, I think the best he's given," and then went on to second its assertions. The boundaries of permissible dissent were clearly set by CNN's Connie Chung, who, after Bush's speech, had this exchange with Democrat Mike Thompson, a Congressman from California:

THOMPSON: Well, Connie, this is the most important vote that I'm ever going to cast, and possibly the most important vote that's ever been cast in Congress. Not only are we going to set up a situation where American soldiers are going to go to war and possibly die, but we're also establishing an international precedent where we're going to use first-strike capabilities, preemptive first strike, in a situation where there appears to be no immediate danger to people here in the United States or to our allies.

CHUNG: Well, let's listen to something that President Bush said tonight, and you tell me if this doesn't provide you with the evidence that you want. Let's play a clip of it.

[*Begin video clip*]

BUSH: Some al Qaeda leaders who fled Afghanistan went to Iraq. These include one very senior al Qaeda leader who received medical treatment in Baghdad this year and who has been associated with planning for chemical and biological attacks.

We've learned that Iraq has trained al Qaeda members in bomb-making, in poisons and deadly gases. And we know that after September 11, Saddam Hussein's regime gleefully celebrated the terrorist attacks on America.

[*End video clip*]

CHUNG: Congressman, doesn't *that* tell you that an invasion of Iraq is justified?

THOMPSON: Connie, we haven't seen any proof that any of this has happened. I have sat through all the classified briefings—

CHUNG: You mean you don't believe—

THOMPSON:—on the Armed Services—

CHUNG:—what President Bush just said?? With all due respect—!

THOMPSON: No, no, that's not . . .

CHUNG:—you know—

THOMPSON:—what I said.

CHUNG:—I mean, what—??

THOMPSON: That's not what I said. I said that there are—there has been nothing in the committee hearing briefings that have substantiated this. If there is substantiation, we need to see that in Congress, not hear it over the television monitor.

That Chung et al. were so aggressive in defense of Bush & Co. was not a symptom of majoritarian timidity, the newsfolk merely telling people what the people wanted to be told. So weak and windy was the White House case that ever fewer Americans would buy it, nor did the president's big speech in Cincinnati make much difference. According to a CNN/*USA Today*/Gallup Poll, national pro-war sentiment had dipped from 74 percent in November of 2001 to 61 percent in June of 2002—with 60 percent approving diplomatic rather than military measures. (The downward trend continued even after Bush's speech in Cincinnati.) A *New York Times*/CBS News Poll released the day of Bush's speech found that while 67 percent "approve of the US taking military action against Iraq to try and remove Saddam Hussein from power," 63 percent said that the United States should "wait and give the UN more time to get weapons inspectors into Iraq"—Scott Ritter's view, which had survived the smear campaign against the man himself. Thus was the press's deference to the White House *not* reflective of broad mass approval. Indeed, the latter poll revealed that 51 percent said that Congress was not "asking enough questions" about Bush/Cheney's war plans, while only 20 percent felt that "too many" questions had been raised. In stigmatizing those who publicly resisted Bush's pitch, then, Chung et al. were not only betraying the First Amendment but doing so against the public will, in favor of Bush/Cheney's coterie and their loud minority of true believers.

And that minority prevailed because the U.S. press refused to do its civic duty—and kept refusing, even as Bush/Cheney's war campaign veered into ever wilder fictions. On January 29, 2003, four months after Bush's Cincinnati speech, there was his State of the Union address, which was even more mendacious than the president had ever been (about Iraq). Now Bush asserted that "Saddam Hussein aids and protects terrorists, including members of al Qaeda," and used that weary bit—which had been publicly discredited—about the aluminum tubes, and claimed that the Iraqis had been working furtively to purchase yellowcake uranium down in Niger, and so on.*

---

*The speech was, in fact, a tapestry of lies not just about the need for war, but on a lot of other subjects: Bush/Cheney's "Healthy Forests Initiative" (the program's very name a lie), the annual amount of U.S. foreign aid (Bush extravagantly hyped it), the widespread benefits of Bush & Co.'s tax-cut plan (92 million Americans, he said, would keep "an average of almost $1,100 more of their own money" in 2003—that use of "average" conjuring a bright mirage of nonexistent tax returns for most of us).

None of this was challenged front and center by the mainstream press, nor was there any audible attempt to analyze, objectively, the contents of Colin Powell's big dog-and-pony show at the United Nations on February 5, which was hailed mainly for the secretary's commanding tone and smooth delivery and for the impact of his fancy visuals. His histrionic deftness was enough, apparently, to make it seem to some as if he'd finally made the case for an Iraq/al Qaeda link, and for the clear and present danger of Iraq's vast arsenal of forbidden weapons. The fact that Powell's performance was devoid of any evidence was lost on many in the U.S. press, including liberals. Even Mary McGrory of the *Washington Post* went starry-eyed, and pledged allegiance in a piece entitled, "I'm Persuaded."

Such press collusion had exactly the effect that it has had in countless other, closed societies, where people, by and large, know only what the government would have them know. After the president's performance on January 29, the downward trend in the opinion polls began to slow and even to reverse as Bush & Co. ramped up the volume, with U.S. reporters serving merely as White House amplifiers. The prospect of a war was still unpopular, but often the resistance was instinctive rather than informed, the necessary facts and arguments being unavailable to any but the most committed activists, who have their own communication networks.

With the press in general supportive of the White House, most Americans were hearing just the White House message. Thus barraged, it is entirely understandable that some two-thirds of the U.S. population soon believed the story that Saddam Hussein had some connection to the terrorist attacks of 9/11, and understandable that few Americans would know of the Iraqi butcher's heavy debt to Reagan/Bush, whose agents broke the law to arm and fund him and lobbied hard *against* congressional sanctions on his government for its appalling violations of

While the Associated Press did a strong little piece on such deceptions, the otherwise mainstream media machine downplayed them if it brought them up at all, and stayed away especially from the numerous untruths about Iraq. "Bush Speech Casts Issues in Simple Terms," AP, 1/29/03. In general, the AP did an excellent job in following up on the worldwide response to Bush's speech.

Iraqi human rights. Thus protected from the truth, many of our fellow citizens bought Bush & Co.'s defective product. In early February of 2003, the *Christian Science Monitor* took oblique note of the national flimflam:

> In the final days before the 1991 Persian Gulf War, a Gallup poll found that 46 percent of Americans felt the situation in Iraq was "worth going to war" over. This time around, the latest Gallup poll finds overall support for an invasion at 58 percent. And according to a recent ABC News/Washington Post poll, a bare majority now say they would support military action even without UN approval.
>
> Given that the administration hasn't even finished making its case—and hasn't actually called for war—analysts say the current level of support is striking. Behind it lies a complex range of factors, from a diminished fear of casualties to a near-universal view of Mr. Hussein as a menace. General trust in Mr. Bush's judgment—and even more trust in Powell's—may also be swaying many Americans, along with a growing sense of the inevitability of war.
>
> "It is very unusual for members of the public to support an operation before the president actually has made his full case," says Eric Larson, a senior policy analyst at RAND who specializes in public opinion and war. "Americans just have a set of beliefs about Iraq and the nature of the threat."

Of course, we did *not* "just have a set of beliefs about Iraq and the nature of the threat," as if we had been born with them or raised on them. That Americans were simply misinformed by their own government and uninformed by their own press, and *therefore* often willing to support the war, becomes quite clear when we compare U.S. mass opinion vis-à-vis Iraq with the prevailing view in countries where the press still functions as it should, even without constitutional protection. Major news outlets worldwide would, naturally, do more than parrot the official U.S. line, and so their readers, viewers, and listeners knew enough to give the U.S. line the credence it deserved. This was the case not only in, say, the region served by al Jazeera, but throughout Europe, in Canada and Mexico, Japan and India, Thailand and the Philippines, and on and on. Despite Israel's enormous interest in the conflict, that nation's press was far less tame than their U.S. counterparts, and, ironically enough, the authors of the First Amendment surely would have deemed the British media far more "American" than ours.

The British people never were convinced by Tony Blair's fantastic allegations, not because they're any smarter than Americans, but because the BBC, the *Guardian*, the *Glasgow Evening Herald*, the *Independent*, and other British press outlets demanded more specifics from the eloquent prime minister, who never could come up with any. That his assertions were contested by a number of trustworthy sources was enough to slow down his war chariot (but not enough to stop it). In contrast, the U.S. press, likewise confronted with a lot of wild and scary charges by the head of state, uttered not a peep of contradiction and kept contrary experts off the air, or, as with Ritter, made all contradiction sound like treason. Bush's statements came and went unchallenged (except out on the culture's margins) and were therefore taken, by and large, as true.

By failing to subject our leaders to tough scrutiny, and by belittling or ignoring the accounts of expert dissidents as well as other valid points of view, the press has failed America; its broad collusion in Bush/Cheney's propaganda plans amounts to institutional treason. The consequences of this crime are grave—graver even than the devastating rule of Bush & Co., which is a problem that the rational majority can solve (unless their votes aren't counted). More daunting than the mere ascendancy of a particular cabal, and more frightening than the media's routinely spreading government disinformation, is the deeper problem of a press that serves no rational purpose whatsoever, but functions mainly as a medium of angry rightist passion. In other words, the threat lies not just in the countless twisted facts per se—errors that can be corrected, by and by. The deeper threat lies in the general *animus* that drives the press to keep on spewing out those fabrications and distortions.

By this I mean far more than that the press maintains a certain "bias" to the right. To call it "bias" is to understate the media's overall belligerent emotionality, and its function as a giant instrument of mass unreason, channeled and deflected for the benefit of rightist interests. Somehow the U.S. mainstream press has long since been transformed into a pure extension of the rightist psyche, urging us, until it was too late, to see the world as Bush & Co. has seen it—which was to see the world as it is *not*. The mainstream media, in short, routinely seconds the apocalyptic worldview that now dominates our government—and that is also thriving elsewhere in the world, frequently *against* this government. It is a Manichaean worldview, purist, fierce, explosive, and uncompromising, yet terrorstricken too and livid with self-hatred. That ancient way of seeing things has itself become, again, a revolutionary influence on politics. The best way to combat that outlook is to match its fantasies against reality; to try to understand what's driving it; and to call the movement out as antidemocratic and antirepublican. It is irrational, authoritarian, divisive, and intolerant—i.e., directly hostile to the liberal and enlightened spirit of America, as it inspired the framers of our Constitution. We are obliged to make that clear, so that our fellow citizens can finally recognize the plot for what it is.

Although I might now accurately label this archaic movement, that academic stroke would no doubt seem provocative to many of my readers, and so distract them from the argument. I will name the movement later in this book, after certain further revelations which may make that name sound less extreme to those who might be offended by it at this point. Rather than invoke inflammatory terms, I want now to demonstrate the movement's *pathological* dimension, for it is based far less on any ideology than on a virulence that has its roots deep in the psyche or the soul. Specifically, the antidemocratic movement here, like others in the past and present all around the world, is based on, and empowered by, incessant and malevolent *projection*, each true believer angrily imputing his own wishes and desires onto the Other, who is thereby made to function as a scapegoat for the true believer's unacknowledged sins.

Under the dominion of the far-right GOP, with the media largely in the party's pocket (and the Democratic Party ineffectual), this fierce projective tendency has taken over U.S. politics. The process started with the fall of communism, which deprived the rightists of their favorite enemy. On the domestic front, the right at once transferred its hatred from the commies to the Clintons, projecting onto *them* the wicked drives that it had long projected onto Moscow. That epic smear campaign resulted in the rise of Bush & Co.——which now projects abroad the animosity that the regime's supporters had projected onto Washington when Clinton was our president. To apprehend the lunacy of the post–Cold War right, and to appreciate the press's role in the spread of that insanity, we must now turn to the extraordinary double standard of the right, and of the press, in their conjoint assault on Clinton/Gore and adulation of Bush/Cheney.

CHAPTER 3

The Wrong Man: I

"It smells like what happened in Germany"

"People can read the handwriting on the wall. It smells like what happened in Germany," observes Paul Hill, a retired aircraft mechanic, as he sits in a café in Hollis, New Hampshire. "Are we going to wait until the horses are all running down the street before we close the barn door?" Such fears and nervous recollections of the Third Reich now find expression all across America. "We don't have a government that serves you," notes one Pennsylvanian. "We have a Gestapo." The fear has spread since the unprecedented terrorist attack on U.S. soil, and the president's apparent exploitation of that nightmare to promote his own perverse political agenda. It was his Reichstag fire, you hear repeatedly. Of course, the mainstream press dismisses all such notions, and derides or even demonizes those who warn of fascism as "paranoids" and "crazies." Only on the margins of the media, in certain paperbacks (which never get reviewed) and magazines with an extremist readership, do journalists dare speak the obvious. There are, wrote one, "a huge range of people," burning, like "a thousand points of heat . . . to escape the tentacles" of Washington, now that this hated president—a "draft-dodger," a "traitor," and a "liar," and a man made rich by shady business deals—has ended up inside the Oval Office.

For all of its uncanny resonance, that paragraph does not refer to the America where I sit writing now. Its subject, rather, is the atmosphere on the far right throughout the second half of Bill Clinton's first presidential term. Back then, "the recent terrorist attack" was the bombing, on April 19, 1995, of the Alfred P. Murrah Federal Building in Oklahoma City. After that catastrophe, and the discovery that it seemed to be the doing not of an Islamist cell but of a fair-haired all-American with "patriotic" views and U.S. military training, the president spoke out against the rightist propaganda network, primarily on radio, that had lately vented countless calls to violence against the U.S. government and incendiary rants on "liberal fascists," blacks, gays, immigrants, environmentalists, "feminazis," and whatever other sector of the population might be deemed a threat to the Republic. In Minneapolis, on April 24, 1995, at the start of an address on the importance of community colleges, Clinton first recalled the grief and heroism on the scene at Oklahoma City, then offered these extemporaneous remarks:

> In this country we cherish and guard the right of free speech. We know we love it when we put up with people saying things we absolutely deplore. And we must always be willing to defend their right to say things we deplore to the ultimate degree.
>
> But we hear so many loud and angry voices in America today whose sole goal seems to be to try to keep some people as paranoid as possible, and the rest of us all torn up and upset with each other. They spread hate. They leave the impression that, by their very words, that violence is acceptable. You ought to see—I'm sure you are now seeing the reports of some things that are regularly said over the airwaves in America today.

The president then quickly reconfirmed that he was not promoting censorship of any kind.

> Well, people like that who want to share our freedoms must know that their bitter words can have consequences, and that freedom has endured in this country for more than two centuries because it was coupled with an enormous sense of responsibility on the part of the American people.
>
> If we are to have freedom to speak, freedom to assemble, and, yes, the freedom to bear arms, we must have responsibility as well. And to those of us who do not agree with the purveyors of hatred and

division, with the promoters of paranoia, I remind you that *we* have freedom of speech, too. And *we* have responsibilities, too. And some of us have not discharged our responsibilities. It is time we all stood up and spoke against that kind of reckless speech and behavior.

Clinton ended by elaborating on that call to democratic action:

> If they insist on being irresponsible with our common liberties, then we must be all the more responsible with our liberties. When they talk of hatred, we must stand against them. When they talk of violence, we must stand against them. When they say things that are irresponsible, that may have egregious consequences, we must call them on it.
>
> The exercise of their freedom of speech makes our silence all the more unforgivable. So exercise yours, my fellow Americans. Our country, our future, our way of life is at stake. I never want to look into the faces of another set of family members like I saw yesterday—and you can help to stop it.

It was an eloquent and necessary statement—Clinton at his best, perhaps—and so I quote its every word in part because it was so truthful at the time, and, like Jefferson's first inaugural address, is now more relevant than ever. And yet my primary aim in quoting it in full is not to celebrate its wisdom but to note the right's hysterical reaction to it.

Although the president took pains to honor freedom of expression, urging only public *refutation* of the bile expended daily by the right, the latter roared as if he had proposed to round them up and jail them. Clinton had kicked off "a post-Oklahoma *Kristallnacht*," charged a Bircherite biweekly called the *New American* ("That Freedom Shall Not Perish"), the author starting with a passage from *Mein Kampf* and noting that, before the Night of Broken Glass, "Nazi propaganda had accused the German Jews of waging a 'hate campaign' against the National Socialist government." "They must have been dancing a jig in the White House when this happened," railed a caller to a radio program in Detroit, "because it gave them an opportunity to make Clinton the dictator."

Without invoking Hitler outright, many prominent rightists likewise charged that Clinton had attacked the Bill of Rights with his "inflammatory statements," as GOP presidential hopeful Lamar Alexander called the president's restrained objection to inflammatory statements. He was threatening to "trample on domestic liberties," warned far-rightist Senator Don Nickles, and, charged rightist shock-jock Armstrong Williams, "trying to label everyone who disagrees with his policies as extremists," and "closing in . . . on the legitimate speech of the political opposition," cried neocon Charles Krauthammer (a "liberal columnist," according to the *New American*). Sputtering in nervous indignation, talk radio's hottest heads also implied that just for speaking freely, they were being gagged by a despotic chief executive. "There is a huge difference between dissent and hate," intoned Rush Limbaugh, taking the high road for a couple of seconds. Oliver North, whose broadcasting career was only one month old, asked rhetorically while on the air (before a gaggle of reporters), "Should Bill Clinton decide what's on this talk show? I don't think so."

The furor was bizarre, because the rightists' claims bore no relation to the president's remarks, which were about as warlike and "inflammatory" as the Psalmist's line, "I am for peace: but when I speak, they are for war." Typically, the mighty propaganda choir appeared to be responding not to anything that Clinton said, but to their own idea of what he *would* say, as Limbaugh had already indicated, in charging— days before the president spoke out—that "they" were eager to shut down the opposition. "The left in this country would love for the right to be permanently disqualified and silenced by virtue of their innuendo [*sic*]," he boomed soon after the attack in Oklahoma City.

If there was a certain shrillness in the right's reactions to the presidential homily, it was in part because they had to know, somewhere inside, that what he'd said was true. Among Limbaugh's many barbarous ad libs was this one, on February 22, 1995:

> I mean, there is a—out West—you go out to Nevada, parts of California, there is—th—the second violent American revolution is just about—I got my fingers a quarter of an inch apart—it's just about that far away because these people out there are sick and tired of a bunch of bureaucrats in Washington driving into town

and telling them what they can and can't do with their land, using all of these federal regulations!

In like seditious spirit, on August 26, 1994, G. Gordon Liddy, who had come to fame, and gone to jail, for having done a bit of Richard Nixon's dirty work against democracy,* advised his listeners on how to deal with pesky agents from the Bureau of Alcohol, Tobacco and Firearms (BATF): "They've got a big target on there, ATF. Don't shoot at that because they've got a vest on underneath that. Head shots, head shots. . . . Kill the sons of bitches." (Even after Oklahoma City, Liddy kept it up, claiming at one point that at a family gathering on Independence Day the year before, he had used stick figures of the Clintons for a little target practice: "Thought it might improve my aim.")† Those were but the most notorious of such utterances, which, as President Clinton noted, had become routine on U.S. radio, both national and local.

However, the intensity with which the right assailed the president for speaking out was no mere symptom of uneasy conscience. (Liddy, for example, seems to have been born without one.) Those strident protestations that the "liberals" were intent on silencing "the legitimate speech of the political opposition" were, of course, themselves attempts at silencing the legitimate speech of the political opposition (such as it was). Those patriots were speaking grimly of themselves. That is, in responding not to what the president had said but to their own idea of what he probably *would* say, they were in fact responding only to what they would have said themselves, for it is *they* who always have confused

---

*Liddy was the wildest member of "the Plumbers," the White House goon squad set up to give the president some extralegal help—burglary, wire-tapping, forgery, blackmail, planning acts of vandalism—in winning reelection.

†After the bombing of the Murrah building, Liddy revisited his "head shots" comment, momentarily pretending, at a press conference during his show, that he would like to take it back. Advising head shots had been wrong, he said—because the head made for too small a target. "So you shoot twice to the body, center of mass, and if that does not work, then shoot to the groin area. . . . They cannot move their hips fast enough and you'll probably get a femoral artery and you'll knock them down at any rate." "Liddy Fine-tunes Advice on How to Shoot Federal Agents," AP, 4/25/95.

dissent with hate and who were always trying, and are trying now, to have the *left* (i.e., all who disagree with them) "permanently disqualified and silenced."

In short, that seeming antifascist chorus was itself protofascist, their strident warnings of a coming wave of Clintonite oppression saying little that was accurate about Bill Clinton's plans—but much, unconsciously, about *their own* desire to crack down on *their* enemies. What they heard in Clinton's reasonable words were their own inner voices clamoring for war; and those wild voices would be vastly amplified when Bush & Co. finally came to power, against the will of the electorate. Even after taking over the entire federal government, in fact, and even with their tribunes omnipresent in the media, the right would still deplore the liberals' endless drive to smash the right, as if the latter had no power and were about to be annihilated.

The Grain of Truth

While the rightists were ferociously off base in their attack on Clinton's statement, and blind as ever to their own wrathfulness, their basic point about the U.S. government was not invalid. Certainly the grassroots right had been appalled—traumatized—by what they took to be strong evidence of looming federal repression. The FBI's shoot-out with Randy Weaver's family at Ruby Ridge in Idaho did turn atrocious, when a sniper's bullet, having missed its target, smashed apart the skull of Weaver's wife as she stood in their cabin doorway with their baby in her arms. The couple's fourteen-year-old son was also killed. (That the Weavers were staunch neo-Nazis, and had been implicated in the fatal shooting of a U.S. Marshal, in no way rights that hideously clumsy wrong.) Eight months later, on April 19, 1993, the danger seemed to have grown exponentially, as federal forces tried to take another and far larger stronghold of millennial resistance, the move this time against the compound of the so-called Branch Davidians in Waco, touching off a conflagration in which seventy-nine people burned to death, twenty-two of them small children. Although a long investigation finally found that the inferno had most likely been ignited by the cult's own leadership and not the FBI (which had aroused suspicions by concealing evidence), the massacre was dreadful, and its horrific impact on a large plurality of other citizens—largely Christians and gun owners—wholly understandable.

And yet Ruby Ridge and Waco were not portents of a federal crackdown by Clinton Democrats. (The Weaver killings had occurred, and the Waco siege begun, when Bush the Elder was in power.) The mass impression of a coming anti-Christian coup was fostered by a flood tide of extremist propaganda. On the ultraright, the killings stood as "proof" of an impending takeover by the nation's Zionist Occupation Government (ZOG), whose Jewish masters planned to wipe out or enslave all Aryan Americans under the evil flag of the UN. Such apocalyptic fantasy—as old as the United States itself—soon grew dimly audible throughout the mainstream, as much the same wild forecast, albeit without the Nazi trappings, resonated far beyond the compounds of the white supremacists. In the Christian right's abundant propaganda, Waco figured heavily as a "holocaust" all too suggestive of the new pro-choice abortion policy of Clinton's White House. No less influentially, the National Rifle Association (NRA) plied its 3.5 million members with Orwellian visions of a police state. Clinton had given "jack-booted government thugs more power to take away our Constitutional rights, break in our doors, seize our guns, destroy our property, and even injure or kill us," wrote the NRA's Wayne LaPierre in a fund-raising letter to the membership on April 13—six days before the Oklahoma City bombing.

All such seeming-libertarian polemic was heavily amplified by GOP operatives, in both the party proper and the corporate media, who cast the Clintons as the most nefarious of power couples, like the Ceaușescus of Romania. The propagation of that fiction was the task of all the public Clinton-haters, whether they portrayed the president as a sophisticated despot, out to crush the people through the latest technological advances (subcutaneous computer chips, black helicopters on the prowl), or as a rougher gangster type, like Hitler on the rise, bumping off his enemies as well as those who "knew too much." (The latter myth took off after the "murder" of Vince Foster in July of 1993.)

Such views of Clinton generally originated way out on the right and then were dumped into the mainstream by excited politicians and a well-heeled national network of demagogic media celebrities. Thus did Representative William Dannemeyer (R-CA)—author of *Shadow on the Land*, a book about "the homosexual's dangerous agenda"—publicize the "Clinton Body Count," a long list of that president's alleged murder victims, which includes the four BATF agents shot in the Waco standoff. (All four had been "Clinton bodyguards." They knew too much.) The list had been concocted by one Linda Thompson, self-styled "acting adjunct general" of the "Unorganized Militia of the United States" and chair of the American Justice Federation, a for-profit propaganda mill that offers, among other works, "Waco: The Big Lie" and "The Traitor Files," which links "Bill and Hillary Clinton to a Marxist-Terrorist network." Headquartered in Indianapolis, the federation calls itself "a group dedicated to stopping the New World Order and getting the truth out to the American public."* Such were the distant sources of the numerous canards assiduously mainstreamed by the *American Spectator*, Rush Limbaugh, Ann Coulter, Lucianne Goldberg, Matt Drudge, and all the rest.

That Clinton craved despotic power was a notion that said more about the people who thus demonized him than it did about his character (or Hillary's). As few of his critics understood, however, there were, especially in his first term, solid grounds for grave concern about the state of U.S. civil liberties—which had been under growing threat since 1980, when the heroic interim of post-Watergate reform was terminated by the jingoism of the Reagan era. Indeed, civil libertarians celebrated Clinton's win in 1992, expecting that the Democrat would halt, at least, the statist trend of Reagan/Bush, with its oppressive "war on drugs," its

---

*Dannemeyer's circulation of the Thompson list is by no means the most significant example of a charge invented by the ultraright and then repeated endlessly by actors better known: Whitewater—the central "scandal" in the epic "case" against Bill Clinton—was largely hatched by vengeful segregationists in Arkansas, and then deliriously propagated by the GOP and major media, not least the *New York Times* and *Washington Post*. On the concoction of Whitewater, see Gene Lyons and Joe Conason, *The Hunting of the President: The Ten-Year Campaign to Destroy Bill and Hillary Clinton* (New York: St. Martin's, 2001). On the obscure far-right origins of much GOP propaganda, see David Neiwert, "Rush, Newspeak, and Fascism: An Exegesis," 8/30/03, available at http://dneiwert.blogspot.com/.

blunt contempt for constitutional niceties—Ed Meese, Reagan's law-breaking attorney general, once called the ACLU a "criminals' lobby"—its drive against pornography, its efforts to curb women's reproductive freedom, and its secret plans to use detention camps in the event of vehement national dissent against the war in Nicaragua.

Clinton dashed the hopes of libertarians, both liberal and conservative: the Cato Institute and the ACLU decried his policies with equal fervor. "Bill Clinton has not been called to account in this campaign for the worst aspect of his presidency. That is his appalling record on constitutional rights," charged Anthony Lewis in 1996. On March 4, 1997, he added, "Bill Clinton has the worst civil liberties record of any president in at least 60 years." The sad truth is that Clinton heated up the "war on drugs" (the number of arrests for pot possession doubled under Clinton, and overall there was a sharp increase in the number of jailed African-Americans). He also pushed the Communications Decency Act, making it a federal crime to transmit "indecent" or "patently offensive" content via the Internet, and/or not to block kids' access to such material; signed the Defense of Marriage Act, a federal ban on gay unions; allowed the FBI to track protestors of "free trade"; and so on. "A single essay cannot do justice to the injustices that the Clinton administration has perpetrated through its far-ranging assaults on free speech and privacy," the ACLU's Nadine Strossen writes in *The Rule of Law in the Wake of Clinton*, edited by the Cato Institute's Roger Pilon and published in 2000.

Perhaps the worst of Clinton's moves against the Bill of Rights was his approval of the Anti-Terrorism and Effective Death Penalty Act (AEDPA), passed in 1996. This was the first bill ever to place temporal limits on the right to habeas corpus, now giving prisoners just one year to file a habeas corpus writ upon exhaustion of their final state appeals. The purpose of this limitation was to speed up the death penalty, which Clinton backed without reserve. The AEDPA also drastically infringed on the constitutional rights of immigrants. It vacated a 1986 statute offering amnesty to illegal aliens, so that 300,000 pending court cases were summarily thrown out. It rendered federal judges powerless to block decisions by the Immigration and Naturalization Service (INS), whose agents could now hastily deport, on the very hazy grounds of "moral turpitude," any green-card holder who has been convicted of a crime.

The act's anti-immigrant measures were driven, we now know, by Clinton's deep concerns about al Qaeda, which he fought stealthily for years. But even if it were permissible to cut back civil liberties to hinder terrorism, Clinton's record vis-à-vis those liberties would be quite poor.* Unless *terrorism* is an infinitely broader term than anyone had ever known, the terrorist threat could hardly be affected by restricting habeas corpus rights, forbidding homosexual marriages, or making it a federal offense to e-mail images that may strike someone as "offensive." The fact is that Bill Clinton, although well acquainted with the issues (having once been a professor of constitutional law), was at best indifferent to the state of civil liberties, and, in this regard, a president far more Nixonian than his supporters had expected. His was "the most wire-tap-friendly administration in history," according to the ACLU's Laura Murphy.

And so when Clinton was condemned by rightist activists for his apparent drift toward tyranny, there was some basis for the charge—especially if we include the constitutional freedom most important to that faction. It was, above all, Clinton's policy on gun control that mobilized the right against him. Passed in November of 1993, the Brady Bill—requiring background checks for would-be handgun purchasers and a five-day waiting period—struck many on the right as a despotic blow against "the right of the people to keep and bear arms," which, in their eyes, is just as crucial to the maintenance of democracy as free speech and freedom of the press. It was the president's attempt to slow the spread of handguns that aroused the NRA against him, its advocates

---

*There is one notable exception: Clinton did a great deal to reverse the federal tendency toward ever greater secrecy. He authorized the broad release of public documents and sought to expedite the process of declassification, working closely with Senator Daniel Patrick Moynihan to make American government more transparent, as it was at the beginning of our history and as it remained, by and large, until the First World War. Clinton's efforts at *glasnost* seem particularly laudable, now that Bush & Co. has established the most secretive regime in U.S. history. See Daniel Patrick Moynihan, *Secrecy: The American Experience* (New Haven: Yale University Press, 1998).

resorting to that vivid antifascist rhetoric deployed by Gordon Liddy and Wayne LaPierre. The latter's evocation of "jack-booted government thugs" oppressing patriots and their families was, after Waco, especially effective on the right, and that vision of the state as a mass murderer of innocents was further heightened by the president's liberal posture on abortion. That toxic mix of images inspired many rightists to wild threats of insurrection (and, at times, to outright violence). "And Miss Reno, I say to you: If you send your jackbooted, baby-burning bush-whackers to confiscate my guns, pack them a lunch—it will be a damned long day," said Harry Thomas, board member of the NRA, in April 1995.

Only such true believers could imagine, or pretend, that Clinton was another Mussolini or Pol Pot. For those loud tribunes of the right, the proper measure of "democracy" lies mainly in the freedom to bear arms and in those symbolically related issues of abortion and apocalyptic Christianity. Here I refer not to principled conservatives who rightly fear the power of unrestricted government or who have reasoned out their opposition to abortion or to gun control. Rather, I refer to those extrem-ists wedded to the rightist creed of armed resistance, for they would have felt unwelcome at the Constitutional Convention, regardless of their anti-Nazi noises. The ideology of the paramilitary ultraright may be summed up as bullets over ballots. By and large, their aim is theocratic rather than republican, as they are eager to "tear down this wall" between church and state and to reinstate the patriarchal order of the Bible as they read it: the menfolk giving orders, the women doing nothing but having babies and preparing meals. The champions of that vision are repelled by secular democracy, in part because that system would disable their own programs. As Lars-Erik Nelson notes, the NRA itself is an undemocratic outfit, because its grassroots membership cannot be trusted to adhere to management's hard line,* nor does the NRA want

---

*Most rank-and-file members, reported Nelson in 1995, "either cannot or do not vote in NRA elections, or even make their opinions known to other members. The NRA is run by a handful of paid staff employees in Washington who determine its day-to-day political strategy and, like bureaucrats everywhere, figure ways to build a bigger empire and bigger budgets for themselves.

"Dave Edmondson, a lifelong NRA member, said this hard-line leadership . . . is

any public referendum on gun ownership because they know that most Americans do not agree with them. Likewise, the foes of legalized abortion do not seek to put their platform to a vote, but operate by stealthy infiltration of state legislatures and the federal judiciary, their cadres effecting secret changes that would quickly be defeated at the polls.

And so their charges that Bill Clinton was a would-be autocrat ring false, as they themselves distrust democracy. Those calling him "a jackboot liberal" (as Cato's Doug Bandow wrote in 1997) necessarily ignored the fact that Clinton was not liberal—and, more important, that his most repressive measures were *opposed* by liberal Democrats and moderate Republicans, but fervently *supported* by the staunchest rightists in the GOP. The AEDPA, Clinton's antiterrorist bill, was defended loudly by Hank Brown of Colorado, Christian reconstructionist Lauch Faircloth, Jesse Helms, and Orrin Hatch. It was opposed by Daniel Patrick Moynihan. "Habeas corpus has little to do with terrorism," he observed.

> Nothing in our present circumstances requires the suspension of habeas corpus. We are dealing with a fundamental provision of law [which] is at the very foundation of the legal system designed to safeguard our liberties. We are putting in jeopardy a tradition of protection of individual rights by federal courts that goes back to our earliest foundation.

Moynihan was joined in his conservative position by five other Democrats and two moderate Republicans, Bob Packwood and Mark Hatfield, both of Oregon. The Senate's entire rightist bloc was for the bill, and in the House the vote was likewise skewed hard-right Republican, with 293 in favor, 133 against.*

---

both alienating longtime political supporters and costing the NRA its old-line members like former President George Bush." Lars-Erik Nelson, "Handguns and Hyperbole," *Newsday* (N.Y.), 5/21/95.

*The opposition view was neatly summarized by Representative Louis Stokes (D-OH): "Mr. Speaker, I share the national outrage expressed against terrorism. America should and must act swiftly and decisively to end these despicable acts. We must not, however, under the guise of fighting acts of terror, sacrifice our constitutional rights.

Bill Clinton, for all the strident rightist diatribes against him, was actually in close agreement with the GOP on civil liberties, as he was on so many other major issues: welfare reform, "free trade," the drug war, media deregulation, banking deregulation, capital punishment. And so there never was a shred of evidence that Clinton was a would-be leftist tyrant trying to force a far-out Democratic program on Americans. Although he did indeed abridge the Bill of Rights, he did so primarily to the benefit of the Republicans, both at the time and in the time to come. Through his efforts to be "tough on crime" and combat terrorism, Clinton greased the skids for Bush & Co., making it all that much easier for the latter to set up the police state now under construction.

By and large, those very rightists who nailed Clinton for his "jackboot liberalism" were, for too long, strangely quiet on the Great Leap Backward taken by Bush/Cheney. Certainly some rightists showed an admirable consistency in their libertarianism, whatever their true motives; soon after 9/11, GOP ex-firebrands Dick Armey and Bob Barr, troubled by Bush/Cheney's growing power, began discreetly working with the ACLU, Representative Dan Burton assailed the White House for its arrogance in dealing with the Senate, and some rightist groups protested the regime's unconstitutional presumption. Judicial Watch sued Cheney for withholding public information, and the Eagle Forum objected formally to the invasiveness of Bush & Co.'s antidrug and antiterrorism policies. And at the grassroots level there have long been some traditional Republicans—genuine conservatives—appalled by Bush & Co.'s preemptive war and vast empowerment of the state.

Until late spring 2004, however, most big wheels on the right were much less scrupulous. Throughout the federal clampdown after 9/11, the Cato Institute was noisily pro-Bush, just like the Hoover Institute, the Heritage Foundation, the Manhattan Institute, and all the other major hives of rightist influence. And so the few exceptions did not alter

As legislators, we must judiciously seek a balanced strategy to diminish the dangers of terrorism and injustice. I urge my colleagues to therefore vote down this measure; preserve our ability to enforce the Bill of Rights." Conference Report on S. 735, Antiterrorism and Effective Death Penalty Act of 1996, *Congressional Record*, 4/19/96.

the disorienting fact that President Clinton, whose civil liberties agenda
was Republican, was often loudly charged with fascist tendencies by the
Republicans, while Bush/Cheney, whose civil liberties agenda is fascistic,
were treated largely with respect and deference by Republicans (*and,*
until 2004, most Democrats), as if the patent despotism of this rogue
administration were appropriate and right for the United States.

The Closing of Some American Minds

That double standard has defined our politics since 1992: Bill Clinton
was attacked relentlessly for crimes he did not commit and errors he did
not make. Bush/Cheney have committed just such crimes and errors on
an infinitely larger scale, so brazenly that they could keep a dozen independent counsels busy for the next ten years, and yet for over three years
they were criticized or censured very little. This paradox has been so dom-
inant, and its consequences so enormous, that the term "double standard"
seems too weak to do it justice. Rather, there has seemed to be *no* "standard" operating, but a raging Manichaean animus; one that has impelled
the corporate media as well as most Republicans. Clinton was routinely
crucified for what he didn't do, while Bush *did* do it, or is even doing it
now, yet everybody acts as if he never did and never would.

What matters here is not the Clinton legacy per se, nor merely Bush
& Co.'s culpability, nor whether Democrats are getting a fair shake or
the Republicans an easy ride. What finally matters, rather, is the all-
important difference between truth and untruth. To set the record
straight about Bill Clinton, therefore, means far more than spinning
things his way or singing praises for his every policy. Indeed, Bill Clinton's policies are not the issue here, except for the canard that they were
"left" or "liberal." In their crusade against the former president, the
rightists tended less to nail his policies than to assail the man himself.
That move was necessitated by the fact that Clinton's policies were *not*
traditionally Democratic, and surely not left wing, but often so conservative that the Republicans were happy to support them, while many
Democrats had reason to complain. (If the GOP were rational, and not
politically dependent on mere rage, they would have hailed Bill Clinton

as a man of compromise, and even as a friend.) Unable to perceive his record, and always needing somebody to hate, the right instead concocted a bizarre mythology about "the Clintons" and hammered at it endlessly (and continue hammering at it still). If a nation cannot tell the difference between truth and falsehood, or if it falls under the sway of a minority incapable of making that distinction (and if the press defers to that minority), that nation can't be a democracy—nor can it even function as a nation.

This Age of Information has turned out to be an Age of Ignorance, in some ways comparable to the so-called Dark Ages, when the priests alone knew how to read and there was nothing to plug in. We live with an unprecedented wealth of information: countless facts and solid arguments and scrupulous researches, all of it (for many of us) just a click away. And yet it is entirely possible, and dangerously easy, to zoom through life with one's head tightly stuck inside a sort of iron bubble, wholly portable and yet completely shatterproof, that lets in just one kind of "information." There is, out there, an entire propaganda universe available to anyone who wants to obsess about one thing and from one point of view. Something like this always has been feasible, of course—for avid readers of a single creed or doctrine, or, prior to that, religious communes of one kind or another. But until now it never has been possible to prearrange so thoroughly one's daily mental diet so that nothing contradictory can ever pierce the bubble and invade one's head.

Thus the right has made for its constituents a new designer consciousness. Having co-opted the media, the right can fill your head all day, all night, wherever you may go, as long as you're plugged in. You can watch only Fox News Channel and MSNBC, listen only to Sean Hannity et al., read only those newspapers that re-echo what you've seen and heard, hit only those Web sites that others like you also hit, and, if you should ever feel like curling up with a relaxing book, buy Bill O'Reilly's latest or Sean Hannity's—all such products having been approved directly or inspired by the White House and the Republican National Committee, if not sources even farther to the right.

As we have seen, the mainstream media, with too few exceptions, either takes up the right's campaigns or largely fails to contradict them at the proper volume. Of course, there are also real reporters in the main-stream trying hard to do the sort of journalism that they once were trained to do, and we are blessed as well by columnists like Paul Krug-man and Bob Herbert and interviewers like Bill Moyers who try to fill us in on what the U.S. press keeps leaving out. The work of such excep-tions is invaluable, and yet it does not do enough to counter the decep-tions of *the news* in general, the daily misimpression of what's happening (apparently), the mainstream institutions mainly failing to stand up and contradict Bush/Cheney's falsehoods or mistakes. (That, of course, does not prevent the mainstream media from being charged endlessly with "liberal bias" *by* the right.)

And so America's minority of rightists walk around completely mis-informed and yet cocksure, belligerently echoing the sophistries and fab-rications that have made it through the bubble so that they themselves are also nonstop propagandists. Meanwhile, other than those plucky few who try to learn what's really happening out there, everybody else, too busy for such extra daily work, feels timid, uninformed, and therefore half-inclined to heed the ones with strong opinions, booming voices, and a lot of "facts." Through such a network has the right deluded millions of Americans just as effectively as any modern oligarchy or medieval faith—just as effectively, in fact, as Bush/Cheney have deceived themselves.

Bush v. Clinton

Although Clinton and the Democrats have been especially disadvan-taged by that national daze (whose primary victims are the poor, here and abroad), this is by no means a partisan concern: on the contrary. A nation thus half-stupefied by *any* winning propaganda system is at risk, no matter what party is in charge, and however "left" or "right" the groupthink. The United States has already been profoundly damaged by the media's readiness to say that peace is war, that black is white. When Scott Ritter went to CNN, and after evidently demonstrating his integrity, Walter Isaacson asked him if he "had any questions or concerns."

> I brought up one: that I, an expert with years of experience, would
> be grilled for over an hour and 45 minutes, is understandable. But

why the double standard? Why didn't CNN have the same standard for when the President, or people in the Bush administration, spoke about Iraq? Why did CNN air everything these people said without question, without demanding to know the source of the statement, the data and the facts to back that statement up? CNN demanded I back up everything I said (I did, in spades). Why not the same standard for the elected representatives of the people?

No one at CNN had an answer, which speaks volumes.

In that case, the media's inversion of the truth has cost us more, perhaps, than we can ultimately bear—untold blood and treasure (untold especially here in the United States). Every one of Ritter's painful moments on TV and every supercilious print piece conduced, in its small way, to the disaster in Iraq and to all the larger consequences of that slaughter. And those programs and networks that would *not* have Ritter on, and those newspapers and newsmagazines that would *not* publicize his expert take, were also complicit in Bush/Cheney's rush to war. And if we go a little further back, we can discern the same thing happening throughout the nineties and beyond, but on a far larger scale: innumerable false stories, items sloppily researched (or not researched), arguments that made no sense, and pertinent findings not reported, all that jive contributing at last to a judicial coup and the establishment of a one-party government resolved to end American democracy.

There is something crucial to be learned from an exact comparison of Clinton and Bush as each was covered by the mainstream press. Although he ran as the un-Clinton, vowing daily to "restore honor and dignity to the White House," Bush was all along, in fact, a man uncannily "Clintonian." Indeed, the more closely we examine Bush and Clinton—or rather, Bush and "Clinton," the rightist *fiction* of that president—the more we can perceive the sameness of those two apparent opposites, somewhat like Dorian Gray's relationship to his horrific portrait. To put it bluntly: Everything that Clinton was *accused* of doing, Bush *has done*; and everything that Clinton was accused of *being*, Bush *is*. And yet, while Clinton mostly had not done those things, nor was he that man, he was assailed relentlessly for doing so, and being so—while

Bush, who is all that, and who has done all that, has been treated with inordinate tact, however serious his crimes and misdemeanors.

A Haircut

From early in his tenure, Bill Clinton was continually cast as an arrogant and hypocritical elitist, secretly contemptuous of the common man for whom he feigned such warm respect. The propaganda mill established for that purpose spun innnumerable canards, some of them "big" stories that went on for months or years, while others were short-lived yet no less effective than the epic tales of Clinton's selfishness and cynicism. One doozy hit the airwaves in the spring of 1993. "At 4:30 in the afternoon on Tuesday, May 18, President Bill Clinton boarded *Air Force One*, at Los Angeles International Airport, after playing a game of basketball with children in the city," wrote Jonathan Schell, in a brilliant retrospective on the nonincident.

> Waiting for him there was Cristophe, a renowned hairdresser of Belgian extraction who catered to Hollywood stars and had on occasion cut Hillary Clinton's hair. At 4:52 P.M., the Secret Service and airport officials closed two of the airport's four runways, as is customary when Air Force One takes off or lands. A few minutes later, they requested a delay of 20 minutes. Meanwhile, Cristophe cut Clinton's hair. Air Force One took off at 5:48.

After Reuters ran a story on the haircut, a UPI reporter in Los Angeles called up the Federal Aviation Administration (FAA) and asked the agency's spokeswoman if any flights had been delayed because of Clinton's trim. There were two such delays, the woman claimed. The wire-service item came out on May 20—the same day that Lois Romano of the *Washington Post* reported that the "stylist" had been Cristophe of Beverly Hills and that his haircuts cost around $200.

The news brought on a hailstorm of derision, started by the press. "Haircut Grounded Clinton While the Price Took off," proclaimed the *New York Times,* and "Presidential Trim Left Travellers in the Air," announced the *Dallas Morning News,* while the *Boston Globe* reported that "Air Traffic Waits for Beverly Hills Haircut," and the Gannett News Service—America's largest newspaper chain—went national with this explosive question: "Clinton: Man of the People or Just Another Elitist?" The same rhetorical jab re-echoed coast to coast for several days, the din maintained by TV comics, opposition pols, and gleeful rightist rabble-rousers. Letterman and Leno had some fun with it, and even Johnny Carson joined the pile-on. "If you're going to try to impress the common man," he said at an awards lunch in New York, "you can't go from a barber with three names to a guy with one. You can't go from Billy Joe Jethro to Cristophe."

From the Republicans, the pseudopopulist attack was more ferocious. "That's Bill Clinton," said Representative Dan Burton (R-IN). "He's really concerned about the middle class. He spent thousands of your tax dollars waiting to get a haircut for 200 bucks from Hillary's hairdresser. He ought to be more concerned about trimming the deficit than his own hair." In the *American Spectator*—soon to be the secret headquarters of the "Arkansas Project," the massive anti-Clinton propaganda effort funded by the far-rightist Richard Mellon Scaife—editor R. Emmett Tyrell, much offended by the haircut, wrote long and scathingly about the Clintons:

> They are the spoiled brats of their generation, and they have not a hint as to what is amiss with shutting down half of Los Angeles International Airport's runways so that a $200 haircut can be administered to one of their selfless advocates of the Noble Cause—any noble cause.

In San Francisco, shock jock "Mancow" Muller got himself suspended from his morning gig at KSOL-FM for blocking the Bay Bridge, so as to satirize the president's alleged folly.* And, predictably, Rush Limbaugh went to town, for days embellishing the incident with whopping lies and raucous anti-liberalism:

---

*"Morning rush-hour traffic was tied up for more than an hour while two KSOL vans came to a halt on the span," reported the AP. "Another radio personality inside one van announced on the air that he was getting a haircut." "Station Gets DJ out of Its Hair after Stunt that Tangled Bay Bridge Traffic," AP, 5/28/93.

This haircut business is the most amazing thing! The way it started, its evolution—we—we want to show you some of the most recent things which have been said. First off, as you know, the president of the United States was on Air Force One and held up traffic for an hour. The—they've run the numbers, by the way: $1.4 million, is what that cost!

Limbaugh ran a video of Linda Bloodworth-Thomason, a Clinton friend and Hollywood producer, trying to defend the president: "Do you think that Bill Clinton, a Rhodes scholar, would say, 'Hey, let's tie up air traffic and do this'?" "Let me tell you something," Limbaugh cracked.

First place, he's not a Rhodes scholar. He never graduated. He didn't finish his second year. Number two, do you know who teaches Rhodes scholars? Marxists.*

Despite the triviality of the alleged incident, the national furor over it had major consequences. Timing is essential to effective propaganda. Coming as it did just at the end of Clinton's first 100 days, and following the loud fuss over his abortive effort to allow gay soldiers in the military, the haircut story badly hampered his political effectiveness, just as his first budget package was moving toward a House vote. As that controversy raged, moreover, there was also news of "Travelgate," the trumped-up "scandal" over Hillary's allegedly improper purge of the White House Travel Office. Those two scandals were now merrily lumped together by the president's detractors on the right—and by the press, which saw those seeming infamies as evidence of dangerous incompetence. It wasn't just the pricey haircut and the inconvenienced travelers; it was the fact that White House staffers could allow it all to happen and then *handle* it so poorly. On CNN's *Capital Gang*, four days

*As the Rhodes Scholarship is not a degree program, no one has ever "graduated" from it. It is a two-year program, with the possibility of a one-year extension. Clinton finished both years of his term and is indeed a Rhodes scholar. Moreover, as the Scholars are allowed to take whatever courses Oxford has to offer, they are not taught by "Marxists," as Oxford University is not, of course, a Marxist institution.

after the LAX affair, the *Wall Street Journal*'s Al Hunt solemnly described a White House on the brink:

> Let me just say something. I've been in Washington for 24 years. This is the most inept White House operation I have ever seen— worse than anything under Carter, worse than John Sununu's-led [*sic*] Bush White House, worse than Donald Regan in his worst days under Ronald Reagan, and I'll tell you something. If this guy doesn't straighten it out pretty soon, he's going to be a subject of such great ridicule it'll be too late. And Mark, I really question whether Bill Clinton is personally and politically secure enough to bring in the kind of tough and skillful people that he needs to give some purpose.

Mark Shields, the program's feisty "liberal," felt the same way:

> I don't know, Al, but boy, you get the feeling that this thing is just—it's just whirling out of control, and I've got to tell you, Ed Rollins, Ronald Reagan's 1984 campaign manager,* says that—told me, he said, "Each President, in turn, there's something about the Presidency they really enjoy." He said, "George Bush thrived on Camp David. Ronald Reagan loved the ceremonial aspect." He said, "Bill Clinton, it's like the rock star aspect of being President." I've got to tell you, Al, this is—It's like Icarus getting awful close to the sun with the wings of wax.

"I think he's finished," put in *Newsweek*'s Margaret Warner. Six days later, on May 27, the *Washington Post* ran a long piece by Joel Achenbach on the front page of its Style section: "Another Failed Presidency

---

*Rollins was not the only Republican invoked on that day's show: Newt Gingrich himself was there, "commenting" on the White House, with no Democrat to answer him. Hunt made his dark assessment after Gingrich had said this, about the haircut debacle: "I pay $9 at Great Clips in Marietta, but I understand the virtue—I understand the virtue of a $200 haircut. The thing that's weird is, we are told that it costs $15,000 to the taxpayer to keep the 747 running for the 45 minutes he got the $200 haircut, so I assume the President will write a $15,000 personal check as part of his sacrifice on the deficit." "The President's Bad Hair Day," *Capital Gang*, CNN, 5/22/93.

Already?" At a "town meeting" that same day on *CBS This Morning*,
Clinton actually apologized for what had happened on the runway, calling it "a boner," "just a mess-up." Two days later, it was announced that
David Gergen, veteran GOP spinmeister and "Washington insider," had
accepted a position with the Clinton team as "White House counselor
in charge of communications," to smarten up the president's PR.

Gergen's stint did not work out, and, overall, Bill Clinton never
ceased to be defamed as a self-indulgent sixties type and phony liberal,
the whole long rightist diatribe climaxing finally in his farcical impeachment and then in the "election" of George W. Bush. By far the biggest
story of his early term, Clinton's selfish haircut was a great boon to his
enemies—and, as it turned out, a fiction from the start. The day after
the alleged incident, *Newsday*'s Glenn Kessler filed a Freedom of Information Act request with the FAA. Some five weeks later, the FAA's reply
made clear that not a single ordinary flight had been delayed by Clinton's twenty minutes with Cristophe. All scheduled flights took off and
landed right on time, while an unscheduled air taxi *was* delayed, taking
off two minutes late. "This haircut business is the most amazing thing!"
Limbaugh had said, and he was right for once, because the thing had
never happened.

Kessler's story—"Bill's Coif: The Myth; Runway Trim Delayed No
One"—ran in *Newsday* on June 30 (on p. 19 of the City Edition). (The
paper also ran Jonathan Schell's commentary, over two weeks later, on
July 18.) The next day, there was a brief corrective item ("Bald Truth
about the Haircut Story") on p. 12 of the *Atlanta Journal-Constitution*.
And on September 17, the *Los Angeles Times* ran David Shaw's exemplary
analysis of both the haircut and Travelgate stories, not just reconfirming
that *both* tales were fiction but also attempting to explain the journalists'
peculiar overreadiness to spread mere damning rumors about the Clintons. And yet such correctives were, of course, too few, too marginal, and
way too late to make a difference. Since they inspired no retractions by
the hundreds of reporters, editors, producers, commentators, stand-up
comics, and cartoonists who had taken full advantage of the myth, those
pieces finally were of interest only to historians and the president's most
loyal partisans. Thus was the myth of Clinton's vanity and pride put over

on Americans, a plurality of whom believed it ardently enough to weaken his position, just when we could least afford a hobbled president. The World Trade Center had been bombed a few months earlier, and Clinton surely grasped the Islamist threat; but the rightist drive against him hampered his ability to fight that danger with the proper force and concentration.

A Bombardment

On September 5, 2001, George W. Bush hosted his first state dinner at the White House, honoring his long-time friend Vicente Fox, the president of Mexico. At 11:00 P.M., the presidential revels ended with a bang, or rather several hundred bangs, and very loud ones. The White House had not thought to warn the public of the huge fireworks display that shook the ground for fifteen minutes. (It was a Wednesday night.) Audible as far north as Mt. Pleasant, Maryland, and as far south as Alexandria, Virginia, the explosions "lit up the sky and rattled windows miles away," the *Houston Chronicle* reported (on September 9).

The unexpected late-night thunder panicked thousands of Americans. "Residents on both sides of the Potomac lit up switchboards after the 11 P.M. display, worried that the fireworks were gunfire, an explosion or a full-scale attack on the capital," the *Washington Post* reported two days later. Startled by the racket, Roberta Synal, forty-four, of Dupont Circle hurried to the window and saw "these huge flashes of light." What with the unexpected booming and the lateness of the hour, she drew the obvious conclusion: "I thought, 'This is it. We're being bombed.'" At first, Daniel Quinn of Adams Morgan figured it was just a car backfiring, but as the din grew louder, waking up his five-year-old, he thought, "My God, there's something blowing up!"

Once they realized that it was not a terrorist attack but a loud party at the White House, the panic turned to anger. "I think it's the height of insensitivity for the White House to wake up its neighbors," Quinn charged. "I've never been woken up on a school night for officially sanctioned . . . bombs." He and many others posted their complaints on the *Post's* Web site the next day, in an online discussion of the night before.

"They're not on the ranch in Crawford, Texas. They're in the middle of the city. I think [Bush] could show us some consideration," said Terrance Lynch, executive director of an ecumenical coalition of local churches. Sutton Snook, a law firm employee in Foggy Bottom, wrote the White House an indignant letter. "I don't know," he told the *Post*, "maybe the president is cocky as hell and thinks the neighborhood [around the White House] is not really a neighborhood. But we're all his neighbors, and we already put up with quite a lot."

That night's barrage was as extravagant as it was thoughtless, as it had cost, reportedly, around a quarter-million dollars. "The federal government may have to take $9 billion from the Social Security surplus just to make ends meet," said Jill Lancelot, spokeswoman for Taxpayers for Common Sense (TCS). "Spending money on glitzy White House celebrations sends a terrible message in this tense budget climate."

Exactly who *had* paid for the bombardment was unclear. Ashleigh Adams, Laura Bush's spokeswoman, said that the State Department covered it, as it was used for diplomatic purposes. "Oh, I was told that it was the White House," a State Department press official told the New York *Daily News*, which added: "Another agency official said only the White House could comment on a state dinner." George Zambelli, whose company did the fireworks, would not say how much it cost (although the TCS's press release revealed that he had given $2,000 to the Bush campaign the year before). Asked about the inconsiderate timing of the show, "Zambelli said he did not question the White House request to start the fireworks at 11 P.M. even though he could not remember a show that began so late. 'You never ask questions like that' of the White House, he said."

Aside from these stray pieces in the *Post*, *Houston Chronicle*, and New York *Daily News*, as well as a brief bit in *Slate*, there was no mainstream coverage of the popular reaction to the White House pyrotechnics. (On *ABC World News Tonight* on September 6, anchor Peter Jennings mentioned that "[t]he White House has apologized for a fireworks display last night in honor of the Mexican President.")* Not that the press

*The item was succinct. Here is the rest of it: "The White House didn't tell the public it was going to occur. Many people either fearful or just upset called 911 to complain."

ignored the fireworks: on the contrary. That festive touch was duly mentioned in a wide range of awed reports and articles on the deluxe affair, the light show merely capping off an evening of luxurious eats and topflight live performance—this despite the worsening economic mess and Bush's manifest unpopularity (his ratings had been plummeting all summer). "Clint Eastwood is here," Campbell Brown told Brian Williams on MSNBC, and then reported that the main course would be "bison, we are told, encrusted in pumpkin seeds." After noting the First Lady's vivid dress ("Her designer describes it as lollipop red"), the correspondent added that the evening would conclude with "fireworks, dancing, and a performance by opera singer Dawn Upshaw. It is indeed the hottest ticket in town!"

Earlier that day, Laura Bush told CNN about the evening's grandiose climax: "After Dawn Upshaw sings, we are going to go out onto this balcony and have fireworks so that'll be a new thing for a state dinner but especially festive, I think." While the First Lady's get-up caused much comment ("She looks wonderful in red," said Arnold Scaasi, her couturier), and the dessert was most deliciously observed ("Tiny paper Mexican and U.S. flags extended from the ice cream," *USA Today* reported), those fireworks were the evening's *pièce de résistance*, as UPI noted: "To close the night, dinner guests were invited onto the White House balcony to view fireworks, a first for a state dinner according to the first lady." The *New York Times* described "a spicy meal of upscale Tex-Mex cuisine, an exclusive gathering and a fireworks display." Other papers gushed even more fulsomely in their accounts of that big-time *soirée*.

From the postprandial orgy of bedazzled reportage a certain late development was missing. "Bush thanked his guests for a 'fantastic evening,'" the *Dallas Morning News* reported, "inviting them to watch fireworks and dance the night away, though he indicated he would be going to bed early." That nobody in Washington could do so, thanks to that imperial celebration, was a fact that went unmentioned by the Washington press corps, whose members, much like Bush, pay little heed to the complaints of commoners. Of all the next day's stories on that "family gathering" (as Bush had called it), only one, in the *Washington Post*, brought up the widespread anger of the locals, and that one mention, in parentheses, was clearly added by an editor, as its lone hint of popular exasperation stood out sharply from its sycophantic context. "In an evening of traditional social values," reported the *Washington Post* (without explaining what that meant),

> the boldest strokes were the bison, the first lady's hotly hued gown and a gorgeous, nearly 20-minute display of pyrotechnic virtuosity. The famed Zambelli fireworks company of Brooklyn set off the fireworks from the Ellipse as guests watched from the balcony off the Blue Room. Bush aides said they did not know the cost of the elaborate display, which lit up the White House switchboard with calls from startled residents upset by the noise. ("I think it's the height of insensitivity for the White House to wake up its neighbors," said Daniel Quinn of Adams Morgan, whose 5-year-old son was awakened on a school night.)*

Here, then, is a typical example of the press's tendency to nail one president for a fictitious crime or error, and then to let another one do something like it, only worse, and do it *in reality*; and of that actual transgression we hear nothing. The framers surely would be outraged by this common reportorial indifference to real grievances among the people. No doubt they would also be perplexed by U.S. journalists' concern for the life, liberty, and happiness of nonexistent persons: Of that alleged multitude of travelers inconvenienced on May 18, 1993, not one came forward to confirm that he or she was incommoded by Bill Clinton's haircut. U.S. reporters went all out on behalf of those offended figments of right-wing imagination. On September 5, 2001, on the other hand, there were hundreds of complaints in Washington—overwhelming 911, the local press, and city councilmen—and yet the press was mute; or, to be more accurate, our journalists were terribly *impressed* by Bush & Co.'s

---

*Note that this incomplete quotation of Quinn's comment, which the *Post* would run in full the next day, leaves out the part concerning unexpected "bombs." The festive gesture surely sounded like bombardment, as it entailed the firing, by Zambelli's men, of 769 shells from the Ellipse. The shells were four to six inches in diameter—smaller than the usual July 4th fireworks, the largest of those being ten to twelve inches wide. However, Zambelli added, "Wednesday night's fireworks may have been just as loud because higher-quality materials were used." "Look! Up in the Sky! It's a White House Wake-up Call," *Washington Post*, 9/7/01.

imperial entertainment, that "gorgeous, nearly 20-minute display of pyrotechnic virtuosity." That it might wake up a lot of working people seems not to have occurred to them. It was exactly as if Bill Clinton *had* delayed a lot of flights to get his hair cut—and the members of the press were on the plane, marveling at Cristophe's superb technique and fancy scissors.

Inconsiderates Abroad

Thus the Bushes put out thousands of Americans, and right in Washington, D.C., and yet that mass disturbance got almost no national coverage. Similarly, when Bush has traveled elsewhere, his movements have caused suffering much worse than being rudely wakened on a weeknight: suffering that the U.S. press reported not at all. On his quick trip to Africa in the summer of 2003, Bush made that brief stop in Senegal, so as to tour the old Slave House on Goree Island and then appear on TV trying to deplore the wickedness of the peculiar institution.

As we have seen, the president had trouble doing that, since he evidently did not know, or want to know, that Africans had been enslaved in the United States. Worse yet, the very Africans to whom he seemed to be addressing those remarks on slavery were themselves enslaved in their own land while he was there. Even as he spoke about the shackled Africans of yesteryear, scores of people there were in detention, having been locked up by Senegal's police, who were acting under guidance of the U.S. Secret Service. The South African newspaper *Cape Times* reported the preventive "round-up" of over a thousand "known lawbreakers," as well as the Bush entourage's reservation of 400 phone lines, which meant that no one in the country could make calls.

Meanwhile, the residents of Goree Island—population 1,000—were hauled off to a soccer field as far away from Bush as possible and kept penned there, without food, from 6:00 A.M. until the early afternoon. "We were shut up like sheep," said one fifteen-year-old. Although Americans were unaware of it, the irony was hardly lost on all those Africans locked up so that our president could stand before the cameras and voice

sympathy for all those other Africans locked up. " 'It's slavery all over
again,' fumed one father-of-four, who did not want to give his name,"
reported Reuters. "'It's humiliating. The island was deserted.' "

In Nigeria a few days later, Bush's presence made things even worse,
his welfare somehow necessitating the complete destruction of an entire
neighborhood in the nation's capital, according to Agence France-Presse.
The item, which appeared in the South African journal *Business Day*,
was published nowhere in this country:

> Armed police backed by bulldozers tore down illegally built homes
> and shops in the Nigerian capital Abuja today ahead of a visit by
> US President George W Bush.
>
> The operation began yesterday after an order from President
> Olusegun Obasanjo to clean up the city ahead of his American
> counterpart's arrival, officials said.
>
> In one residential quarter of the city a reporter saw around 60
> buildings—ranging from brick-built structures to makeshift
> wooden shanties—ploughed down as hundreds of residents looked
> on in despair.
>
> "They didn't give us any warning," wailed tailor John Emeka,
> who saved his sewing machine but lost much of his stock when a
> joint taskforce of police and environmental protection agents
> pulled down his business.
>
> Nearby a stock of computers lay mangled in the wreckage of an
> electronic goods store, and the owner of a grilled meat stand argued
> with officers attempting to condemn his barbecue.
>
> The police came armed with assault rifles and tear gas, but there
> was no violence as the bulldozers rolled in.

The point here is not that Bush & Co. was necessarily to blame for
all that devastation in Nigeria (although it seems unlikely that the Secret
Service had no influence in Senegal). Nor do I necessarily suggest that
such acts of high thoughtlessness, whether in Dakar or in Washington,
D.C., were major crimes demanding in-depth coverage by the U.S.
press. What is significant about such huge nonstories, rather, is their

total difference from the hostile and exaggerated tales about the former president. If Bush were covered by the Clinton standard, he would have been impeached, and probably imprisoned, long ago. (In fact, he never would have been "elected.") In any case, our press's penchant for reporting lies as truth about one president, and then suppressing truths about another, demonstrates a sort of cognitive disorder actually more worrying than any simple "bias," liberal *or* "conservative." What this grand disorder has produced, in these United States, is a press system as irrational as those in power. Never fearing that the press might act on *our* behalf, they simply use it to define reality for us, so that it has worked here as it has worked in closed societies, where truth remains negotiable—things meaning always, and only, what Bush/Cheney's GOP interprets them to mean. "Whatever the Party holds to be the truth, *is* truth. It is impossible to see reality except by looking through the eyes of the Party." Thus O'Brien of the Inner Party tells the hapless Winston Smith in *1984*; and thus it is here, too, although the propaganda here is far more colorful and festive than it is in Orwell's dismal Oceania.

Taken together, the stories of Bill Clinton's selfish haircut and Bush/Cheney's "gorgeous" pyrotechnics tell us this: that Bush is "Clinton." That is to say, *this* president, and not the one who came before him, is the actual "Clinton" of the two: feigning warm concern for average folks while actually despising them, and working secretly to lord it over them while breaking every rule to have his way. We learn the same disorienting lesson every time we study a particular feature of both presidents' biographies, always taking care to match the common view—the view purveyed or just unchallenged by the U.S. press—with what we can learn only from extensive, careful reading.

Draft-Dodger

George W. Bush was a draft-dodger, whereas Bill Clinton did *not* dodge the draft; and Bush did not just dodge the draft but blew off his entire last year of service in the Texas Air National Guard (TANG). The equation "Clinton = draft-dodger" and the tacit myth that Bush fulfilled *his* military obligations together represent a most successful propaganda fiction, devised by Clinton's enemies and circulated by the press, which, as of this writing, never has provided all the facts.

Clinton's case was complicated by the same profound ambivalence afflicting countless other patriotic youngsters at that time. Loving his country but hating its war, he could never comfortably decide whether to fight in Vietnam, or fight the war itself from Canada, or go to jail, and his dilemma was compounded further by his frank intention to become a politician. Thus racked, he tried at first simply to *put off* the moment when he might be sent to Vietnam. In the spring of 1968, as a soon-to-be graduate of Georgetown University and a prospective Rhodes Scholar bound for Oxford in the fall, Clinton found himself reclassified 1-A (i.e., available for military service) after Nixon's government canceled most deferments for graduate students. He asked his draft board back in Arkansas to delay the process for him, so that he might at least get started on his first year overseas—an allowance made routinely for Rhodes Scholars at the time. This favor granted, he went off to study in Great Britain.

In the middle of his first year at Oxford, he was notified that he must take his preinduction physical, and did so at a nearby U.S. military base. In February, his Arkansas draft board sent him an induction notice, but by surface mail, so that he received it in Britain too late to report on the date stipulated. He returned home and arranged to join the Reserve Officer Training Corps (ROTC) at the University of Arkansas, where he intended now to transfer as a law student. ROTC would not exempt him from the draft, but it would give him a few years' grace and training as an officer before he went to Vietnam—a half-solution, and in any case an option that he ultimately would not take because it meant that some Arkansan less well connected would be sent to Vietnam instead of him. Having spent the summer in his hometown—"where everyone else's children seem to be in the military, most of them in Vietnam," as he put it in a letter to his friend Richard Stearns—he turned against the ROTC plan: "I am about resolved to go to England come hell or high water and take my chances."* Soon after he wrote that letter on September 9, he returned to England and, later that month, asked his stepfather to let the draft board know that he was eligible once again. He was reclassified in late October.

Clinton could therefore have been called up at any time—until December 1, when the national draft lottery took place and he drew a number high enough (311) to improve the odds against his being conscripted soon. He then wrote his notorious letter to Colonel Eugene Holmes, director of the ROTC program at the University of Arkansas, to explain his change of plan. The letter was extraordinarily ingenuous:

> I decided to accept the draft in spite of my beliefs for one reason: to maintain my political viability within the system. For years I have worked to prepare myself for a political life characterized by both practical political ability and concern for rapid social progress. It is a life I still feel compelled to try to lead. I do not think our system of government is by definition corrupt, however dangerous and inadequate it has been in recent years.

And its final paragraph:

> And that is where I am now, writing to you because you have been good to me and have a right to know what I think and feel. I am writing too in the hope that my telling this one story will help you to understand more clearly how so many fine people have come to find themselves still loving their country but loathing the military, to which you and other good men have devoted years, lifetimes, of the best service you could give. To many of us, it is no longer clear

---

*By contrast, Richard Cheney managed to get five deferments during the war, and never seemed to worry about others fighting in his place. When the government announced that married men with children would henceforth be subject to the draft, unless the child had been conceived by a particular date, Cheney got right down to business, swiftly impregnating Lynne, so that the couple's first child might arrive upon the scene in time to keep him out of uniform. (Mary Cheney was born nine months and two days after the expansion order was announced.) Cheney used to be quite frank about his selfish motives: "I had other priorities in the '60s than military service," he told the *Washington Post* in 1989. Laura Flanders, *Bushwomen: Tales of a Cynical Species* (London and New York: Verso, 2004), p. 257.

what is service and what is disservice, or if it is clear, the conclusion
is likely to be illegal.

In the presidential race of 1992 (and then throughout the next eight
years), the Republicans reduced this complicated story to a propaganda
mantra: "Clinton dodged the draft." That line was based on a tendentious version of the full account. Clinton's letter to Colonel Holmes
came in for much provocative quotation. His frank avowal of political
idealism was cast as proof of moral obtuseness or mad ambition, and his
point about *why* young Americans had come to "loath[e] the military"
was used to smear him as seditious and unpatriotic. Clinton might
appear to have been guilty of a certain indecorum, having written such
a candid, leftish letter to an army colonel over twice his age. In any case,
the GOP's dark view of his relationship with Holmes seemed to be
bluntly reconfirmed when, on September 7, 1992, Bush/Quayle released
a stinging affidavit signed by Holmes, who, now confined to a nursing
home, had been induced to write, or certify, that Clinton had "purposely
deceived me, using the possibility of joining the ROTC as a ploy to work
with the draft board to delay his induction and get a new draft classifi-
cation. These actions cause me to question both his patriotism and his
integrity," and so on, at great length.

The affidavit, it turned out, had been obtained by Cliff Jackson, a
devoted anti-Clintonite who had smeared the candidate before, and
would again. (Later, Jackson tried to publicize the sexual fantasies of
three disgruntled Arkansas state troopers, whose tale of Clinton's epic
lechery was known as "Troopergate," until it was debunked.) Moreover,
the affidavit contradicted Holmes's prior relations with Bill Clinton,
whose course of action back in 1969 the colonel had apparently approved.*
Those facts came up in passing in about a dozen preelection print pieces

---

*In late September 1992, *U.S. News & World Report* took pains to put the Holmes
account into a broader context:

> All these complicated charges against Clinton ought to be treated with cau-
> tion, not least because they appear so close to Election Day. Holmes, now
> 76 and a resident of a nursing home, praised Clinton warmly in 1978 when
> he was running for governor of Arkansas—and responded to questions
> about Clinton and the draft at the time by saying he remembered nothing

by American reporters—whereas Holmes's seemingly baleful view of Bill Clinton got a lot of press, not only prior to Election Day but for years afterward. Full quotations from the affidavit ran in *U.S. News & World Report*, the *Boston Globe*, *Los Angeles Times*, *Chicago Tribune*, and—especially—the *Wall Street Journal*, as well as in an item from the Associated Press, and, far more audibly, on CNN, NPR, and ABC's *Nightline*.

More generally, disturbing stories of the Clinton/Holmes relationship appeared in five *Washington Post* articles and one *New York Times* piece prior to Election Day—and, *after* Clinton was elected, in three more *Post* articles as well as two more pieces in the *Times*, including Michael Kelly's withering profile ("The President's Past"), which ran in the *New York Times Magazine* on June 10, 1994. Stoked by Limbaugh and his peers, as well as far-right propaganda classics like *The Clinton Chronicles*, a wild video flogged by Jerry Falwell, and Floyd G. Brown's defamatory paperback *Slick Willie*, that old story never died nor would it fade away: "Vietnam a steady source of controversy for Clinton," Agence France-Presse reported on July 11, 1995.

The presidential race of 1996 was largely cast, both by Bob Dole's campaign and by the press, as a great tragic clash between an amoral hippie-type draft-dodger and a disabled Grand Old Veteran of the Greatest Generation. As late as the fall of 1998, Holmes's affidavit was still re-echoing throughout the rightist media—Fox News Network, Steve Dunleavy's column in the *New York Post*, and countless organs farther to the right—while Clinton's reputation as a "draft-dodger," for years unchallenged by the U.S. press, had long since sunk into the public mind.*

Although *everybody knows* that Clinton dodged the draft, although he

wrong. Holmes says the prospect of Clinton as commander in chief is what spurred him. His daughter Linda Burnett, who once worked in a GOP campaign, released his remarks in a written statement culled from what she said were extensive tapes of his recollections. She said Holmes could not answer questions himself because of ill health and she would not release the tapes. "An Ill Draft Blown Over Clinton's Camp," *U.S. News and World Report*, 9/28/92.

*That mass impression did not seem to lessen Clinton's stature among veterans, however. In 1992, 41 percent of the veteran votes went to Clinton, while George H. W. Bush pulled 37 percent, with H. Ross Perot attracting 22 percent. E-mail from Jennifer De Pinto at CBS News, 3/14/04.

didn't, few members of the U.S. press would dare report the fact that George W. Bush *was* a draft-dodger. On May 27, 1968—twelve days before he would lose his student deferment—Bush found easy refuge from the draft, and therefore Vietnam, in the 147th Fighter Wing of the TANG. Here the young man, flying the friendly skies of Texas, would be safe from antiaircraft fire, captivity by vengeful Asian communists, and, above all, boredom, as he would be based in Houston, not Da Nang. By that time, Americans were dying in Vietnam at a rate of roughly 460 per week.

Although he showed little promise as an airman—he had scored 25 percent, the lowest grade acceptable, on a pilot aptitude test—and, more important, even though there were some 100,000 other kids in line before him, Bush was ushered right on in because he had in family connections what he lacked in aeronautical ability. Indeed, the 147th was nicknamed the "Champagne Unit" because it housed so many rich men's sons.* And it had another telling nickname, according to Jake Johnson, a former Texas legislator: "It was sometimes called Air Canada. What that meant was you didn't have to go to Canada to stay out of Vietnam."

When similar news had broken back in 1988, about another candidate aspiring to the presidential plane, that former Guardsman was subjected to protracted grilling by the U.S. press. Indeed, the antijournalistic cliché "feeding frenzy" seems first to have been coined by Bush the Elder in response to the ordeal of his young running mate, another rich guy who used family pull to save himself from Vietnam through service in the National Guard (in his case, Indiana's). Whereas the strings pulled on Dan Quayle's behalf were major news in 1988, the strings that pulled the younger Bush to safety were, at first, of major interest to the press— and then abruptly dropped before the contest even started. From July through September of 1999 (with one last exposé, in the *Chicago Tri-*

---

*The TANG was well known for its openness to lads of means. "In addition to Bush and [Lloyd] Bentsen [III]," the *Washington Post* reported in July of 1999, "many socially or politically prominent young men were admitted to the Air Guard, according to former officials; they included the son of then-Sen. John Tower and at least seven members of the Dallas Cowboys." "At Height of Vietnam, Graduate Picks Guard," *Washington Post*, 7/28/99.

bune, coming out in January of 2000), there was a healthy spate of long newspaper articles revealing that the young Bush had been shoehorned into the Champagne Unit at the urging of Ben Barnes, speaker of the Texas legislature, who had been asked to make that call by a rich Houston businessman named Sidney A. Adger, close friend and neighbor to Representative George H. W. Bush (R-TX). For whatever reason, that hot story simply died some months before the parties' nominating conventions, whereas the same story stuck to Quayle for years, and Eugene Holmes was linked to Clinton, evidently, for all time.*

Bush's military history went unexamined by the U.S. press from 1999 until February 2004, when the sudden strength of John Kerry's candidacy and a deft wisecrack by Michael Moore reopened Bush's case, Kerry's heroic wartime service having made the issue visible again. The press was also loath to face the glaring inconsistencies in Bush's ever-changing story of his attitude toward the war in Vietnam. According to *A Charge to Keep*, his campaign "autobiography," the war weighed heavily on the minds of Bush and all his student pals at Yale. "The other reality in spring of 1968 was Vietnam," wrote Bush (or rather, Karen Hughes).

> The war became increasingly personal as friends who had graduated the year before went into the military. The war was no longer something that was happening to other people in a distant land; it came home to us.

In person, Bush would bluntly contradict that brooding reminiscence with blithe memories of how *un*concerned he and his friends had been

---

*Quayle believes himself to have been slurred by the inevitable comparisons of his own case with Clinton's, which he regards, of course, as far more reprehensible. "Four years later, Bill Clinton would be hammered over his draft record, and a lot of comparisons would be made between his situation and mine. I resented them, because there's not much of a parallel. Clinton, who during his college years [*sic*] wrote a letter admitting that he 'loathed the military,' sought every way to get out of serving [*sic*]; I did not. I did not base my choices on some hypothetical future political career, whereas he did." What this self-defense leaves out, aside from any accurate details of Clinton's situation, is the fact that Quayle, like Bush the Younger, backed the war in Vietnam and yet chose not to fight in it himself. Dan Quayle, *Standing Firm: A Vice-Presidential Memoir* (New York: HarperCollins, 1994), p. 32.

about the war. "I don't think we spent a lot of time debating it. Maybe we did, but I don't remember," he told the *Washington Post*, and told *GQ* that "I don't remember any kind of heaviness ruining my time at Yale."* And would Bush have gone to Vietnam, if that had been a possibility? It surely would have been the proper thing to do, as Bush was a supporter of the war—and so he sometimes said that he would certainly have done his bit in southeast Asia. "Had my unit been called up, I'd have gone . . . to Vietnam," he told the *Washington Post*. "I was prepared to go." This despite the fact that on his application for the 147th Fighter Group, where it asked if the aspiring pilot would serve overseas, Bush checked the box that said, "DO NOT VOLUNTEER."

While all such stark self-contradiction made no news, neither was the press concerned about the very issue that would later serve to lower the presidential ratings: Bush's failure to report for his Guard duty from May 1, 1972, to April 30, 1973.

On May 24, 1972, Bush requested a transfer from the TANG to the 9921st Air Reserve Squadron in Alabama—a nominal National Guard unit where he could "serve" while working on the Senate campaign of former postmaster general Winton "Red" Blount, a wealthy business-man who did much to build the GOP in Alabama. Bush took off for his new gig before his request for reassignment was considered by the Air Reserve Personnel Center in Denver, whose director turned it down. Bush stayed on in Alabama, reporting nowhere for his days of military service, as he was then in legal limbo with no orders. Since he was not showing up in Texas, meanwhile, his absence there was duly noted by his superiors, Colonel William D. Harris Jr. and Lieutenant Colonel Jerry B. Killian. (Bush was also grounded there for failing to undergo his annual physical exam.) Bush finally applied for his new Alabama orders in September of 1972 and was assigned to Dannelly Air Force Base near Montgomery for service with the Air National Guard Tactical Recon-naissance Group. Ordered to report to Lieutenant Colonel William

*"Of some dozen Bush associates from that time," reported the *Chicago Tribune*, "none recalls a conversation with Bush about his views of the war." "The Son Also Rises," *Chicago Tribune*, 1/18/00.

Turnipseed on October 7–8 and November 4–5, Bush did not comply. "To my knowledge, he never showed up," Turnipseed told the Associated Press in late May of 2000. "I believe that I would have remembered him." (Turnipseed's recollection was confirmed by Lieutenant Colonel Kenneth Lott, his former administration officer.)

Confronted with that testimony, Bush flatly denied it; and the press accepted that denial. The media's see-no-evil attitude back then was obvious in the coverage by the *New York Times*, whose Jo Thomas thus dispatched the controversy in a long piece headlined, "After Yale, Bush Ambled Amiably into His Future":

> Questions about Mr. Bush's military service arose in May when The Boston Globe quoted Mr. Turnipseed, who retired as a general, as saying Mr. Bush never appeared for duty.
>
> In a recent interview, the general took a tiny step back, saying, "I don't think he did, but I wouldn't stake my life on it. I think I would have remembered him. The chances are 99 percent he didn't."
>
> In an interview, Mr. Bush disagreed. "I was there. I know this guy was quoted as saying I wasn't, but I was there."
>
> Emily Marks, who worked in the Blount campaign and dated Mr. Bush, said she recalls that he returned to Montgomery after the election to serve with the Air National Guard.
>
> National Guard records provided by the Guard and by the Bush campaign indicate he did serve on Nov. 29, 1972, after the election. These records also show a gap in service from that time to the previous May. Mr. Bush says he made up for the lost time in subsequent months, and guard records show he received credit for having performed all the required service.

Bush's story was unlikely on its face, and would have been even if those officers had not so clearly contradicted it. "I was there," the candidate insisted, as if no one had noticed him at Dannelly Air Force Base—a notion rather difficult to swallow, given Bush's status, rank, and personality. A famous cutup from his days at Phillips Andover (where he was known to everybody as "The Lip"), Bush never ceased to stand out in a crowd, and as an airman and a junior officer, moreover, he was hardly likely to have struck a mouselike presence. He was, as well, the son of someone eminent—a fact that certainly had not been any secret to his peers or his commanders back in Houston.* Despite all this, *no one* can remember seeing Bush at any drills in Texas *or* in Alabama all throughout that missing year, even though a group of angry veterans offered a reward of several thousand dollars to any airman willing to attest that Bush was there.

And yet, the press largely accepted Bush's claim, as well as Bush's documentary "evidence" that he had duly served. The *Times* was quick to validate the campaign's seeming proof of Bush's service. Those "records provided by the Guard and by the Bush campaign" amounted to "a torn piece of paper in his Guard records, a statement of points Bush apparently earned in 1972–73, although most of the dates and Bush's name except for the 'W' have been torn off." Thus the *Washington Post* described those "records," in its *one* article on Bush's missing year of military service, an eleventh-hour piece that came out on November 3— four days prior to Election Day—and cast not as a story on the candidate's peculiar record but about the desperate Democrats' attempts to make an issue out of it: "2 Democrats: Bush Let Guard Down; Gore Surrogates Revive Issue of Apparent Laxity in Candidate's Military Service." (The *Post*, recall, had, prior to the '92 election, run *five* articles on Clinton's ROTC dealings.) The tone of that short article, by George Lardner Jr. and Howard Kurtz, was as dismissive as the *Times* had been:

> Two high-profile surrogates for Vice President Gore, in an 11th-hour attempt to exploit a dormant issue, yesterday castigated George W. Bush over allegations that he did not fulfill some of his National Guard duties in the 1970s.

---

*"Two members of the Air National Guard unit that President George W. Bush allegedly served with as a young Guard flyer in 1972 had been told to expect him and were on the lookout for him. He never showed, however; of that both Bob Mintz and Paul Bishop are certain." "Bush a No-Show at Alabama Base, says Memphian," *Memphis Flyer*, 2/13/04.

After Election Day 2000, that "dormant issue" went into a sort of coma. Turnipseed was hardly quoted anywhere until the spring of 2003, when the rising carnage in Iraq had started prompting reconsiderations of the president's own military record (mostly among veterans, who knew the score), and even then, the references appeared primarily in editorials and letters to the editor (and in a column by Gene Lyons in the *Arkansas Democrat-Gazette*). Meanwhile, the mainstream press, far from questioning the president's own soldierly commitment, lustily applauded his tough posture as a soldier's kind of guy, as if they were his courtiers and not our fellow citizens.

Bush is not guilty of desertion, or even, technically, of being AWOL. If the Guard had punished him for his long truancy, he would have been declared an "unsatisfactory participant" for having missed nine or more drills during his term of service. Still more serious a misdemeanor was Bush's failure to report for his annual physical examination in 1972. For that failure Bush's flying status was suspended on August 1 of that year, but his punishment should have been more severe, according to the rule. A missed flight physical is no trivial matter, as the training of an aviator represents a large investment by the government ($1 million is the figure often cited). The Guard is therefore strict in prosecuting those who are delinquent. Ordinarily, a missed flight physical would call for the convention of a Flying Evaluation Board, which could in turn order the removal of the offending airman's wings. Bush ought to have been grounded and demoted. At the very least, there would have been a formal narrative report composed by his commanding officer, explaining why Lieutenant Bush's name had been removed from the flight duty roster.

That crucial document is only one of many that has never been made public, notwithstanding the White House's showy release, on February 13, 2004, of over 400 pages from the president's TANG service file: a weighty trove of unimportant scraps, such as the record of Lieutenant Bush's dental exam on January 6, 1973, including a complete chart of his teeth. Although portrayed as comprehensive—"The president felt everything should be made available to the public," said White House press secretary Scott McClellan—that batch of odds and ends included nothing of his blown-off physical, nor anything to prove that Bush had fully served his term: pay stubs, retirement point-sheet, W-2 forms. As James C. Moore reports, such pertinent records are on microfiche at the Air Reserve Personnel Center in Denver, and at the National Personnel Records Center in St. Louis. If Bush would simply sign a release-authorization form—as John McCain did in 2000, and as John Kerry did in 2004—his entire service history would be an open book. That, however, is a book that Bush & Co. wants us not to read, despite McClellan's stilted declaration: "There were some who sought to leave a wrong impression that there was something to hide when there is not."

The history of Bush's service file should by itself have sunk him long ago. Moore notes that when he and other Texas journalists asked to see the file when Bush was getting set to run for president, they received 160 pages: "the entirety of the record," they were told. By 2004, that "record" had swelled magically to over 400 pages, and yet that variable folder still contained no evidence in Bush's favor. Moreover, since 1998 there has been solid testimony that the paper file was sanitized by Governor Bush's minions, so as to make no problems for the presidential candidate-to-be. In 1997, according to Bill Burkett, a retired lieutenant colonel in the TANG, Joe Allbaugh, Governor Bush's chief of staff, ordered General Daniel James, the TANG's commander (and a Bush appointee), to "get rid of the embarrassments" in Bush's file. As State Plans Officer, Burkett worked closely with the general, and so was there when Allbaugh gave the order via speakerphone. Soon Burkett came upon another general, John Scribner, sorting through a hefty stack of documents, and noticed "twenty to 40 pages" lying in a large waste basket: "Bush, George W., On Lt" was written at the top of the first sheet. They were "performance documents and payroll-type documents," claims Burkett, who went public with the story in 1998.

An old soldier with a reputation for integrity, Burkett has staunchly reconfirmed his story all these years, despite broad reportorial indifference, frequent threats of violence, and, as usual, prolific slander by the Bush machine.* He finally earned a bit of national attention in mid-Feb-

---

*Scribner's act was also witnessed by Chief Warrant Officer George Conn, who repeatedly confirmed Bill Burkett's story—until mid-February 2004, when he abruptly changed his tune, insisting now that he had "no recall" of those events in

ruary 2004, when John Kerry forced the president's TANG record into public view. On MSNBC's *Hardball*, Chris Matthews cross-examined him, then sent him on his way; and the *New York Times* reported Burkett's charges in a single article, running it on p. A33. Thus it was left to Kerry to sustain an issue that the members of the press, it seems, would just as soon have all of us forget.

In the matter of his military history the president is obviously guilty, not of any legal misdemeanor (that we know of yet) but of a moral and a civic wrong. The military ethic is fraternal and collective, each service member coming through for everybody else. That Bush used his Guard service to keep himself away from Vietnam—a war that he supported, as long as other people had to fight in it—and that he then blew off his obligation and even missed that crucial physical, suggests a man indifferent to his duty, and unmoved by any feeling of responsibility toward his fellow citizens-in-arms.* And yet Bush has never ceased to posture as a gung-ho soldier's soldier, a patriot devoted to his comrades, and, as their commander, always looking out for them.

On May 1, 2003, Bush, dressed up like a navy pilot, made (or was

---

1997. A longtime friend of Conn's, Burkett believes that fear of unemployment motivated the reversal, Conn having lately gone to work for the Department of Defense as a civilian contractor. Eric Boehlert, "Bad News Doesn't Get Better with Age," *Salon*, 2/14/04 (www.salon.com/news/feature/2004/02/14/burkett/index_np.html).

The best account of Bush's military history is James Moore, *Bush's Quest for Reelection: Iraq, the White House and the People* (Hoboken, N.J.: John Wiley, 2004). Despite—or because of—its wealth of information about Bush's case, Moore's book has received scant media attention: only one review, and it was hostile.

*However, there is also evidence that Bush may have been suspended from flying because of a stringent new military screening program designed to keep unreliable pilots from access to nuclear weapons and delivery systems. The Human Reliability Program applied to all U.S. Air Force and Air Guard units when Bush was serving, and the TANG had nuclear-capable jets. See Bill Mordin and Karen Dorn Steele, "Bush's Partial History: Stringent military screening program may explain gaps on president's record," *The Spokesman-Review.com*, 3/14/04 (http://www.spokesman review.com/breaking-news-story.asp?submitDate=200431401040). The article also provides a vivid sense of the official wall of silence that, concerning Bush's military record, has been imposed at every level of the government.

said to have made) a gorgeous and unnecessary landing on the aircraft carrier *Abraham Lincoln*, which was bringing troops home from the Gulf. Although the ship was only forty miles from San Diego, and therefore easily accessible by helicopter, Bush's image-men saw fit to fly him most dramatically onto the scene, "in the co-pilot's seat of a Navy S-3B Viking after making two fly-bys of the carrier," as CNN's Web site reported.

The spectacle was clearly meant to give the audience a major rush, as at the start of *Triumph of the Will*, and to provide Team Bush with several *Top Gun* moments for the "reelection" propaganda blitz in 2004. Otherwise, it benefited no one. The sailors and Marines on the *Lincoln* had been separated from their families for months—and yet Team Bush delayed the ship's return for one full day so that the president could have a picturesque "sleepover" with our brave men and women. (The *Lincoln* also was diverted from its proper course so that the sun would look just right on Bush. "If you looked at the TV picture," one aide said later, "you saw there was flattering light on his left cheek and slight shadowing on his right. It looked great.") The carrier's extra day at sea cost U.S. taxpayers $3.3 million.*

It was a moment of Neronian self-indulgence; Clinton would have had to put a hot tub on board *Air Force One* and frolicked in it for a week at LAX to outdo Bush's inconsiderate stunt. Throughout the epic photo op, the *Lincoln* was triumphantly adorned with a gigantic banner, imprinted brightly with the legend "MISSION ACCOMPLISHED," those proud words stamped across a lustrous twirl of Stars and Stripes. After a quick costume change, Bush reappeared in mufti (dark Oxxford suit, red tie, Old Glory on lapel) and took his place beneath the banner, standing at a solemn podium to give his victory speech, which compared the occupation of Iraq with World War II:

> The character of our military through history—the daring of Normandy, the fierce courage of Iwo Jima—the decency and idealism

---

*That is the daily cost of keeping a carrier task force at sea, according to the World Policy Institute. Frida Berrigan, "Progress in Iraq?" posted to the Web site of the Institute Arms Trade Resources Center, 11/10/03 (http://www.worldpolicy.org/projects/arms/updates/111003.html).

that turned enemies into allies is fully present in this generation. When Iraqi civilians looked into the faces of our servicemen and women, they saw strength and kindness and goodwill. When I look at the members of the United States military, I see the best of our country, and I'm honored to be your commander in chief.

Thus Bush—first "a pilot," then "the president"—appeared as if he'd won that war all by himself, as a can-do airman *and* a great commander (and a Great Emancipator) in one superpatriotic package.

And yet, of course, the war had not been won, nor had the president himself been a victorious flyboy in that other war, but an inglorious exploiter of the National Guard, which he had entered, over many others, through his family connections. Especially as Bush was doing his fictitious military history to sell the nation on preemptive war, the U.S. press was obligated to report all this—and to note also that this president was now the first in U.S. history to dress up like a military man in public. Ours being a civilian government, not one of our chief executives, including all those seasoned generals who had moved on to the White House, ever thought to flaunt his military uniform in office. But while Washington, Jackson, Grant, and Eisenhower never would have crossed that line, George W. Bush, who dodged the draft and then deserted, jumped right over it, and this gross impropriety the U.S. press ignored.

Indeed, far from telling any of the truths suppressed by that impertinent performance, our journalists were on their knees before it, oohing at his swagger like so many groupies. On a CNN Live Event Special, Kyra Phillips and Miles O'Brien had this exchange:

PHILLIPS: He looks like a fighter pilot!

O'BRIEN: Yes. He's got the look, doesn't he? Yeah! That's—

PHILLIPS: He sure does! Look at the stroll!

O'BRIEN: I'm telling you, that is the fighter pilot strut if I ever saw it. He's got it going!

PHILLIPS: Tom Cruise! Look at him!

"I don't know what more I can add," interjected Judy Woodruff, "but we are watching President Bush as he strides across the deck of the *Abraham Lincoln* saluting, being saluted to, wearing the uniform of a pilot." "The images all say 'wartime leader,' " she later added helpfully. "It is quite a photo op!" Later, on the *CBS Evening News*, Cynthia Bowers likewise marveled at the president's "first-of-a-kind photo op," noting that "with his dramatic flight onto this decorated carrier, the White House has sent a clear signal: It is pulling out all the stops choreographing this finale to the war." In her pretaped story, she elaborated lyrically:

> BOWERS: After nearly ten months at sea, there was one last landing, and this one was anything but routine. From stem to stern, all eyes scanned the heavens, straining to be the first to pick out that flash of silver in overcast skies, because out of the thousands of landings this crew has seen, this one could be called historic. The president chose to fly in on a Navy jet because he wanted to experience landing on a carrier's short deck and the adrenaline rush that comes with it.
>
> PO3 WINSTON BANTON (U.S. Navy): He was, like, catching his breath. He was just like, "Wow," you know?
>
> BOWERS: He was?
>
> PO3 BANTON: He had to take a little time to pause for a second.

On the ABC News Special Report, Peter Jennings also made an effort to convey the utter awesomeness of Bush's landing:

> The President has had the kind of day that many of us will envy, a chance to fly in a Navy plane out to the *Abraham Lincoln* and land on its deck. An exhilarating experience, as he later said it had been.

Most U.S. journalists appeared to be as wowed by Bush's flight as Seaman Banton was, or, if not wowed by the flight itself, wowed by the ingenuity and boldness of the Bush team's effort to wow everybody else. (Upon landing, wrote David Sanger in the *Times*, the president "emerged for the kind of photographs that other politicians can only dream about.") According to the press, that master stroke of propaganda dazzled *everybody.* "Even the Democrats said it was a John Wayne moment," Diane Sawyer told Charles Gibson on ABC's *Good Morning America* the next day. And when the Democrats *did* get their act together and deplore the spectacle as exploitation, their deviation from the party line went unreported by the media or was jeered as bluntly as Scott Ritter's arguments had been before the war. "To me," said Senator Robert Byrd, "it is an affront to the Americans killed or injured in Iraq for the president to exploit the trappings of war for the momentary spectacle of a speech." Our troops "shouldn't have to be props," said Senator Henry Waxman, "in a campaign event. This was to launch the re-election campaign of George Bush." And Representative Robert Menendez (D-NJ) had a more practical objection: "It would have been much easier and much less costly to the taxpayers to have just visited them at port."

On May 8, Chris Matthews had G. Gordon Liddy on *Hardball* to promote his latest book, *When I Was a Kid, This Was a Free Country.* After playing clips of Byrd et al., the bumptious host asked Liddy, "What do you make of this broadside against the USS *Abraham Lincoln* and its chief visitor last week?" Asked that loaded question, Liddy fired away:

> Well, I—in the first place, I think it's envy. I mean, after all, Al Gore had to go get some woman to tell him how to be a man.*
>
> And here comes George Bush. You know, he's in his flight suit, he's striding across the deck, and he's wearing his parachute harness, you know—and I've worn those because I parachute—and it makes the best of his *manly characteristic.*
>
> You go run those—run that stuff again of him walking across there with the parachute. He has just won every woman's vote in the United States of America! You know, all those women who say size doesn't count—they're all liars. Check that out!
>
> I hope the Democrats keep ratting on him and all of this stuff so that they keep showing that tape.

*This was a reference to reports that Gore had sought campaign advice from feminist Naomi Wolf, who allegedly advised him to wear earth tones.

As Liddy paused to calm himself, Matthews gleefully assailed the Democrats for their wrong-headedness:

> MATTHEWS: You know, it's funny. I shouldn't talk about ratings. I don't always pay attention to them, but last night was a riot because, at the very time Henry Waxman was on—and I do respect him on legislative issues—he was on blasting away, and these pictures were showing last night, and everybody's tuning in to see these pictures again.

> LIDDY: That's right.

> MATTHEWS: And I've got to say why do the Democrats, as you say, want to keep advertising this guy's greatest moment?

Contemplating Bush's package, Liddy started losing it completely.

> LIDDY: Look, he's—he's coming across as a—well, as women would call in on my show saying, what a stud, you know, and the guy—they're seeing him out there with his flight suit, and he's— and they know he's an F-105 fighter jock. I mean it's just great.

> MATTHEWS: Let's let him talk for himself. Here's President Bush expressing his confidence that he did the right thing.

[Begin video clip]

> BUSH: It was an honor for me to go on the USS *Abraham Lincoln*. I appreciate the chance to thank our troops. It was an unbelievably positive experience, and not only was I able to thank our troops, I was able to speak to the country and talk about not only their courage but the courage of a lot of other men and women who wear our country's uniform.

[End video clip]

> MATTHEWS: You know what struck me about that? The part that couldn't have been faked, which is the faces of the troop[s].

> LIDDY: Yes. Did you see when they—when they ran the Clinton one? Pretty much the same thing. They're all there just like that, stone faces, and here, they're just all over him.

MATTHEWS: They just love him.

LIDDY: They're loving him.

MATTHEWS: I think that's a bonding that we're seeing right there. We're watching it now, Gordon. It's pretty impressive bonding between him and these guys. I mean they did win the war together, and he was their commander in chief. Why not have a—we don't have an Arc de Triomphe in this country like the French do. Isn't it okay to—

LIDDY: Please don't mention the French!

Here again, as when Scott Ritter dared dissent, the media invoked the president's mere *word* as if it clinched the case: "Here's President Bush expressing his confidence that he did the right thing." Here we see him say it, so it must be true; and since those soldiers on TV are visibly entranced—"that's a bonding that we're seeing right there"—there can't be any argument that Bush did wrong, either in showboating on that aircraft carrier or, by implication, hustling the United States to war.* Journalistically, the moment was grotesque, even if we don't consider Liddy's wild fixation on the presidential crotch ("Check that out!"). On a show called *Hardball,* two ostensibly tough pundits gush like schoolgirls at the sight of Bush in uniform and praise the seemingly euphoric unanimity of all those troops, while ridiculing all who see it differently. That they might mention anything to contradict the propaganda picture, or even complicate it, was unthinkable, as their function clearly was to keep on saying "Yes!" and thereby have us all saying "Yes!" to Bush, his propaganda, and his war.

As it happened, only time would finally do the journalists' job, the gradual accretion of horrific news from Over There eventually disproving Bush & Co.'s upbeat suggestion that the "mission" was "accomplished." Actually, the war was just beginning, and the president's flyboy tableau therefore became a huge embarrassment in retrospect, as did

---

*While not unusual for the protofascist Liddy, such prostration was a bit surprising for Chris Matthews, who had vociferously opposed the war for months, both on his show and in his syndicated column.

Bush the Elder's Clint Eastwood–style promise never to raise taxes ("Read my lips!") after Bush the Elder *did* raise taxes. By late October, the uncanny gap between the younger Bush's air show and his lasting war had grown so flagrant that the press was finally moved to notice it, and so the president felt moved to lie about it.

> REPORTER: Mr. President, if I may take you back to May 1st when you stood on the USS *Lincoln* under a huge banner that said, "Mission Accomplished." At that time you declared major combat operations were over, but since that time there have been over 1,000 wounded, many of them amputees who are recovering at Walter Reed, 217 killed in action since that date. Will you acknowledge now that you were premature in making those remarks?
>
> BUSH: Nora, I think you ought to look at my speech. I said, Iraq is a dangerous place and we've still got hard work to do, there's still more to be done. And we had just come off a very successful military operation. I was there to thank the troops.
>
> The "Mission Accomplished" sign, of course, was put up by the members of the USS *Abraham Lincoln*, saying that their mission was accomplished. I know it was attributed somehow to some ingenious advance man from my staff—they weren't that ingenious, by the way.

Afterward, Press Secretary Scott McClellan gamely tried to make the story true. The banner, he said, "was suggested by those on the ship. They asked us to do the production of the banner, and we did. They're the ones who put it up."

In fact, the banner was the handiwork of White House propagandist Scott Sforza (a former ABC producer) who had concocted similar banners for past photo ops. "The members of the USS *Abraham Lincoln*" had nothing to do with it. Although thoroughly misleading, that lie reconfirmed a certain truth, for it was just one more example of the president's actual *esprit de corps*, Bush always having been quite ready to let others do his fighting for him and otherwise to cover for him. In this case, however, those Americans fighting in Iraq, so that this Bush can look tough on TV, are paying an excessive price. Despite the president's public statements of "support" for them, and his assurances that all of them are good to go, with the best possible equipment, training, leadership, supplies, etc., our troops have in fact been poorly served by this administration.

Bush likes to say the opposite: "They must have the best pay, the best equipment and the best possible training!" he told a cheering audience in Milwaukee on October 3, 2003. In fact, our troops have been supremely stiffed on all three counts. While handing Halliburton billions, the regime has taken every opportunity to slash the modest income of our military personnel.

In April of 2003, Congress voted raises for those fighting in Iraq and Afghanistan: $75 added to the troops' imminent danger pay, for a total of $225 per month, and $150 added to the family separation allowance paid to service members with dependents, for a monthly total of $250. The raises would continue only through October—and through the summer Bush & Co. quietly lobbied Congress not to keep that money coming to the troops, deeming the raises "wasteful and unnecessary." Public anger finally forced the White House to back off; and yet the regime has succeeded in eliminating many benefits. On November 11, 2003, the *Army Times* threw down the gauntlet. The Pentagon was closing at least nineteen commissaries, and considering the sale or closure of fifty-eight schools on fourteen U.S. military bases. "The two initiatives are the latest in a string of actions by the Bush administration to cut or hold down growth in pay and benefits, including basic pay, combat pay, health-care benefits and the death gratuity paid to survivors of troops who die on active duty."*

The most egregious rip-offs have been stopped by Congress. Now troops flying home on leave have their whole airfare covered (whereas, formerly, the Pentagon would only pay the fare from Baghdad to a "gate-

* Bush/Cheney and congressional Republicans have also pushed enormous cuts in veterans benefits: $14.6 billion over the next ten years. Considering the weekly casualties in the "war on terrorism," such cuts are especially ill-advised. "If they are trying to cut us now," remarked a member of Disabled American Veterans, "you can just imagine what's going to happen to all these kids over there in Iraq." Phoebe Sweet, "Bush, GOP Take Aim at Veterans' Benefits," *Town Online*, April 11, 2003 (http://www.townonline.com/allston/news/local_regional/ab_covabvets04112003.htm).

way airport" in Atlanta, Baltimore, Dallas or Los Angeles).* Nor are the troops recovering from wounds in U.S. military hospitals required to pay for their own meals (a policy that started under Ronald Reagan). On the other hand, the government has been quite slow to get our troops "the best equipment," notwithstanding Bush's claims. Only 40,000 of the troops now fighting in Iraq have serviceable body armor. The rest must pay for it themselves. When they learned that Sergeant David Zvosechz was without such crucial gear, his fellow citizens in Henrietta, Ohio, chipped in to buy it for him. "I started out investigating, and found out so many didn't have the right vest," Zvosechz's mother told the Associated Press. And the troops need more than Kevlar vests. According to an unofficial study circulating through the army in the spring of 2004, scores of Americans killed in Iraq—20 percent of the first year's fatalities—were driving Humvees, which are "light-skinned," or unarmored. As Rumsfeld is fixated on developing a lighter, high-tech military, our troops do not drive proper combat vehicles. Of all those soldiers killed in Humvees, *Newsweek* reported, "perhaps one in four of those killed in combat in Iraq might be alive if they had had stronger armor around them. . . . Thousands more who were unprotected have suffered grievous wounds, such as the loss of limbs."

Far from giving them "the best equipment," Bush & Co. does not even adequately feed our troops. Throughout the summer of 2003, they were short on water, and their meals have often been inedible. In December of 2003, it came out that the troops were being served filth-

*While the troops were partly paying their own airfare, Bush & Co.'s Pentagon officials were illegally taking pleasure trips for free, using public funds to bump their tickets up to first-class status.

Military and civilian defense officials improperly used government credit cards to buy 68,000 first-class or business-class airline seats when they were supposed to fly coach, congressional investigators concluded Thursday.

Several high-ranking political appointees were among the 44,000 people who bought premium tickets that cost $124 million over two years. The investigators' report did not estimate how much extra money that meant. Coach tickets can cost anywhere from a few dollars to thousands of dollars less.

"Report: Pentagon Officials Fly in Style," AP, 11/7/03.

ily by the Halliburton subsidiary Kellogg Brown & Root—Dick Cheney's outfit, which Bush & Co. had very generously hired to feed the U.S. service members in Iraq. Although Halliburton had overcharged us hugely for its services, the food that they provided, and the facilities in which they cooked it, were unsanitary. "The Pentagon reported finding 'blood all over the floor,' 'dirty pans,' 'dirty grills,' 'dirty salad bars' and 'rotting meats . . . and vegetables,' " NBC reported, citing documents from the Department of Defense.

The troops are undermanned as well as ill-equipped. (There are up to 20,000 mercenaries—"security contractors"—fighting in Iraq, making them the third-largest bloc within "the coalition of the willing.")* So dire is the shortage of combatants that the military has deployed troops who were "mentally unfit," UPI reported in the spring of 2004. Such was, at any rate, the Pentagon's explanation for the startling incidence of pathological behavior among U.S. soldiers: an inordinate number of suicides (nineteen in 2003 alone), an untold number of attempted suicides, and "hundreds of medical evacuations for psychiatric problems"—a type of illness that accounts for one in ten evacuees. The Pentagon might also have referred to the numerous sexual assaults on female troops by their male comrades in the Gulf theater. In late January 2004, the *Denver Post* reported that thirty-seven soldiers had sought trauma counseling after their ordeals at other soldiers' hands (and found themselves mistreated or ignored by the authorities). Such widespread symptoms of derangement indicated that the military's screening methods were at fault, the Pentagon suggested in October of 2003: "Variability in pre-deployment screening guidelines for mental health issues may have resulted in some

---

*Among these "contractors" are professionals whose background would not seem to suit them for a struggle to create democracy. "A South African killed in Iraq two weeks ago once worked for a secret apartheid death squad known as the Civil Co-operation Bureau. The CCB specialised in assassinating civilians who sympathised with black liberation movements." The mercenary presence in Iraq includes at least 1,500 South Africans. Gavin du Vinage, "Apartheid Assassins Meet Match in Iraq," *The Australian*, 4/27/04. As far as we know now, however, such ex-colonial assassins have performed no more barbarically than any other private forces hired to help out with the U.S. occupation.

soldiers with mental health diagnoses being inappropriately deployed."

Surely such a bureaucratic snafu may account for the sick conduct of "some soldiers." However, it alone cannot explain the special madness of this war, which was based entirely on a fantasy, and largely prosecuted, from the start, with pathological brutality. Certainly this sense of madness was not just infused into the war by crazy soldiers. First of all, the war itself has driven soldiers crazy. Iraq is far more dangerous for U.S. troops than Vietnam was forty years ago; for in this war there is no DMZ, no relatively safe place like Saigon, but everywhere, at any time, the possibility of death. "You can get shot in the head when you go to buy a Coke,"* said Larry Syverson, the father of two boys serving in the Gulf, in August 2003. Already worn by such incessant risk, and by the sense of helplessness against guerrilla methods, our troops are maddened further by the Pentagon's capriciousness. They do not know how long they might be stuck there, battling a whole nation that increasingly detests them. That fatal quandary is sure to drive them past the breaking point, when they risk dying in some far-off slaughter whose official pretext is unclear. Hard enough for full-time troops to bear, such inexplicable and open-ended service is especially punishing for our reservists, whose lives back home may be collapsing as they strike out at the omnipresent enemy.

The bitterness can only be augmented by the fact that their ordeal is routinely whitewashed by a Pentagon and White House that care more about their public image than about the welfare of our troops *or* the Iraqi people. The cost among Americans in physical destruction has been vastly understated by the Pentagon. By the end of 2003, there were, officially, about 2,000 U.S. casualties—a sum persuasively disputed by Colonel David Hackworth, who observed in late December that the occupation of Iraq had thus far led to *22,000* casualties. By early May 2004, our military had conducted 40,000 medical evacuations from Iraq and Afghanistan since the beginning of the war (a datum noted casually by Aaron Brown on CNN). And yet, while systematically played *down* by the corporate media—who were, of course, accused by the Republi-

* That had happened to a U.S. army sergeant in Baghdad.

cans of playing it *up*—the toll in U.S. lives and limbs received more press attention than the spiritual and moral toll of this atrocious occupation.

Even with the endless censorship and spin, it was apparent from the outset that the U.S. war against Iraq—just like conditions at Guantá-namo, and the roundup of "suspected terrorists" throughout the home-land—betrayed a flagrant racist animus much sharpened by religious bigotry. Notwithstanding Bush's claim that U.S. troops receive "the best possible training," the wartime conduct of our fighting men and women has, too often, been reflective less of any military discipline than of an angry bullying contempt for those whom they purportedly were sent to liberate. "We're here to give you your fuckin' freedom, now *back off!*" one GI shouted at a crowd of Shi'ite protestors soon after the U.S. inva-sion. "They don't see the Iraqi people the way we see them. They view them as untermenschen," a British officer complained in April 2004 (without, perhaps, enough awareness of the British soldiers' attitudes toward "the Iraqi people"). This attitude has been apparent throughout the "war on terror" in Iraq as in Afghanistan, the United States using tac-tics on civilians that our government would surely *not* deploy against white Christian populations.

The U.S. invasion smashed the nation's infrastructure, most of which remains unreconstructed, and allowed the nation's cultural treasures to be trashed or hauled away; as the war intensified, our military tactics actually did recall some of those German methods that Rumsfeld had invoked with such approval. (See p. 12.) Our bombers blasted mosques, our snipers picked off women, children, anything that moved amid the rubble of Fallujah, and elsewhere.* *Overkill* would seem the most appro-priate descriptor for the U.S. tactical approach to those Islamic lands: a gift to those Islamist radicals who had killed thousands in their effort to provoke just such atrocities, so as to make their cause more popular with

---

*So coarse have U.S. tactics been that the British high command deplores them: "It is trite, but American troops do shoot first and ask questions later," one British officer told the *Telegraph* (UK). "My view and the view of the British chain of com-mand is that the Americans' use of violence is not proportionate and is over-responsive to the threat they are facing." "US tactics condemned by British officers," Sunday *Telegraph*, 4/11/04.

Muslims everywhere. Our troops contributed to this effect, often following their orders with a certain gleeful zest. "US soldiers driving bulldozers, with jazz blaring from loudspeakers, have uprooted ancient
groves of date palms as well as orange and lemon trees in central Iraq as
part of a new policy of collective punishment of farmers who do not give
information about guerrillas attacking US troops," reported Patrick
Cockburn in the Sunday *Independent* (UK) in October 2003.

And then there was the vast sadistic horror visited upon civilians of
both sexes, and all ages, most controversially inside Abu Ghraib, Saddam
Hussein's notorious central dungeon, but also in the secret prisons operated globally by the United States throughout Iraq, and in Afghanistan,
and at Guantánamo, and on the island of Diego Garcia. (The similar
treatment of Americans locked up in many U.S. prisons is a problem
that demands much greater scrutiny.) On the orders of military intelligence, agents of the CIA, and certain private "contractors"—orders that
originated higher up, and back in Washington—U.S. troops, both male
and female, tortured and debased Iraqi prisoners, and, to make their victims feel still more degraded, merrily shot countless photographs and
videos of the ordeal, and avidly exchanged them. (Some soldiers used
such images as screen savers on their computers.) Once this story came
to light—thanks to the heroic whistle-blowing of a very few—Bush
claimed to find the images "disgusting" and "abhorrent," arguing that all
the rape and torture was the freelance evil-doing of a few bad apples, in
no way reflecting on our nation, our troops, or, of course, Bush himself
or any of his cabinet.*

At the very least, the scandal shattered Bush's claim that U.S. troops
receive "the best possible training." Some of the interrogators had no
military training whatsoever, but were only cooks and drivers working
for the private companies involved. Whoever their employers, the tor-
turers knew nothing of the Geneva Accords, and therefore carried out
their orders, evidently, with no paralyzing qualms. Staff Sergeant Chip

*Thus Bush blames the soldiers for his own regime's misdeeds, just as he did in
claiming that that White House banner had been "put up by the members of the USS
Abraham Lincoln.

Frederick, one of the accused, told CBS: "We had no support, no training whatsoever. And I kept asking my chain of command for certain things . . . like rules and regulations." That any of our fellow citizens would need to be told not to gang-rape women, or sic police dogs on naked men, or sodomize prisoners with mop handles, or videotape the rape of adolescent boys, suggests a national catastrophe far worse than 9/11: an absolute collapse of those great moral principles on which this nation was originally founded.

This breakdown starts at the top. Indeed, far from giving U.S. troops the "best possible training," Bush/Cheney are themselves the authors of this breakdown, having pushed the "war on terror" as a national exercise in violent revenge. For all his early photo ops with U.S. Muslims, and his faint praise for Islam as a "peaceful" creed "hijacked" by extremists, Bush sent a very different message to our troops, and to Americans in general, by harping on Iraq's alleged complicity in 9/11, and by hyping the fictitious "terrorist threat" posed by that nation. Because of such inflammatory propaganda, our troops were motivated mainly by a craving for revenge, as after the destruction of Pearl Harbor. Throughout the march to war, and through the first year of the war itself, *payback* was on everybody's mind. "The one thing that motivates all the soldiers fighting in Iraq is payback for Sept. 11, 2001," reported Reuters on the second anniversary of the catastrophe. "There's a picture of the World Trade Center hanging up by my bed and I keep one in my [flak jacket]," one Army corporal told the *London Evening Standard.* "Every time I feel sorry for these people I look at that. I think, 'They hit us at home and, now, it's our turn.' I don't want to say payback but, you know, it's pretty much payback."

That lust for righteous vengeance has helped push our troops toward barbarism—which is often frightening even to themselves. Having joined the Army to give "some payback" to the terrorists, a GI from Buffalo expressed his fears to a reporter with the Associated Press: "I'm afraid of going back home again. I don't want to bring the mentality I have here back to my mother and little brothers." Thus Bush has done our troops a deeper injury than any they could suffer from the snipers and the hidden bombs, or from the "mystery pneumonia" or any other of the baffling ailments that the Pentagon will not explain (or do too much to cure). Beyond the many deaths and lasting wounds, our troops are getting maimed in spirit, their youthful hearts and minds distorted by too close a union with atrocity. And that great cost was long ignored completely, by both the Pentagon and the U.S. press, whose antiseptic version of the war preserved the rest of us in comfortable and dangerous denial.

And those who dare to tell the truth to members of the press are often bawled out for their honesty or punished more severely, being under constant pressure *not* to speak their minds about this war for "freedom and democracy." Meanwhile, their president is always quick to use them as the backdrop for another photo op, devised for use in future campaign advertising. When, in 2003, Bush paid his "surprise Thanksgiving visit" to the soldiers stationed at the Baghdad International Airport, he certainly appeared to be real glad to see them, and they him. Getting teary-eyed, and proffering a large delicious-looking turkey on a platter, Bush posed manfully in his flight jacket, looking every inch the kind commander loved by all his men.

And yet the soldiers and the press had been strictly ordered not to say a word to one another. That audience of troops had been preselected. The turkey, it turned out, was not for eating, but a display item of the kind that only *looks* delectable for advertising purposes.* The whole trip, finally, was no last-minute matter, meant to boost the troops' morale (as Bush had said), but an exercise that had been planned weeks before, mainly to upstage a visit to Iraq by Senator Hillary Clinton.

While the president devotes enormous effort to such cheery photo ops with service members who are in one piece (and vote Republican), Bush

---

*"The troops actually ate the equivalent of TV dinners," notes Larry Syverson, whose two sons have been stationed in Iraq. "But that's not all of the story. There are about 5,000 troops that eat at that cafeteria. And Bush closed down half of it for over four hours. The wait for those other troops' Thanksgiving dinner grew from 30 minutes to three hours. Many soldiers went to their bunks and ate MREs as a protest against the president." Speech by Larry Syverson delivered in Richmond, Va., 3/21/04 (available online at http://www.mfso.org/Syv21.html).

evidently has not had much time to mark the sacrifice of those Americans who have been killed, disabled, or disfigured in the occupation of Iraq. Before his war began, he gave the very clear impression that he would be there to solace the bereaved. "There's only one person who is responsible for making the decision to go to war, and that's me," he said to Barbara Walters on ABC's *20/20* on December 13, 2002:

> And there's only one person who hugs the mothers and the widows, the wives and the kids on the death of their loved ones. Others hug, but having committed the troops, I've got an additional responsibility to hug, and that's me, and I know what it's like.

Despite that seeming vow, the president has not, as of this writing, bothered to attend a single military funeral consequent upon his war, nor has Dick Cheney been to any.* On the other hand, both men have pressed the flesh at scores of big fund-raisers for their "reelection." In 2003—and starting when the occupation had been raging for some months—Bush/Cheney made it to 100 fund-raisers between them, amassing an unprecedented war chest of $130 million. Meanwhile, as the military death toll mounted from the hundreds to the thousands, the president apparently did not remember his "additional responsibility to hug" the mourners. The White House did, however, send the grieving families official letters of condolence: form letters, which Bush himself may or may not have signed.

---

*As further evidence of the regime's concern for those who have served in our military, Bush/Cheney, in their budget for 2006, proposed a cut of $910,000,000 in funding for veterans. "2006 Cuts in Domestic Spending on Table," *Washington Post,* 5/27/04.

CHAPTER 4

The Wrong Man: II

Crook

Bush would seem to be the seasoned "crook" that everyone deemed Clinton for eight years, whereas the latter was, in his own business dealings, actually a paragon of probity. At party fund-raising, of course, that president certainly did bend the rules, as did Al Gore—and as all U.S. politicians must, in this corrupted system. Of course, the fact that everyone is guilty of it does not make it right in Clinton's case. If, however, we consider the wild charges hurled at him relentlessly for his extraordinary abuse of campaign finance laws, we must admit that Clinton/Gore's exertions, although at times improper, were not unusual. Indeed, their dirty doings in this regard were minimal compared with Bush's, and with Cheney's, and with Tom DeLay's, and Grover Norquist's, representing the new far-right GOP forever whoring after giant contributions with a diligence and sleaziness that put the Clinton venture in the shade (and that even top the Nixon operation).

Whereas Bill Clinton was condemned, and rightly, for his lodging wealthy donors in the so-called Lincoln bedroom, Bush/Cheney have hardly been rebuked for far more brazen doings of that kind. Their donors too have often been rewarded with nights inside the White House, all amenities included. (The White House has refused to say which presidential guests have spent the night inside the Lincoln bedroom, as if it would make any difference if they had been bedded down in any other chamber of the presidential home).

What puts Bush/Cheney in a whole new league, however, is their open sale of our entire government to corporate interests, which now run the U.S. for themselves. Certainly this sort of quid pro quo has long been an unwholesome feature of American politics, but Bush & Co. has pushed it to unprecedented heights (or depths), with their very governance based mainly on the sale of such indulgences. From the airlines to the big utilities, from agribusiness to the oil cartel, from pharmaceuticals to corporate media, from nursing homes to chemical companies, mining firms to huge retailers, superbanks to weapons manufacturers, Enron to Halliburton to Alcoa to Microsoft to General Electric to Enron to Halliburton, the industries and corporate entities that have paid off the regime have had their calls returned and problems solved, with their own people now in charge of the very governmental system that was built to regulate them.

So fervent is the GOP's eternal quest for cash that their top dogs make no attempt to hide the crassness of their enterprise. Fixated on their plutocratic base, Bush/Cheney dig for dollars more aggressively than any prior presidential team, and have thereby raised unprecedented sums for campaign propaganda. And yet the press has largely let them off the hook.

The *New York Times* ran some tough pieces on the subject once it was apparent that the "mission" in Iraq was *not* "accomplished": on May 22, 2003, a piece on Bush's plan to use the war to fill the party's coffers; on October 31, 2003, an article on Bush & Co.'s tendency to favor corporate donors in contracting for the reconstruction in Iraq and Afghanistan; on November 23, a strong lead editorial on all the recent Bush & Co. fund-raisers in wartime:

> That averages about three a week for the two men, most of them much farther away from the White House than Dover Air Force Base, where the bodies of the dead soldiers arrive back home.

And yet the *Times* has covered such self-salesmanship with far more restraint than marked their stories about Clinton/Gore's fund-raising. The paper noted Clinton's search for cash over 100 times, with the latest piece (as of this writing) in August 2002. The *Times* was even more obsessed with Al Gore's partisan solicitations, mentioning his notorious fund-raising gaffes—the Buddhist temple photo op and Gore's legalistic claim to have been subject to "no controlling legal authority"—238 times. (Only 48 of those allusions were quotations from Republicans). Considering the *Times*' agenda-setting power, its relative leniency toward Bush & Co. may help explain the general failure of the other major media—TV in particular—to notice this administration's record-breaking sales pitch. At this point, TV appears to have done nothing, and the print press very little, on Bush/Cheney's wartime gold rush or their sweetheart deals with, say, Halliburton and Bechtel, even though such wrongs are far more glaring and more consequential than Clinton/Gore's self-salesmanship at its most vigorous.

In any case, apart from his fund-raising, Clinton, both as governor and as president, was squeaky clean as far as money was concerned: a point made inadvertently by Kenneth Starr. That real-life Javert spent over $40 million hunting for an illegality in Bill and Hillary Clinton's innocuous and unrewarding business deals. Nor was that the only effort made by the Republicans to dig up something—anything—that might reveal or hint that the First Couple were a pair of thieves. Promising a "complete, thorough and impartial investigation" of Whitewater, former U.S. Attorney Robert B. Fiske Jr., a Republican, did just that from January 20 to June 30 of 1994. His report, released on July 1, not only determined that Vince Foster had indeed committed suicide (and not been killed by the First Couple), but wholly cleared the Clintons and their people of the charge that they had tried to cover up some crime involving Whitewater. There was no crime to cover up, Fiske found:

> After a review of all the evidence, we have concluded that the evidence is insufficient to establish that anyone within the White House or the Department of Treasury acted with the intent to corruptly influence [a] R[esolution] T[rust] C[orporation] investigation. Therefore, the evidence of the events surrounding the contacts between the White House and the Treasury Department

does not justify the prosecution of anyone for a violation of Section
1505. We have also concluded that the evidence does not justify a
criminal prosecution for violation of any other federal statute.

And there it should have ended, Fiske having proved, and pointed
out, what Starr would prove again (without admitting it): that, far from
ripping anybody off, the Clintons had themselves been ripped off by the
ailing and erratic Jim McDougal, who took their $40,000 stake in
Whitewater and blew it on his own ill-fated schemes. Since that was not
the story that the anti-Clinton faction wanted to believe, Fiske's conclusions sparked much rightist lamentation, as well as the decision (made
largely by Chief Justice Rehnquist) to order Starr to try again. Forty million dollars later—in addition to the mere $6 million spent by Robert
Fiske—Starr proved not just that the president had had that thing with
Monica Lewinsky, but also that as governor of Arkansas he had always
played it absolutely straight with other people's money, making not one
dime beyond his salary.

And yet Clinton's *crookedness* was hyped for years, by his rightist enemies and, no less vehemently, by the mainstream press, which drove the
story from day one. As Gene Lyons shows in *Fools for Scandal*, "Whitewater" was a load of hogwash all along, and would have been dismissed
as such if it had not been wildly misreported by the *New York Times* and
the *Washington Post*, whose misimpressions were routinely publicized by
all three networks and the cable giants and the tribunes of talk radio,
with *Time* and (especially) *Newsweek*, as well as the *New Yorker*, also on
board. So many were the stories that it would take quite some time to
quantify them. ("Who could possibly count that high?" asks independent journalist Bob Somerby.)* While worthless as journalism, that flood
tide of false reports worked brilliantly as propaganda, establishing the
Clintons in the public mind as an outrageous pair of cheats, like Jim and
Tammy Faye Bakker, or Ferdinand and Imelda Marcos.

That *Bush* committed fiscal crimes, on the other hand, there *is* abundant evidence, and yet the U.S. press has looked away, by and large

*James Carville estimates that Whitewater generated over 80,000 stories in the
mainstream press.

ignoring it throughout the presidential race and ever since.* During the campaign of 2000, few reporters would go near the story of Bush's highly dubious involvement with Harken Energy—an outfit as corrupt in reality as Whitewater was in rightist fantasy. In fact, few reporters would go near the tangled tale of Bush's history as a businessman: an odd narrative of upward failure, with the young entrepreneur consistently grub-staked, and repeatedly bailed out, by various wealthy interests keen on forging links to his important father.

The younger Bush's maiden enterprise, Arbusto Energy, was formed in 1977, with the help of Houston aircraft broker James R. Bath, who put $50,000 into the concern. A buddy of Bush's from the National Guard, Bath had made his living partly by investing money in this country on behalf of two extremely wealthy Saudi sheikhs: Kalid bin Mahfouz was a major shareholder in the infamous Bank of Credit and Commerce International (BCCI), aka "the Bank of Crooks and Criminals International," a heinous global entity that made a lot of bad news in the early eighties.† Salem M. bin Laden, eldest son of the Saudi con-

*The Center for Public Integrity broke the story of Clinton and the Lincoln bedroom—and it has tried for years to get the press to cover the far worse corruption of Bush/Cheney. Charles Lewis, the center's director, commented astutely on the double standard: "Having broken the Clinton 'Lincoln bedroom' scandal, I was deeply involved in hundreds of media interviews and the feeding frenzy that occurred particularly in 1997, but with a memorable flourish the last month of the '96 campaign (40 media calls a day, highest ever in our history). There is one very salient point to recall, which gnaws away at me today. The campaign finance scandals had multiple congressional committees (Thompson in the Senate, Burton in the House, especially) tracking the Clinton/Gore excesses furtively, and of course feeding the press. [There were also] at least two independent counsel investigations, plus an internal, 'Public Integrity' Justice Department investigation." All those hearings yielded "an extraordinary amount of fodder for the press." Under Bush/Cheney, there is no such activity—primarily because the GOP controls the Congress, and since 9/11, a new secretiveness enwraps the White House and the entire executive branch. "It is a deadly combination," Lewis concluded. Only occasionally can the best reporters break through with an important story. E-mail from Charles Lewis, 12/13/03.
†According to the Executive Summary of a 1992 report by the U.S. Senate Foreign Relations Committee, "BCCI's criminality included fraud by BCCI and BCCI customers involving billions of dollars; money laundering in Europe, Africa, Asia, and

struction magnate Mohammed Awad bin Laden (died 1968), ran the family's immense construction business along with certain of his fifty-three siblings. (Osama bin Laden, Salem's youngest brother, was not an active player in the firm, being only twenty-three at the time.) In a trust agreement struck in 1976, Sheikh bin Laden had named Bath as his business representative in Texas—George Bush Sr., then head of the CIA, having hooked Bath up with his Saudi business partners on the recommendation of George Jr. With no money of his own, Bath—director of Bin Laden & Associates, a procurement company for the Saudis—fronted for the sheikhs not only with Arbusto but also in U.S. ventures of all kinds. "He really was their figurehead as these enterprises cannot legally be owned by foreign nationals," recalls Bill White, Bath's onetime business partner. "He was the point man in that respect for their business interests." (Bath's relationship with Sheikh bin Laden ended when the latter's light plane crashed in San Antonio in 1988.)

Arbusto was a failure, having mainly drilled dry holes. In 1984, renamed Bush Exploration, the company merged with Spectrum 7 Energy, which absorbed Arbusto's losses and made Bush CEO, paying him an annual salary of $75,000 and awarding him 1.1 million shares of Spectrum 7 stock. Leveraged to the hilt, Spectrum 7 didn't make a dime for its investors. Its oil drilling program also failed, and the company came close to bankruptcy. In 1986 it merged with Harken Energy, which absorbed Spectrum 7's losses, put Bush on the board, and made him a consultant for "investor relations and equity placement," with the right to buy the company's stock at 40 percent of its face value. (That bailout was effected by "the Arabs," White recalls.) By 1989, Harken too was leaking badly. That year the company lost $12 million against revenues

---

the Americas; BCCI's bribery of officials in most of those locations; support of terrorism, arms trafficking, and the sale of nuclear technologies; management of prostitution; the commission and facilitation of income tax evasion, smuggling, and illegal immigration; illicit purchases of banks and real estate; and a panoply of financial crimes limited only by the imagination of its officers and customers." Senator John Kerry and Senator Hank Brown, "Executive Summary," in "The BCCI Affair: A Report to the Committee on Foreign Relations, United States Senate," 1992. The summary is online at http://www.fas.org/irp/congress/1992_rpt/bcci/01exec.htm.

of $1 billion. Also that year, Bush was paid $120,000 in consulting fees and awarded stock options worth $131,250. He had also been voted a director. Harken enjoyed a booming reputation, although it made no money, and its creditors were threatening to foreclose.

If all this sounds suspiciously like Enron's way of doing business, it is because back then the management at Harken was indeed engaged in just the sort of profitable scams that Kenneth Lay et al. would later make notorious. Soon after Harken's acquisition of Spectrum 7, the company forged a close relationship with Harvard Management Company, the muscular investment arm of Harvard University. (The board member responsible for the endowment's energy investments was Robert Stone Jr., an oilman and strong advocate for Bush the Elder.) In studying the Harvard/Harken symbiosis, *Wall Street Journal* reporter Glenn Simpson found evidence of "two heretofore little-noticed deals, both endorsed by Mr. Bush, to allow the Texas firm to stave off creditors. One, critical to the company's survival, involved a partnership used to move troubled assets and large debts off the company's balance sheet—much like the controversial investments that Enron Corp. set up before it filed for bankruptcy-court protection." The setup obviously benefited Harken Energy and Harvard Management—and also Bush himself, since Harvard's quiet assistance enabled him to maintain his winning posture as a self-made player.

" 'It seems to be a simple case of Aeneas [Harvard Management's venture-capital arm] bailing out Harken,' " Bala Dharan, an accounting professor at Rice University's Jones Graduate School of Management, told Simpson. "Because Harken owned less than 20 percent of the partnership, it no longer was required under accounting rules to include the debts and assets on its balance sheet. Mr. Dharan argues that a true reflection of Harken's financial health would have included them. In effect, the partnership raised money without taking on new debt."

Just as Bush's image as a fiscal whiz was threatening to collapse—by the end of 1990, Harken posted an annual loss of $40 million—the company was, as it were, born again in January of that year, when the lucky little firm won an exclusive thirty-five-year contract to drill for oil and gas in and near the island kingdom of Bahrain. Industry insiders

were astonished, as Bahrain had broken off negotiations with the able
giant Amoco in favor of what *Time* called an "obscure, money-losing
company with no refineries and no experience in offshore oil exploration."

Of course, what Harken *did* have was a major Bush connection. The
contract was awarded through the efforts of another wealthy Saudi,
Sheikh Abdullah Bakhsh, who had been on Harken's board since 1987,
as part of an elaborate deal with Stephens, Inc., a huge investment bank
in Little Rock (run by Jackson Stephens, a very giving Arkansas Republican), and the London branch of the Union Bank of Switzerland (UBS).
(Stephens, UBS, and Bakhsh all had close connections with BCCI.)
Harken was hired by the Bahrainis at the suggestion of Michael Ameen,
a Houston oil consultant friendly to the Saudi royal family, connected to
BCCI, and a close friend of Sheikh Abdullah Bakhsh. The deal was
reportedly cemented by Charles Hostler, a wealthy San Diego real estate
developer and generous donor to Republicans, and lately tapped by Bush
the Elder to be U.S. ambassador to Bahrain. Clearly, Hostler hinted
to the kingdom's representatives, it would be in Bahrain's interests to
include the president's son in their new project. Hostler's lobbying evidently did the trick. For the Bahraini project, Bush raised the crucial
capital from the billionaire Bass family of Ft. Worth, a clan of venerable
angels to the GOP. Because of this good news, Harken's stock price
jumped a dollar, climbing to $5.50 in just weeks.

Everything was right on track, until word came of possible U.S. military intervention in the Gulf, the rift between Saddam Hussein and
Kuwait's al-Sabah dynasty beginning to appear irreparable. Smith Barney came out with a very negative report on Harken's prospects, and the
drilling in Bahrain was not due to begin until the following year. What
Bush did next is well described by J. H. Hatfield:

> On June 22, 1990, Bush suddenly unloaded 60 percent of his
> Harken stock—212,140 shares—for a tidy profit of $848,560,
> more than two-and-one-half times their original value. The trans-
> action came a week prior to the end of a quarter in which the com-
> pany lost $23.2 million. A quarterly report issued in 1990, only

days after Iraq's invasion of Kuwait, documented the loss and company stock plummeted to $2.37 a share. Bush, who sold at $4.12 per share, denied having any inside knowledge at the time, although he sat on Harken's board, its audit committee, and a panel looking at corporate restructuring which had met in May and worked directly with the Smith Barney financial consultants.

Two months after Bush sold out, Harken posted second-quarter losses of $23 million, and that news drove the stock price down even further, to $1.25 by the end of 1990. Bush, moreover, took eight months to notify the government of the sale of stock that generated this windfall— an obvious violation of the Securities and Exchange Act of 1934, which gives company insiders just ten days to file a report called a Form 4, publicly disclosing all stock purchases and sales.*

When the *Wall Street Journal* reported that delay, the Securities and Exchange Commission (SEC) mounted, or at least announced, an investigation of possible insider trading. The case was obviously strong. (Thirteen years later, Martha Stewart went down for much less.) That Bush was eight months late in filing his Form 4 there was no doubt. As an active member of the board, moreover, Bush had to know that Harken was about to tank. What with his father in the Oval Office, furthermore, it's also likely that he knew how close Saddam Hussein and the Kuwaitis were to war, which certainly would not be good for business. Eleven days after Bush's sale, Iraq launched its invasion. That angle was, however, left to the occasional journalist to ponder, as it was of no interest to the SEC. Despite all that, the investigation, which began in April 1991, was cursory, with no one interviewing George W. Bush himself or any other of the firm's directors.

Such laxity was unsurprising. Richard Breeden, the commission's

---

*The president's son claimed to have sent the Form 4 in on time, but that it somehow got lost at the SEC. That claim would have been more believable, perhaps, if Bush had not been similarly casual about the necessary paperwork three times before. He had taken nearly three months to disclose a buy of 25,000 Harken shares on June 16, 1989; over four months to disclose a buy of 80,000 shares on December 10, 1986; and over five months to disclose his gain of well over 200,000 shares pursuant to the Spectrum 7/Harken merger.

chair, had spent four years as a senior policy adviser to the elder Bush (who appointed Breeden to the chairmanship).* James R. Doty, the SEC's general counsel, had, as a private lawyer, lately represented Bush the Younger. (Doty formally recused himself from Bush's case.) There were other links as well: Doty was a partner at James Baker's powerful Houston law firm Baker and Botts. Breeden too had been a lawyer there, and so was Richard W. Jordan, Bush's lawyer in the SEC case (and, in October 2001, appointed U.S. ambassador to Saudi Arabia). The firm had given generously to the Bush/Quayle campaign in 1988 and would go on to handle other touchy matters for the House of Bush.

And so the agency eventually dropped the case, deciding that the president's son would not be prosecuted. Bruce A. Hiler, associate director of the SEC's enforcement division, sent Bush's lawyer a letter saying that "the investigation has been terminated as to the conduct of Mr. Bush, and that, at this time, no enforcement action is contemplated with respect to him." Thus the case was closed, apparently. Once the agency had let it go, Bush quit the board of Harken to devote himself to his political career. When he ran for governor, he used the Hiler letter to assert his probity, and he used it later when, as president, the story popped, belatedly (and briefly), into public view. In mid-July of 2002, the news of Halliburton's no-bid contracts revived press interest in the president's own past financial dealings. As Bush had so far failed to bring the Enron managers to justice, or to reform the practices of crony capitalists, the Halliburton mess inspired a spate of mainstream articles. Once again, Bush used the SEC to clear himself. "The SEC has already looked into this in its entirety," Ari Fleischer told the press. "You know the conclusions, you know the reasons, and you have everything you need." The White House re-released the Hiler letter, and the press largely reechoed Bush's view of it: "The key document said there is no case."

The "case was dropped," reported the Associated Press. "The securities commission dropped the investigation," reported Elizabeth Bumiller

*"George Bush is Breeden's Mao: The walls of Breeden's office are lined with photographs of President and Mrs. Bush; additional pictures and other Bush memorabilia are strewn about the Breeden home, even in the downstairs bathroom." Stephen Labaton, "Wall Street's Ambitious Top Cop," *New York Times*, Business World Magazine, 3/24/91.

in the *New York Times*, "and in a letter to Mr. Jordan said that 'at this time no enforcement action is contemplated.'"* "The president was cleared of insider trading by the SEC," the *Houston Chronicle* reported. "Will Democrats Turn Harken into Whitewater?" *Salon* asked in a testy headline. "The SEC cleared Bush after looking into whether he had insider knowledge of an upcoming quarterly loss at Harken," the *Boston Globe* reported. On this affair "the liberal media" were largely in agreement with the propaganda outlets of the right. "Bush did not do anything wrong," wrote Byron York in the *National Review*. The *Washington Times* dragged Clinton into it: "The SEC's decision to close the Bush insider-trading investigation, occurring after President Clinton took office [*sic*], almost certainly was not a whitewash or politically motivated, as some have charged, the securities lawyers said." That exculpatory take was shared by PBS and NPR. "I think the president, what the president wants to do, *should* do, is put it behind him and get it over with," Mark Shields told Jim Lehrer on PBS's *NewsHour*. "There is a certain shopworn quality to the Harken story," which, he noted, was no Halliburton. (David Brooks, as ever, sat there gently beaming.) And on *Talk of the Nation*, NPR's Don Gonyea let Bush have the final word:

> So those things prompted an investigation. It was deemed not actionable by the SEC back in the early 1990's, meaning that they didn't pursue it. So the president says, "This is old news. Democrats keep bringing this up." He said they brought it up in '94 when he ran for governor. They brought it up in 2000 when he ran for president, and he says, "Well, looky here, it's an election year in 2002, and here it comes again. This is old news." And to quote him, he said, "There's no there there."

Technically, in fact, the SEC had *not* cleared Bush. Generally unnoted, and unquoted, in the rush to get him off the hook was the inconvenient

---

*Five days later, in a *Times* piece cowritten with Richard A. Oppel Jr., Bumiller quoted Hiler's letter once again: "The S.E.C. investigated on suspicions that the transaction was conducted on the basis of insider information, a potential crime, but dropped the investigation in 1993, saying that 'at this time no enforcement action is contemplated.'"

caveat that the agency's decision to abort the inquiry "must in no way be construed as indicating the party has been exonerated or that no action may ultimately result from the staff's investigation of that particular matter." This fact came up in just a handful of reports: in the *Boston Globe* and *Dallas Morning News*, from United Press International, and on NPR's *Morning Edition*, Bob Edwards interviewing a defensive James R. Doty. Edwards's introduction was entirely accurate: "Doty recused himself from the SEC investigation, and the agency ultimately took no action in the case. Neither did it exonerate George W. Bush." The erstwhile general counsel of the SEC* rejected that account. "You say that the SEC did not exonerate Mr. Bush," he said, sounding strikingly unlike a man who had recused himself from the investigation:

> That is a campaign line from [an] unsuccessful opponent in his first campaign for governor [i.e., Ann Richards]. She had no more basis for making that statement then than anyone has for making it now. And, in fact, the SEC, looking at this, taking a careful look at it and then deciding not to go forward and issuing a 5310 letter, as we say, in which they tell him they have no more questions, go in peace, that is, in fact, what happened here.
>
> EDWARDS: But isn't it also in that letter that it specifically says that it should not be taken as exoneration?
>
> DOTY: No, actually it simply says that the agency reserves the right to reopen the file if subsequent facts come to their attention that indicate that they should.
>
> EDWARDS: Well, let me find it. Let me find it. It says "must in no way be construed as indicating that the party has been exonerated."
>
> DOTY: I think the release prohibits adopting the letter, prohibits people representing it as exoneration. But the facts of the matter are that the SEC, after looking at many cases like this, issuing that letter, has had ten years to reopen that file and has not done so.

---

*After leaving the agency, Doty went on to represent Jeffrey Skilling, CEO of Enron.

Doty was in fact correct in noting that that stipulation is a standard feature of such letters from the SEC. That it is boilerplate, however, does not mean that Bush was cleared—nor would it, surely, if it had been Clinton in the spotlight. If Bush's predecessor had thus claimed to have been formally absolved and such a letter came to light, it would have finished him. For Bush, however, it was not even a problem worth reporting—and yet his malfeasance had tremendous consequences for his personal fortune, whereas Clinton's misdeed would have been inconsequential even if he had committed it.

First of all, the profits from that timely sale of Harken stock turned Bush into a multimillionaire. With his Harken gains, he paid back the $500,000 bank loan that he had taken out to buy his small piece (under 2 percent) of the Texas Rangers, an investment that would ultimately pay off thirty-fold. For the far-flung consortium that had bought the Rangers in 1989, and arranged for the construction of its new stadium in Arlington (paid for by local taxpayers), Bush served as the official Texan face and best-known statewide booster. Such work was much appreciated by his richer partners—who also owed him big-time for the giant favors he had done them since becoming governor in 1994. (His election to that post required his buddies' generous contributions.) When Bush's crony Tom Hicks bought the team in 1998—for a quarter of a billion dollars, triple the amount that Bush et al. had paid for it—the lucky politician did quite well, as Joe Conason reported in *Harper's* in February of 2000: "The other members of the Rangers partnership fattened Bush's payout six times over, by awarding him additional shares in the team at the time of the sale that brought his 1.8 percent share up to 12 percent. Without that extra consideration, his investment would have earned far less."

Thus Bush made $15 million—"more money than I ever dreamed," he said. That he had repaid the crucial bank loan with the profits of insider trading casts his sudden fabulous enrichment less as a fantastic stroke of luck than evidence, perhaps, of racketeering—as it would no doubt be considered, and investigated, if Bill Clinton were the lucky man in question.

Aside from all that money, Bush's rise in politics was yet another of the benefits resulting from his having been "exonerated." Once that SEC stuff was behind him, he declared himself a candidate for governor—and now a politician far more viable than he had been some years before, when, fresh out of Yale, he had mounted an inconsequential run for Congress. Back then, he had been easily derided as a rich boy from Connecticut who had done nothing down in Texas but lose money and exploit his family name. Now, it seemed, *he* was the owner of the Texas Rangers, *he* had kept the team at home, and *he* had built them that nice stadium in Arlington. (Bush took shrewd advantage of his status as the Rangers' public face, using it to pitch that winning image of *himself* as the most valued player in the enterprise.) Thus ostensibly accomplished, and with a fearsome knack for Texas politics, Bush made it to the top in Austin, and then in Washington, with a little help from all his daddy's friends.

And there he has been just the kind of president you would expect such a slick customer to be. When the top executives at Enron, World-Com, Tyco, Qwest, et al., exposed the ultimate effects of Bush's kind of business, the president assured us that he would go after them, and then did little. He pledged tough reforms of U.S. corporate business practice, then did nothing to develop any. Being who he is and coming from the world he came from, Bush *could not* have cleaned those stables out, because he himself had always done, and is still doing, his business there, along with all those friends to whom he's selling off the U.S. government. Thus would we, the people, have been duly served if our reporters had illuminated Dubya's financial history instead of clamming up about it. And so would we have been well served if our reporters had *not* harped relentlessly on *Clinton's* putative misdeeds, which broke no laws and harmed no one—and yet eventually helped harm us all, by weakening the White House in a time of nascent terror.

Liar

Bush's frequent blunt assertion that the SEC had "cleared" him, much like his riff about the banner on the aircraft carrier, brings us to still one more of those "Clintonian" attributes that Bush has long revealed more clearly and consistently than Clinton ever did. So often have Bush/Cheney lied in public, and so baldly have they lied, that they seem to have established a new standard of political mendacity, creating, as Senator Edward Kennedy observed in April 2004, "the largest credibility gap since Richard Nixon." Although entirely apt, that reference is a bit misleading, for it obscures the fact that Bush & Co. have introduced into the politics of the United States a type of lying ultimately un-American in its perversity, deliberateness, and shamelessness. Theirs is not, in other words, the standard hooey of America's elected representatives or those of any other democratic system.

All politicians spin, select, exaggerate, extenuate, make promises they know they'll have to break, etc. Such prevarication is a tiresome but inevitable feature of the democratic process, as people must be brought around, whatever your agenda. While such white lies have often served democracy, the giant black untruths of Bush & Co. bespeak the spirit of quite different forms of government. Bush/Cheney lie like Bolshevist commandos, like Nazi propagandists, or any other power-mad elite whose public statements sound like what the Party tells its members in George Orwell's Oceania.* When it comes to lying, this regime, in short, is off the charts (and, for that matter, in a brave new zone where the word *lying* may in fact be inappropriate, as we shall see).

This regime's definitive lies are not those desperate ad hoc whoppers of the kind that Bush used to disown "the 'Mission Accomplished' sign." He lied that way again when he tried to put a lot of daylight between himself and Enron. "Ken Lay is a supporter," the president told a roomful of reporters on January 10, 2002,

---

*Conservative TV pundit Tucker Carlson was astonished by the brazenness of Karen Hughes' mendacity when she was squiring Governor Bush around the country during the 2000 campaign. "I've obviously been lied to by a lot of campaign operatives, but the striking thing about the way she lied was she knew I knew she was lying, and she did it anyway. There is no word in English that captures that. It almost crosses over from bravado into mental illness." Kerry Laverman, "You burn out fast when you demagogue," *Salon*, 9/13/03, http://www.salon.com/books/feature/2003/09/13/carlson/index_np.html.

and I got to know Ken Lay when he was a head of the—what they call the Governor's Business Council in Texas. He was a supporter of Ann Richards in my run in 1994, and she had named him head of the Governor's Business Council, and I decided to leave him in place, for the sake of continuity. And that's when I first got to know Ken and worked with Ken, and he supported my candidacy for—and—but this is what—what anybody's going to find, if—is that this administration will fully investigate issues such as the Enron bankruptcy to make sure we can learn from the past and make sure that workers are protected.

Bush had in fact known Lay for years, as most of those reporters no doubt knew and as Lay himself had publicly made clear. It had been a "difficult situation" when Dubya "decided to run for the governor's spot," Lay told PBS's *Frontline* in March of 2001.

> I'd worked very closely with Ann Richards also, the four years she was governor. But I was very close to George W. and had a lot of respect for him, had watched him over the years, particularly with reference to dealing with his father when his father was in the White House and some of the things he did to work for his father, and so I did support him.

In 1994, Lay had given candidate Bush $37,500—three times more than the $12,500 that he gave to Governor Richards. Thus was the president's improv a reckless and gratuitous fabrication, bolder even than the constant lies of Richard Nixon, which tended mainly to be stealthier, more trivial fibs.

While they are certainly pure Dubya, such rambling falsehoods are not typical of Bush & Co.'s untruthfulness, which tends to be (as Bush would say) more "disciplined," more "focused": more succinct. The regime generally works its old black magic through flat-out and deliberate contradictions of reality: what Hitler called "big lies." Like any other seasoned body of authoritarian propagandists, Bush/Cheney's troops (including Bush and Cheney) use two very basic tricks to take us in. The more obvious device, and seemingly the more astounding, is the wholly false assertion made as frequently as possible by everyone involved. This is, of course, the "talking point," but always, in Bush/Cheney's case, a blunt *inversion of the facts*, expressed with a convincing self-assurance that suggests *not* conscious lies so much as angry wishful thinking, or mass deception based on *self*-deception. "The larger point is, and the fundamental question is, did Saddam Hussein have a weapons program?" Bush asked rhetorically on July 14, 2003.

> And the answer is, absolutely. *And we gave him a chance to allow the inspectors in, and he wouldn't let them in.* And, therefore, after a reasonable request, we decided to remove him from power, along with other nations, so as to make sure he was not a threat to the United States and our friends and allies in the region. I firmly believe the decisions we made will make America more secure and the world more peaceful (emphasis added).

Although surprising, this invention—rightly noted by *Slate*'s Timothy Noah as the "Whopper of the Week"—was merely Bush's somewhat heightened version of a propaganda line that had been floating all around for over a year, largely unchallenged—indeed, sometimes circulated—by the U.S. press: that, in 1998, the UN weapons inspectors in Iraq had been *thrown out by Saddam Hussein*. In fact, the U.S. government had ordered UNSCOM out of the country so that our military could start Operation Desert Fox, a lavish application of cruise missiles to many sites throughout Iraq, the campaign lasting for four days. At least from June of 2002, that fact was often pointedly denied by Bush & Co.'s public instruments. "And Paul, if you'll remember," said Representative Mike Pence (R-IN) to Paul Begala on *Crossfire* in mid-June of 2003, "I think you were in the Clinton administration in those years when Saddam Hussein threw out the weapons inspectors in 1998 [*sic*]." (Begala did not set him straight.) "And of course," Donald Rumsfeld told the House Armed Services Committee on September 18, 2002, "the country that threw the inspectors out was *not* the United States. It was *not* the United Nations. It was *Iraq* that threw the inspectors out." Later that day, Rumsfeld said the same thing on PBS's *NewsHour with Jim Lehrer*:

> So there clearly is a role in our world for inspections but it tends to be with a cooperat[iv]e partner, and we have seen the situation with

Iraq where they have violated some 16 UN resolutions and finally threw the inspectors out.

Jim Lehrer did not challenge that assertion, which likewise went uncontradicted by the entire White House press corps when Ari Fleischer said it a month later. "Why," asked Helen Thomas on October 15, was the president "sending thousands of soldiers and people to the Persian Gulf, including planes and tanks and carriers and so forth, if he's not planning a war?" "Well," Fleischer answered fragmentarily, "I think if you take a look at the actions of Saddam Hussein, he threw out the weapons inspectors in 1998." Whereas the U.S. press let that one go (perhaps bewildered by its logic), an Arab journalist in Bahrain was more assertive when, on January 24, 2003, Douglas J. Feith, U.S. undersecretary of defense for policy, repeated the canard on al-Jazeera, referring back to "when those inspectors were thrown out back in 1998." "You said Iraq threw the inspectors out in 1998," one of Feith's interviewers objected,

> but I think we all know that UNSCOM chief Mr. Butler summoned them out because the U.S. was preparing for Desert Fox, in December 1998, to strike Iraq. So they left for their own safety, at the request of UNSCOM. I won't go into this, but you can correct me or comment, of course.

> FEITH: You are *mistaken*. You are *mistaken*. The *Iraqis* threw the UNSCOM inspectors out.

On October 13, 2003, Ann Coulter, with a knowing grin, reasserted the now-ancient lie, much to Joe Conason's bemusement. On CNN's *Paula Zahn Now*, she reasoned thus about Saddam Hussein:

> COULTER: He gave up his administration, his life, his sons' lives, all of this because he refused to let the U.N. weapons inspectors come in and show them, "I have no weapons of mass destruction."

> CONASON: Actually, he did let them in. He did let them in.

> COULTER: No.

> CONASON: Yes, he did!

COULTER: That's why we went to war with him!

CONASON: Ann, he let them in!

COULTER: [*Unintelligible*] have them! [*Unintelligible*] did not show them!

CONASON: They can run tape right—they can run tape right now!

The purpose of that Bush/Feith/Rumsfeld/Fleischer/Coulter* line was to revise the past: that is, to "rewrite history," as Bush put it on June 16, 2003 (in a sideswipe at "revisionist historians," by which he meant not his own propaganda team but anyone still harping on the facts of recent history).† Although Bush/Cheney do this often, they are mainly interested in obfuscating what is happening now and/or ill-preparing us for what will happen soon. Certainly this is a venerable tactic in the realm of politics, in the United States and elsewhere; but no American regime has ever used it so consistently or zealously. In his third debate with Al Gore in 2000, Bush had this to say about U.S. foreign policy:

> I just don't think it's the role of the United States to walk into a country and say, "We do it this way, so should you." . . . I think one way for us to end up being viewed as "the ugly American" is for us to go around the world saying, "We do it this way, so should you." Now, we trust freedom. . . .
> I think the United States must be humble and must be proud and confident of our values, but humble in how we treat nations that are figuring out how to chart their own course.

This was, to put it mildly, a deceptive pose, as Bush & Co. was then intent on realizing its proud dream of "global leadership"—i.e., "to maintain American military preeminence, to secure American geopolitical leadership, and to preserve the American peace," as they had put it

---

*The line has been perpetuated not by outright Busheviks alone. In *Plan of Attack*, Bob Woodward seconds it repeatedly. Bob Woodward, *Plan of Attack* (New York: Simon & Schuster, 2004), pp. 39, 182, 245.

†"Now, there are some who would like to rewrite history," he told an enthusiastic audience in New Jersey. "The revisionist historians, is what I like to call them."

in "Rebuilding America's Defenses," their foreign policy vision statement drafted by the Project for the New American Century.

One could, of course, defend the governor's kind-and-gentle act as an
electioneering feint, no more reprehensible than any other candidate's sly
campaign promises. That defense would be less unconvincing if the president did not continue to delude the national audience even after he'd
been hoisted into power, and to do it incessantly. Interviewed by CNN's
Candy Crowley on January 18, 2001, the president-to-be implied that,
on the drug war, he might take a softer line. Noting "the disparity in sentencing for powder cocaine versus crack," and the inordinate number of
black people locked up on drug charges in this country, Crowley asked
if Bush was planning to address "the very real concern and frustration
within the African-American community about that." "If people feel like
our criminal justice system is unfair, then we better look at the reasons
why, the underlying concerns," he answered.

> You mentioned drug-users. One of the things that we have got to
> make sure of in our society is that our drug-prevention programs
> are effective. And I think a lot of people are coming to the realiza-
> tion that maybe long minimum sentences for the first-time users
> may not be the best way to occupy jail space and/or heal people
> from their disease. And I'm willing to look at that.

Bush then hinted that he understood the fears of African-Americans
regarding capital punishment. He first defended his own long support of
the death penalty in Texas: "But I understand," he added. "I can hear the
concerns. And to the extent the law is unfair, then I think we need to
analyze the unfairness." He was interested, he said, in "making sure the
powder-cocaine and the crack-cocaine penalties are the same. I don't
believe we ought to be discriminatory." Surprisingly, he then concluded
on a note that was not punitive but therapeutic.

> But my point to you on the drug use is that one of the things we've
> got to do a better job of in our society is helping people cure them-
> selves of an illness.   .
>   Addiction to alcohol or addiction to drugs is an illness. And we
> haven't not done a very good job [sic], thus far, of curing people
> from that illness. And it's one of the reasons why I believe so

strongly in faith-based programs to help people first change their lives, which would then change their habits.

Maybe Bush's goal here was to try to calm the boiling opposition to John Ashcroft, whom he had named as his attorney general on December 22. (He announced the pick right after formally resigning as the governor of Texas; it was his first official act as president-to-be.) Certainly, throughout his confirmation hearings, which had begun on January 16, Ashcroft pointedly refrained from talking tough about the war on drugs, even taking pains to stress the need for "education, prevention and"—especially—"treatment." ("I think if we don't understand that remediation of that particular problem is a part of this, I think we are kidding ourselves.") Only after he had been confirmed did Ashcroft sound like his old self—and not at all as Bush had sounded in his chat with Candy Crowley: "I want to escalate the war on drugs," he told Larry King excitedly on February 7.

> I want to renew it. I want to refresh it—relaunch it, if you will. We'll enforce the law with vigor and with intensity. We've got to stop this upswing in drug use.

A few months later, Bush further demonstrated his commitment to the therapeutic view by naming John P. Walters as his new "drug czar." A creature of the Heritage Foundation, and protégé of antidrug hardliner (and renowned blackjack enthusiast) William Bennett, Walters was notorious for not believing that "addiction to drugs is an illness." Long perceiving drug use as a sin, the fervent Walters backs retaining the disparity in sentencing for crack and powdered cocaine, jailing more people for marijuana, and spending billions less on "curing people" than on busting them. So antitherapeutic is his ideology, in fact, that even his ferocious predecessor, General Barry McCaffrey, sees him as extreme, as the *Workplace Substance Abuse Advisor* (and hardly any other publications) reported in the wake of his appointment: "According to McCaffrey, Walters has suggested 'there is too much treatment capacity in the United States,' a statement he found 'shocking.' " Walters is especially gung-ho on military partnerships with governments like Colombia's and

Peru's. He has played a major role in Bush & Co.'s post-9/11 drive to make the "war on drugs" an adjunct to the "war on terror"—a reconception that has only meant more funds for hardware and surveillance and that much less for education, prevention, and treatment.*

Thus has Bush & Co. deceived us all along, its public gestures so consistently and carefully devised to contradict the truth that it is difficult to name one that was *not* deceptive. Certainly such suasive artifice was not invented by Karl Rove; Richard Nixon was relentless in his (futile) efforts to project himself as he was not, and Ronald Reagan's team perfected the new science of deceptive visuals—positioning that president as cheerfully outdoorsy, so as to make the viewers think that he liked forests more than lumber companies, or placing him, beer mug in hand, amid a jolly crew of hardhats in a tavern after hours, to foster the impression that his economic policies were really good for average Joes. As cynical as Nixon was, however, and as expertly produced as Reagan was, those two sly dogs were as ingenuous as Joan of Arc, compared to the imagineers in charge today. Michael Deaver, Reagan's brilliant "Vicar of Visuals," has rightly marveled at the ingenuity and boldness of Bush/Cheney's propaganda posse, who have brought the art of mass delusion to a whole new level. (Of course, Deaver words it differently.)

Bush's *Top Gun* moment was, as we have seen, just such a fake-out, concealing the explosive situation in Iraq by claiming grandly, both through his cocky flyboy pose and with that vivid banner, that the "mission" was "accomplished." (The soldiers still stuck in Iraq knew otherwise.) Bush had similarly conned the U.S. audience with his stout self-portrayal as "a patient man," who would "deliberate" and "consult"

---

*Like the occupation of Iraq, this new militarization of the "war on drugs" may well have been anticipated prior to Bush & Co.'s placement in the White House, even though U.S. drug policy did not appear to change dramatically until after 9/11. Walters surely was the man for such a job. In the nineties, he was president of the New Citizenship Project (NCP), an entity well funded by such far-right angels as the Bradley and Olin Foundations, Richard Mellon Scaife's Carthage Foundation, and the Sarah Scaife Foundation. The NCP begat the Project for the New American Century (PNAC), Bush & Co.'s foreign policy think tank. According to the PNAC Web site, "The Project is an initiative of the New Citizenship Project (501c3)" (http://www.newamericancentury.org/aboutpnac.htm).

before taking any military steps against Saddam Hussein. (See pp. 67–68.) And Bush & Co. did likewise, and with immense success throughout the world, by staging that apparent mass insurgency in Baghdad's Firdos Square on April 9, 2003. As represented by the global media, it looked like a spontaneous and jubilant uprising by thousands (tens of thousands?) of Iraqis who appeared to topple that imposing statue of Saddam Hussein and then stomp happily on its face. As glossed by Bush and Rumsfeld, among others, it was a liberatory moment comparable to the collapse of Soviet and European communism; and it sure looked that way if you just watched it on TV or read about it in some mainstream daily or newsmagazine.

And yet, to see what really happened, one had only to glance at CNN's Web site, or the BBC's, which ran a Reuters photograph that told another story. That aerial photo made it clear that there were just a few hundred Iraqis clustered at the pedestal in Firdos Square, while, all around, the lone and level grounds stretched far away without a soul in sight. The square, you could see clearly from above, was right beside the Palestine Hotel, which housed the foreign press, so that the photo op had been delivered to the journalists' very doorstep. Also from above, one could perceive almost as many journalists and U.S. Marines as there were local demonstrators—none of whom, it turned out, was exactly "local": that seeming multitude of everyday Iraqis was in fact the entourage, or private army, of Ahmed Chalabi, the dubious Iraqi exile who had long aspired to run the show after Saddam Hussein. (A favorite of the Pentagon, that "friend" would ultimately be exposed as an agent of Iran.) The Marines had organized the whole faux-revolutionary spectacle. The perimeter had been sealed off with razor wire.

At times, Bush & Co.'s more ambitious lies have been exposed to all Americans, *despite* the U.S. press. The tale of Private First Class Jessica Lynch was one such failed invention. Her seeming story of intrepid heroism under fire (she was badly wounded and went down shooting!), her suffering at the hands of the Iraqis (they tortured her, we think!), and then her sudden liberation by a crack platoon of able U.S. troops (they kicked the doors down, and they got her out of there!) were all recounted by the flacks at the Department of Defense, and then hyped breathlessly, no questions asked, by U.S. journalists, as the media started churning out postmodern variations on the old "captivity narratives" of white women forced to dwell among the Indians. Only after John Kampfner had reported the true story in a documentary for the BBC did that heroic fantasy come into question. Later, Lynch herself confirmed Kampfner's report and also pointedly deplored the propaganda drive that had distorted her ordeal. She had not been wounded, nor had she gone down shooting, but was badly injured when her jeep crashed during an Iraqi ambush (which apparently resulted from incompetent command). "I'm no hero," she told Diane Sawyer, expressing sorrow that her comrade, Private First Class Lori Piestawa, *had* been killed and *had* gone down shooting and yet her sacrifice had gone unsung.* Moreover, Lynch had not been harmed by the Iraqi doctors who took care of her, and who at one point even tried to take her back to the Americans. (They had to turn and flee when U.S. soldiers opened fire on the approaching ambulance.) The Iraqi soldiers having long since left the hospital, there was no need for Lynch's rescuers to play the mission like an episode of *S.W.A.T.* They could have walked right in and brought Lynch out with them; but then the U.S. military's video of the event, released at once to all the U.S. networks, would have been a lot less cool.

Most of Bush & Co.'s official fantasies are not thus thoroughly refuted, or even lightly questioned by U.S. reporters, and so are left to resonate within most hearts and minds, driving home the wrong impression. So it was with Bush's many firm denials of the truth about his tax cuts, which in fact *were* only for the rich, benefiting no taxpayers of modest means, and which could *not* help strengthen this wartime economy, but surely will calamitously weaken it if they are not repealed. (The

---

*This inequity had everything to do with race: Lynch, blonde and blue-eyed, looked the part of the fair maiden taken prisoner by a bunch of dusky savages. Piestawa, being Native American, would have been iconologically unsuitable.

This was true also of Shoshana Johnson, another of Lynch's comrades, and an African-American. Johnson too was taken prisoner on that day and also went down shooting, but for her there was no hoopla in the news or afterward. Although shot in both ankles, the army moved to give her only 30 percent of her disability pay, while giving Lynch 80 percent of hers. "Jessica Backs POW Pal; Woman Shown on Iraq TV Will Get Less Disability Pay," *Daily News* (N.Y.), 10/25/03.

mainstream voices making these sound counterarguments were very few, *New York Times* columnist Paul Krugman standing out heroically among them.)

Bush & Co. has managed to suggest that it has cracked down really hard on corporate crime, when it has actually done nothing to prevent its happening again, or even from recurring *now*; nor have most perpetrators felt the lash of proper punishment. Very showily—out on the street—the FBI handcuffed John Rigas, the founder of Adelphia Communications, and his two sons, as TV cameras caught the scene for national propagation.* The arrest of ImClone's former CEO Sam Waksal was also pretty rough, as was the treatment of his good friend Martha Stewart, inside trader (and big donor to Democrats). While such stray images have surely served to reinforce the *claim* that Bush & Co. is tough on corporate crime, the status quo is quite unchanged—and the very worst perpetrators, being close to Bush & Co., have paid no price at all. On Common Dreams News Center, Glenn Scherer asks why "the biggest corporate swindler in U.S. history, Kenneth Lay, the CEO of Enron who deprived his own employees of millions in retirement savings, has not been charged with any crime, remains untried, unfined, and unjailed?" (The U.S. press has not asked that good question, nor have the Enron-tainted Democrats, and so Bush & Co. is not obliged to answer it.)

However dangerous, such flagrant contradictions of the truth are somewhat less insidious than Bush & Co.'s other basic propaganda trick, which is to contradict reality more subtly, by crafting *epithets* that are themselves negations of the truth. This regime is especially given to attaching such Orwellian names to heinous strokes of legislation and lawless military actions, so as to make the bills seem harmless and the wars entirely just. In February of 2002, Bush announced his new "Clean Skies Initiative," along with his "Global Climate Change Initiative," both of which were meant to *weaken* the Clean Air Act while taking *no* "initiative" to combat global warming. "Clean Skies," noted Friends of

---

*Although generous in his philanthropy, Rigas was a modest donor to the GOP and had given small amounts to the McCain *and* Bush campaigns.

the Earth, "trades real health protections now for hypothetical gains later," by setting standards *lower* than those mandated by existing law; by letting industry *delay* pollution reductions by up to a decade longer than the Clean Air Act permits; and by *ignoring* the effect of carbon dioxide emissions. Thus "clean" means "dirty," whether it refers to sky or air. In August of 2003 Bush unveiled "Healthy Forests" ("an initiative for wildfire prevention and stronger communities"), which, despite its leafy name, is meant to turn the nation's woodlands over to the lumber companies. According to Defenders of Wildlife, HR 1904, the bill advertised by the "Healthy Forests Initiative," is part of "a near-total overhaul of the national forest regulatory and policy system as the administration rewrites practically every important forest policy on the books. A major focus of this administrative overhaul is the elimination of safeguards and procedures designed to sustain environmental values and ensure an effective role for the public in public forest management." Thus "healthy forests" means tree stumps, hotter climate, toxic runoff, vanished species.

On November 1, 2001, Bush signed Executive Order 13233. The purpose of this order was to gut the Presidential Records Act of 1978, a post-Watergate reform mandating that presidential papers be made public expeditiously, once the chief executive is out of office. This order allowed Bush to *seal* all presidential papers from 1980 on. The order's title: "Further Implementation of the Presidential Records Act." On October 29, 2002, Bush signed HR 3295, mandating the elimination of all paper balloting in the United States and its eventual replacement by touch-screen computer voting. (See p. 276–77.) The "Help America Vote Act" would be better named the "Help America Vote Republican Act," since its aim is to ensure that Democratic votes can never add up to a victory. When the White House and/or Congress move to "strengthen," "save," or "improve" Social Security, or Medicare, or Head Start, or any other federal social program, it means that they intend either to scale the program back or to abolish it. Such euphemism makes protest less likely, as no one who believes in, say, Head Start could possibly object to any plan to "strengthen" it. And protest is especially unfeasible if e-mail is your medium of choice. In the summer of 2003, Bush/Cheney made it harder to get through to them that way. "Under a system deployed on the White House Web site for the first time last week," reported John Markoff of the *New York Times* on July 18, "those who want to send a message to President Bush must now navigate as many as nine Web pages and fill out a detailed form that starts by asking whether the message sender supports White House policy or differs with it." "Over all, it's a very cumbersome process," commented Jakob Neilsen, a California Web consultant. "It's probably designed deliberately to cut down on their e-mail." According to White House spokesman Jimmy Orr, the system is considered an "enhancement."

Thus the president would feel at home in Orwell's Oceania, where they say that "war is peace," as Bush also has said, albeit less concisely: "I just want you to know," he said in Washington in June of 2002, "that when we talk about war, we're really talking about peace." And, just as in *1984*, Bush & Co.'s euphemisms are especially sinister when they invoke the ideals of progressive humanism and turn them inside out. "Operation Iraqi Freedom" is an odd name for a war of occupation,* entailing national disenfranchisement, thousands thrown in prison on no charges, routine torture, U.S. appropriation of Iraqi assets, and the suppression of dissenting journalism. In Senegal, Bush tours the Slave House on Goree Island and afterward salutes the Africans' "belief in freedom," while the whole local population is "penned up like sheep," for his security. And when Bush speaks of "democracy," it sounds just as convincing as it once did in the German Democratic Republic: this president has been installed against the will of the electorate; his party has seized control of both the government and the national media; and his police are free to track his party's adversaries, crush all public demonstrations of dissent, and lock up anyone whom he might see as somehow dangerous to "national security."

And yet, despite all this, it is not Bush but *Clinton* who has been stigmatized as the most lying president we've ever had—a bigger liar than

---

*The operation was originally named "Operation Iraqi Liberation," until some observant planner noticed that that title makes for a subversive acronym.

LBJ, an even bigger liar than Nixon, and, it goes without saying, a bigger liar than Reagan and George Bush the Elder put together. On this myth of Clinton as the Father of Lies—as on his other mythic sins—the ultraright is in complete agreement with the rightists who are closer to what used to be the center, and on the subject of Clintonian prevarication, those self-described "conservatives" have often sounded like extremist nuts. For it is not *just* "Slick Willie"—or "Clinton the Liar and Deciever [*sic*]" (as the group Citizens for Netanyahu puts it), or the "lying, Jew-collaborating traitor that Bill Clinton is" (as neo-Nazi William Pierce once put it), or Clinton "the pathological liar" (as Christopher Hitchens has put it repeatedly)—who figures as an arch-falsifier in their minds. Rather, they are thus repelled by *all* who share his alien creed, who come from his detested clan. "We have a President who has a problem: he lies when he doesn't really have to," wrote William Safire in the *New York Times*. It was not just that president who had this problem. His closest comrade had it too, as Safire noted often: "Americans of all political persuasions are coming to the sad realization that our First Lady—a woman of undoubted talents who was a role model for many in her generation—is a congenital liar." Such were the mendacious, ever-shifting would-be King and Queen of the United States, the spiritual parents of "those lying Democrats."

So well established was the Clinton-as-Satanic-liar line that it was easy to extend it to Al Gore throughout the presidential contest in 2000. Building both on Clinton's legendary dishonesty and on Gore's apparent history of little fibs, Bush's propaganda team cast Gore as a compulsive fabulist as well as stiff and haughty. "This is a man who has difficulty telling the truth," said Karl Rove on NBC's *Meet the Press* on October 8, 2000. "He constantly exaggerates and embellishes." "The vice president has consistently and repeatedly made up things, exaggerated, embellished facts. And that's a warning sign," said Karen Hughes on *Fox News Sunday* that same day. ("Now, unlike Al Gore, Gov. Bush doesn't just make up facts," she added.) The anti-Clinton brigadiers all went for it: "The guy can't tell the truth!" yelled David Bossie, coauthor of *Slick Willie: Why America Cannot Trust Bill Clinton*, on Fox the following day. "He doesn't exaggerate, he *lies!*" (Bossie was discredited two years before, for the extensive doctoring of transcripts that he then tendered as evidence to the House Government and Reform Committee, chaired by Dan Burton.) "More than anything," claimed Rupert Murdoch's *New York Post*, "Al Gore's campaign has been about lies. He's the serial exaggerator, the political Pinocchio, the frequent fibber, the king of the whoppers."

That view was merely bolstered by the coverage of the "controversy," which echoed all the accusations without scrutinizing any of them. "There are a lot of people with significant doubts that Gore is a trustworthy figure," said CNN's William Schneider, while *Newsweek* did a cover story on Gore's alleged "fib factor." Such "neutral" punditry was hard to tell from outright propaganda. "Why does Al Gore do it? Why does he exaggerate and embellish his stories—and his resumé—when he really doesn't have to?" asked Cokie and Steven Roberts, sounding just like William Safire.

> Gore is not in Clinton's class when it comes to prevarication. No finger-wagging denials of sex with interns. But his fibs are magnified because they remind folks of Clinton at his worst. As Ronald Reagan might say, "There they go again."

Outside the mainstream, meanwhile, some meticulous observers—most notably Bob Somerby, through his sharp Web site *The Daily Howler*—were demonstrating that the myth of Gore as "serial exaggerator" was itself a series of exaggerations or inventions. Gore's notorious "fibs" turned out to be either true, or harmless errors, or, more often, instances of gleeful misreporting by the press. Gore never said that he'd invented the Internet, or that he'd discovered the toxic waste dump at Love Canal, nor did he "make up" the "story" of how much his mother paid for her arthritis medicine, or hype his military record, or make any other of those weird "delusional" remarks that were imputed to him by the GOP, the *New York Times*, and David Letterman, among many others. (According to Erich Segal, furthermore, Gore *was* a model for *Love Story*'s central character.)

Bush, meanwhile, was keeping mum about his checkered military

service, hedging on his prior use of drugs, dissembling on the SEC investigation, and frequently suppressing or misstating facts about his record
as the governor of Texas. And yet it was Gore, always Gore, whom the
reporters kept on charging with mendacity, their take identical to the
Republicans', and therefore finally serving no one but the most fanatical
and bigoted Bush partisans, like the author of this fervent posting on
freerepublic.com:

> I am so stunned that people would vote for this chronic liar. How
> can anyone want to be associated with the Democrats and be rep-
> resented by the likes of, not just Algore [*sic*] & the Lying Clintons,
> but Al Sharpton, Jesse Jerkson [*sic*], Maxine Waters, Henry Wax-
> man, Major Owens, etc. Such obvious liars & hippocrits [*sic*].

For his part, Clinton too was, as a speaker, much more honest than
the man who ran as his antithesis. The myth of Clinton's devilish lying
had far more to do with the mentality of those attacking him than with
the actual history of his remarks. That Clinton could be glib there is no
doubt, and with the charge that he lied baldly to the public about Monica Lewinsky there can be no argument, but that he somehow lied more
ably or compulsively than any other politician is itself a paranoid delusion, or a lie, intended to define his strengths—great charm and keen
intelligence—as signs of evil.

The fierce distrust of Clinton felt and propagated by his rightist
adversaries is a bit mysterious, in part because when Clinton did fake
people out, they usually were people on the left, for whom he tended to
reserve his wildest campaign promises—not proof of an extraordinary
immorality, but just a function of the fact that Clinton was a centrist
Democrat who ran, at first, as more progressive than he was.

To this assessment, naturally, a lot of people would assert that Clinton was a perjurer—the only perjurer who ever occupied the Oval
Office, as only he, of all our presidents, *lied under oath*. Those who
would make that argument would surely also point out that while Bush
may tell some lies from time to time, or even if he tells lies every day, he
has *not* done it under oath, and so is *not*, at least, a perjurer, like Clinton. No doubt it will come as a surprise to such defenders of this presi-

dent that he also has committed perjury—has, indeed, committed it more clearly than his predecessor did. For Clinton's testimony under oath, while certainly not honest, was still not necessarily perjurious in the strict legal sense. The point is literally academic, as legal scholars have been arguing about it since Charles Ruff, the president's attorney, seemed to blow the case to smithereens at the impeachment hearings. By contrast, Bush's crime appears to have been more obvious than Clinton's. It was also far more consequential, pertaining not to a consensual love affair but to an apparent case of corporate criminality that injured hundreds, maybe thousands, of bereaved consumers.

Funeralgate

In early 1998, Eliza May, then chief regulator for the Texas Funeral Services Commission (TFSC), received complaints about two funeral parlors owned by Service Corporation International (SCI), the world's largest mortuary company, headquartered in Houston. Corpses, May was told, had been improperly embalmed by junior staffers not yet licensed, with macabre results. Laid out in an open casket at the funeral, one man's body had been pumped so heavily with embalming fluid that the goo was dribbling from his eyes and nose and mouth, traumatizing the man's younger brother. Another unhappy customer, Gayle Johnson, mother of a well-liked TV newscaster in Wichita Falls, reported that when she went to mourn at the mausoleum where his body lay, "it was infested with gnats," as *Newsweek*'s Michael Isikoff wrote later, "and a malodorous maroon-colored fluid oozed out of her son's crypt." In March, on the basis of such information, May denied licenses to a number of SCI-owned properties. For this she was castigated by the head of the commission *and* by SCI's lawyer, Johnnie B. Rogers. To strengthen her case, she issued subpoenas for fifteen months' worth of documents from SCI. A week later, Rogers told her that his client would not comply, and the next day, Joshua Kimball, a provisional licensee employed at one of the contested sites, called up the offices of the commission and said, "I'm going to kill all of you."

May filed a police report, then sent a team of inspectors, armed with subpoenas, to inspect two SCI sites unannounced. This outraged the corporation's CEO, Robert Waltrip, who called and threatened to have the TFSC abolished by the Texas legislature. He then wrote Governor Bush a letter denouncing the inspectors' "storm-trooper" tactics and demanding that the state's investigation stop at once. With Rogers at his side, Waltrip walked the letter over to the office of the governor. There he was met by Bush's chief of staff, Joe Allbaugh, who had the two men come into his office for a chat.

According to May's lawsuit, and, later, Rogers himself, Bush poked his head into the office, saw Waltrip, and asked him, "Hey Bobby, are those people still messing with you?" When Waltrip said they were, Bush, Rogers claims, then turned to him and asked, "Hey, Johnnie B! Are you taking care of him?" Johnnie B. said he was doing his best, and Bush popped out again.

The governor's concern was understandable, as Waltrip was a generous client from way back. He had donated $100,000 for construction of the elder Bush's presidential library and would later invite that Bush to address a big convention of funeral associations, for an honorarium of $70,000. He had contributed $10,000 to the younger Bush's first run for governor, and SCI's political action committee contributed another $70,000 for the governor's second run. Waltrip had also put the corporate jet at Bush I's disposal and provided him with other plush amenities. Such largesse was an easy matter for him. With funeral homes and crematoria on five continents, SCI pulls in $2.5 billion per annum. (It is said to bury one in nine Americans.) And the money for such gifts was certainly well spent, considering the gruesome quality of Waltrip's product, which would not have made him quite so rich, perhaps, if it were not so shoddy.

After the confab in Allbaugh's office, Bush's apparat began to lean on May explicitly. That week three senior Bush aides pressured her by phone. In May, Allbaugh summoned her into his office, refusing to allow a court reporter to come with her, and browbeat her in front of Waltrip; Senator John Whitmire, who represents Waltrip's home district; and Bush's general counsel, Margaret Wilson. According to May, "the meeting ended with Allbaugh, in a hostile and peremptory tone, demanding that TFSC's staff deliver to him by 1:00 P.M. that afternoon a letter stating exactly what documents TFSC required to close the investigation." As threatening as Allbaugh was (his self-imposed nickname was "the Enforcer"), May did not give in. That summer the commission fined SCI $450,000 for its illegal practices. May was once more summoned to see Allbaugh, this time by herself. (He would not let her bring a colleague in with her.) "Allbaugh," she attests, "simply demanded more information about the status of the SCI investigation and finally announced, 'This isn't going anywhere.' "

SCI did not pay the fine. In the fall of 1998, the governor discussed the situation briefly with Charles "Dick" McNeil, then chair of the TFSC (and a Bush appointee). In a later deposition, McNeil testified that Bush had asked him, "Have you got—you and Bob Waltrip—are you and Mr. Waltrip got your problems worked out [sic]?" McNeil said that they were still working on it, and hoped that the commission had not caused Bush any "embarrassment." Bush assured him that McNeil was no embarrassment, and then said, "Do your job."

May was fired on February 8, 1999. On March 23, she filed suit against the TFSC, SCI, and Waltrip. Although Bush was not named in the litigation, May wanted to depose him. On July 20, in order to prevent a deposition, Bush swore as follows in an affidavit:

> I have had no conversations with Texas Funeral Services Commission officials, agents or representatives concerning the investigation of SCI by the Texas Funeral Services Commission or any dispute arising from it. I have had no conversations with SCI officials, agents, or representatives concerning the investigation or any dispute arising from it. I have no personal knowledge of relevant facts of the investigation nor do I have any personal knowledge of relevant facts concerning any dispute arising from this investigation. I have never asked anyone to take a role or to become involved in any way in this investigation or any dispute arising from it or given direction to anyone who might be involved in the SCI investigation or dispute.

That sworn affidavit was entirely false. In response, May's lawyers called the court's attention to the exposé by *Newsweek's* Michael Isikoff, who had key figures in the controversy, on the record, contradicting Bush's claim, as well as other evidence that Bush's affidavit was perjurious. The case dragged on as Bush & Co. stonewalled for the next few years; and it went wholly unreported all throughout the presidential race, aside from Isikoff's article and a few brief pieces in the Texas press. Despite its relevance to Bush's pose as Clinton's opposite (and the heroic efforts of a researcher named Roses Prichard, who struggled ceaselessly to get the U.S. press to pay attention), the story never did appear, and never has appeared, while Bush continues both to service his big donors at the citizens' expense and to lie about it.

Scofflaw

From the start, "Clinton" was a man of devilish indifference to the law, despite his fancy LLD from Yale. "A president cannot operate by the lax ethical standards customary to Arkansas politics," wrote Floyd G. Brown in *Slick Willie*. "As president, Bill Clinton cannot continue the kind of behavior that characterized his Arkansas governorship." The charge of lawlessness persisted all throughout the GOP's failed efforts to confirm it. It always was, and still is now, catnip, or a shot of moonshine, to the ultraright. "To put it plainly," said Charley Reese in August 1998, the prolific columnist* rousing an assembly of his comrades, "Bill Clinton is a sociopath, a liar, a sexual predator, a man with recklessly bad judgment—and a *scofflaw*!" That line got plenty of applause. Campaigning for president in April of 2000, Alan Keyes elaborated on the theme of Clinton's lawlessness. His topic was the late rescue of Elian Gonzalez. "They were, in fact, committing a lawless act in the lawless style of this lawless administration!" Keyes shouted.

> They were, once again, showing their willingness, not just to do the bidding of Bill Clinton's communist masters, but now to do it in

---

*Reese, for many years a syndicated columnist for the *Orlando Sentinel*, became a freelancer in 2001. His many articles include "Choose the Right Gun," "Disregard Laws That Violate Conscience," and "Are You Confederate but Don't Know It?"

their communist style! I saw again what I had seen when this administration began. Then it was a lawless abuse of force that pointlessly took even innocent human lives at Waco. Now, it is a pointless abuse of force that ignores the requirements of the human heart in Miami. But, it is the same!

Like the right, the U.S. press maintained that marginal view beyond the Clinton years and even into Bush's reign. "Bill Clinton, in some ways, is a lawless human being," Hugh Sidey said to Larry King on February 8, 2001.

He has done it in his personal ways. He has this elegant facility to talk about major social issues. And it is good. Let me tell you, he is right. And then in his personal life, he violates all the rules. Now, you—as somebody said, we need a psychiatrist for this.

Thus spake Sidey—just a few weeks after Bush & Co. had frankly seized the Oval Office, thereby initiating a regime that would turn out to be the most unlawful in this nation's history. On his wildest day, the "lawless" Clinton could not hold a candle to the outlaws now in charge. A summary is in order, not merely to refresh our memories but, still more important, to stress the ruling party's un-American extremism. Certainly it is old news; and yet it never was sufficiently reported and can never be reemphasized enough:

Against the will of the majority, Bush was made our president through an immense infringement of the nation's laws: the illegal disenfranchisement in Florida of over 90,000 citizens, primarily African-Americans and Democrats; polls in largely Democratic precincts ill-equipped and understaffed, or closed or moved elsewhere on Election Day, with voters—mostly African-American and Democrats—often intimidated by police (and not only in Florida); and on that night, the race deliberately miscalled in Bush's favor by John Ellis—one of Bush's cousins and the man in charge of the decision desk at Fox, the first news outlet to cast Al Gore as the likely loser; NBC's quick seconding of that disinformation, at the personal insistence of Jack Welch, then CEO of General Electric, the network's parent company—and, as things turned out, a major beneficiary of the Bush regime. (Welch's rare appearance in the

202

Mark Crispin Miller

studio, and his pro-Bush agitation there, were caught on tape, and yet the network simply blew off a congressional subpoena for the visuals.)

For the next thirty-six days, the GOP struggled unrelentingly to seize authority, and in so doing routinely broke the law. On Wednesday, November 22, a "mob" of wrathful partisans, shouting threats and swinging punches, forced its way into Clark Center in Miami, halting the court-ordered recount of the votes cast throughout Miami-Dade County (a Democratic stronghold). The recount never started up again, so shaken were the staff by that efficient burst of violence—for which no one was prosecuted, even though the perpetrators were all recognizable as staffers to congressional Republicans in Washington. (The Bush campaign saluted them and several hundred other party activists the following day, with a nice Thanksgiving dinner in a hotel ballroom in Ft. Lauderdale. Both Bush and Cheney personally thanked the rioters by telephone, and then Wayne Newton wowed them by performing his Teutonic Golden Oldie, *Danke Schoen*.)* Each day, meanwhile, another, larger mob would gather on the street outside the vice presidential mansion and chant "Get out of Cheney's house!" That action too was orchestrated by the party; Doro Bush, the governor's sister, liked to sneak into the crowd and shout along. As the Gore family was still living there, it

---

*The rightist commentariate winked at that action—or extolled it: "a bourgeois riot," Paul Gigot called it with approval, as if it had been a spontaneous and wholly righteous protest by the local tax-paying community, and not an orchestrated act of thuggery committed by a party goon squad.

While hailing that obstructive violence, whose purpose was to stop the recount, Bush/Cheney's propagandists vilified the peaceful demonstration led by Jesse Jackson Jr., whose purpose was to get the recount going again, as ordered by the Supreme Court of Florida. On *Imus in the Morning*, Mary Matalin referred to Jackson's fellow marchers—who were mostly black—as "rent-a-rioters." "The way we're covering it is an outrage," she complained in an interview with the *Washington Post*. "We're fomenting turbulence. It's awful." Meanwhile, she had only praise for those (white) rioters whose "turbulence" had stopped the recount in Miami. Howard Kurtz, "On the Airwaves, Election Aftermath Is All Talk, All the Time," *Washington Post*, 11/11/00.

(Aside from Howard Kurtz's article, which also ran in a newspaper in New Jersey, the only journalists who mentioned Matalin's racist crack were Mary C. Curtis and Joe Conason, in op-ed pieces for, respectively, the *Charlotte Observer* and the *New York Observer*.)

was a harrowing experience for them—as Al and Tipper Gore explained to Barbara Walters on a special episode of ABC's *20/20*. The part about the mob outside their house, however, was censored by the network, which put it out on its Web site instead. (For a transcript of that exchange, see Appendix.)

On the same day as the "riot" in Miami, Representative Steve Buyer, Republican of Indiana, used his status as a member of the House Armed Services Committee to ask the Pentagon to rush him contact information for those Florida servicemen whose absentee ballots had been disqualified because of various flaws. Buyer, a veteran of the 1998 impeachment effort, then hooked those soldiers up with U.S. journalists, who duly amplified the myth that Gore's campaign was disenfranchising "our troops." That move was but one part of the Bush/Cheney propaganda drive to pressure Florida election officials to accept, as the *New York Times* eventually (and only once) reported, "ballots without postmarks, ballots postmarked after the election, ballots without witness signatures, ballots mailed from towns and cities within the United States and even ballots from voters who voted twice. All would have been disqualified had the state's election laws been strictly enforced." In its study of the 2,490 Florida ballots cast successfully by U.S. citizens abroad, the *Times* discovered 680 "questionable votes"—in itself enough to have made the difference for Al Gore, who "lost" by an official margin of 537.

Wrong though they were, however, all such misdeeds are less troubling than the great judicial travesty that *stopped the vote count* so that Bush could be alleged to have prevailed. The U.S. Supreme Court should not even have heard the case, as Bush, not being a Florida voter, had no standing to present it, and there were no statutory grounds for his petition. Bush's legal team invoked the Fourteenth Amendment's equal protection clause, to argue that the recount of the votes in Florida would somehow do Bush "irreparable harm," which evidently meant that he would lose if the people had turned out to vote against him. (That complaint allegedly bore some relation to the fact that there was no statewide standard for the tabulation of the vote in Florida— although there is no single standard of that sort in many states.) In other words, the clause that Congress passed, in 1868, to certify the civil rights

of the emancipated slaves, was invoked now by a *candidate* petitioning to
keep the people's choice *suppressed*—a "victory" whereby five members of
the Supreme Court replaced, with their own small consensus, the ballots
cast by roughly fifty million of their fellow citizens.

Thus was the Bush administration put in place through a collective
crime unprecedented in American judicial history, for in torturing our
nation's laws to serve their party's interests, and otherwise to suit their
own convenience, the Rehnquist Five serenely broke the oath of office
that each had taken just before admission to the highest bench in all
the land:

> I, _____, do solemnly swear (or affirm) that I will
> administer justice without respect to persons, and that I will faith-
> fully and impartially discharge and perform all the duties incum-
> bent upon me as a justice of the United States Supreme Court
> under the Constitution and laws of the United States. So help me
> God. (U.S. Code, Section 453, Title 28)

Having violated that essential oath, the court's rightist partisans were
guilty of a crime far worse than perjury*—a felony so great, in fact, that
the authors of the code apparently could not imagine it, as no penalty
is stipulated there for breach of that crucial vow. Certainly the gravity
of such a wrong cannot be overstated: that our leading jurists would
despise, and take advantage of, the very law that we entrust them to
interpret to the nation. Although it is anomalous, however, that betrayal
must now be recognized for what it really was, as Vincent Bugliosi has
made clear:

> While the conduct of the five conservative [*sic*] Justices doesn't fall
> within the strict language of treason, the essence of treason, clearly,
> is an American citizen (which each of the Justices is) doing grave

---

*Clarence Thomas seems to have perjured himself before the Senate Judiciary
Committee at his tumultuous confirmation hearing. As Jane Mayer and Jill Abram-
son reveal in their investigative classic, *Strange Justice*, and as David Brock, formerly a
spirited pro-Thomas propagandist, confirms in *Blinded by the Right*, Thomas's cate-
gorical denials of Hill's charges, as well as certain other of his claims, were false.

and unjustifiable damage to this nation, which the Justices surely
did by stealing the office of the presidency for the candidate of
their choice. How much of a distinction is there between helping
an enemy hurt us, and hurting us yourself, whether at peace or war?

Thus the Bush regime was illegitimate at birth. The court's crime was
indeed a doozy, and yet our estimation of it should not blind us to the
many other crimes committed by Bush/Cheney, even from the start of
their campaign. The very ticket was unconstitutional: "The Electors
shall meet in their respective states," begins the Twelfth Amendment,
"and vote by ballot for President and Vice-President, *one of whom, at
least, shall not be an inhabitant of the same state with themselves*" (emphasis added). When he stood up as Bush's running mate, Cheney was a fellow Texan to George W. Bush, having lived in Dallas County for eight
years: voted there, got his driver's license there, registered his autos there,
and paid his taxes there. And yet he hurried up to Jackson Hole to reg-
ister as a Wyoming voter on July 21, 2000—three days before he joined
the ticket. "It was a transparent attempt to evade the Constitution,"
noted David Prindle, professor of government at the University of Texas.
(Prindle was thus quoted in the school's own daily paper.)

If Cheney really did live in Wyoming (he kept a mountain cabin
there), then he had committed fraud against the state of Texas. On his
$1.6 million mansion on Euclid Avenue in Highland Park, he had been
granted a residential homestead exemption of $347,654. "As every Texas
homeowner knows," attorney Robert Dennis noted on Tompaine.com,
"a homestead exemption is only granted on a property 'occupied as his
[or her] principal place of residence.' " If Cheney's candidacy did not
violate the Twelfth Amendment, then he had certainly ripped off the taxpayers of Texas, and yet he was allowed to run *and* keep the money:
Judge Sidney Fitzwater, a Reagan appointee to the Circuit Court in
Texas's Northern District, found that Cheney *did* live in Wyoming,
mainly on the grounds that Cheney said he did.* (The judge did not

---

*It is pertinent that Fitzwater's nomination had been challenged by Democrats in
Congress, because of reports that, as a Texas magistrate, he had tried to keep black
Texans from the polls.

address the fraudulent exemption.) And so that crime slipped down the memory hole, as the media—which barely mentioned Cheney's problem in the first place—dropped the subject for all time, leaving only a few thousand angry citizens to pursue the matter further, to no end, through litigation. (Ultimately, the Supreme Court refused to hear the case.)

That past was prologue. To do justice (so to speak) to Bush & Co.'s crimes would take another volume. Suffice it to say here that they are not peccadilloes but offenses grave enough to merit at least impeachment, and not just of Bush alone. Ignoring the courts' orders—four, at last count—to release the pertinent documents concerning Bush & Co.'s energy policy, stonewalling the inquiry into 9/11, launching a preemptive war with bogus evidence (and profiteering from that war), flouting the Presidential Records Act of 1978, trashing the Clean Air Act, and violating the Intelligence Agents Identification Act of 1982—a deed that clearly threatened national security—are all high crimes, in no way comparable to a consensual fling. And yet there are still millions of Americans, members of the press among them, who persist in seeing *Clinton* as a "lawless" president, and Bush as basically upright. No doubt Bush himself sees Clinton as a "lawless" individual—and so he must, or be confronted by the fact of his own lawlessness.

The Big Picture

Bush's pose as Clinton's opposite, in other words, was finally not so much a conscious propaganda tactic as a psychological imperative—just as it always is in hate-based propaganda movements, which draw their all-important energy from the feverish internal efforts of their leaders and their followers alike to extirpate the Other *in themselves*. This is not to say, however, that such movements are not also calculating. Propaganda must be organized and soberly administered; if it breaks down into mere screams of rage, its triumphs will be brief and its appeal restricted only to the weird folk on the margins. It takes a certain discipline to craft the most effectual projective shots, which serve not just to stigmatize the Other but to obscure the aims, and obfuscate the character, of the attacker(s). "The propagandist will not accuse the enemy of just any misdeed; he will accuse him of the very intention that he him-self has and of trying to commit the crime that he himself is about to commit," writes ethicist and theologian Jacques Ellul.

> He who wants to provoke a war will not only proclaim his own peaceful intentions but also accuses the other party of provocation. He who uses concentration camps accuses his neighbor of doing so. He who intends to establish a dictatorship always insists that his adversaries are bent on dictatorship.

He continues, "The accusation aimed at the other's intention clearly reveals the intention of the accuser. But the public cannot see this because the revelation is interwoven with facts."

Ellul describes a rational process of deception, or distraction, pertaining mainly to the *actions* that the propagandist's own team secretly intends. We might extend Ellul's conception to the realm of "character," as the propagandist—especially in the culture of TV—will also loudly charge the enemy with *being* what the propagandist, or his leader, is him-self, behind closed doors. Here is a fail-safe way to hide out in plain sight, as he who makes the accusation *first* always appears as somehow purged of all the nasty vices or shortcomings that he rails at in his adversary, even if his own defects are infinitely worse. As represented to the public by the Bush campaign, *Al Gore* was the fancy-pants elitist ("Prince Albert," who grew up in a Washington hotel and went to *Harvard*), which caricature served perfectly to kill all thought of Bush's vastly greater privilege (Prince George grew up summering in Kennebunkport and wintering in Hobe Sound, and went to Yale *and* Harvard). Likewise, the biggest liars in the campaign tagged *Gore* as the biggest liar in the campaign; the biggest spenders in the race called *Gore* the biggest spender in the race ("This man has outspent me!" Bush falsely com-plained); and *Gore* was charged with trying to steal the race by those who had already planned to steal the race, and who were stealing it, and who then, having stolen it, charged *Gore* with having tried to steal it.

Here, it seems, were quite clear instances of Bush's propagandists con-sciously deploying the exquisitely disorienting tactic noted by Ellul—although it really is not clear to what extent Bush/Cheney were engaged in a deliberate ruse, as opposed to merely lashing out at their projection of their own elitism and dishonesty. Certainly Bush/Cheney knew that their campaign was wealthier than Gore's, and knew that they were acting in the interests of the very rich. But did they also *see themselves* as liars? This is in fact the central ambiguity of all hate-propaganda drives, whose most committed people are at once fanatical and opportunistic, true believers and detached manipulators, seeing through, yet also still believing in, the tricks they use to take the masses with them. Such is "doublethink," to use the coinage analyzed so cogently by George Orwell in *1984*. It takes us well beyond the sphere of simple lies or ideology, and out into the twilight region of pathology, where all hate propagandists partly dwell, and where many operate full-time.

CHAPTER 5

They Have Met the Enemy

Mirror, Mirror

On May 26, 1792, the bold New Yorker Alexander Hamilton, secretary of the treasury, fired off a long and heated letter to Edward Carrington, who had lately been appointed U.S. marshal for Virginia. Deeming Carrington a likely ally in the South, Hamilton made a damning case against his leading adversaries in the government: James Madison, the highly influential figure in the House of Representatives, and, especially, Thomas Jefferson, secretary of state. Those two Virginians were in stealthy league against him, Hamilton complained, their motivation at once meanly personal and dangerously political: "Mr. Madison, cooperating with Mr. Jefferson, is at the head of a faction decidedly hostile to me and my administration; and actuated by views, in my judgment, subversive of the principles of good government and dangerous to the Union, peace, and happiness of the country."

Between the secretaries—President Washington's top men—there had been some trouble over jurisdiction. Hamilton had strayed into the diplomatic province of his colleague, undercutting Jefferson's negotiations with the British (who benefited from such interference, as Hamilton was secretly a British agent, code-named "No. 7" back at Westminster). That turf war was no petty conflict, but the unrecognized result of a profound and, ultimately, fatal ideological divide between a

New Yorker and a Virginian.* The Northerner, intent on building up the
young republic's credit and on generating a great flow of liquid capital
through the creation of a national bank, envisioned the United States as
a commercial powerhouse sustained by manufacturers and investors, and
thereby growing into an empire. The Southerner regarded such a plan as
deeply threatening to the interests of the nation's agricultural foundation
and, more generally, inimical to the agrarian ideal of a republic uncor-
rupted by financial schemes, unblemished by enormous cities, but
mainly populated, and intelligently ruled, by yeoman farmers. That
essential disagreement soon brought party politics into the U.S. government and—variously complicated by concerns about the franchise,
America's economic bifurcation, and the archaic curse of slavery—ultimately pushed the nation into civil war.

That there were genuine disagreements between Hamilton and Jefferson does not, however, quite explain the scope, duration, or ferocity of
Hamilton's attacks. The letter to Carrington was his first shot against his
seeming enemies, devised to move the South to back his cause and block
the eminent republicans. The letter also was an outline of the propaganda
drive to come, for Hamilton would shortly take his campaign public,
publishing through the summer and fall a lot of tortuous and largely
baseless calumnies, pseudonymously fulminating as "Amicus," "Catullus"
and "Metellus," "An American" and "A Plain Honest Man."† In his eyes,
Jefferson's and Madison's antipathy to him was as intense and unremitting
as his antipathy to them: a notion that is not supported by the others' correspondence. While Jefferson and Madison were certainly opponents of
his project, their letters concentrate on that and not on him, whereas
Hamilton, both in his correspondence and in his published screeds,
repeatedly and pointedly defames *them*, denigrates their *motives*, doubts
their *loyalty*. Jefferson, writes "Metellus," is "the interested, ambitious and

---

*Hamilton's pro-British machinations were impelled primarily, although not
exclusively, by the dependence of his economic plan on unrestricted British imports.
The secretary of state, for his part, wanted the United States and Britain to compete
commercially as equals, with British markets open to American goods.

†A reluctant controversialist, Jefferson did not reply himself, but was publicly
defended by his allies, also using pseudonyms.

intriguing head of a party." The Virginians, writes "Catullus," are "the Catilines and the Caesars of the community," who "endeavor to intoxicate the people with delicious but poisonous draughts to render them the easier victims of their rapacious ambition."

That Hamilton's agenda had its merits—which Jefferson could not perceive—there is no doubt. Nevertheless, his diatribe does not reflect reality. Jefferson, wrote Hamilton to Carrington, is "a man of profound ambition and violent passions." Jefferson is "the intriguing incendiary, the aspiring turbulent competitor," "Catullus" writes.

> How long it is since that gentleman's real character may have been *divined*, or whether this is only the *first time* that the *secret* has been disclosed, I am not sufficiently acquainted with the history of his political life to determine; but there is always a "*first time*" when characters studious of artful disguises are unveiled; when the visor of stoicism is plucked from the brow of the epicurean; when the plain garb of Quaker simplicity is stripped from the concealed voluptuary; when Caesar *coyly refusing* the proffered diadem, is seen to be Caesar rejecting the trappings, but tenaciously grasping the substance of imperial domination.

To anyone familiar with the works and deeds of Thomas Jefferson, that characterization is preposterous—indeed, a trifle mad. For anyone familiar with the works and deeds of Alexander Hamilton can see that his attack on Jefferson did not in fact refer to Jefferson at all. Hamilton's "violent passions" and "profound ambition" were quite clear to his contemporaries, and grew clearer over time. Eight years later, after Hamilton had attacked John Adams even more intemperately, Noah Webster, a fellow Federalist, accused him of "insanity" and told him that he had become notorious as "the evil genius of the country." Thus was the propagandist always on a suicidal course, for in his vehement attack on Jefferson, writes Dumas Malone, "Hamilton must have been looking in the glass."

Such angry projectivity appears to drive all hostile propaganda, however ruinous or benign the cause concerned. Religious or antireligious, communist or anticommunist, fascist or antifascist, Zionist or anti-Zionist, the aroused projector sees, and propagates, the universe as split in two: the good "out there" projective of himself as he would like to be (and would like everybody else to be), the bad "out there" projective of the evil that he feels, but will not recognize, within himself. It is from that endless, agonizing inner conflict, and not from any rational aim, that hate propaganda draws its necessary vigor and persistence.

As we survey the history of hate propaganda, that motivating projectivity stands out most clearly in the cases of the maddest and most infamous projectors. In his review of *Hitler's Second Book: The Unpublished Sequel to Mein Kampf*, Omer Bartov notes the awful clarity of Hitler's projectivity: "When Hitler wrote his second book, he was staring into a mirror."

> It is truly astonishing to see how every sin that Hitler ascribed to "the Jew" became part of his own policies as he himself outlined them in his second book and later implemented them: the destruction of entire nations by the elimination of their elites, their mass deportation, and in the case of the Jews, their outright genocide. And it is just as mind-boggling to note that the endless depravity attributed by Hitler to the Jews became the reality of German conduct under his rule, which deprived the Reich of every remnant of moral constraint and finally drove it into an insane storm of self-destruction. What Hitler said would be done to Germany, he did unto others; and he and his people became victims of the nemesis that he prophesied for his enemies.

That fatal glitch in Hitler's vision has been much examined by the students of the tyrant's psyche, and so has the projective tendency of Hitler's monstrous fellow, Josef Stalin, whose propaganda bogeys also were unconsciously reflective of his own destructiveness and rage. "So it was that the villain-image of the enemy came to represent . . . everything that Stalin rejected and condemned in himself," writes Robert C. Tucker. "All that belonged to the rejected evil Stalin—the errors, flaws, and elements of villainy that had no place in his hero-image of himself—tended to be incorporated into his picture of the enemy, especially the picture of the internal enemy as villain of party history." The "enemy" residing in themselves, both dictators had to push the fight unto their own annihilation, in the process taking with them millions of their real and seeming enemies, and millions of their own supporters.

Certainly those two are in a class all by themselves, and yet there is a danger in regarding as unique the feral projectivity of those epic slaughterers, for if we take such comfort in their infamy, we will be blind to that same animus as it now threatens us and what is left of this democracy. No less than the populations of the Reich or of the Soviet Union, we also have been long subjected to extremist propaganda, and here no less than there, that propaganda is the output of well-disciplined projective minds. Wherever livid propaganda has an infrastructure and an audience, projectors are drawn naturally to the profession, which needs their hostile energy and scorched-earth dedication. Here too, war propaganda offers them the perfect outlet for their impossible, unending drive to kill the Other in themselves.

Here in the United States, that impulse has been rampant since the Bushes were dethroned in 1992. Certainly the anti-Clinton movement was maintained by such projective types. Throughout his years inside the anti-Clinton cult, David Brock was struck repeatedly, and eventually brought to his senses, by the movement's violent epidemic projectivity. He describes the mania of Barbara Comstock, a colleague of Ted Olson's (and now John Ashcroft's spokeswoman), who grew so obsessed with Clinton that she nearly lost her mind. "She once dropped by my house to watch the rerun of a dreadfully dull Whitewater hearing she had sat through all day. Comstock sat on the edge of her chair shaking, and screaming over and over again, 'Liars!' " At one point Brock was startled by the power of her projective animus:

> Comstock remarked that maybe she couldn't get Hillary's sins off her brain "because Hillary reminds me of me. I am Hillary." In this admission a vivid illustration of a much wider "Hillary" phenomenon can be seen. Comstock knew nothing about Hillary Clinton. Comstock's "Hillary" was imaginary, a construction composed entirely of the negative points in her own life.

Although it rarely finds such frank expression, that projective impulse has now come to dominate the global stage, as U.S. foreign policy itself has turned into a serial projective reflex, with Bush & Co. repeatedly attacking foreign others for the "evil" that they harbor in themselves. Thus Bush/Cheney's international comportment is a larger and far more destructive version of the great domestic witchhunt that absorbed and paralyzed this nation for eight years. Forever ranting at his legendary sexual immorality, Clinton's public persecutors were themselves no paragons of chastity. In fact, most of them led just the sort of personal lives that they routinely savaged Democrats for leading or tolerating— even though the Democrats (Gary Condit and Joe Lieberman excepted) seldom sermonized about fidelity or abstinence. Thus were Clinton's persecutors often leading private lives far dirtier than his: for they see sexuality as something dirty, and yet have blithely violated their own seeming rules. As Susan McDougal put it with her usual acuity, "The president's pursuers were a bunch of middle-aged, moralistic morons who were obsessed with sex."

Certainly such moralists are grossly hypocritical, and yet that term is not entirely apt. The staggering duplicity of William Bennett and Rush Limbaugh, of Dr. Laura and Matt Drudge, and their distinctive shame-lessness on being exposed, suggest a certain swaggering moral blindness that is finally somewhat different from hypocrisy per se. Hypocrisy— from the Greek *hupokrites*, for "pretense" or "acting on a stage"—is essentially dissimulation, either by a conscious and manipulative feigner, like Tartuffe, or by a sanctimonious poseur merely complacent in the certainty of his or her own spotlessness. In either case, hypocrites are always thinking mainly of themselves: their advantages, and their stand-ing in the world, or the persuasiveness of their performances.

And yet in Clinton's wilder critics there appears to be imposture of another, stranger kind, driven by a perfect inability to recognize the error of their ways. If they did it, it cannot be wrong, as they can do no wrong, no matter what they do, for they are who they are, and they are good. And yet such "good" requires reconfirmation day by day, hour by hour: that is, incessant accusation, condemnation, persecution of the "bad"— who are relentlessly constructed by "the good," out of their own internal demons. In other words, that sense of super-rectitude comes not from any inner certainty, but rather is contingent on an endless furious denial of one's own "bad" aspects, which are imputed—much exaggerated and distorted—onto one's enemies, whoever they may be (and they are legion). Unlike the hypocrite, in short, the mad projector, although self-absorbed and self-promoting, is forever brooding on the Other, and always searching for new opportunities to smear him, bring him down, do him injury, make him suffer: kill him, kill his family and his friends, his colleagues and his followers, and finally wipe out everyone who's even slightly like him.

It's about the Anger

That desperate need to be continually redeemed may help explain the odd sadistic fury that, on the right, appears to be a kick more tempting and delicious than whatever carnal pastimes they condemn. This is surely not to argue that the Bush Republicans prefer to sublimate their lusts, as it is no secret that the rightists are, behind closed doors, as lewd as anybody else in Washington. However they delight themselves in private, out in public they do not restrain themselves from venting their enormous wrath: a moral failing infinitely more destructive than the furtive gropings of the lechers in both parties. While they surely take their share of bawdy pleasures, wrath is the emotion that they most brazenly indulge, and what they seem most to enjoy.

"If it feels good, do it," Bush has often said, "and be sure to blame somebody else if you have a problem." He said it all throughout the campaign of 2000; and as of this writing, he has said it publicly some forty times. Of course, he has not meant it as a call to hedonistic irre-sponsibility: on the contrary. That line has been Bush/Cheney's way of paraphrasing what they take to be the ethos of those self-indulgent baby boomers who, as rampant shaggy potheads way back when, nearly brought this sacred nation down, what with their orgies in the streets, their spitting on our troops, their hanging out with Negroes. Such was the "destructive generation" (to quote one of Bush's gurus, David Horowitz) that spawned the Clintons and Al Gore—and also, providen-tially, George W. Bush. Even at the time, Bush knew that "the counterculture" was a really bad idea, and now deplores it, preaching "the responsibility society"—i.e., "a culture in which each of us understands that we're responsible for the decisions we make in life." Thus, while Clinton and his merry pranksters never left the bus, Bush keeps speaking out against "the sixties" with the repetitious fervor of a sinner who was lost but now is found. "My generation," as he puts it, has finally been redeemed through him. "At times, we lost our way," he said in his acceptance speech at the GOP convention in 2000. "But we're coming home."

And yet this Bush, and his abettors, are quite obviously big believers in that hedonistic axiom, "If it feels good, do it"—a claim that we can safely make without exploring the unappetizing question of their sex lives. "If it feels good, do it." On the evening of March 20, 2003, the president went on TV to tell the world that he had just begun his war. "Less than a minute before going on the air, while seated at his desk, Bush looked around the room, pumped his fist and said, 'Feel good,' " the *Dallas Morning News* reported.* The day before, speaking at the City Club in Cleveland, Antonin Scalia recalled the moment when he and certain of his colleagues stopped the recount of the presidential vote in Florida: "In response to a student's question," reported the Cleveland *Plain Dealer*, "Scalia said it was 'a wonderful feeling' to have led the Supreme Court's rejection of a recount of the Florida vote, thus handing the election to Bush." Months after that aborted vote, the *New York Times* did an investigative piece revealing that the military ballots in the presidential race had been manipulated to the GOP's advantage, with some service members even voting twice for Bush.

One of the double voters, Nicholas Challen, 40, a senior chief petty officer in the Navy who cast his second vote from Jacksonville on

*The *Mirror* (UK) played up the difference between Bush's off- and on-air demeanors: "Later, just seconds before he went on TV to tell the world war had started, he vigorously pumped his fist and declared: 'I feel good.' The extraordinary gesture was in stark contrast to the furrowed brow and look of concern he adopted for the subsequent broadcast." "US Surprise Attack Fails to Kill the Iraqi Leader; I Feel Good: Bush Reaction after Sending in Bombers," *Mirror* (UK), 3/21/03. This was uncannily reminiscent of his father's comportment toward the start of Operation Desert Storm in 1991. Although his spokesmen claimed that he was agonizing over that decision, his high excitement was apparent to everyone around him.

Election Day, reacted with jubilation when told that both of his votes counted. He raised both arms as if he had just scored a touchdown and savored the two votes he had delivered to George W. Bush.

"Yes!" he said, beaming.

"I was lifted up by a wave of vengeance and testosterone and anger. I could feel it," Bush retrospectively exulted, describing his performance with the bullhorn at Ground Zero on 9/14. That giddy moment led, eventually, to countless others. "To take a guy out," explained a U.S. Marine sniper on the outskirts of Fallujah, "is an incomparable adrenaline rush."

In every case, as if a war or national election were an especially barbaric football game, the celebrant "feels good" because the other side is hurting. This would appear to be the signal temperamental difference between rightists and their adversaries, who, by and large, do not get such nasty joy out of their enemy's unhappiness. It certainly distinguishes the rightists of today from true conservatives of any period, who have tended not to relish others' misery. "I really want to hurt him. I want him to feel pain," Ann Coulter said in June of 1999, in contemplating a campaign to unseat Representative Christopher Shays, a moderate Republican. "I know something about Bill and Hillary Clinton right now," wrote Rachel Abrams, wife of Elliott, when several prosecutors had been unleashed on the White House.

I know how their stomachs churn, their anxiety mounts, how their worry over the defenseless child increases. I know their inability to sleep at night and their reluctance to rise in the morning. I know every new incursion of doubt, every heartbreak over bailing out friends . . . every jaw-clenching look at front pages. I know all this, and the thought of it makes me happy.*

*"'I feel like a mother who wants to defend her child,' says Abrams' wife Rachel, beaming benignly as she sits Indian-style in their Northwest Washington home, caressing the head of their 5-year-old daughter. 'I would like to take a machine gun and mow Anthony Lewis down.'

"At the State Department, Abrams grins when told of his wife's remark. 'I wouldn't waste the bullets,' he chortles. 'I would rather have them go to the contras. They would use them to more effect.'" Lloyd Grove, "Elliott Abrams in the Hour of Combat," *Washington Post*, 1/13/87.

"We will fuck him. Do you hear me? We will fuck him. We will ruin him. Like no one has ever fucked him!" shouted Karl Rove in his office, about some unnamed victim-to-be, as reporter Ron Suskind sat outside, marveling at the violence of Rove's outburst, the propagandist's face turning pink from the exertion.*

The right commonly denies its special fury, claiming that the Democrats are worse, or just as bad, or did it first. Starting in the fall of 2003, in fact, this line became the basis of a rightist propaganda drive intended to shut down all criticism of the president, by charging that such "Bush-bashing" was excessive and irrational. Charles Krauthammer, the rightist columnist and erstwhile practicing psychiatrist, even came up with a "Bush Derangement Syndrome," thereby using his professional credentials in the finest Soviet tradition. Needless to say, Krauthammer never voiced such outrage over Clinton's treatment by his enemies (Krauthammer then being one of them). Indeed, the very loudest and most vitri-

---

*"As a reporter, you get around—curse words, anger, passionate intensity are not notable events—but the ferocity, the bellicosity, the violent imputations were, well, shocking. This went on without a break for a minute or two." Ron Suskind, "Why Are These Men Laughing?" *Esquire*, 1/1/03.

David Brock was similarly stunned by the reaction of Judge Laurence Silberman and his wife, Ricky, when they called to tell him how much they enjoyed a certain chapter of his manuscript, "The Real Anita Hill." In the course of the Hill/Thomas hearings, the Republicans on the Judiciary Committee had mischievously leaked the FBI file of a pro-Thomas witness. Brock covered for them in his chapter, by concocting a scenario that made Democratic Senator Paul Simon seem to be the guilty party: "Ricky and Larry were literally squealing with joy about the case I had constructed implicating Simon, a vocal critic of Silberman's during the judge's own confirmation hearing. They were passing the phone to each other, marveling at my 'genius' at the top of their lungs. 'You got him. You nailed him. You fucked him. You killed him,' they sang. The state of manic euphoria that gripped the Silbermans that evening is impossible to describe to a normal person, but I would see more and more of it—in others, and eventually in myself—as I rose through the ranks." *Blinded by the Right: The Conscience of an Ex-Conservative* (New York: Crown, 2002), p. 113.

Notwithstanding his judicial post, Silberman was, behind the scenes, a dedicated and extremely devious anti-Clinton operative throughout the nineties, Brock reports. In February of 2004, Bush/Cheney appointed Silberman to the nine-person panel charged with investigating the intelligence failures that led up to the occupation of Iraq. "Senator Assails Silberman as Too Partisan for Panel; White House rejects call for his removal from intelligence review," *Los Angeles Times*, 2/12/04.

olic of the anti-Clintonites themselves now holler bloody murder over what this president is going through, although Bush never was the object of the sort of threats and insults that were hurled routinely at his predecessor, who was subjected to a long assault at least as vitriolic as the drive against the Roosevelts.

Lest we forget, Senator Jesse Helms warned publicly—on the eve of November 22, the anniversary of JFK's assassination—that Clinton "better watch out if he comes down" to North Carolina ("He better have a bodyguard"), Representative Dan Burton called Clinton "a scumbag," Representative Bob Dornan called Clinton a "traitor," and Darrell Issa, Senate hopeful for the GOP in California, called the president a "slut." Of course, Hillary Clinton too has been the object of extraordinary virulence, as when Trent Lott opined wistfully that lightning just might strike her, and prevent her coming to the Senate. Under his office desk at Fox News Channel, Bill O'Reilly keeps a doormat embroidered with a likeness of her face. Even Chelsea Clinton has been mocked and threatened, Rush Limbaugh referring to her as "the family dog." And—in February of 2001—the *National Review Online* posted an article (which is, as of this writing, still online) by John Derbyshire, calling for her murder:

> Chelsea is a Clinton. She bears the taint; and though not prosecutable in law, in custom and nature the taint cannot be ignored. All the great despotisms of the past—I'm not arguing for despotism as a principle, but they sure knew how to deal with potential trouble—recognized that the families of objectionable citizens were a continuing threat. In Stalin's penal code it was a crime to be the wife or child of an "enemy of the people." The Nazis used the same principle, which they called Sippenhaft, "clan liability." In Imperial China, enemies of the state were punished "to the ninth degree": that is, everyone in the offender's own generation would be killed and everyone related via four generations up, to the great-great grandparents, and four generations down, to the great-great-grandchildren, would also be killed.

No calumny remotely like the anti-Clinton diatribe has ever been flung at this Bush by any prominent Democrat or liberal propagandist, nor has the press, or any TV comic, ever taken personal shots at Bush or any member of his family.* (Such tact is all the more remarkable in light of the Bush clan's dense and various arrest record, the many shady business dealings that involve most of the presidential siblings, the lurid personal lives of Neil and Jeb, and the family's drinking problem.) And yet the right seems to believe that Bush has been assaulted unrelentingly by those offensive Democrats with their groundless personal attacks.

All such "attacks," however, have been perfectly responsible, not ad hominem at all, which suggests that the right cannot perceive the "huge difference between dissent and hate," to quote Rush Limbaugh. On September 18, 2003, Ted Kennedy spoke bluntly in an interview with the Associated Press, making two important charges. "He expressed doubt about how serious a threat Saddam Hussein posed to the United States in its battle against terrorism," the AP reported. "There was no imminent threat," said Kennedy.

> This was made up in Texas, announced in January to the Republican leadership that war was going to take place and was going to be good politically. This whole thing was a fraud.

The senator also noted that Bush/Cheney had accounted for just $2.5 billion out of the $4 billion "being spent monthly on the war." " 'My belief is this money is being shuffled all around to these political leaders in all parts of the world, bribing them to send in troops,' he said."† On

*When Buddy, Clinton's chocolate Labrador, was hit by a car and killed in early January 2002, CNN's Aaron Brown offered this condolence: "The former president may have acted like a dog; Buddy was the real thing." *NewsNight*, CNN, 1/3/02. As late as December 3, 2003, at a formal ceremony honoring Hillary Clinton for her work on the environment, Bill Maher, serving as emcee, cracked several jokes about those blowjobs, with Mrs. Clinton sitting in the front row, right before him. "Rush and Malloy," *Daily News* (N.Y.), 12/8/03.

†Kennedy backed this charge with a long list of extraordinary disbursements: an $8.5 million loan package for Turkey (from whom we were requesting 10,000 troops), $700 million in economic support funds for Jordan (where the United States was staging operations), and, for Egypt's acquiescence, $300 million in economic support funds as well as $2 billion in loan guarantees. Kennedy also noted $200 million to support a multinational division run by Poland. Moreover, he claimed that the regime

both counts Kennedy was absolutely right—and so Bush/Cheney charged him with excessive rudeness: Bush called his remarks "uncivil," and Tom DeLay got very personal indeed. Kennedy, he said, was guilty of "the most mean-spirited and irresponsible hate-speech yet." MSNBC's Joe Scarborough called it "wrong," "sick," and—his memory of the nineties having evidently gone—"unprecedented in modern politics." "As ad hominem attacks go, this one is a classic," wrote shouting-head Lynn Woolley for NewsMax.com, a rightist Web site owned by Richard Mellon Scaife.

Likewise, Howard Dean touched off a rightist firestorm when, on December 10, 2003, he addressed the "theories" of the president's fore-knowledge of the terrorist attacks on 9/11:

> There are many interesting theories about it. The most interesting theory I've heard so far—which is nothing more than a theory that can't be proved—is that he was warned ahead of time by the Saudis. Now who knows what the real situation is? By suppressing that kind of information, you lead to those kind of theories, whether they have any truth to them or not, and they get repeated as fact.

Now, whether Riyadh warned the president ahead of time is not yet known for sure, although it would be no surprise, as Bush *had* been fore-warned repeatedly, and with a rising urgency, by his own CIA. He was also warned by Egyptian president Hosni Mubarak, and the government of Jordan (and also possibly Morocco's), while U.S. intelligence had been forewarned by the Mossad.* Shortly after 9/11, moreover, it also came

---

had spent, in the current fiscal year, $800 million to "reimburse key cooperating nations for providing logistical and military support."

The *Washington Post* account continued: "Finally, Kennedy cited a number of spending initiatives included in the administration's recent $87 billion supplemental spending request to support military operations and reconstruction in Iraq and Afghanistan, including $1.4 billion to reimburse Jordan, Pakistan, and other cooperating nations for logistical, military and other support to U.S. military operations and $200 million in economic support funds for Pakistani debt forgiveness." "Kennedy Fuels Sharp Debate," *Washington Post*, 9/24/03.

*The likelihood of such a terrorist attack had also been spelled out with startling clarity in *Road Map for National Security: Imperative for Change*, the authoritative

out that France had warned the FBI of an al Qaeda operative in search of flying lessons in this country; that Russia had warned the United States of al Qaeda's terrorist infrastructure in Afghanistan; and that Germany confirmed that an Iranian spy detained in Hamburg had warned the United States "several times" that terrorists had planned to strike the World Trade Center.* And yet Republicans tore into Dean's restrained and sensible remarks as "political hate-speech," as if mere reference to the question of the president's foreknowledge were the same as calling for impeachment or assassination.

The stridency of such reactions indicates not simple calculation but a sincere vengeful fury. That anyone would dare even to *question* what they do, much less denounce them frankly, strikes the rightists as outrageous, even though their own routine attacks are toxic well beyond the bounds of prior political invective, for the Busheviks do not just call their adversaries names and charge them with sedition, but gloat at their misfortunes and strongly hint, or say outright, that they would like to see them dead.

Like any common bully, the right can dish it out but can't take it. They bellow like gored oxen whenever someone puts it to them straight, as they did when Clinton spoke against hate radio in 1995, the rightists crying that his plea for more debate was actually a threat to jail them for their views; and as they did again when, at Senator Paul Wellstone's

---

three-volume report released in September 1999 by the United States Commission on National Security, which was co-chaired by former senators Gary Hart and Warren Rudman. While the Clinton administration took that warning very seriously, as Daniel Benjamin and Steven Simon show in *The Age of Sacred Terror* (New York: Random House, 2002), the mainstream press largely ignored the commission's findings.

Five days before 9/11, in a face-to-face meeting with Condoleezza Rice, Hart made a desperate final plea for some protective action. "Her only response was, 'Well, I'll speak to the vice president about it.' And that was disheartening." Ron Hutcheson, "Counterpunch on 9/11 is in Rice's hands," *Miami Herald*, 4/4/04.

*Moreover, erstwhile FBI translator Sibel Edmonds has tried valiantly to tell the public, through Congress and the 9/11 commission, what she knows about the Bureau's foreknowledge, but she has been silenced by John Ashcroft. James Ridgeway, Mondo Washington," *Village Voice*, 6/1/04.

memorial on October 30, 2002, Trent Lott was booed by a few people in that grieving multitude. Although the boos were minimal—a momentary lowing in the distance—the right reacted to that tiny chorus of disapproval (there were 20,000 people in the hall) as if Lott had been bedaubed with excrement in Wellstone's name.

Wellstone was the leftmost member of the Senate. If, say, Tom DeLay, the rightmost figure in the House, had been thus mourned by 20,000 of his keenest followers, and, say, Ted Kennedy had shown his face, the mass reaction would have been much uglier. Such a ritual, moreover, surely could not match the warmth and idealism of Wellstone's memorial, which never mentioned any of the right's attacks on him. Indeed, that very atmosphere of nonbelligerent solidarity appears to have provoked the rightists' bile. Frightened by the prospect of an optimistic, unifying politics, they seem to have projected their own hatefulness onto the ceremony, using Trent Lott's tribulation as their pretext, and so did they project their cynicism onto the memorial, asserting that the whole heartfelt event was nothing but a "partisan" manipulation. They did not hesitate to jeer at those bereaved by Wellstone's death. The next day, Texas Governor Rick Perry, campaigning for reelection, had Dick Cheney come to Austin for a rally demonstrating party unity. The turnout was unimpressive. Tom DeLay was there: "I know we could have thousands [here] if we just had a memorial service," he cracked. "The comment drew hoots from those who recognized DeLay's reference to the funeral of U.S. Sen. Paul Wellstone, D-Minn., which critics contend resembled a Democratic political pep rally with 20,000 attendees," the *Houston Chronicle* reported.

No Democrat would make a crack like that, or otherwise mimic the peculiar malice of the Bush Republicans. After Senator Jim Jeffords left the GOP for saner fields, some rightist wag stuck Jeffords's photo in the urinal on the first floor of the Capitol Hill Club, "a gathering place for GOP folks that sits adjacent to Republican National Committee headquarters," *Roll Call* reported in June of 2001. A number of fun-loving partisans took aim at Jeffords's likeness, until "a peeved member of the club ripped the photo out of the urinal, fearing it would be seen as yet another symbol of the party's alleged intolerance." The Democrats did not do likewise when Senator Ben Nighthorse Campbell left their party for the GOP in 1995, nor can one easily imagine that they ever would do such a thing.

Nor can one imagine any Democratic counterpart to the incomparable Ann Coulter, who has become a star by virtue of her golden tresses and maniacal hostility. "We need to execute people like John Walker in order to physically intimidate liberals, by making them realize that they can be killed too. Otherwise they will turn out to be outright traitors," she once suggested at a rightist conference. After 9/11, she wrote: "We should invade their countries, kill their leaders and convert them to Christianity." (That last line appeared on a Pakistani Web site calling for a defensive holy war against the West, her blunt prescription serving, understandably, as "proof" that the United States and Israel plan to wipe out Islam.)

That no one on the left would make such genocidal jests was made clear by a pro-Coulter op-ed in the *Wall Street Journal*, which argued that such wisecracks have for years been common on the left. "We have been programmed to think," wrote Melik Kaylan in the summer of 2002, "that such impassioned outrage, and outrageousness, are permissible only on the left . . . and certainly not from nice blonde Connecticut-born Republican girls." Kaylan's examples: "From Lenny Bruce, George Carlin, Angela Davis, Reverend Farrakhan, yes. Ann Coulter—heaven forbid." All that this list proved was Kaylan's inability to make his argument. Lenny Bruce—deceased since 1966—was not a leftist, but a beat comedian, much like George Carlin, who in fact is just as hard on Volvo liberals as he is on Christian moralists. Neither one of them, moreover, ever once made jokes (if "jokes" they are) about exterminating those they disagreed with. Nor has Angela Davis—the only leftist on the roster—ever ranted like La Coulter; or, if she did, it may have been a put-on at a dinner party to amuse some friends. A revolutionary communist, the cerebral Davis never got much airtime even when she was notorious, and has not had much, if any, since. Louis Farrakhan, of course, *has* made bloody demagogic statements, as did the infamous Khalid Abdul Muhammad, Farrakhan's late disciple, delivering long genocidal diatribes against the whites, "the Jews." Ann Coulter *does* recall those orators—who were not leftists. Racial supremacists and true believers in "black capital," the Nation of Islam is way out there on the *right*, promoting a worldview that owes far more to Hitler than it does to Marx.* Despite Kaylan's assumption that all African-Americans are "on the left," his coy comparison of Coulter with those other figures merely proves the opposite of his contention that liberals always say the vilest things.

While Stalinists engaged in wild invective, that was quite some time ago, and their shrill calumnies were rarely quoted in the U.S. mainstream press, but were restricted, in this country, to their own small publications. In certain of their screeds one does hear Coulter's tone (although the Stalinist polemics tended not to be as openly bloodthirsty as she is). Nowhere on the post-Stalin left, however, is there anyone as vicious as Ann Coulter—who, naturally, accuses *liberals* of relentless "slander," just as the major figures in the anti-Clinton slime machine often referred to *Clinton's White House* as "the slime machine." (Coulter's book *Slander* is a how-to manual packaged as an exposé.) Thus have the rightists ceaselessly imputed their own hatred to the very objects of that hatred, raging at *the liberals* for a rage that is their own.

This projective stroke eventually became the party's favorite weapon, once the Democrats began to call a spade a spade. At first, the Dean and Clark campaigns, the boldest in the field of Democratic aspirants, were singled out especially for deploying "hate speech" in their broadsides at Bush/Cheney. Once John Kerry took their place, his speech too was scored as foul and mean, with Ed Gillespie, chairman of the Republican National Committee, warning grimly on February 13, 2004, that the

*Thus spake Muhammad at a typical performance: "You see everybody always talk about Hitler exterminating 6 million Jews. That's right. But don't nobody ever ask what did they do to Hitler? What did they do to them folks? They went in there, in Germany, the way they do everywhere they go, and they supplanted, they usurped, they turned around and a German, in his own country, would almost have to go to a Jew to get money," etc. Muhammad made these remarks at Kean College in New Jersey, 11/29/93. The Anti-Defamation League maintains a Web site titled "Khalil's Abdul Muhammad: In His Own Words," http://www.adl.org/special_reports/khalid_own_words/khalid_own_words.asp.

Democrats were going to run "the dirtiest campaign in modern presidential politics."* Thus the right, as usual, confused dissent with hate, while obfuscating their own hatefulness, and nervous centrist commentators pitched right in to help the rightists out, admonishing *the Democrats* for their unseemly rhetoric and complaining wanly of the incivility "on both sides." "Liberals have now become as intemperate as conservatives," fretted Nicholas Kristof in his *New York Times* column on November 12, 2003, "and the result—everybody shouting at everybody else—corrodes the body politic and is counterproductive for Democrats themselves." Such even-handedness was but a gift to the Republicans. By scolding everyone for brawling, instead of pointing clearly to the most belligerent party, Kristof and other such apologists recalled the family court judge who, confronted with a case of wife-beating, advised both wife *and* husband to lay off each other, as if "both sides" were equally at fault. The two went home, and then the husband beat the wife to death.

"Come out, I know I'm in there!"

Although the right's self-hatred is a psychological phenomenon, its context is historical and cultural. Indeed, the history of the rightist seizure of the U.S. government since 1992 is, in large part, the history of U.S. rightist projectivity. Suddenly bereft of its familiar bogeys on the wrong side of the Iron Curtain, the U.S. right decided to "bring the war home," as the sixties' student left once put it. Now the enemy became at once more proximate and even more demonic, as the Soviets gave way to the

*The day before Gillespie leveled that indignant charge, Matt Drudge publicized the myth that Kerry had been having an affair with a young intern, who had lately fled the country. That story raged in a score of dailies, and throughout cyberspace (Rush Limbaugh also weighing in), until it quickly fizzled five days later, when Alex Polier, the young woman in question, forcefully denied the whole account in every detail. (Meanwhile, the White House was desperately impugning the great reportorial effort to determine whether Bush had served his full stint in the National Guard. Unlike the Kerry/Polier fabrication, Bush's true military history was, of course, a worthy story *and* exceedingly suspicious. Nevertheless, Scott McClellan, the president's press secretary, kept accusing the inquisitive press of "trolling for trash." "White House Toughens Stance on Bush's National Guard Service," AP, 2/11/04.)

inchoate homegrown evil of "the left"—not only blacks, Jews, and Hispanics, but gays, feminists, environmentalists, defenders of abortion rights, and every other "special interest" that, in one way or another, would obstruct the corporate cartel and the troops of the religious right. Throughout the Cold War, the right's projective tendency had been obscured by the inarguable fact that the Soviet Union did exist and was opposed to the United States. (The same was true of the hardliners in the Kremlin, *their* paranoia likewise masked by the reality of U.S. force and influence.) Once communism ceased to be a military threat, and the right looked homeward for the enemy, their projectivity became more obvious, as any rational person could at once perceive the vast discrepancy between, say, Clinton and the hated "Clinton," whereas it always had been hard to measure the veracity of anti-Soviet propaganda, because one saw very little for oneself.

The actual Clinton has long been perceptible to us, however—and so have his detractors, and their strange fixation on the presidential genitals. The anti-Clinton drive was all about the sex. His noisiest assailants were obsessed with it. However awesome his libido really was, Bill Clinton could not possibly have thought about his crotch one-tenth as much as his detractors did (and do). It was not he but they who seemed incapable of focusing on anything but Clinton's Johnson: its history, its "distinguishing characteristics," its whereabouts at every moment. ("Clinton is in love with the erect penis," Ann Coulter said on Fox on February 6, 2000.)*

To some extent, that prurient obsession was a sign of simple dirty-mindedness, as Susan McDougal notes in her account of her ordeal at the hands of Ken Starr, the crusading puritan who was "obsessed with sex." That interpretation certainly befits the likes of "Judge Starr" as the TV news presented him, awkwardly galumphing from his front stoop to his car door bright and early every morning, his glinting spectacles and bashful grin defining him as someone who does not get out much. Such a closeted naïf would surely get a secret thrill out of the president's lubri-

---

*Six months earlier, on August 2, 1999, Coulter, on CNBC's *Rivera Live*, stated that Clinton "masturbates in the sinks."

cious ways. And yet that laughable persona—Starr liked to stay at home
on Saturday nights to shine his shoes, or so we heard—was not entirely
accurate. The façade, in fact, was very useful to him, as it obscured his
oversized ambitions (he wanted to be on the Supreme Court) and his
partisan fanaticism. Starr was not the hapless nerd he seemed, but a ruth-
less operator capable of crossing any line to suit the party and enhance
his own career.

Of course, that sounds a lot like "Clinton," and, indeed, "the president's pursuers" were not merely titillated by his legendary sex life. They
were incensed by Clinton's sexuality, not because they were mere prud-
ish innocents but out of sheer projective desperation to annihilate the
"evil" *in themselves.* That drive, again, was not based on hypocrisy per
se—although the anti-Clinton movement did get pretty far on that old
vice, which in our time has been especially epidemic among televangelists and moralizing politicians. As Joe Conason wrote in *Big Lies* (and as
the U.S. press was always too polite to tell their audience), many of the
president's congressional assailants were themselves no angels in the
Godliness Department, leading personal lives in fact more colorful than
Clinton's, that man, unlike them, never having postured as a paragon
of "family values": Newt Gingrich, Henry Hyde, Helen Chenoweth,
Robert Livingston, and many others would have been in serious trouble
if the press had ever thought to spotlight *their* affairs.*

---

*Clinton did preach sexual self-restraint to others, insofar as he deplored the rising
trend of unwed motherhood, urging abstinence on poor young women. In doing so,
however, he did not sermonize and certainly did not imply that he himself was sexually pure.

While charging liberals with compulsive immorality, Gingrich was having an affair
with a twenty-seven-year-old staffer named Callista Bisek. (In 1993, when the liaison
began, Gingrich was fifty.) In May of 1999, Gingrich called his wife, Marianne, who
was with her mother to celebrate the latter's birthday. He told her that he wanted a
divorce. (That callousness recalled Gingrich's treatment of his first wife, who, when he
came in to tell her that he wanted out, was in a hospital bed for treatment of ovarian
cancer.)

For eight years, Henry Hyde had an affair with another man's wife. (He called it
"a youthful indiscretion," although the congressman was in his forties at the time.)
Representative Robert Livingston—a moralist whom the Christian Coalition rated at

Among the major anti-Clinton propagandists not in government, the most hypocritical, perhaps, was William Bennett, who, while publicly deploring Clinton's horrid self-indulgence, was squandering millions in Las Vegas and, less frequently, Atlantic City. The author of *The Book of Virtues*, *The Child's Book of Virtues*, *The Broken Hearth*, and—most pertinent here—*The Death of Outrage* (a screed lamenting Clinton's stubborn popularity) dropped some $8 million in casinos over just ten years (once blowing $1.4 million in one evening), and then he tried to blather his way out of it, just as "Clinton" would. Gambling was legal! It didn't hurt his family! He'd paid the taxes! He "always broke even"! And, most notably, he argued that he'd never aimed his moral fire at gambling, which is no sin, as every Catholic Bingo player knows. All that energetic casuistry—and most of the press coverage of his plight—steered carefully around the implications of the fact that Bennett had dropped all that dough in *Vegas*, where gamesters go, as columnist Frank Rich pointed out, not just to gamble but to have one hell of a good time.

Casino gambling is legal in 28 states, many of which are far closer to his Maryland home; he could play his beloved slots as nearby as Delaware. Maybe he was drawn by the same attributes that appeal to many Americans: big drinks, big shows, big breasts. Maybe he liked the fact that Vegas, after a brief effort to offer family-friendly attractions in the early 90's, had reverted to its Rat Pack roots. As The Los Angeles Times declared two years ago, the sin is back in Sin City with an explosion of sex shows on and beyond the Strip.*

100 percent—had multiple affairs, which Larry Flynt was set to publicize at the height of the Lewinsky scandal, forcing Livingston's tearful public resignation. Representative Helen Chenoweth, an especially vocal critic of Clinton's "personal conduct," was so sexually active as a legislator back in Idaho that one GOP insider from that state told journalist David Neiwert, "Helen is living proof that you can fuck your brains out."

The facts concerning Gingrich, Hyde, Livingston, and Chenoworth, among others, are available in Joe Conason's *Big Lies: The Right-Wing Propaganda Machine and How It Distorts the Truth* (New York: Thomas Dunne Books, 2003), pp. 109–27.

*Rich goes on acutely: "Mr. Bennett's compulsive, prolonged visits to a town that exuberantly epitomizes everything he was against in American culture is the hypocrisy

Here the point is not to fault the man for such behavior, which is a matter between him and his own conscience, and his wife, and his God. Bennett's high times in Las Vegas are his business, as are the Clinton haters' other secret recreations, whatever indoor sports they like (except for those entailing nonconsensual violence). The sin at issue here is not this naughty game or that, but the unwholesome tendency of certain players to damn everybody else who likes to play as well. In this great secular republic, each of us is free to have his or her fun, and then atone for it, or not, as he or she sees fit. What is immoral—and quite dangerous—is that oppressive tendency to punish other people just for doing what you do yourself, or for even trying to do what you will do as soon as you get the chance. That peculiar sin is common to the former president's most ardent persecutors.

Bennett's equal in humiliation,* and maybe in hypocrisy, was Rush Limbaugh, the party's jovial propaganda titan, daily scourge of all things countercultural, merciless advocate of lockin' 'em up and throwin' away the key, and tireless heckler of "our pot-smoking president." He was also, it came out, a voracious pill-head, avid money-launderer, and the mellowed beneficiary of countless late-night parking-lot transactions with drug dealers. For over four years this went on despite Limbaugh's well-

_____

that truly resonates—far more so than the gambling itself. If his slots habit has wreaked havoc on his family and bank account, that's his own private business. But the hypocrisy he has long practiced as a cultural warrior inflicted damage far beyond his immediate household." Frank Rich, "Tupac's Revenge on Bennett," *New York Times*, 5/18/03.

*In William F. Buckley Jr.'s eyes, the sinner was excommunicate: "Bill Bennett is through. . . . He is objectively discredited. He will not be proffered any public post by any president into the foreseeable future. He will not publish another book on another virtue, if there is any he has neglected to write about. It is possible that the books written by him on the subject, sitting in bookstores, will work their way to the remainder houses. These are the consequences of the damage he has done to himself." William F. Buckley Jr., "Bennett and his Enemies," *National Review Online*, posted 5/13/03 (http://www.nationalreview.com/buckley/buckley051303.asp).

Buckley underestimated the resilient Bennett, and, apparently, the moral fussiness of the contemporary right. On April 15, 2004, Bennett was reborn as national radio pundit, hosting his show *Morning in America*, under the auspices of Salem Radio Network, a well-established right-wing operation.

aired hard line on recreations such as his. "Let's all admit something," he said in 1995.

> There's nothing good about drug use. We know it. It destroys individuals. It destroys families. Drug use destroys societies. Drug use, some might say, is destroying this country. And we have laws against selling drugs, pushing drugs, using drugs, importing drugs. And the laws are good because we know what happens to people in societies and neighborhoods which become consumed by them. And so if people are violating the law by doing drugs, they ought to be accused and they ought to be convicted and they ought to be sent up!

And that meant whites as well as blacks!

> [T]oo many whites are getting away with drug use. Too many whites are getting away with drug sales. Too many whites are getting away with trafficking in this stuff. The answer to this disparity is not to start letting people out of jail because we're not putting others in jail who are breaking the law. The answer is to go out and find the ones who are getting away with it, convict *them* and send *them* up the river, too!*

When the story broke, Limbaugh was unapologetic, making various excuses for himself just as Bennett had (although claiming to "take full responsibility"). He'd had back surgery! He was in a lot of pain! And anyway, they were *prescription medications*, hence not "drugs" like that "stuff" bought and sold by hardened criminals (i.e., black people). Such self-exculpatory jive would not have helped him much with any serious narcotics officer. "OxyContin® has become the number one prescribed Schedule II narcotic in the United States," reports Asa Hutchinson, director of the Drug Enforcement Administration. "Increasing abuse of OxyContin® has led to an increase of associated criminal activity." Nevertheless, Rush was not "sent up the river," but merely sentenced to a

---

*Within hours of Kurt Cobain's suicide on April 5, 1994, Limbaugh referred to the drug-addicted rocker as a "worthless shred of human debris." *Rush Limbaugh*, Multimedia Entertainment, Inc., 4/11/94.

rehab program, doing "five intense weeks" (as he put it) in a comfortable
retreat, as opposed to years of hard time in a federal cell.* (He also
became the subject of an ongoing criminal investigation, which he
would milk on-air for audience sympathy.) If he was ever struck by the
injustice of his easy ride or by the great divide between his Jack Webb
rhetoric and his druggy doings, he kept it to himself: "I know the sky
probably seems brighter to you no matter where you are," he said on his
first day back at work. "The air is cleaner, the water is purer, and it's not
because of the environmentalist wackos. It's because I'm back, right?" He
spoke a while about his rehab, then tore into Teddy Kennedy.

From the start, the anti-Clinton drive was fueled by the projections of
such secret reprobates, yearning, deep inside, to be made clean. Lee
Atwater was the first to make an issue out of Clinton's "skirt problem."
As early as 1989, Atwater, former chairman of the Republican National
Committee and Bush I's top campaign propagandist (Willie Horton's
fame was largely his creation), could see the threat that Clinton posed to
Poppy Bush's reelection, and set about at once to have him smeared,
especially as a lecher—an unsurprising move, perhaps, as Atwater was
himself an infamous sex addict. "As early as 1984," according to Gene
Lyons and Joe Conason, "the long-married Atwater's reputation for compulsive, reckless womanizing was so well-known, at least among fellow
Republicans, that George Bush's closest advisers had urged Bush to avoid
him altogether."† Late in 1989, Atwater was almost nailed for his phi-
landering by the *Washington Post*, but he pressured the reporter into
dropping it, insisting that "innocent bystanders would be hurt." Meanwhile, Atwater was busily using every rumor he could glean about Bill

*Limbaugh was desperate not to go to prison, no doubt fearing what might hap-
pen to him there. Later, when the revelations about Abu Ghraib resounded through
the media, Limbaugh claimed that they were no big deal. He likened the torture in
Iraq to a fraternity hazing in the United States, arguing that the perpetrators were just
"letting off steam."

†"He reveled in telling stories of conquests, sharing details with office colleagues,"
writes John Brady, Atwater's biographer. "Disposable sex without commitment was a
huge piece of his ego, a badge of honor." Gene Lyons and Joe Conason, *The Hunting
of the President: The Ten-Year Campaign to Destroy Bill and Hillary Clinton* (New York:
Thomas Dunne Books, 2000), p. 3.

Clinton's sex life to destroy the governor's political career, and thereby prolong Bush the Elder's.

Once Clinton was elected, the campaign against him heated up, attracting a rogues' gallery of militant projectors. The campaign made the name and fortune of Matt Drudge, propelling the inventive Walter Winchell wannabe from rank obscurity to rank celebrity, despite his sloppy work and trivial concerns.* Drudge first came to fame by hyping the sensational and groundless charges of Kathleen Willey that the president had "fondled" her, or, as Drudge put it, "made sexual overtones towards her." That such an outrage, even if it had occurred, would shock the cyberjournalist is not believable, considering his own private life. As David Brock reveals, Drudge is a longtime regular at certain gay bars, despite his longtime collaboration with the homophobic right, for whom he's done a lot aside from smearing Clinton. In the summer of 2003, Drudge ran a story to punish Jeffrey Kofman of ABC for daring to report the restiveness of U.S. soldiers in Iraq: "ABC News Reporter Who Filed Troop Complaints Story—Openly Gay Canadian." (Drudge soon deleted "openly gay" from the Web site, but not before the news, such as it was, had got around.) He also pandered to the right by claiming frequently, and falsely, that the "Trench Coat Mafia," the outcast coterie at Columbine High School, were gay. "Kids who are members of the Trench Coat Mafia say they aren't gay. Kids who hate the Trench Coat Mafia say they aren't gay. Yet Matt Drudge continues to beat this dead horse trying to find a gay angle. Enough already," said John Aravosis of Wired Strategies, in an interview with *Gay Today*. The invidious thrust of Drudge's gambit was not lost on his intended readers.†

*Notwithstanding his explicit propaganda function and his major defects as a journalist, Drudge was encouraged by the corporate press. In 1998, as if to mark his contribution to the president's impeachment, he was Tim Russert's guest on NBC's *Meet the Press* and was also asked to speak before the National Press Club.

†One of them, having been sent Drudge's cybercolumns on Columbine, replied thus to his correspondent: "Your emails prove that the two male Colorado students that committed the mass murder at their high school were sodomites who were filled with homosexual rage." The sender also urged that his friend "not use the word 'GAY.' . . . You could use the word 'FAG' or 'Queer' or 'Sodomite' or 'Faggot'." He then suggested a visit to antigay crusader Fred Phelps' Web site—www.godhatesfags.com—to

It was Drudge who spread the tale that Sidney Blumenthal, a top Clinton aide, had "a spousal abuse past." " 'There are court records of Blumenthal's violence against his wife,' one influential republican [*sic*], who demanded anonymity, tells the *Drudge Report*." Blumenthal sued Drudge for libel,* and in his own investigation of the case discovered that the "influential" author of the slander was John Fund, an editorial writer for the *Wall Street Journal* and a longtime propagandist for the GOP. (Fund was also Rush Limbaugh's ghostwriter.) Aside from his anti-Clinton writings (which included some of the attacks on Clinton aide Vince Foster, whose suicide left the author gleeful), Fund also was a frequent shouting head on MSNBC and CNN, hammering forever at the Clintons' moral turpitude. He was especially horrified by Clinton's randy ways, as well as shocked, apparently, by Blumenthal's mistreatment of his wife, Jackie. It was, to some, therefore a bit of a surprise when, on February 23, 2002, Fund was hauled in by the NYPD for beating up his girlfriend, Morgan Pillsbury. (Fund was hiding from the cops in the Manhattan Institute, a neoconservative redoubt.) Given all his prior criticisms of Bill Clinton's kinky ways, it was strange to learn that Fund had been not only Morgan's lover (and got her pregnant, then got her an abortion), but also, years before, her mother's lover, and that he had a lot of other lovers, too. (Fired from both the *Journal* and MSNBC, Fund went on to become a commentator for the Christian Broadcasting Network. These days he is often back on CNN, holding forth for Paula Zahn.)

In case after case, Clinton's most dogged detractors stood exposed as having done themselves what they deplored in others. Long obsessed with Clinton's sex life, gay British rightist Andrew Sullivan has also been a constant critic of the irresponsibility of other gays, charging them with hedonistic recklessness—"libidinal pathology," he's called it—in the Age

---

get "statistics about fags." "Trench Coat Mafia 'Gay' Angle Critiqued," *Gay Today*, 4/23/99 (http://www.gaytoday.badpuppy.com/garchive/world/042399wo.htm).

   *The case dragged on for years, as Drudge refused to sign an apology. Finally, as it grew clear that Drudge was using the lawsuit for his own publicity, Blumenthal decided to scrap the case in 2001. (Sydney Blumenthal, *The Clinton Wars* [New York: Farrar, Straus and Giroux, 2003], pp. 784–85.)

of AIDS. "He considers gay marriage the only healthy alternative to 'a life of meaningless promiscuity followed by eternal damnation,' " writes Richard Goldstein. "He has hectored gay men for their obsession with 'manic muscle factories,' and written at length about the need for 'responsibility' in the age of AIDS." In the spring of 2001, Sullivan was caught in a most embarrassing self-contradiction:

> Using the screen name RawMuscleGlutes, Sullivan posted on a site for bare backers (the heroic term for gay men who have sex without condoms). He was seeking partners for unsafe anal and oral intercourse. Sullivan revealed that he was HIV-positive and stated his preference for men who are "poz," but he also indicated an interest in "bi scenes," groups, parties, orgies, and "gang bangs." This hardly fit the gay ideal Sullivan had created in his book *Virtually Normal.* In fact, RawMuscleGlutes is just the sort of "pathological" creature who raises Sullivan's wrath.

"Dr. Laura" Schlessinger, the radio scold and columnist for World NetDaily.com (a Scaife enterprise), is another rightist homophobe, although not gay herself (and *not* in favor of gay marriage). Homosexuality is "deviant," she likes to say, and "a biological error." And, of course, she too has zealously condemned the Clintons, whose bad example she so loathes that in 2002 she claimed that she would run for president if Hillary declared, so as to block another Clinton victory:

> Everything I've read about her . . . the book the FBI guy who was in the White House, Gary Aldrich—I mean, you read that book and you realize the two of them are perverse, disturbed and destructive. And immoral. And legalities mean nothing to them. This is not a role model. But this is what happens when you have such ferocious bias in the media and only one picture is painted. It's scary. If Hillary runs, I'm going to feel a need to run against her.

What with her unforgiving moralism, Dr. Laura took some heat when it came out that back when she was married, she had had her lover take some hot nude pictures of herself, which turned up on the Internet in 1998. ("After first denying that the photos taken in the 1970s were of her," reported *Adult Industry News*, "Schlessinger eventually admitted

they were real but said that she had changed her lifestyle and should not
be blamed for past errors in judgment.") This from the woman who
scored ABC's Barbara Walters for appearing in her bathrobe in a promotion for *The View*. A firm believer in the Fifth Commandment, furthermore, Schlessinger apparently forgot to honor her own mother, who,
in the summer of 2003, was found dead in her condo, where the body
had been lying for three months. Dr. Laura told the press that she and
Yolanda Schlessinger had been "estranged" for quite some time. As usual,
she was both appalled and mystified by the indignation at her double
standard, decrying the "hate campaign" that, she claimed, had been
launched against her.

And then there's Michael Savage—"the most exciting and controversial radio host in America," according to NewsMax.com, and for a while
a bellowing head on MSNBC. That gig ended in early July of 2003,
when Savage finally went too far, excoriating a gay caller on the TV version of his show, *The Savage Nation* (which had been the object of gay
protests since March 8). "Oh, you're one of the sodomites!" snarled the
author of *The Enemy Within*.

> You should only get AIDS and die, you pig! How's that? Why don't
> you see if you can sue me, you pig? You got nothing better than to
> put me down, you piece of garbage? You have got nothing to do
> today, go eat a sausage and choke on it!

Savage had the same warm feeling for the Clintons, and often vented it,
sometimes with a passion reminiscent of *Mein Kampf*. He said this in
October 1999:

> We are now living through the equivalent social chaos that the Ger-
> mans experienced in the Weimar Republic in pre-Hitler Germany
> before 1933. We have the same radical political leadership that
> caters to pornographers, drug dealers, perverts, foreign immigrants,
> foreign competitors. . . . It disdains church, family, fathers, moth-
> ers, children, and decency.

The problem with prewar Germany, in other words, was not Nazism but
the liberal order that the Nazis too despised. "Believe me, there is no
essential difference between Bill Clinton's and the leadership of the

Weimar Republic. It's the same mentality, the same diseased mind that's come back to haunt us again." Savage ranted on about the "anarchy and social decay," the "decadence" of Clintonism, and about the "rights" of "average people" being "mocked," and their "values" made the "brunt of filthy humor."

Listening to such diatribes, one would surely not suspect that "Michael Savage" is a Jew, born Michael Weiner in the Bronx, and that for years he was an ardent counterculturalist, selling herbs and celebrating trees in northern California. Listening to his homophobic rants, on the other hand, one might *not* be surprised to learn that "Savage" has, as they say, some issues in his closet. In his *Vital Signs*, an autobiographical novel published in 1983, the central character, Samuel Trueblood, is haunted by the memory of an emasculating father: " 'You're not a fag, are you Sam?' the little man would say each time the boy dared wear a colorful shirt or flashy trousers." Always "filled with fears," the adult Trueblood struggles to get free of his anxieties, which drive him close to madness even after he has moved to Marin County to become an herbalist and start a family. Writing in *Salon*, David Gilson paraphrases the first phase of Trueblood's spiritual deliverance:

> Eventually, Trueblood seeks solace in chasing skirts. (Though he admits to being drawn to "masculine beauty," he confides that "I choose to override my desires for men when they swell in me, waiting out the passions like a storm, below decks.") While his wife stays home with the kids, he beds a young "cockswell" with a "dykish haircut" and skin "softer than that Northern Indian prostitute in Fiji whose covering was as soft as that of my own penis." And so it goes for another 50 pages.

You Either *Are* Us or You're Not

The same projective energy that galvanized the anti-Clinton propaganda now impels this president to flog Bush/Cheney's scorched-earth foreign policy. Certainly that policy has been determined by a number of objective interests, including oil and the demands of Cheney's cronies in the corporate sector. And yet there also is a certain messianic ardor in the president's pursuit of "evil," in part reflective of the dreams of his constituents on the Christian right, and—as Bush himself is way out on the Christian right—in part expressive of the president's own Manichaean psychology. "Id-control was the basis of Bush's approach to the presidency. . . . Bush was a man of fierce anger," Bush speechwriter David Frum has written, noting the peculiar animus that Bush conceives as an *external* danger, out there threatening all good people.

As Bush and his constituents see it, the universe is split between the godly (Us) and the demonic (Them). Despite the frequent anti-narcissistic broadsides against the "Me Decade" and the selfish hippie types, the president's either/or cosmology is wholly narcissistic, if not solipsistic. For your choice is not just to support, or not support, his side. Your true choice, rather, is to *be one with* him and his team, or to be naught in Bush's sight and therefore marked for extinction: "You're either with us or against us." What this ultimately means is that either *you are "us"* or *you are not "us."* If Bush/Cheney perceive you as a "good person," a "real American," in other words, it means that they perceive you not merely as in agreement with them, but as a member of their body: a being finally not to be distinguished from themselves.

"A man who loves his wife as much as I love mine"

On the world stage, this sort of projectivity became apparent prior to 9/11, when Bush betrayed his strange affection—at that time distressing to the right *and* left—for Vladimir Putin, the cold-eyed president of Russia. Notoriously, Bush claimed to have perceived a sympathetic "soul" within those frigid baby-blues:

> I looked the man in the eye. I found him to be very straightforward and trustworthy. We had a very good dialogue. I was able to get a sense of his soul—a man deeply committed to his country and to the best interests of his country. And I appreciated so very much the frank dialogue.

Bush went on to make it clear that he so liked Putin—seemed, indeed, to love Putin—because the latter was, in Bush's eyes, another Bush (or an incarnation of the *good* Bush): "I very much enjoyed our time together. He's an honest, straightforward man who loves his country. He loves his family. We share a lot of values."

However radiant his charms behind closed doors, to call that KGB old-timer "honest" and "straightforward" seems preposterous on its face, and no doubt got a hearty laugh from many of the Russian president's former colleagues—who, at Putin's whim, have taken over Russia's government, tilting it increasingly toward fascism.* On the other hand, Bush probably considers his own father "honest" and "straightforward," a man who "loves his family" and one "deeply committed to his country and to the best interests of his country," even though the elder Bush is just as dedicated to—and, as Kevin Phillips demonstrates, as much a creature of—the CIA as Putin is a product of the KGB. Bush may see a bit of Poppy in the Russian spook, or he may not. In any case, as time went on, he spoke of Putin more and more as of his double. Seeing himself in Putin, Bush liked what he saw, and called it good.

> BUSH: He is a physical fitness person† and I bet he'd like to go for a long walk.
>
> REPORTER: He's probably seen nothing like [your ranch].
>
> BUSH: I'd love to show him the canyons. I will show him the canyons. And I think he'll like it out here. . . . I think he'd like to spend some time in Washington and do both, go to Washington and Crawford.

And, after 9/11:

---

*From 1975, Putin was a KGB spy, stationed in East Germany and Leningrad. Unusually skilled and highly dedicated, he eventually became the head of the Federal Security Service, the KGB's successor organization.

Reportedly, Bush's instant bond with Putin was, at least in part, based on the latter's Christian piety. At their first meeting, Putin showed Bush the Russian Orthodox crucifix that he wears around his neck, and told of its dramatic rescue from an office fire. "Then you are close to eternal life," Bush said to him. David Aikman, *A Man of Faith: The Spiritual Journey of George W. Bush* (Nashville: W Publishing Group, 2004), p. 152.

†Bush too, of course, "is a physical fitness person," spending much time in the White House gym and jogging miles each day, whenever possible.

And it's my honor to welcome to Central Texas a new style leader, a reformer, a man who loves his country as much as I love mine, a man who loves his wife as much as I love mine, a man who loves his daughters as much as I love my daughters, and a man who's going to make a huge difference in making the world more peaceful by working closely with the United States.*

The Bad Guys

While Bush *likes* Putin because Putin seems to Bush to be a sort of Dubya on the Volga, the leaders Bush particularly hates seem also to appear to him as versions of himself. As Putin is a "good Bush" in the mind of Bush, Kim Jong-il is a "bad Bush," our president's inordinate hatred of the North Korean dictator betraying what would appear to be a displaced *self*-hatred. Otherwise, his animus is inexplicable.

Bush's hatred of the North Korean tyrant came as quite a shock to Kim Dae-Jung, South Korea's president, when he came to Washington on March 7, 2001, expecting Bush to bless his efforts to resolve the tensions between North and South. Instead, Bush stunned his guest by casting North Korea as a predatory threat. First he sounded an alarm that would become familiar after 9/11: "We want to make sure that their ability to develop and spread weapons of mass destruction was, in fact, stopped, they're willing to stop it and that we could verify that in fact they had stopped it." Bush then doubted North Korea's inclination to

---

*Interestingly, Bush was speaking of the Russian as an ally in the U.S. "war on terror" as early as July of 2001—two months before the terrorist attacks of 9/11. "As you know, I'm going to see him in a couple of weeks," Bush said on July 6. "I look forward to continuing what has been a very good relationship. And it's important that I have a good relationship with Mr. Putin, because it's good for the—it's good for our nations, and it's also good for the world, so we can work together to make the world more secure.

"And we share common interests. He's deeply concerned about extremism and what extremism can mean to Russia. And, as you know, I am, too. He recognizes there are new threats in the twenty-first century. The United States is not a threat. And we can work cooperatively to address the new threats of the twenty-first century."

observe bilateral agreements: "Part of the problem in dealing with North Korea, there's not very much transparency."

Bush thus set back the Korean reconciliation effort, pushed the North Koreans to speed up nuclear arms production, and soured U.S. relations with both South Korea and Japan. After 9/11, with Iraq obsessing him, he sought to calm our allies in the East, whose fears he had just deepened by including North Korea in his "Axis of Evil," the nonexistent global network Bush had startlingly propounded in his State of the Union speech on January 29, 2002. On February 20, he made remarks suggesting a disinclination to make war on North Korea, although he could not help deploring, once again, the menacing opacity of that grim garrison state. "I love freedom," said the president. "I worry about a regime that is closed and not transparent."

Certainly there was a material dimension to the president's hard line, as Kim Jong-il was Bush & Co.'s main excuse for spending billions on "missile defense." However, that motive alone cannot account for the intensity of Bush's personal hatred for the tyrant. That feeling soon exploded into view, for no apparent reason. On May 27, 2002, Bush strode into the Mansfield Room for what was meant to be a quick pro forma meeting with the Senate Republicans before a ceremony honoring Nancy Reagan in the Capitol Rotunda. The president had just been badly jarred, however, by the news that he had actually been warned beforehand, in a general way, about 9/11. "No question, when he walked into the room he was shaken," said one Republican to *Newsweek*'s Howard Fineman. Bush then shocked his fellow partisans with "a jut-jawed, disjointed discourse with a tinge of diatribe and a crescendo of podium pounding."

The final object of the president's wrath was Kim Jong-il, whose name apparently provoked the maddest podium-bashing. "He's starving his own people!" Bush shouted, and complained that Kim was jailing intellectuals in "a Gulag the size of Houston." He compared the North Korean to "a spoiled child at a dinner table," and called him a "pygmy." "Stunned senators didn't know quite what to make of the performance," Fineman reported. " 'It was like in church, when the sermon goes on too long and you're not sure what the point is,' one told *Newsweek*. 'Nobody

dared look at anybody else.' " And a few months after that, in August—
as the charges that "Bush Knew" continued to resound—the president
launched into yet another diatribe against the North Korean tyrant, this
time in a taped exchange with Bob Woodward, who was doing the background interviews for *Bush at War*:

> I loathe Kim Jong Il.—I've got a visceral reaction to this guy
> because he is starving his people. It appalls me.—I feel passionate
> about this.—They tell me, well we may not need to move too fast,
> because the financial burdens on people will be so immense if this
> guy were to topple.—I just don't buy that.

Bush's reason for thus "loathing" Kim Jong-il was unconvincing, and
not just because this president has shown no empathy for *any* suffering
masses, except at photo ops and packed churches. First of all, while
North Korea's Stalinist regime has clearly used the famine to keep certain
regions of the country hungrier than others, such triage is not terror
famine, and in any case the North's grave shortages—a national catastrophe since the mid-nineties—were not created by the government but
are a consequence of economic breakdown, flooding, heavy winters, and
the cutoff of the supplementary aid that used to come from China and
the Soviet Union. While dire indeed, moreover, North Korea's famine
certainly is not the only such acute food crisis in the world. For several
years now, famine has been devastating Africa, particularly the nations of
the Horn, as well as Eritrea, Ethiopia, and Mauritania. The situation in
Zimbabwe is critical, as it was when Bush was ranting about Kim Jong-
il. The problem there has been much worsened by the racist and illegal
land redistribution policy of dictator Robert Mugabe, and yet Bush has
not made any moves to help *those* starving millions, nor has he called
Mugabe names.

There is no doubt that North Korea is a grim, fanatical dictatorship
whose paranoid worldview, mammoth army, and latent nuclear capability pose a considerable threat to other nations in the region and to world
peace. That fact calls for statesmanship, not wrathful personal attacks—
whose strange intensity would seem to come from something within
Bush himself. "A spoiled child at the dinner table"? Who does that

remind us of? Bush himself was certainly a very pampered child—and, some might say, still is—and has quite a temper. He often bangs the table or the lectern when frustrated, as he did toward the climax of that very tantrum, with its "crescendo of podium pounding." It is perhaps significant that Bush exploded on those senators in May 2002, just when he had been accused of having known beforehand that the terrorists were getting ready to attack. If it is true that Bush was culpable *in any way* for 9/11—whether through incompetence or something worse—those charges would have been enough to drive him not to tell the truth, of course, but to attack *Kim Jong-il* for killing *his* "own people."

In any case, the president's indictment of the North Korean tyrant was also a self-indictment. "I worry about a regime that is closed and not transparent." So do we all. That the government is tightly closed in North Korea, however, ought to matter less to any sane American than that "there's not very much transparency" in these United States, which, under Bush, has turned into a land of secret warrants and closed tribunals, where the president feels free to tell an eminent reporter, "I do not need to explain why I say things."*

Of course, Saddam Hussein has been the most notorious of the president's dark *Doppelgangers*. "This is a man who continually lies. This is a man who does not know the truth. This is a man who's a threat to peace," Bush said on September 26, 2002—by which time it was apparent to the world that Bush himself was such a man, and one more powerful by far than the Iraqi despot. As war approached, despite the opposition of the world at large and the majority of Bush's fellow citizens, and as the weakness of his case became overt, Bush's inadvertent self-indictment grew more obvious, that very propaganda drive itself presenting *him* as the unprecedented menace he was warning us against: "These are the actions of a regime engaged in a willful charade," he said on March 6, 2003. "These are the actions of a regime that systematically

---

*The president's ire over Kim Jong-il's oppression of North Korean "intellectuals" is similarly telling, as Bush himself bears little love for the intellectuals in his own country, and would no doubt confine them if he could.

and deliberately is defying the world." That *Bush* was thus "defying the world" had been quite obvious for months.

> REPORTER: What do you make of the fact that millions of people across the globe are taking to the street to protest your approach to Iraq? And if you decide to go to war, how do you wage a campaign in the face of such stiff opposition?

> BUSH: Two points: one is that democracy is a beautiful thing, and that people are allowed to express their opinion and I welcome people's right to say what they believe.
> Secondly, evidently some in the world don't view Saddam Hussein as a risk to peace; I respectfully disagree. Saddam Hussein has gassed his own people, Saddam Hussein has got weapons of mass destruction, Saddam Hussein has made—defied the United Nations, Saddam Hussein is providing links to terrorists, Saddam Hussein is a threat to America, and we will deal with him.
> You know, I—war is my last choice, but the risk of doing nothing is even a worst [*sic*] option, as far as I'm concerned. I owe it to the American people to secure this country; I will do so.

Although democracy is "beautiful," in other words, and people can say anything they like, this president is not obliged to listen to them. All he need do is *assert* the charges against Saddam Hussein, and that's enough.

> I don't spend a lot of time taking polls around the world to tell me what I think is the right way to act. I just got to know how I feel. I feel strongly about freedom, I feel strongly about liberty, and I feel strongly about the obligation to make the world a more peaceful place. And I take those responsibilities really seriously.

Thus guided by mere whim ("I just got to know how I feel"), Bush actually appeared to be *more* dictatorial than Iraq's dictator: Here he was promoting a preemptive war on his say-so alone, whereas Saddam Hussein was trying only to seem strong enough to stay in power. And as it was *Bush* who was defying world opinion, so was it *Bush* who was "defying the United Nations," even as he posed as the UN's defender: "This is a man," he said indignantly about Saddam Hussein on October 28, 2002, "who has made the United Nations look foolish"—and *in the next breath* made the United Nations look foolish, much to the amusement of his audience in New Mexico:

> I went to the United Nations; I said to them as clearly as I could, in Western language—[*Laughter, cheers*]—I said, "You can be an effective body to help us keep the peace, you can be an effective U.N., or you can be the League of Nations."

The president's aggressive condescension made it clear that he was telling the United Nations what to do—a unilateral directive to the world's central multilateral institution:

> "It's your choice to make. You have the choice as to whether or not you will allow this dictator to continue to defy the United Nations, and therefore weaken you, or you can join with the United States and disarm him like he said he would do [*sic*]."

As the United States moved ever closer to preemptive war against Iraq's dictator, Bush's own demeanor grew more dictatorial. On New Year's Eve 2002, a journalist presumed to raise a timely question:

> REPORTER: Mr. President, looking ahead here, with a possible war with Iraq looming, North Korea nuclear conflict as well as Osama bin Laden still at large, is the world safer as we look ahead to 2003?
>
> BUSH: . . . You said we're headed to war in Iraq. I don't know why you say that. I hope we're not headed to war in Iraq. I'm the person who gets to decide, not you.

The reporter had *not* "said we're headed to war in Iraq," but Bush imagined that he had, so jealous is this president of his command (and, as well, so prone to blurting out the very thing he's trying to hide).* And

---

*Also worth noting is the president's puerile locution: "I'm the person who *gets* to decide" suggests that that decision struck him not as agonizing but as pretty cool. Otherwise, he would have said that he was the person who *has* to decide, implying a painful rather than a neat prerogative.

yet, despite his swagger, and his matchless military power, and the fact that he was the aggressor in this situation, and Saddam Hussein his target, Bush seemed to think it was the other way around. In other words, his drive against Saddam Hussein was not just cynical, the president deliberately concocting a false case against the despot in furtherance of a simple plot for oil or global dominance. Bush, in his projective way, apparently believed *himself* to be the target of *Saddam Hussein*. He saw his prey as predator, his own predation as pure self-defense.

> There's no doubt his hatred is mainly directed at us. There's no doubt he can't stand us. After all, this is the guy that tried to kill my dad at one time.

The president was here referring to the alleged Iraqi plot to assassinate the elder Bush while he was visiting Kuwait in April 1993. Whether Bush believed the plot to be authentic (there is evidence suggesting it was not) or a Kuwaiti fabrication, his statement was remarkable, as he appeared to have forgotten, or never to have understood, the fact that if Saddam Hussein did try to kill the president's dad, that dad had tried to kill Saddam Hussein: for weeks in 1991, Bush the Elder had deployed the full resources of the U.S. military with the not-so-secret purpose of "decapitating" the Iraqi government. His eldest son either could not remember or did not perceive that sequence of events, but automatically projected all the "hatred" in that conflict onto the Iraqi ("There's no doubt he can't stand us"), while casting "us"—the Bush family, the United States—as wholly peaceable.

With the war looming, but unannounced, the president pretended that he had not made his mind up yet, while the people of Iraq, and the military families of the United States, were quietly terrified of what the U.S. president might do. But throughout that period of painful international suspense, the U.S. president was deeply worried about what *Saddam Hussein* might do to *us*. Around the time that Bush reminded people that "the guy [had] tried to kill my dad," the Pentagon was preparing to "shock and awe" the people of Iraq and then obliterate the Ba'athist government—and yet the president was lying awake night after night, in fear of what might happen *here*, through the apocalyptic medium of Iraq's "weapons of mass destruction" or Iraq's connection to al Qaeda. (Iraq had no such weapons or connection.) "Four months ago," rightist pundit Peggy Noonan wrote in late January of 2003,

> a friend who had recently met with the president on other business reported to me that in conversation the president had said that he has been having some trouble sleeping, and that when he awakes in the morning the first thing he often thinks is: I wonder if this is the day Saddam will do it.
>
> "Do what exactly?" I asked my friend. He told me he understood the president to be saying that he wonders if this will be the day Saddam launches a terror attack here, on American soil.*

Cheney too, despite his reputation as "the man behind the curtain" at the White House, was not *pretending* to be frightened of Saddam Hussein's fictitious terrorist capacity. "Cheney, say those who know him, is in no way cynically manipulative," *Newsweek* reported in November of 2003. "By all accounts, he is genuinely convinced that the threat is imminent and menacing." Genuinely scared of what Saddam Hussein might do, Bush/Cheney used that fear quite masterfully to drag the country into war, to shut off public criticism of themselves, to change the subject every time they seemed to get in trouble, and generally to keep their ratings high. "After all," Bush said of Saddam Hussein after the latter's capture, "he stayed in power by fear, by ruling through fear." True enough about Saddam Hussein; and no less true of Bush & Co., for whom the radically enabling tragedy of 9/11 was, at best, a dream come true.

---

*In a mid-December interview with Barbara Walters, the Bushes seemed to confirm this story:

MRS. BUSH: Sure. I mean, you know, we have a lot of challenges in our country. We're facing something we've never faced before, something very different from anything Americans have faced. I have a lot of confidence. I have a lot of confidence in my husband, I have a lot of confidence in the American people; but, you know, there are moments when you wake up at night and say a little prayer.

WALTERS: You comfort each other?

PRES. BUSH: You bet.

20/20, ABC, 12/11/03.

To Rid the World of "Evil"

That both Bush and Cheney were terrified of a fictitious evil, when they themselves were doing the terrifying, suggests that what the two feared most was something in themselves. Certainly al Qaeda was, and still is, a danger to be reckoned with, but the objective fact of *that* grave threat bears no relation to Bush/Cheney's wild projective fears of what *Saddam Hussein* might do, as that tottering strongman had no more connection to the Islamists than Kim Jong-il had. The regime's eagerness to smash Saddam Hussein—an eagerness that drove them from Day One—was thoroughly irrational (especially since the Ba'ath's abuse of the Iraqi people had perturbed the Cheney/Rumsfeld circle not at all throughout the eighties).

What strikes fear in the hearts of Bush and Co., then, is no real evil-doer living in the world, but something evil in the hearts of Bush and Cheney—as the president himself has often inadvertently confessed, in random bursts of accidental truth:

> We are resolved to rout out terror wherever it exists **to save the world from freedom**!

> The more we value the ability to worship God the way we see fit, the more they hate us.
> [*Cheers, applause.*]
> The more we honor church and synagogue and mosque, the more they hate us. The more we speak our mind freely, the more they hate us. The more free our press is, the more they hate us.
> And therefore, since **we're not going to yield to our freedoms**, since we're not going to yield the values we hold dear, we've got to do everything we can to defend the homeland.

> **Our most important job is to protect an enemy which still exists and still hates**, from taking other lives. People say, well, you know, are you sure they're still out there? Yeah, I'm sure. And I know they still hate.

They understand it doesn't matter how long it takes, no matter what the cost, we're going to do our duty, and that is to defend freedom, and **to defeat the enemy of terror!**

The second pillar of peace and security in our world is the willingness of free nations, when the last resort arrives, **to retain aggression and evil by force.**

And who struck the United States on 9/11?

No, the enemy hit us, but they didn't know who we were hitting!*

Such clumsy revelations are not funny, as they tell us what we're really up against. American democracy is threatened by no mere cabal of scheming oilmen or titanic business cronies, slyly playing on the people's fears. There is such a cabal, of course, but this one is compelled by fear as well as greed, is generally persuaded by the lies it tells the rest of us, and will not stop pursuing its own demons until everybody else is dead. Until the people rise to reckon with it—reasserting the ideals, and honoring the laws, that gave this nation its extraordinary promise—the apocalyptic movement now in power will trample us and all the world,

---

*According to the president, the enemy is an inveterate lurker—and so is Bush himself. "I fully understand the enemy still lurks out there and the enemy still would like to hit us," he said on January 15, 2002. "One of the things that we're finding is that our enemy is shadowy," he said on May 14. "They lurk behind civil institutions, and then they strike." "And they're still out there," he said on June 12. "These people— you know, these—these—these killers are—they're still lurking around." "We're still at risk here in America," he said on October 9. "We're at risk because there's some enemies still lurking around out there." "People must understand," he said on October 18, "that there's still an enemy which lurks and desires to hurt." He put it just a little differently on November 1, when he claimed that "there's still an enemy that lurches around, which hates America." Thus "lurking" is, in Bush's universe, a terrorist activity; so it was somewhat disconcerting when, on September 21, 2002, he used it to refer to his own function:

> The United States is no longer secure because we've got oceans. We're vulnerable to attack, as we learned so vividly. My job is to not only deal with problems—*kind of run around and lurk*; my job is also to anticipate problems.

flattening the earth in ever larger circles, like a mad elephant in hot pursuit of its own tail.

To stop it, we must not only take an honest look around, but also take a long look back at our own history, for the danger now upon us is, although unprecedented in our government, one that the American people faced, and overcame, at the beginning of the history of this republic.

CHAPTER 6

The Clear and Present Danger

The Revenge of Salem

Bush's projectivity—or Cheney's, or Karl Rove's—is finally not a matter for the clinical psychologist, although the president's own case is rich, and has been analyzed persuasively by various mental health professionals. There is no doubt, for instance, that Bush shows all the psychic symptoms of the "dry drunk" syndrome—his hypersensitivity, intransigence, stark dualist perception of the world, and angry quickness to blame others for his problems all betraying the profile of the alcoholic who, disdaining therapy, has *forced* himself to give up drinking, and so spends every waking moment struggling *not to drink*. (In Bush's case, this diagnosis also would shed light on his compulsive exercising.) Oliver James, a British child psychologist, has come up with a subtler and no less persuasive reading based closely on the details of the president's biography. James argues that Bush, deeply angry at his parents, "jailed his rebellious self" by adopting the repressive creed of Christian fundamentalism, channeling his anger "into a fanatical moral crusade to rid the world of evil."

A psychoanalytic view of the United States' projective warriors would surely be enhanced by some discussion of the nation's postwar foreign policy, which has consistently entailed the sudden transformation of an erstwhile client, or ally, into an enemy. "Saddam Hussein has gassed his own people, Saddam Hussein has got weapons of mass destruction," claimed the president—overlooking, or forgetting, the fact that the

United States, and the elder Bush's regime in particular, had *given* the
dictator many of those "weapons of mass destruction." When, in 1988,
Saddam had "gassed his own people" at Halabja, the Bush White House,
while issuing a wan official protest, privately assured the murderer that
all was well between the United States and Iraq, and the Bush regime
came down *against* congressional sanctions for that crime. Throughout
the eighties, Reagan/Bush were ardent suitors to "the beast of Baghdad,"
whom they deemed not "a threat to America" but a useful instrument,
inclined to do as he was told. (As to his seizure of Kuwait, the Iraqi
cleared his plans beforehand with the State Department.)

The Arab "freedom fighters" who evolved into al Qaeda also started out
as creatures of the U.S. government. Their anti-Soviet troops were armed
and funded by the Reagan team. Even earlier, the United States equipped
the Islamists to harass the Soviets along the border with Afghanistan,
provoking a long war designed to "bleed" the Soviet Union. (Thus Zbigniew Brzezinksi, Jimmy Carter's national security adviser, chucklingly
admitted to *Le Nouvel Observateur* in early 1998.) A government thus
prone to turning longtime clients into sudden demons would appear to
be peculiarly hospitable to the projective warrior, who has the self-
unconsciousness and ever-ready rage for just such mad reversals.*

And yet the U.S. tendency toward policies that result in "blowback,"
as important as it is, still does not sufficiently enlarge the psychological
discussion, for the suicidal projectivity of which we speak is surely not
restricted to Americans of any sort, but marks all movements finally
based on animosity alone. Such hatred never quite perceives itself.
Instead it postures as its very opposite, imputing hatred only *to the enemy*;
or those who hate exult in their own hatred, deeming it a necessary zeal
learned *from* the enemy, and now essential to the enemy's annihilation.

---

*Donald Rumsfeld has a marked propensity for such Orwellian U-turns. It was
Rumsfeld who flew to Baghdad in 1983, specifically to make nice with Saddam Hussein (on the orders of George Shultz, Reagan's secretary of state). And as a member of
the board of ABB, Rumsfeld was instrumental in providing North Korea with "the
design and key components of two light-water [nuclear] reactors," *Fortune* reported
in the spring of 2003. Richard Behar, "Rummy's North Korea Connection," *Fortune*,
5/12/03.

Such has been the fighting spirit of all militant religious sweeps against the infidel, and of America throughout her "savage wars" against the Indians, and, later, of the Turks against the Armenians, the Nazi drive against "the Jew" and other *Untermenschen*, the Stalinists against their endless enemies at home and everywhere. Whatever movement has proposed so radically to cleanse the nation, or the world, or "the community," of "evil," "heresy," or "barbarism" dooms itself to self-extinction, for its own soldiers, forever apprehending their own inner "evil," can never cease to *need* an enemy, and therefore keep inventing new ones, even after the most obvious "barbarians" or "heretics" have been cut down.

Such is the suicidal fighting spirit of Bush/Cheney's base, the quasi-Christian right; and also of al Qaeda, for that matter, and of the warlike Hindus of the Bharatiya Janata Party in India, and of the most relentless champions of Greater Israel. It is the paranoid quintessence of all fervent otherworldly movements that despise the secular constraints of worldly law.* That spirit is inimical not just to democratic practice, but to peace and order generally, as the early champions of our Constitution understood. In their time, it was a certain angry variant of Christianity that posed the greatest threat and that required the total separation of all churches from the powers of the state. As the Americans knew well from Europe's bloody history, the divisive purism of sectarian Christianity must never be allowed to wield the instruments of government. "The word Christianity is equally as vague as the word religion. No two sectaries can agree what is it. It is *lo here* and *lo there*. The two principal sectaries, Papists and Protestants, have often cut each other's throats about it," writes Tom Paine.

> The Papists call the Protestants heretics, and the Protestants call the Papists idolaters. The minor sectaries have shown the same spirit of rancor, but as the civil law restrains them from blood, they content themselves with preaching damnation against each other.

---

*This is not to say that such an animus drives only true believers in some religious creed or other. Christopher Hitchens, for example, might best be described as a fanatical atheist.

The framers were intent on keeping the United States secure from such dogmatic anarchy and, no less, from the tyranny of theocratic rule, such as the Puritans had introduced into New England. It was to keep the people's freedom thus preserved from the oppressive troops of *any* faith—and thereby keep religious liberty itself alive—that Jefferson and his associates deliberately conceived our *godless* Constitution, as historians Isaac Kramnick and R. Laurence Moore have aptly termed it. Americans can worship as they please, or not at all, because our government must never be transformed into an instrument or agency of any faith. "It does me no injury for my neighbor to say there are twenty gods or no God. It neither picks my pocket nor breaks my leg," wrote Jefferson, who was so proud of having realized that libertarian conception of religion that he asked to have his epitaph make mention of Virginia's statute for religious freedom. He made his libertarian intentions very clear in his account of an attempted emendation in the wording of that law's preamble:

> Where the preamble declares that coercion is a departure from the plan of the holy author of our religion, an amendment was proposed, by inserting the word "Jesus Christ," so that it should read "a departure from the plan of Jesus Christ, the holy author of our religion." *The insertion was rejected by a great majority, in proof that they meant to comprehend within the mantle of its protection the Jew and the Gentile, the Christian and Mahometan, the Hindoo and infidel of every denomination* (emphasis added).

The United States, in short, was quite deliberately *not* formed as a "Christian Republic": a fact that was reconfirmed a few years into U.S. history, when George Washington—another of the many Founders dubious about fanatical religions, Christianity included—signed the Treaty of Tripoli in 1796: "The Government of the United States of America is not, in any sense, founded on the Christian religion."*

*The line comes from Article 11, which thus reads in its entirety: "As the government of the United States of America is not in any sense founded on the Christian Religion,—as it has in itself no character of enmity against the laws, religion or tranquility of [Muslims],—and as the said States never have entered into any war or act

The pointed godlessness of the U.S. Constitution was its boldest feature and most radical departure from tradition. "We were (in our own
view of ourselves) 'founded' not by an oracle or by a God or by mythic
figures or by some writings but by a particular group of people at a particular time and place with a particular set of rather clearly articulated
ideas, about which they argued," writes William Lee Miller. "And one of
those ideas was freedom of 'conscience' or belief." The document's
unprecedented secularity was a stroke at once exhilarating to the champions of the Enlightenment worldwide, and reassuring to a broad majority of thoughtful Christians in this country—and, predictably, anathema
to those Americans who wanted the United States to be a Protestant
theocracy. The Constitution did not just offend the theocrats' religious
scruples, but threatened them with social and political demotion, as that
faction comprised the erstwhile rulers of the British colonies, especially
in New England, where the clergy had been powerful enough to banish
heretics and order witches executed.

The anticonstitutional reaction was intense, invoking fears that sound
familiar to us now. In January 1788, the *New York Daily Advertiser* ran
an article imagining the social consequences of abolishing religious tests
for would-be office-holders—the purport of Article VI:

> 1st. Quakers, who will make the blacks saucy, and at the same time
> deprive us of the means of defence [Quakers being abolitionists
> and pacifists]—2ndly. Mahometans, who ridicule the doctrine of
> the Trinity—3dly. Deists, abominable wretches—4thly. Negroes,
> the seed of Cain—5thly. Beggars, who when set on horseback will
> ride to the devil—6thly. Jews etc. etc.

Keen on a Christian commonwealth *instead* of what the framers had
conceived, the theocrats kept up their agitation, which came to a

---

of hostility against any Mehomitan nation, it is declared by the parties that no pretext
arising from religious opinions shall ever produce an interruption of the harmony
existing between the two countries." The vow not to use religious differences as the
pretext for a war with Libya was reconfirmed in an amendment to the treaty, signed
by Jefferson in 1806. (See Article XIV.) The text is online at http://www.yale.edu/law
web/avalon/diplomacy/barbary/bar1796t.htm.

crescendo in the presidential race of 1800. Their wrath was heavily exploited by the Federalists, who, much like Bush/Cheney's GOP, preferred the most restricted franchise possible, and so had nothing much to offer but fear-mongering propaganda of the crudest kind.

This meant translation of the choice between the Federalists and the Republicans into a Manichaean struggle between good and evil, light and darkness, decent order and infernal chaos. To vote for Jefferson, the preachers thundered from their pulpits (and the Federalists repeated), was to vote for Satan, as the Republican had been seduced to revolutionary atheism in France, where he had served as the U.S. ambassador. He was an "anti-Christ," "French infidel," a "howling atheist," the zealots of his day apparently projecting onto him—a man profoundly influenced by Jesus—their own doubts, sense of guilt, subversive longings:

> Can serious and reflecting men look about them and doubt, that if Jefferson is elected, and the Jacobins get into authority, that those morals which protect our lives from the knife of the assassin— which guard the chastity of our wives and daughters from seduction and violence—defend our property from plunder and devastation, and shield our religion from contempt and profanation, will not be trampled upon and exploded?

Jefferson's election would bring down on the United States "the just vengeance of insulted heaven," which would entail a hellish orgy of apocalyptic punishment: "dwellings in flames, hoary hairs bathed in blood, female chastity violated . . . children writhing on the pike and halberd." The choice was crystal clear, as one campaign placard put it:

> GOD—AND A RELIGIOUS PRESIDENT;
> or impiously declare for
> JEFFERSON—AND NO GOD!!!

Despite his own intense religious faith, Jefferson refused to answer such outrageous charges, complaining only in his private correspondence. "The floodgates of calumny have opened upon me," he wrote to a friend, and in the midst of the campaign, bedeviled by his clerical antagonists, composed what is perhaps his most enduring line about the freedom of the mind of man: a line that many of us know, but whose crucial context is unknown to most of us. If he had time to express them properly, his views on Christianity, he wrote to Benjamin Rush on September 23, 1800, would "displease neither the rational Christian nor Deists, and would reconcile many to a character they have too hastily rejected." He suspected, on the other hand, that nothing he could ever say or do could mollify the "irritable tribe of priests": "I do not know that it would reconcile the *genus irritabile vatum* who are all in arms against me. Their hostility is on too interesting ground to be softened." That animus, he reckoned, was based on an inordinate appetite for worldly power. A misreading of the First Amendment

> had given to the clergy a very favorite hope of obtaining an establishment of a particular form of Christianity thro' the U.S.; and as every sect believes its own form the true one, every one perhaps hoped for this own, but especially the Episcopalians & Congregationalists. The returning good sense of the country threatens abortion to their hopes, & they believe that any portion of power confided to me, will be exerted in opposition to their schemes. And they believe rightly: for *I have sworn upon the altar of God eternal hostility against every form of tyranny over the mind of man.* But this is all they have to fear from me: and enough too in their opinion, & this is the cause of their printing lying pamphlets against me (emphasis added).

Jefferson weathered that storm, of course, and went on to reelection four years later. The agitation of the theocrats, however, never did subside entirely. Indeed, it flared up to new heights in Jefferson's old age, when, in a letter to Thomas Cooper, he noted grimly that "[t]he atmosphere of our country is unquestionably charged with a threatening cloud of fanaticism, lighter in some parts, denser in others, but too heavy in all." "This," he concluded, "must be owing to the growth of Presbyterianism," which Jefferson described in terms that resonate uneasily today. "The blasphemy and absurdity of the five points of Calvin, and the impossibility of defending them, render their advocates impatient of reasoning, irritable, and prone to denunciation." He compares the calm religious atmosphere in Charlottesville—where "there is a good degree of religion, with a small spice only of fanaticism"—with those "districts where Presbyterianism prevails undividedly."

> Their ambition and tyranny would tolerate no rival if they had power. Systematical in grasping at an ascendancy over all other sects, they aim, like the Jesuits, at engrossing the education of the country, are hostile to every institution which they do not direct, and jealous at seeing others begin to attend at all to that object.

In the short term, that crisis might be lessened by "the progress of Unitarianism." The ultimate solution, Jefferson concludes, can only be "the diffusion of instruction" (and so his letter then proceeds to a discussion of religious teaching at the University of Virginia).

Jefferson himself, of course, prevailed against the "lying pamphlets" of his adversaries at that time, and yet the larger conflict never ended, and may never end. Between the compromising spirit of a rational democracy and the domineering temperament of paranoid religiosity—"impatient of reasoning, irritable, and prone to denunciation"—there can be no ultimate agreement, but an eternal stalemate, with that millennial tendency contained (or else the conflict ends). The late resurgence, or persistence, of that backward drive was manifest throughout the 1990s in the Christian rightists' drive against "Bill Clinton," who very easily replaced the hated "Jefferson" in *their* apocalyptic campaign propaganda: "To vote for Bill Clinton is to sin against God," warned the fiery "pro-life" cleric Randall Terry in one influential pamphlet that appeared in 1992, and that pious warning echoed and reechoed many millionfold throughout that campaign year and then again in 1996. To demonstrate that the regressive animus of 1800 has returned to plague our politics today, however, we need not point to Clinton as a surrogate for Jefferson, for Jefferson *himself* is still, or once again, a figure wildly and routinely slandered on the Christian right (or, as we shall see, pointedly misrepresented as an ardent theist). By his current detractors he alone is blamed for fostering the "myth" of church/state separation, his tolerant and rational theology dismissed as "out of step" with the evangelistic zeal of Franklin, Madison, George Mason, Washington, et al., and his absence from the Constitutional Convention—he having been (where else?) in Paris at the time—deemed "providential," as God's way of protecting that great synod from the Jacobin's demonic influence.

Although his thought has always irked our native theocrats, Jefferson's belief in nonreligious governance is now especially offensive to that movement, which, since the seventies, has undergone a major transformation—a sea change quite unnoticed by the U.S. press. While reporters were engrossed in the sensational affairs of televangelists like Jimmy Swaggart and the Bakkers, and then attending to the racist thuggery of the Christian Identity cultists in the far Northwest, an elite theocratic movement of extreme commitment and considerable wealth was fast becoming the most influential force on the religious right. This is the postmillenarian movement known as Christian Reconstructionism. A peculiarly American derivative of orthodox Presbyterianism, but now a transdenominational ideology, Christian Reconstructionism—also known as "dominion theology"—was thoroughly articulated in the masterwork of maverick theologian R. J. Rushdoony, whose mammoth summa on the creed, *The Institutes of Biblical Law*, was published in 1973 (although Rushdoony had been propagating since the fifties, as an acolyte of the conservative Presbyterian theologian Cornelius Van Til). A self-conscious elaboration on John Calvin's *Institutes of the Christian Religion*, Rushdoony's text explains the worldly pertinence—specifically, the necessary *legal* application—of the Ten Commandments, which ought to be the ultimate foundation of *all* institutions, here and everywhere.

"Reconstructionism argues that the Bible is to be the governing text for all areas of life—such as government, education, and law—not merely for 'social' or 'moral' issues like pornography, homosexuality and abortion," writes investigative journalist Frederick Clarkson. "Reconstructionists have formulated a 'Biblical worldview' and 'Biblical principles' to govern and inform their lives and their politics"—which is to say, *our* lives and *our* politics as well. For the Reconstructionists, the Bible—and, in particular, the Pentateuch, especially Leviticus—should be the basis of society itself, much as Islamists see the place of the Koran and the hadith in the great caliphate that *they* are working to establish everywhere. Whereas the focus of traditional evangelism is the world to come, the Reconstructionists want *this* world to be transformed absolutely, every humanistic institution wiped out root and branch. "The Christian goal for the world," says Reconstructionist David Chilton, "is the universal development of Biblical theocratic republics, in which every area of life is redeemed and placed under the Lordship of Jesus Christ and the rule of God's law."

These Christian nations would be just as tolerant and democratic as Iran under Khomeni, or Afghanistan under the Taliban. Non-Christians would be disenfranchised,* if not executed or enslaved (as slavery is permissible, according to the Bible), while those acceptable as citizens would be forever subject to a penal code far harsher than *shari'a* law: death by stoning for adultery, for abortion, for homosexuality, for premarital unchastity (in women), "for every one that curseth his father and his mother," or anyone who dares work on the Sabbath, or otherwise blasphemes, or who has been found guilty of apostasy, or heresy, or witchcraft, or astrology. The totality and urgency of the new way find clear expression throughout the fundamental writings of the Reconstructionists, as in this passage from Rushdoony's *Institutes*:

> Now man needs regeneration. Thus, the *first* step in the mandate is to bring men the word of God and for God to regenerate them. The *second* step is to demolish every kind of theory, humanistic, evolutionary, idolatrous, or otherwise, and every kind of rampart or opposition to the dominion of God in Christ. The world and men must be brought into captivity to Christ, under the dominion of the Kingdom of God and the law of that kingdom. *Third*, this requires that, like Paul, we court-martial or "administer justice upon all disobedience" in every area of life where we encounter it. To deny the cultural mandate is to deny Christ and surrender the world to Satan.

---

*"The long-term goal of Christians in politics should be to gain exclusive control over the franchise. Those who refuse to submit publicly to the eternal sanctions of God by submitting to His Church's public marks of the covenant—baptism and holy communion—must be denied citizenship, just as they were in ancient Israel." Gary North, *Political Polytheism* (Tyler, Tex.: Institute for Christian Economics, 1989), p. 87. A prolific propagandist for the cause, North is the late Rushdoony's son-in-law.

Thus the Reconstructionists are (among themselves) quite frank in their desire to *go back* to what they think the world was like before the bad detour of the Enlightenment, and the pestiferous Jefferson. "We live in a deeply anti-historical age," laments Reconstructionist P. Andrew Sandlin.

> Thomas Jefferson believed, "The earth belongs to the living," not the dead. Today the implicit Jeffersonians are everywhere. Most are secular humanists. To these folks, history and tradition are considered not so much irrelevant as *unreal*—they are not within the purview of the reality in which most of us live.
>
> In conscious reaction to this New A-Historical Reality, many conservative Christians and churches, the Historicists, have deliberately recovered a profound sense of the historical. We read books of history. We read great biographies. We have heroes. We love the ancient confessions of faith. We romanticize about Calvin's Geneva, Puritan New England, and the Scottish Covenanters. This is all good.
>
> Let us never forget that there *is* a glorious Christian culture in the past—in *our* past. This is medieval Europe. This is Reformation Europe. This is southern Europe and Russia. This is colonial America, and even the United States, to an extent.

Hostile to the worldly "Jeffersonians," the Reconstructionists also condemn those Christians—*pre*millenarians—who wait passively for Jesus's return, as opposed to the sort of militant preparatory *action* that the Reconstructionists demand. Despite the harshness of its language, the revolutionary Christian program is itself theoretically not violent but gradualist, based on the thorough preparation of religious cadres in private Christian schools (like Islamic *madrassas*), and their eventual infiltration into every cultural, political, and social institution, leading to a national conversion, which will in turn lead to conversion of the world. "They feel that the power of God's word will bring about this conversion. No armed force or insurrection will be needed; in fact, they believe that there will be little opposition to their plan. People will willingly accept it if it is properly presented to them." Once that New World Order is in place, however, the Bible's laws will be relentlessly enforced with all the requisite brutality, on everyone—wrong-headed Christians no less than witches and astrologers. "All who are content with a humanistic law system and do not strive to replace it with Biblical law are guilty of idolatry," Rushdoony writes. "They have forsaken the covenant of their God, and they are asking us to serve other gods. They are thus idolaters, and are, in our generation, when our world is idolatrous and our states also, to be objects of missionary activity. They must be called out of their idolatry into the service of the living God."

The movement's luminaries are all members of a highly secretive organization called the Council for National Policy (CNP), based in Alexandria, Virginia. Formed in 1981, the exact identity of the council's founders is unclear: some sources claim that rightist propaganda genius Richard Viguerie established it, as "The Right's quiet and heady answer to the Left's Council on Foreign Relations (CFR)," while others name the Texas billionaires Nelson Bunker Hunt, Herbert Hunt, and T. Cullen Davis, and still others credit Tim LaHaye. Whoever set it up, the CNP has, of course, had R. J. Rushdoony as a member, along with all the leading Christian antihumanists, including Jerry Falwell, Pat Robertson, Ralph Reed, Paul Weyrich, Donald Wildmon, Oliver North, and Howard Phillips, as well as erstwhile members of the Reagan team. (Former Attorney General Ed Meese was the council's president in 1996, and Reagan pollster Richard Wirthlin is on board.) Also on the CNP is California billionaire Howard Ahmanson, founder of the Chalcedon Institute, a Reconstructionist think tank/propaganda mill. Others of the superrich include Richard DeVos of Amway, Pierre S. DuPont IV, and several members of the Coors clan. (Although he sees *himself* as the Messiah, the Reverend Moon has been a generous contributor to the council, perhaps in expectation that its members will decide to glory in him after all, if Jesus takes too long to get back down here.)

The GOP's current national leadership is heavily represented on the council: Tom DeLay is a member, as are Representatives Dan Burton and Ernest Istook, and Senators Trent Lott, Lauch Faircloth, and Don Nickles. Such retired legislators as Dick Armey and Jesse Helms are on board also. Other major rightist politicians, while not formally affiliated, find the council a receptive place: John Ashcroft has spoken at CNP meetings. Indeed, it would be hard to find a (Protestant) Bush cohort, or anti-Clintonite, who has not at least had friendly dealings with the CNP. John Whitehead, an ex-student of Rushdoony's, and introduced by him once at the council as a man "chosen by God," directs the Rutherford Institute, a legal arm of the Chalcedon Foundation (which until his death was run by Rushdoony and funded by Howard Ahmanson). Rutherford's important mission is to fight the legal battles on behalf of Reconstructionism. It also represented Paula Jones in her lawsuit against Bill Clinton, and was therefore instrumental in the rightist campaign to destroy that president.

As a candidate for president in 1999, George W. Bush made a pilgrimage to the CNP, and gave a speech there that his campaign then refused to make available to journalists, and that has not been published yet. (Some months later, Gov. Bush officially designated June 10 as "Jesus Day" in Texas.) Moreover, Marvin Olasky, the ex-Maoist who coined the phrase "compassionate conservatism," and who long served as a key adviser to the Bush campaign, is a dedicated protégé of Ahmanson, who has evidently subsidized Olasky's late career as a polemicist. Throughout his works, Olasky gratefully acknowledges the influence of leading Reconstructionists, in one book (*Prodigal Press: The Anti-Christian Bias of the American News Media*) praising Rushdoony's explication of the Ninth Commandment—wherein Rushdoony argues that the Holocaust has been exaggerated—and, in another (*The Tragedy of American Compassion*), profusely thanking Reconstructionist George Grant, who once asserted that the only legal right that homosexuals enjoy is the right to a fair trial. In general, Olasky has espoused the Reconstructionist agenda, even at its most perverse. In *Fighting for Liberty and Virtue*, he takes pains to note that, "[w]hile Scripture makes defense of slavery in some modes impossible and in other modes difficult, it does not simply ban all of its modes." (Introduced to Olasky by Karl Rove sometime before the presidential race, Dubya was much impressed by the professor, who became the governor's top adviser on welfare.)

Whatever Bush promised the assembly at the CNP, his commitment to the theocratic cause has much impressed the movement's most devoted activists. Those who take the longer view are not much fazed by his occasional transgressions. Late in his first term, Bush keenly disappointed many on the right: Michael Savage called for his impeachment, so disgusted was he, as were others, by the president's employer-friendly immigration policy, and many rightists felt betrayed when he did nothing to forbid all those gay marriages in San Francisco. With their eyes on the future, those at work on forging an all-Christian USA are overjoyed that Bush is president, for they correctly see the regime's imposition on the people as itself a signal victory for their movement.* In February of

---

*The pro-Bush faction on the Supreme Court has shown its antidemocratic animus not only by aborting the election in 2000, but also, in several cases, by explicitly endorsing theocratic principles. In 1989, at the request of the Arizona GOP, Sandra Day O'Connor wrote a letter urging that Republicans adopt a party resolution stating (incorrectly) that the Supreme Court has held the United States to be "a Christian nation . . . based on the absolute law of the Bible, not a democracy." Clarence Thomas has routinely spoken as a sympathetic guest at Christian rightist gatherings, and Antonin Scalia, the prime mover behind *Bush v. Gore*, has faulted secular democracy for its "tendency . . . to obscure the divine authority behind government." The entire passage—a complicated apologia for capital punishment—is worth quoting:

> The mistaken tendency to believe that a democratic government, being nothing more than the composite will of its individual citizens, has no more moral power or authority than they do as individuals has adverse effects in other areas as well. It fosters civil disobedience, for example, which proceeds on the assumption that what the individual citizen considers an unjust law—even if it does not compel *him* to act unjustly—need not be obeyed. St. Paul would not agree. "Ye must needs be subject," he said, "not only for wrath, but also for conscience sake." For conscience sake. The reaction of people of faith to this tendency of democracy to obscure the divine authority behind government should not be resignation to it, but the resolution to combat it as effectively as possible. We have done that in this country (and continental Europe has not) by preserving in our public life many visible reminders that—in the words of a Supreme Court opinion from the 1940s—"we are a religious people, whose institutions presuppose a Supreme Being." These reminders include: "In God we trust" on our coins, "one nation, under God" in our Pledge of Allegiance, the opening of sessions of our legislatures with a prayer, the opening of sessions of my Court [*sic*] with "God save the United States and this Honorable Court," annual Thanksgiving proclamations issued by our President at the direction of Congress, and constant invocations of divine support in the speeches of our political

2003, Lou Sheldon, founder of the Traditional Values Coalition and a longtime activist for the religious ultraright, was asked if Bush was generally in sync with Sheldon's overall agenda. Sheldon answered, "George Bush *is* our agenda!" Lately, several other Reconstructionists have also reconfirmed that jubilant equation, as Bush himself is ever more explicit in his claims to be an instrument of God.

By Their Fruits Ye Shall Know Them

The radical collapse of all distinction between church and state, and the promotion of an angry "Christianity" as the USA's official state religion, have grown increasingly apparent as the Bush regime has turned more grandiose and reckless after 9/11. That revolutionary program has gradually come into view despite the press's failure to expose it, and despite the random efforts of the White House to conceal it ("Well, I—first of all, I would never justify—I would never use God to promote policy decisions," Bush said, without conviction, to Brit Hume in an interview on September 22, 2003). A cursory survey of Bush/Cheney's foreign and domestic innovations will make clear that this regime has, from the start, been hard at work transforming the United States into a theocratic system, and, globally, at the gradual creation of a nominally Christian New World Order.

Although the president made quite a show of mounting *no* rhetorical attack on Islam or on Muslims in the dark days after 9/11, as if to reassure the world that the United States was *not* intent on waging a religious war, that tolerant pose was shortly overwhelmed, those words of peace obliterated, by much graphic counterevidence. The United States was obviously mounting a "crusade"—as Bush himself so tactlessly announced on September 16, 2001. All he meant was "a broad cause," Ari Fleischer reassured reporters two days later, and yet Muslim residents

---

leaders, which often conclude, "God bless America." All this, as I say, is most un-European, and helps explain why our people are more inclined to understand, as St. Paul did, that government carries the sword as "the minister of God," to "execute wrath" upon the evildoer.
Antonin Scalia, "God's Justice and Ours," *First Things* 123 (May 2002), pp. 17–21.

of the United States (and of Afghanistan) could not be blamed for thinking otherwise. At once John Ashcroft's troops began to sweep illegally
through Muslim neighborhoods, hauling off "suspected terrorists" by the
hundreds and treating them as enemy aliens, and there was like harassment by police departments all across the country. Soon, moreover,
some of Bush's best-known co-religionists and sometime spiritual advisers started venting anti-Muslim propaganda. Franklin Graham called
Islam "a very evil and very wicked religion," and Pat Robertson, who
compared the Koran to *Mein Kampf*, declared, projectively, about the
Muslims: "They want to coexist until they can control, dominate and
then, if need be, destroy." Said Jerry Falwell: "I think Muhammad was a
terrorist." The White House offered no rebuke.

Bush himself has carefully avoided venting such anti-Islamic senti-
ments in public. He has also tried not to repeat the word "crusade," or
otherwise betray the war-like zeal that motivates his strain of Christianity. At this he has been less successful, unable, as he is, to mask his true
intentions and desires. Five months after urging his "crusade" on 9/16,
he did it once again in speaking to our troops in Anchorage. (The Cana-
dians, he said, "stand with us in this incredibly important crusade to
defend freedom, this campaign to do what is right for our children and
our grandchildren.")* I am not a fanatic, Bush sometimes tries to say—
and then, as ever, contradicts his wan pretense at moderation and humil-
ity with some insanely grandiose remark. "I'm surely not going to justify
war based upon God," he awkwardly assured Bob Woodward. However,
Woodward also reports the president's explanation for his refusal to consult his dad for guidance: "You know, he is the wrong father to appeal to
in terms of strength. There is a higher father that I appeal to." God told
him to run for president, Bush says, and God told him to strike al
Qaeda, and God told him to occupy Iraq. "I haven't suffered doubt,"
Bush said to Woodward (adding, without irony, "I hope I'm able to con-

*Bush has otherwise made clear that he could not care less about Muslim sensibil-
ities. "One of the ways to deal with oversupply is to sell our pork in foreign markets,"
he told the World Pork Expo in Des Moines on June 7, 2002. "We ought to be selling our hogs all across the world."

vey that in a humble way"). For all his weak demurrals, Bush does in fact perceive the "war on terrorism" as a new crusade, as a member of his family makes explicit:

> George sees this as a religious war. He doesn't have a p.c. view of the war. His view of this is that they are trying to kill the Christians. And we the Christians will strike back with more force and more ferocity than they will ever know.

Of course, it would be comforting to see this only as a case of individual mania, which reasonable people—Christian and non-Christian—might shrug off. And yet this is no laughing matter, as Bush is not alone in his apocalyptic frame of mind, but aided and abetted very powerfully. Having variously seized our nation's government, the GOP also pursues "religious war." In a fund-raising letter mailed on March 3, 2004, Marc Racicot, director of the Bush/Cheney's "re-election" drive, again deployed the c-word, Muslim perceptions notwithstanding: "From leading a global **crusade** against terrorism to signing into law two of the largest tax cuts in history," the letter reads, "[Bush] has provided strong, steady leadership during difficult times." Questioned by reporters, Racicot was unapologetic, claiming that the word need not denote a holy war. However, he then sounded something like a holy warrior himself, in offering the ecstatic statement that the letter's focus, and therefore Bush's goal, is "to protect the cause of freedom—not just for a moment, not for a day, not for ten years, but for a hundred years." Although he stopped short of "a thousand years," that millenarian utterance would have come as no surprise.

Apparently the U.S. military also is on board for Bush & Co.'s grand new drive against the Saracens. The spirit of crusade shines forth from the hearty countenance of Army Lieutenant General William G. "Jerry" Boykin, deputy undersecretary of defense for intelligence, who caused a momentary stir by giving talks, sometimes in his military uniform, at fundamentalist churches, where he would call America "a Christian nation," assert that Bush had been "appointed by God," and tell the rapt believers that our enemy in the "war on terrorism" is "a guy named Satan." Christians believe in "a real god," whereas the god of Islam is "an idol." He would also show the audience a photograph that he had taken in Somalia, clearly demonstrating "a demonic spirit over the city of Mogadishu." That Bush & Co. did not replace or even reprimand the general (who did not apologize, insisting, quite sincerely, that he was "not a zealot") stood out as mere further evidence of just how militant the regime's Christian doctrine really is.*

Shortly after the invasion, U.S. troops stationed in Iraq received a booklet called "A Christian's Duty," adjuring them to pray for Bush and even mail the president a special tear-out form assuring him that, while dodging potshots and firing on civilians, *they* were praying for *him*. Meanwhile, the ravaged theater of the occupation has been overrun by Southern Baptist missionaries seeking to exploit Iraqi misery for Jesus' sake. Laden with clean blankets, bottled water, bread, and bandages— and countless Bibles—the Christian soldiers of the International Mission Board use such material inducements to convert as many Muslims as they can, waging what their Web site calls a "war for souls":

> Southern Baptists must understand that there is a war for souls under way in Iraq. . . . Even as Islamic leaders try to tighten their grip on the country and its people, cult groups like the Mormons and Jehovah's Witnesses are sending hundreds of their missionaries into Iraq to spread their pseudo-Christianity.

Muslims have been horrified by such spiritual carpetbagging. "The Iraqi people are in a state of siege—they lack, food, water, everything—and to come to exploit it and to give it in the name of Jesus Christ the Lord is unacceptable," Ali Abu Zarkuk of the American Muslim Council told

---

*Boykin was promoted after that brief storm blew over. For a full account of Boykin's power in the "war on terror," and more on his checkered career, see Seymour Hersh, "Moving Targets," *The New Yorker*, 12/15/03. It was the pious Boykin who demanded that the brutal interrogatory methods at Guantánamo be used also at Abu Ghraib (or "Camp Redemption," as the prison's grimmest dormitory was christened by the Pentagon in May 2004, in a bid to quell Muslim fury at the revelation of "abuses" in Saddam Hussein's old jail). Sidney Blumenthal, "The Religious Warrior of Abu Ghraib," *The Guardian* (London), 5/20/04; "Reporters given tour of improved Abu Ghraib," *USA Today*, 5/18/04.

the BBC in April of 2003. "You will be perceived as either dying by the bullet or dying by the Bible through Muslim eyes." Eight months later, Islamic terrorists in Yemen bombed the Jibla Baptist Hospital, killing all three mission workers, and thereby inflicting "the worst tragedy in the 156-year history of the IMB," reported *APB News* in December 2003. The U.S. Christian presence has amounted to a dangerous provocation in Iraq, although our press has rarely mentioned it.

Bloody are the consequences also of the U.S. government's impossibly hard line on Israel—a partiality dictated less by well-connected Zionists inside the Pentagon than by the president's millennial co-religionists, who call the shots in this administration. On July 14, 2003, Condoleezza Rice met secretly with 40 "Christian Zionists," including Jerry Falwell, Gary Bauer, and Tom DeLay, to hear their views about a future Palestinian state. (They opposed it.) Such confabs are routine. In May 2004, a stray e-mail revealed that Elliott Abrams, the National Security Council's major expert on the Middle East, regularly holds long meetings with the Apostolic Congress, "the Christian Voice in the Nation's Capital." Asked why the Congress deems itself "*the* Christian Voice," rather than *a* Christian voice, Pentecostal minister Robert G. Upton answered, "There has been a real lack of leadership in having someone emerge as a Christian voice, someone who doesn't speak for the right, someone who doesn't speak for the left, but someone who speaks for the people, and someone who speaks from a theocratical perspective."

Thus prompted, Bush has given up all possibility of honest mediation, in favor of the Manichaean paradigm that dominates his consciousness and theirs: Israeli violence is good, and Palestinian violence is evil. This apolitical and antidiplomatic view is based entirely on the dictates of apocalyptic Christian eschatology: the Jews must stay in Israel so that a number of them (i.e., 144,000) can turn into Christians prior to Jesus' return.* On the basis of Romans 9-11, Reconstructionist Greg Bahnsen prophecies the magical effect of Jewish mass conversion:

*The Reconstructionists advise that every Jew had better turn to Jesus Christ ASAP. See Gary North, *The Judeo-Christian Tradition: A Guide for the Perplexed* (Tyler,

When the world sees "all Israel" become saved (through Jewish longing for the saving blessing experienced by the Gentiles), there will be yet further and greater blessings from God upon the whole population of the world because Christ will then be internationally recognized and exalted among men.

On July 30, 2003, the Christian Zionist bloc that dictates U.S. foreign policy displayed its power when Tom DeLay, openly rejecting the regime's half-hearted "road map," heated up the Knesset with a faith-based message of eternal nonconciliation:

> The war on terror is not a misunderstanding. It is not an opportunity for negotiation or dialogue. It's a battle between good and evil, between the Truth of liberty and the Lie of terror.
>
> Freedom and terrorism will struggle—good and evil—until the battle is resolved. These are the terms Providence has put before the United States, Israel, and the rest of the civilized world.
>
> They are stark, and they are final.*

That the White House would permit a congressman and Christian Reconstructionist—and, at foreign policy, a frothing amateur—to make so visible and partisan a public statement on, and in, the Middle East suggests that faith, not reason (and not Colin Powell), drives Bush/Cheney's foreign policy. And the result has been predictably disastrous: Israeli/Palestinian relations at their worst, the death toll at unprecedented levels, extremists on both sides resolved and popular among their own, and mounting worldwide hatred for the Jews.

Stateside, meanwhile, the theocrats continue to exert their wonder-working powers, as they have been doing ever since the president's first

---

Tex.: Institute for Christan Economics, 1990). "The Messiah has come," North concludes. "Do not pray for His return if you deny that He has come. When He returns again, it will be to enforce the eternal sanctions of his Covenant. There will be no escape then" (p. 174). The book contains an edifying appendix: "On Evangelizing Jews."

*DeLay did generously note that some might disagree with his approach: "Those who call this world-view 'simplistic' are more than welcome to share their 'sophisticated' theories at any number of international debating clubs."

public act, which was to make John Ashcroft his attorney general. That step alone should have made clear to all that Bush was no "uniter" but *averse* to "reaching out," and, indeed, uninterested in solving any worldly problems, dedicated as he is to stealthily theocratizing this republic.

Thus the White House has an "Office of Faith-Based and Community Initiatives," while each of the Departments of Labor, Commerce, Health and Human Services, et al., boasts a departmental "Center for Faith-Based and Community Initiatives"—a grand administrative stroke that blurs the crucial line dividing church and state. This move has served both to legitimize the political activism of pro-Bush churches and denominations and to further propagate the view that social services should be performed not by the government but by religious groups, whose charity should take the place of federal programs. Although advertised as purely altruistic, and as an equal boon to the communities served by churches, synagogues, and mosques alike, this innovation is primarily intended to abet the proselytizing efforts of the Christian right, whose "armies of compassion" can now save souls under the auspices of Uncle Sam.

Bush & Co. also pushes for theocracy by loading the judiciary branch with jurists who would gladly serve a "Christian" order. In the eighties, the now-controversial Charles Pickering of Mississippi was president of the Southern Baptists in that state, allying himself with the "inerrantists," who read the Bible as a factual history from the mouth of God. His appointment blocked by Senate Democrats concerned about his racial views, Pickering made the bench despite that opposition, as the president resorted to a recess appointment after Congress was adjourned. In February of 2004, Bush used the same tactic to seat William H. Pryor Jr., a judge both less distinguished and far more extreme than Pickering. "An advocate for a greater Christian influence in government," according to the *New York Times*, Pryor has referred to *Roe v. Wade* as "the worst abomination in the history of constitutional law." In his first year as attorney general of Alabama, he spoke at a Christian Coalition rally on behalf of a state judge's campaign to post the Ten Commandments in his courtroom—a cause that God Himself supported, Pryor told the crowd.

Thus Bush would have the federal bench well stacked with men inclined to favor the levitical constraints and punishments that the

Christian Reconstructionists believe in, and that Bush & Co. apparently supports. On gay sexuality, for instance, it is hard to see much difference between Bush & Co.'s views and, say, Rushdoony's. Pryor once signed a Supreme Court brief asserting that the abolition of a Texas law forbidding homosexual relations would somehow pave the way for "prostitution, adultery, necrophilia, bestiality, possession of child pornography and even incest or pedophilia." (The brief did not explain how this might work.) Two months later, Senator Rick Santorum (R-PA) also invoked the domino theory in defense of the abolished statute:

> If the Supreme Court says that you have the right to consensual sex within your home, then you have the right to bigamy, you have the right to polygamy, you have the right to incest, you have the right to adultery. You have the right to anything. Does that undermine the fabric of our society? I would argue yes, it does. It all comes from, I would argue, this right to privacy that doesn't exist in my opinion in the United States Constitution.

Santorum would gladly outlaw all "behavior that's antithetical to strong, healthy families. Whether it's polygamy, whether it's adultery, whether it's sodomy, all of those things are antithetical to a healthy, stable, traditional family."

From there Santorum went on to denounce the notion of gay marriage:

> Every society in the history of man has upheld the institution of marriage as a bond between a man and a woman. Why? Because society is based on one thing: that society is based on the future of the society. And that's what? Children. Monogamous relationships. In every society, the definition of marriage has not ever to my knowledge included homosexuality.
>
> That's not to pick on homosexuality. It's not, you know, man on child, man on dog, or whatever the case may be. It is one thing. And when you destroy that you have a dramatic impact on the quality—

"I'm sorry," interrupted the reporter. "I didn't think I was going to talk about 'man on dog' with a United States senator, it's sort of freaking me out." Ignoring her distress, Santorum forged ahead, and finally voiced the theocratic view of private freedom:

> And that's sort of where we are in today's world, unfortunately. The idea is that the state doesn't have rights to limit individuals' wants and passions. I disagree with that. I think we absolutely have rights because there are consequences to letting people live out whatever wants or passions they desire.

Although neither Pryor nor Santorum mentioned stoning, nor has the Bush administration openly suggested it, the only option that such thinking leaves for gays is abstinence—or else. Outraged by gay promiscuity, the regime is just as hostile to gay marriage, pushing for a constitutional amendment to forbid that civil practice. (It would be the first prohibitive amendment since the passage of the Volstead Act in 1919, outlawing the manufacture, sale, and/or purchase of liquor.) This double bind suggests a wish to have gay people *disappear*, just as the Reconstructionists would like them to;* Bush & Co.'s AIDS policy would seem to be designed for just that purpose, as it too is based entirely on religious bigotry. Although it is a scientific fact that condoms greatly cut the risk of HIV transmission, this regime's much-hyped program against the illness disallows the distribution, or even the mention, of that practical safeguard, in favor of unending propaganda on behalf of abstinence—a form of "treatment" that, although religiously correct, has been proved *not to work.*

On women's issues, the regime likewise pursues the theocratic line. As another of the president's judicial nominees once put it, in a 1997 article in *Arkansas Catholic*, "the wife is to subordinate herself to her husband," and "the woman is to place herself under the authority of the man." That patriarchal notion has been amply reconfirmed by the administration's policies on women's health. To the FDA's Reproductive

*Andrew Sullivan noted rightly "that the fundamentalist core of the Republican Party is opposed not just to gay sex but to gay love. Gays will be condemned for promiscuity, and they will be condemned for monogamy. The point is the condemnation." "Washington Diarist: Revolution, Televised," *New Republic*, 3/1/04.

Health Advisory Committee—a crucial body that approves particular drugs for reproductive and contraceptive purposes—Bush has appointed Dr. Joseph Stanford, who will prescribe no contraceptives of whatever kind, and Dr. David Hager, who has treated premenstrual syndrome (PMS) by recommending prayer and Bible reading. (As a member of the Christian Medical Association, Hager signed a petition to the FDA urging revocation of approval for mifepristone, the "morning-after" contraceptive also known as RU-486.) The ban on "partial birth abortion" was another signal victory for the Christian right, the signing of the legislation witnessed with much manly beaming by a special audience including Lou Sheldon, Jerry Falwell, Cardinal Edward Egan, John Ashcroft, and Adrian Rogers, former head of the Southern Baptist Convention. Bush & Co.'s desire to prosecute the ban with vigor was made very clear in February 2004, when Ashcroft sought to subpoena hospital records nationwide: ostensibly to help the government determine whether such procedures have been medically necessary, but in any case a violation of women's privacy.

In line with the theocratic right, Bush/Cheney's Federal Communications Commission, aroused by the notorious display of Janet Jackson's breast during the halftime show of the Super Bowl, began a "decency campaign," increasing the fine for any on-air "indecency" from $25,000 to $250,000 and calling for a five-second delay in all television broadcasts, to enable rapid interference with whatever sudden word or image might strike people as "indecent."* Bush/Cheney's Department of Education has now deemed some 200 TV programs "inappropriate" for closed captioning, as a measure to protect deaf viewers against corruptive entertainment—such as *I Dream of Jeannie* and *Bewitched*, pro-

---

*On February 24, 2004, under the pretext of routing out "indecency," Clear Channel Worldwide—the nation's largest radio station owner and a corporation with close ties to the White House—abruptly dropped the daily program of shock jock Howard Stern. This move made Stern's show unavailable in six major U.S. markets. Stern had lately turned against the Bush administration. "There's a real good argument to be made that I stopped backing Bush and that's when I got kicked off Clear Channel," Stern commented on March 1, 2004. Stern, in fact, was one of numerous Clear Channel employees who paid a price for speaking out against the president and his policies. Maureen Farrell, "As the Worm Turns: Stern, Sully and the Bush Backlash," BuzzFlash, 3/2/04 (http://www.buzzflash.com/farrell/04/03/far04006.html). See also Michael Hiltzik, "After Janet Jackson's Prank, the Truly Indecent Behavior," *Los Angeles Times*, 3/1/04.

scribed for celebrating devilish practices. And the regime supports a broad range of educational "reforms" long cherished by the Christian right—the abolition of sex education, the dumbing down of math instruction, and, not least, the teaching of creationism, to begin undoing the enormous damage wrought by Darwin's theory. "We are increasingly getting both socialism and a moral breakdown with flagrant lawlessness as a result of evolutionary thinking," writes Rushdoony. "The only alternative to this decline and fall is a renewal of biblical Christianity, which requires a return to creationism. . . . Not only is creationism a *necessary* faith: *it is an inescapable fact.*"

While thus promoting its crusades abroad, and quietly Christianizing life at home, the regime also serves the program of that revolutionary theocratic movement by working to terminate environmentalism, for such attempts at conservation also are offensive to the creed of Reconstructionism. According to Rushdoony's followers, environmentalists are at once neo-pagan pantheists and latent Stalinists. On the one hand, by casting humankind as part of nature, they contradict God's first command to Adam. "That man is called to dominion over nature," writes Ruben C. Alvarado, "is made explicit in God's initial commandment to him (Genesis 1:26–28). He, as made in the image of God, is above nature, and he is called to fill the earth and subdue it. The implications of this command are decisive." By placing nature above man, the greens encourage statism: "The socialistic impulse is pervasive among environmentalists, because salvation is seen to lie in the hands of a planning elite," writes Alvarado, paraphrasing Gary North. In short, environmentalism is a form of blasphemy: "Its idolatry condemns it to outlandish and ineffective programs for the stewardship of the natural heritage, and subjugation to political expediency. May the Church be prepared with its own program for the righteous stewardship of God's creation, derived from His Word."

Although it is unlikely that, say, Gale Norton, Bush's secretary of the interior, has closely read a lot of Reconstructionist theology, the general antienvironmentalist thrust of Christian rightist dogma has undoubtedly confirmed the Bush Republicans in the peculiar recklessness of their agenda for the planet (and, as well, for outer space, which they intend to fill with high-tech weaponry). Indeed, the blitheness with which Bush & Co. ignores the ever-worsening threats of global warming, air pollution,

and the disappearance of endangered species—among many other looming ecological disasters—can only be explained as an expression of their
faith. To such apocalyptic types, the prospect of a ruined Earth is no big
deal, as long as God can be alleged to go for it. Such fatal equanimity is
common among theocratic rightists, whether crackpot theologians or
professional provocateurs like Rush Limbaugh, or Ann Coulter—who
once said this on *Hannity & Colmes*: "God gave us the earth. We have
dominion over the plants, the animals, the trees. God said, 'Earth is
yours. Take it. Rape it! It's yours.' "

The only legal way to halt the nation's slide into theocracy, it seems,
would be to open serious investigations by the Congress and the press,
begin a robust national debate, and finally vote the zealots out of power
(and keep them out). But that electoral possibility is also threatened—
how severely we do not yet know—by the overzealous Bush Republicans. The Help America Vote Act (HAVA), passed in 2002 at the urging
of the White House and the party, mandates the eventual use, in every
state, of computerized touch-screen voting machines. Now set up in
nearly thirty states, these machines appear to be the ultimate device for
the subversion of democracy. They can be programmed to cook the
numbers—halve them, double them, erase them, misdistribute them—
however the programmer may desire. They leave no paper trail, so that
their tallies cannot be objectively confirmed. Their programming codes
are not public knowledge, but have been held back by the manufacturers as "proprietary information." They are so insecure, moreover, that a
clever twelve-year-old could easily hack into them. (In fact, a clever
twelve-year-old did so in 2004.) And, most important, the machines' top
manufacturers—Diebold and ES&S—are companies closely tied to
Bush Republicans. Before he turned to politics, Nebraska Senator
Chuck Hagel was the CEO of ES&S; and when he left that post in 1996
to run for Congress, he held on to a substantial interest—up to $5 mil-
lion—in ES&S's parent company, McCarthy Group. (Nebraska used
ES&S machines in the elections of 1996 and 2002. In both elections,

Hagel won some 85 percent of all the ballots cast, even in black precincts.) And in August of 2003, Wally O'Dell, the CEO of Diebold, Inc. (and a Bush Pioneer), sent a fund-raising letter to Ohio Republicans (Diebold is headquartered there) stating that he was "committed to helping Ohio deliver its electoral votes to the President next year."

Subversives

From the beginning of his national political career, the Bush Republicans have charged Bill Clinton with that most despicable and dangerous of public crimes: subversion. In 1992, the Bush campaign alleged that Clinton had served somehow as an agent of the KGB, because of a youthful trip he took to Prague and Moscow, among other cities. (That smear followed the campaign's illegal search of Clinton's State Department file.) In the summer of 1997, Senator Fred Thompson (R-TN) startled Washington with the announcement of "a Chinese plan to subvert our election process" and initiated hearings of the Senate Governmental Affairs Committee, in an attempt to prove that Clinton somehow hadn't tried to stop the Reds from using campaign contributions to improve their nuclear missile capabilities. The issue fizzled out, although it never ceased to agitate the right.* And Clinton's gross

---

*The "scandal" was then born again in 1999, when the *New York Times* alleged that Wen Ho Lee, a Taiwanese-born scientist at Los Alamos, had been involved in espionage. The GOP ran amok: Representative Christopher Cox (R-CA) released a vast report on "Chinagate," in May, with much fanfare, and after other partisans had broadcast much accusatory innuendo.

As it turned out, Wen Ho Lee was innocent (a fact that came out only after he had done nine months in solitary confinement), and Cox's heavily ballyhooed report had in it not a word of evidence. By late August the whole case was dead, although, again, it never lost its luster for the right. Lucinda Fleeson, "Rush to Judgment," *American Journalism Review* (November 2000), p. 207; Eric Bohlert, "How the *New York Times* Helped Railroad Wen Ho Lee," *Salon,* 9/21/00 (www.salon.com/news/feature/ 2000/09/21/nyt/); Wen Ho Lee, with Helen Zia, *My Country Versus Me:The First-Hand Account by the Los Alamos Scientist Who Was Falsely Accused of Being a Spy* (New York: Hyperion, 2001).

betrayal of America has been much hyped since 9/11, with *his* perfidy, *his* negligence, *his* lack of patriotic decency, etc., named repeatedly as the true cause of that catastrophe.

As usual, those seeming patriots who charge Bill Clinton with subversion are themselves the genuine subversives. It is they, not he—and they *more* than the Islamists—whose aim is to undo the framers' work and force an alien form of government on the United States. Their absolute commitment to that cause may help explain the startling ease and readiness with which they lie. History's winning propagandists, by and large, have been those capable of at least half-believing what they have to say, or have had the histrionic talent to believe it only when they're saying it. Even those propagandists who have most admired their own ostensible emotional detachment as manipulators— Goebbels, for example—have had the knack for what George Orwell called "doublethink," permitting them to be at once fanatically convinced that what they say is true, *and* well aware that they're engaging in deception. At least a little of that passion is essential to convincing multitudes to do or think whatever benefits the cause, whatever that may be.

The rightists in this country are immensely aided in their propaganda work by their intense conviction that there is no wrong in telling lies to aid their cause, which is to wreck American republican democracy. The Christian Reconstructionists are quite explicit on this point (although not in public). Unsurprisingly, perhaps, those tough ex-Birchers are, in this regard, exactly like the legendary Reds of yesteryear, whose devilish skill at lying was a constant point of anticommunist polemic. As Frederick Clarkson demonstrates, the Reconstructionists believe in stealthy "infiltration" of the government, so as to "smooth the transition to Christian political leadership," wrote theocrat Gary North in 1981. "Christians must begin to organize politically within the present party structure, and they must begin to infiltrate the existing institutional order."

Although it seems immoral, such duplicity is necessary, according to the theocratic doctrine. In 1959, Rushdoony addressed the issue in a commentary on the Biblical story of Rahab (Joshua 2:1–24), the Canaanite harlot who hid two Israelite spies from the forces of the king of Jericho, and thereby helped effect the conquest of Canaan by the Israelites. (She and her family were spared when the Jews sacked Jericho, and she later married the Israelite Salmon, and was an ancestress of Jesus.) In the New Testament, Rahab's story serves to illustrate the necessity of good works in addition to faith. ("Likewise also was not Rahab the harlot justified by works, when she had received the messengers, and had sent them out another way?" James 2:25) In Rushdoony's universe, Rahab's action demonstrates that the Christian obligation to be truthful "does not apply to acts of war. Spying is legitimate, as are deceptive tactics in warfare." And, as Clarkson notes, since Rushdoony and his followers believe that Christianity is in a state of constant war with other faiths, lying always is a necessary ruse for pious Christians. As Fawn Hall, Oliver North's secretary, famously observed at the Iran/contra hearings in 1986, in extenuation of her boss's crimes in that adventure, "Sometimes you have to go above the written law." In 1993, Michael Farris, the Republican candidate for lieutenant governor of Virginia (and an ordained minister and constitutional lawyer), used Rushdoony's argument to exculpate the controversial North: "What Ollie North did was basically the moral equivalent of what the spies and Rahab did in Jericho. Rahab lied to protect lives."

As a co-conspirator in the anti-Clinton movement, David Brock observed the same amoral dedication in Paul Weyrich, a CNP member and, by his own description, "Melkite Greek Catholic Deacon." "We are no longer working to preserve the status quo," Weyrich has said. "We are radicals, working to overturn the present power structure of the country." The rural far right is the movement's power base, claims Weyrich, who as a tactician deems himself a "Maoist": "I believe you have to control the countryside, and the capital will eventually fall." He too has made it clear, internally, that lying for the cause is not a sin. "One booklet on political tactics published by the Weyrich organization," Brock reports, "included a section saying that for the right reasons lying was to be regarded as a permissible 'mental reservation.' " Brock adds that Reverend Moon has taught his operatives the same pragmatic lesson: "that lying is necessary, even under oath, when one is doing 'God's work.' " Such abstract counsel came home vividly to Brock as he perceived the anti-Clinton forces—even jurists—lying baldly and incessantly in their crusade against the president (whom they consistently condemned, of course, for his outrageous lies).

Such is the standard moral practice of the movement that, not being genuinely Christian (many evangelicals deem Reconstructionism dangerous), should be known as "Christo-fascism," to use an epithet proposed by David Neiwert. While that influence cannot be overemphasized, the right's extreme deceptiveness is not entirely a reflection of that doctrine. While those who follow the dominion theologians base their guile on an extreme interpretation of the Bible, Bush & Co.'s great neoconservative cabal has found its rationale for lying in a very different realm: the neo-Hobbesian philosophy of Leo Strauss, a conservative German émigré who taught at the University of Chicago and died in 1973. A contemporary of critical theorists T. W. Adorno and Herbert Marcuse, and like them a refugee from Hitler's Reich, the rightist Strauss stands out, *Der Spiegel* notes, as "the only German emigrant to establish a philosophy movement that became widespread in the United States, a movement whose influence extends to within today's inner circles of power in Washington."

As Strauss's writings are exceedingly complex and subtle, and concerned more with antiquity than with the present, it would be inaccurate to cast him simply as the neocons' intellectual Svengali. His influence was often indirect, as his philosophy was variously interpreted and passed along by other academics, such as Harvey Mansfield, who taught William Kristol; Allan Bloom, who taught Paul Wolfowitz; and especially Albert Wohlstetter, a mathematician and RAND strategist whose students included Wolfowitz, Richard Perle, and Ahmed Chalabi. Whatever Strauss's own exact political position (which is not easy to discern in his philosophy), his writings strengthened in the neocons of Bush & Co. a paranoid suspicion of democracy and a Machiavellian attitude not only toward the masses but also toward the prince himself, who must routinely be deceived by his own advisers for the sake of national strength and public order. As Perle et al. read Strauss, the men behind the ruler must, in influencing him, observe an axiom somewhat more Nietzschean than Platonic: that *they*, not he, are the true rulers of the state, by virtue of their clearer understanding of reality. According to Strauss, notes Shadia Drury of the University of Calgary, "those who are fit to rule are those who realize there is no morality and that there is only one natural right, the right of the superior to rule over the inferior."*

Although the Straussians are not believers (Strauss himself was probably an atheist), they have in common with the Christian Reconstructionists a powerful distaste for secular society—"the worst possible thing" in their view, Drury notes, because "religion is the glue that holds society together." In the Straussian worldview, according to Jet Heer, secular society "leads to individualism, liberalism and relativism, precisely those traits that might encourage dissent, which in turn could dangerously weaken society's ability to cope with external threats." The church/state separation was a very bad idea, according to the Straussians, who are on that point in full agreement with Rushdoony's followers and other Christian rightists. Also like the Christian Reconstructionists, the Straussians believe themselves to be above the law—as Perle inadvertently revealed, when, speaking in London during Bush's visit there in November of 2003, he told his audience, on the subject of the occupation of Iraq, "I think in this case international law stood in the way of doing the right thing." (That admission, which flatly contradicted the official line of both Bush/Cheney and the Blair administration, caused an understandable to-do in Britain, and yet went unreported here in the United States.)

And yet the influence of such amoralist doctrines can explain only so much, for the compulsive lying of the right, like the peculiar sadism per-

*Strauss's opposition to democracy was largely based on his own contemptuous observation of the anarchy of the Weimar Republic, which had allowed the rise of Hitler.

vading rightist rhetoric, also has a pathological dimension, which finally
constitutes the common ground of the rightist factions now in power
through Bush & Co. Outside the murky precincts of the psyche, or the
soul, there is no tidy explanation for the acid, sanctimonious perverse-
ness of Ann Coulter, or Sean Hannity, or Michael Savage. This or that
extremist ideology alone is but a carrier or a symptom of disease, not the
disease itself. Certainly a comprehensive academic study of the problem
will enlighten our attempts at understanding that aggressive frame of
mind. The psychological effects of social class and economic interest,
and the profound impact of sexual acculturation, as well as the deep
marks left by ethnic and religious bigotry, shed much light on that militant unreason. Yet, ultimately, such inquiry is beside the point, itself
being just a bit too rational to solve the mystery of that projective rage.
And, more important, such inquiry in itself will not protect us from the
rising civic danger of that paranoid advance, which wants the world, and
wants it now, and takes you for an enemy if you resist or even question
it, and even if you never heard of it.

Persecution Complex

Although its motivation is mysterious, we can with some assurance trace
the *history* of the Reconstructionist conspiracy. According to Frederick
Clarkson, this revolutionary theology grew out of two austere and suspicious prior movements: Orthodox Presbyterianism, and the John
Birch Society (JBS). "Most leading Reconstructionists have either been
JBS members or have close ties to the organization. Reconstructionist
literature can be found in JBS-affiliated American Opinion bookstores."
Rushdoony himself, in fact, approved the structure of the JBS as a modern adaptation of the "early church." "The key to the John Birch Society's effectiveness," he wrote in the *Institutes*, "has been a plan of
operation which has a strong resemblance to the early church; meetings,
local 'lay' leaders, area supervisors or 'bishops.' "
   This legacy is unsurprising, as the Reconstructionists maintain the
projective zeal of Cold War anticommunism, which at its maddest was

itself reflective of the very movement that it fought so bitterly for years and years. Faced with the Soviets' matchless *evil*, some U.S. Cold Warriors prescribed a national attempt to *match that evil*, as it could be defeated, they asserted, only by those strong enough to replicate it in themselves.

> It is now clear we are facing an implacable enemy whose avowed objective is world domination by whatever means and at whatever loss. There are no rules in such a game. Hitherto acceptable long-standing American concepts of "fair play" must be reconsidered. We must develop effective espionage and counter-espionage services and must learn to subvert, sabotage, and destroy our enemies by more clever, more sophisticated and more effective methods than those used against us.

This was the conclusion of General James Doolittle and his colleagues, who had been asked by President Eisenhower to assess the CIA, lately flush with its successes in Iran and Guatemala. In its classified report, turned over to the president in 1954, the committee noted certain failings in the leadership of Allen Dulles, recommended stricter measures against leaks of secret information, and otherwise advised improvements in the young bureaucracy. The heart of the report, however, lay in that overt acknowledgment of the apparent need for the United States to use the devil's means to fight the devil. Such immoralist practice had been urged before; indeed, the National Security Council had been hammering at that theme since its own founding at the Cold War's start in 1947. Doolittle's version was unusual in its explicitness, however—and in its advice that Eisenhower teach the public to accept that starkly un-American new view: "It may become necessary that the American people be made acquainted with, understand and support this fundamentally repugnant philosophy."

That advice went nowhere, as Eisenhower, writes H. W. Brands, "had no intention of declaring that the United States had abandoned its claim to moral superiority in the Cold War and henceforth would operate under the same rules of bleak efficacy that governed Moscow's behavior." Aside from that, however, Eisenhower was in full agreement with Doolittle's chilly pragmatism, and thenceforth gave his covert operatives permission to play epoch-making dirty tricks in country after country—Vietnam, Cambodia, Laos, Indonesia, Syria, the Philippines, Cuba, and the Congo, among others—thereby honoring Doolittle's paranoid advice, and so transforming the United States into a subversive power at least as dangerous as its adversary, while Americans themselves knew nothing of it. And even if they had been told, a certain number of them would no doubt have been untroubled by the policy, as God was on our side, and the Soviets were agents of the Devil.

Today the Reconstructionists are likewise urging the abandonment of moral scruples, so as to win their twilight struggle with the forces of the damned.* This time the enemy is not the Soviets, of course, because their state has ceased to be. This time, it's *the Democrats* who, devoid of moral scruples, are threatening to transform America; and so the godly soldiers of this Christian nation must behave like *them*, or lose this most important of religious wars. From February 2001 until November 2003, the Web site for the Chalcedon Foundation ("Faith for All of Life") highlighted an essay called "Slash and Burn Politics," by Val Finnell, an army officer and fervent Christian Reconstructionist. His take on the election of 2000 is another clear example of malevolent projection—and, although not meant for anyone outside the fold, a vivid warning to all those who cherish the ideals of our great secular republic:

> The Florida elections [*sic*] have taught us that the Democrats with
> their liberal/socialistic worldview will stop at nothing to seize control

---

*As is al Qaeda. "We believe that the biggest thieves in the world and the terrorists are the Americans. The only way for us to fend off these assaults is to use similar means," Osama bin Laden has asserted. John Miller, "Greetings, America. My name is Osama bin Laden," *Esquire*, February 1999.

of the government. For the government is the instrument whereby the legislator and the courts shape man into what they want.

Instead of half-hearted and compromising responses from so-called conservatives, we need an explicitly Christian response in politics that has its own worldview, an agenda, and courageous men to implement it confrontationally.

Although the theocratic goal is hardly universal on the right, that paranoid perception of "the Florida elections" *is* common to Bush/Cheney partisans. Even as the crisis raged in Florida, thousands of Americans turned up there to prevent a *Democratic* coup, some of them with guns and the resolve to use them to ensure that Bush and Cheney be rightfully "elected." That line has been assiduously propagated ever since, in heated and selective "histories" like *At Any Cost*, by *Washington Times* reporter Bill Sammons, and in wisecracks and asides all over rightist radio and television, as well as in the casual reminiscences of Bush's family. "I find myself thinking of Al Gore and what he must be feeling," Barbara Bush writes. "I'm sure he thinks he won the race, although I don't. I do feel sorry for him."

Such minds believe what they prefer, and therefore are not to be changed by contrary evidence, however copious, or by any reasonable argument, however strong. Here I am not trying to convince those partisans that they did *not* win that election. My purpose, rather, is to warn the rational majority, whose minds have not been closed by propaganda, that the activists who stole the last election also plan to steal the next one, as it is not in them to accept defeat, or to observe the law, as we have seen. They would have "won" the White House last time even if Ralph Nader never had been born, and they will "win" this next one, come what may, unless the people keep a watchful eye on them and on the media. Otherwise we may well have no more elections in this country— no doubt for reasons of "security," the times no longer being right for so unsafe and decadent a system as democracy.

And yet we also must look well beyond this next election, for, whatever may occur because of it (assuming that it does take place), the danger represented by Bush/Cheney will not disappear. Whoever ends up in the White House, and whichever party dominates in Congress, the threat of that projective animus will not abate, because the movement driven by it is too wealthy, well entrenched, and smartly organized to melt away, and the broad emotional appeal of such resentfulness will certainly abide, particularly through disorienting times like these. The U.S. media system too is likely not to change for quite some time, so that it will not soon refute the rightist lies with all due clarity and force, or cry shame on the smears and maledictions. The Democrats being overly dependent on their corporate donors, they too will have trouble speaking truth to power, and with no fervent opposition party fully dedicated to the realization of American democracy, the people will have trouble speaking out and being heard.

And yet the theocratic movement will remain the gravest threat to our democracy, for that self-hating drive is evidently inexhaustible. As we have seen, their stated program is to dominate the nation, and eventually the world, and yet, of course, *they* see *themselves* as dominated. "Like it or not, the Christians of America are in bondage," Pat Robertson lamented in 2000.

> We're in bondage to nine old men [*sic*] in black robes of the Supreme Court. We're in bondage to the ACLU. We're in bondage to Planned Parenthood, we're in bondage to a bunch of homosexuals. . . . How did they get this power? We are under bondage, and it's time the Christian church stood up and said, "No more!" . . .
>
> We vastly outnumber the atheists. . . . Why should we put up with abortion? Why should we put up with all of these laws that are being put on us? Why should we submit to unrighteous laws and unrighteous government and take it lying down? We shouldn't, we shouldn't!

Such is the Christian Right's defining plaint. Subtract that cry, and there is nothing left of most such rightist sermonizing, which is all *about* the dangers posed to *them* because of *us*. Christians are oppressed by hateful liberals. Thus David Limbaugh vehemently argues in his *Persecution:*

How Liberals Are Waging War against Christianity (whose cover shows a hungry lioness about to pounce). The book was warmly blurbed by various champions of the religious right, such as Sean Hannity, the author of the similarly paranoid *Deliver Us from Evil*:

> At last—some sense in the Church/State debate! In his great new book "Persecution," David Limbaugh shows how liberals have undermined our Constitution and are waging undeclared war on the very people—Americans of faith—who have made America the beacon of freedom and justice that it is. Buy this book, read it, and send a copy to every politician, judge, and Supreme Court Justice you can find.

Notwithstanding such emphatic plaudits, and all of Limbaugh's anecdotes, the claim that Christians suffer daily persecution is preposterous on its face. Christians in this country worship openly and freely; the "conservatives," moreover, build and fill gigantic churches, speak out loud and clear on every issue of the day, and organize politically without constraint; furthermore, the best-known rightist Christians have more access to the media than any of their leftist counterparts. What they take as "persecution"—now as in the days of Jefferson—is any question raised about, or criticism of, their role in party politics and in the government. They see themselves as *persecuted* by defenders of the Constitution and by any effort at a rational response to their fanaticism. What they take as "persecution" is, in short, whatever steps are sometimes taken to prevent the imposition of their faith on everybody else—which is to say, *their* would-be persecution of all other un-like-minded worshippers, all unbelievers and agnostics.

The Christian right's agenda for our persecution is quite blatant in the jeremiads of Pat Robertson and Jerry Falwell, as it is throughout the writings of R. J. Rushdoony and his followers:

> God has a plan for the conquest of all things by his covenant people. That plan is His law. It leaves no area of life and activity untouched, and it predestines victory. To deny the law is to deny God and His plan for victory.

Polemicists like Limbaugh fervently deny that such theology has any-thing to do with them. "What do you say to the people on the left," an interviewer asked him, "who claim that conservative Christians want to turn the US into a theocracy?" His response:

> I'd say that's absolute hogwash. Christianity stands for freedom, we don't want to impose our religion on everyone else. We just don't want secular humanist values or homosexual values to be forced upon us under the guise of anti-harassment laws, speech codes, hate crime laws, or sensitivity training. We want to be free to think and express our views in the public arena or anywhere we want to. We want to be free to practice our religion with impunity because that was central to our founding in this country. We will accord you the exact same rights, whoever you are. You have the right to freedom of worship, but we just want a level playing field. We don't want to be singled out, discriminated against, or treated without tolerance by those for whom tolerance is the highest virtue.

The fact is that Christians are entirely "free to practice their religion with impunity," and also wholly "free to think and express their views in the public arena." They are also "free to think . . . anywhere [they] want to," although *not* free to "express their views anywhere [they] want," if by "express their views" Limbaugh meant "preach the Gospel." Nor should Christians, or anybody else, feel themselves entirely free to hatemonger. Limbaugh's implication is that *he* is "persecuted" as a Christian by attempts to get him not to vent his Christian hatred of, say, gays. A hate crime law, or speech code, that would mute his homophobia amounts, in his mind, to "homosexual values being [forced] on us."

In any case, the links between "conservative Christians" and the Christian Reconstructionists are now too numerous and close to permit us to accept Limbaugh's denial. However, leaving aside Reconstruction-ism per se, there is still abundant evidence that such "conservatives" are prone to persecuting liberals, and not the other way around. That ten-dency is everywhere apparent in the barbarous public discourse of the Bush Republicans. Pervading all the jokes and threats—not only the apocalyptic curses of Pat Robertson and Jerry Falwell, but also Ann

Coulter's slanders, Rush Limbaugh's cracks, the bilious name-calling by the likes of Bill O'Reilly, Sean Hannity, Michael Savage, and Bob Grant, and the incessant grassroots virulence displayed on Web sites like free republic.com and Lucianne Goldberg's lucianne.com, and on and on— there is a clear presumption that the enemy is not mistaken or misled, nor merely sinful, as all God's human creatures are. Rather, "those lying Democrats," the "feminazis," "the black activists," "the homosexual lobby," "the environmentalist wackos," etc., are *demonic*. That is, they are "evil," but not in any way that St. Augustine would have recognized—as persons who have turned themselves away from God yet always are redeemable. For they are not "persons" just like everybody else, nor is there really any place for them in Christian doctrine. Rather, they are figments of the Manichaean heresy, envisioned as a swarm of darkling malefactors: evil not to the extent that they are turned from God (and always able to turn back again), but evil *in themselves*, created *not* by God but by the Devil; and so their fate is not to be redeemed and then assimilated, but to be driven from among us, and exterminated.

The right sees no distinction between "liberals" here and "terrorists" abroad, obsessively conflating them, both in their domestic propaganda and, at a higher level, in their actual "antiterrorist" countermeasures. At its annual jamboree in 2003, the Conservative Political Action Committee featured all sorts of eliminationist amusements. Aside from simple anti-Islamic novelties, such as a bumper sticker reading "No Muslims = No Terrorists," there were decks of playing cards modeled on the anti-Ba'ath cards carried by the soldiers in Iraq, but showing the faces of such traitors as Sean Penn, Barbra Streisand, and Tom Daschle. According to Michelle Goldberg of *Salon*, the Reverend Lou Sheldon was there, showing off "a makeshift carnival game called 'Tip a Troll,' in which players were invited to throw gray beanbags at toy trolls with the heads of Osama bin Laden, Saddam Hussein, Hillary Clinton and Tom Daschle, or trolls holding signs saying, 'The Homosexual Agenda,' 'Roe V. Wade' and 'The Liberal Media.' "

Ubiquitous on the far right, such propaganda items are no more than jokey reexpressions of current federal policy, which tends to cast dissent as terrorism. The Patriot Act, as well as other legislative and administrative strokes, have now defined as "terrorist" a startling range of groups and actions critical of Bush & Co. Meanwhile, the Democrats themselves are indirectly libeled as Islamist fellow travelers and/or part of the pro-Ba'ath resistance (as in a TV ad asserting that Democrats were "attacking Pres. Bush for attacking the terrorists"). Increasingly, moreover, the U.S. military's tactics overseas have been applied to public protest actions here in the United States. American police crack down on U.S. demonstrators with a heavy hand approximating how our troops police Iraqi protests (so far, U.S. police have been deploying rubber bullets), and their martial practice also emulates the Pentagon's incorporation of the press. At the FTAA demonstrations in Miami, police units had reporters functioning along with them as "embeds"—dressed as cops and taking all their notes as members of the unit, as if the protesters were just as lethal as the Ba'athist *fedayeen*.

Bush & Co.'s exterminationist conception of the foreign enemy is blatant in the president's own language on the subject. That he sees them as "evildoers," and that he plans to "rid the world" of them, is clear enough—as is the fact that our whole military operation is pervaded by that same crusading zeal. Moreover, as the Associated Press reported months ago, Bush maintains a special "scorecard" of al Qaeda operatives, "crossing off the faces with an 'X' as members were captured or killed." In his State of the Union speech in 2003, the president boasted openly of all those killed thus far by U.S. forces:

> All told, more than 3,000 suspected terrorists have been arrested in many countries. Many others have met a different fate. Let's put it this way—they are no longer a problem to the United States and our friends and allies.
>
> [*Applause.*]

Such eliminationist language is unpromising, and not only for moral reasons. (When Bush said that those 3,000+ "*suspected* terrorists" were now "no longer a problem," he sounded less like a U.S. chief executive than like Saddam Hussein.) His notion of those others as *nonhuman* also bodes ill for the "war on terror" itself, as it betrays a deep strategic misconception. Because he sees "the terrorists" as demons or as vermin, he often casts them as his quarry. Each and every one of them, he tells us often, will be caught and stopped—until that day when they're all gone.

> We're tracking down terrorists who hate America one by one. We're on the hunt. We got 'em on the run, and it's a matter of time before they learn the meaning of American justice.

But "the terrorists" are not a fixed and finite population of crude predators, like rats or sharks. Presumably, a major pesticidal operation, comprehensive and sustained, *could* rid the world, or the United States, or New York City, of its rats (although it surely would take care of certain other species, too). No human population can, however, be thus thoroughly wiped out, at least not by conventional military means, for people tend to take it ill when they or their loved ones are hurt or killed in "antiterrorist" operations, and that sort of "collateral damage" always happens—even when those at the top are *not* indifferent to such suffering. What this means is that Bush/Cheney's war cannot succeed as they imagine, since every heavy-handed strike and gruesome accident—no less than all the torture and humiliation—has only turned *more* people into enemies of the United States. Far from picking off the bad guys one by one, the U.S. "war on terrorism" has succeeded only in creating countless fresh new cells of terrorists and in enlarging that great human sea in which those predatory fish can swim forever. Thus has Bush & Co. used the teachings of the Prince of Peace to bring us warfare without end.

Public Trust

Many a dictator has reduced his nation, and destroyed himself, by knowing just what he preferred to know and hearing only what he wanted to be told. Here in America, we have an easy time imagining the terminal condition of such isolated tyrants: Hitler in his bunker, shouting crazy orders for his shattered military and ranting on about the danger of "world Jewry"; Stalin huddling in his office at the Kremlin, getting ready to suppress yet one more vast imaginary plot against him (also, in his view, a Jewish plot); Saddam Hussein in one of his palatial hiding places, certain to the end that the Americans would not attack him. Well informed about the antidemocratic features of such closed societies—the "state-controlled press," the "rubber-stamp assembly"—we find it unsurprising, and appropriate, that their exalted leaders should end up locked in total ignorance, preoccupied with fantasy, and broken by reality.

It is less easy for us to perceive the same apocalyptic self-deception at the helm of our own country. After all, this nation runs on business, which cannot afford quasi-psychosis at the top. Unlike the Soviet Union or the Ba'ath's Iraq, moreover, we seem to have unfettered media everywhere, so that our rulers cannot possibly conceal themselves as thoroughly as Mao or Stalin could. And, finally, we keep hearing it asserted, by a constant chorus of authoritative voices, that we still inhabit a democracy, one that even seeks to form democracies abroad. All such

facts and factors—and, of course, the press's daily abdication of its constitutional responsibility—have made it difficult for us to see, as clearly
as we should, that the United States today is governed by delusion.

Bush does not represent the will of the American majority, and never
did—not even when this nation was most badly traumatized by 9/11,
however high his ratings may have climbed. He does not speak for
rational Americans, but rather is the president—America's first president—of the American irrational. Our projector-in-chief, George W.
Bush lives in, and is trying to rule, the malevolent dreamworld of the
right. In that dominion, truth is always written off as "propaganda,"
while propaganda comes at us as "truth"—Bill O'Reilly's "No-Spin
Zone" and Fox News Channel's "fair and balanced" news, communicat-
ing just as honestly as *Pravda* (which means "truth" in Russian) did
throughout the heyday of the Soviets. In that dominion, "deficits don't
matter," "CO2 is not a pollutant," "we're making good progress in Iraq,"
and war is peace, and $2 + 2 = 5$, and if you see things differently, you are
the enemy.

This is not a problem of mere posturing, the president and all his men
pretending to see black as white for their own hidden reasons. In this
regime there *is* no reason, but instead a deep presumption of infallibility, a feeling of divine entitlement, and an insatiable desire for power.
What rules them here and now is the same brutal messianic egotism that
the Enlightenment attempted to restrain, with mixed results; but most
successfully, perhaps, in the design of our republic. The movement now
in power is a stark throwback to the centuries of unreason in the West,
when one could not distinguish "history" from "story," and the pursuit
of science was heretical. For Bush himself sees truth as propaganda, and
vice versa. On the one hand, he opposes making manufacturers of packaged food list all ingredients clearly on their labels, deeming *that* a "propaganda" ploy.* On the other hand, he has extolled as "history" mere

---

*"I sense they want to run a propaganda campaign," he said. "There needs to be
scientific labels as to whether something is safe or not. What I'm for is for there to be
truth in advertising that enables a product manufacturer to clearly state nothing in
this product is harmful to your health, for example." It would be "scientific," in other

concoctions by his propagandists: "You know," he said on September 17, 2002,

> I think one of the most defining moments of the recent American history was [United Airlines] Flight 93. Flight 93 is a amazing lesson [*sic*]. Laura and I had the honor of going to the site there in Shanksville, Pennsylvania, the other day to hug and cry and visit with—and smile with, if they wanted to smile—with the family members of those brave souls who were on that airplane.
>
> But it's a lesson of people loving freedom so much and loving their country so much that they're willing to drive a plane into the ground to save other people's lives. What a powerful message, that part of being an American is to serve something greater than yourself; part of being a citizen in this great land is to not only take from the land, but to give.

That Flight 93 went down that day there is no doubt; and it is likely that Todd Beamer, as reported, said "Let's roll!" before the end, since that is, according to his widow, what the FBI was told by the Chicago operator who received his final phone call. As for the rest of it—the storming of the cockpit by the fearless passengers who crashed the plane on purpose "to save other people's lives"—that thrilling tale is just as scrupulously documented as the other fictions used to sell us on whatever war was going on or coming next: "the rescue of Private Jessica Lynch," Saddam Hussein's complicity in 9/11, his close collaboration with al Qaeda, his arsenal of WMDs, and so on. As for Flight 93, there is no evidence that any of the passengers gained entry to the cockpit.* In any case, Bush's statement that the passengers deliberately committed suicide is not just groundless—how could he know what they intended?—but preposterous on its face. Why would they have chosen

---

words, for the manufacturer *not* to list all his ingredients, but merely to assert that "nothing in this product is harmful to your health"—which, in fact, would be a stroke of propaganda. "Bush Doubts Federal Report of Hungry Children in Texas," *Ft. Worth Star-Telegram*, 12/18/99.

*The plane's black boxes were impounded by the FBI, which will not release the tapes or publish transcripts.

to get killed if they could somehow manage a crash landing? Did they think the plane was *programmed* to collide with some important building—like the White House—so that they had no choice but suicide "to save other people's lives"?

Bush used the story of Flight 93 to bolster one of his most frequent moralisms: that it's important "to serve something greater than yourself." And yet what higher value is there than the truth? While moralizing on the "history" of 9/11, Bush was vigorously lobbying against formation of a panel to inquire into that very history—and so, once more, betrayed his animus against democracy. For if we were, at last, to learn the truth about that fatal day, we would no doubt be mobilized to call for some reforms and certainly some resignations (and no doubt some criminal proceedings). Rather than use 9/11 to remind the people of their power to govern this republic, Bush has understandably preferred to laud those passengers for their euphoric self-*destruction*, as (according to his view) they gladly killed themselves in order to protect him and his house.

"To serve something greater than yourself in life," as Bush says time and time again, is actually a noble thing—and indispensable to the revival of American democracy. The first Republicans invoked it often, referring to it as the classical ideal of *civic virtue*. "Is there no virtue among us?" asked Madison in 1788. "If there be not, we are in a wretched situation. No theoretical checks, no form of government can render us secure. To suppose that any form of government will secure liberty or happiness without any virtue in the people, is a chimerical idea." By "virtue" Madison did not mean sexual chastity, but self-denial for the sake of the collective good—the moral cornerstone of classical republicanism. "The only principles of public conduct that are worthy of a gentleman or a man are to sacrifice estate, ease, health, and applause, and even life, to the sacred calls of his country," James Otis wrote in 1761.

In order to return this nation to its rightful track, toward the fulfillment of our constitutional ideals, we must rediscover something of that virtue. To do so, we might well begin by recognizing that the Bush regime provides an excellent negative example. No administration in our history has been so utterly devoid of civic virtue. Against that old ideal (and while relentlessly attacking *Clinton* for his self-indulgence), Bush/Cheney celebrate mere license—for themselves, their donors, and their co-religionists. After 9/11, when millions of Americans were clamoring to know what they could do, how they might give, to aid the victims and to help their battered country, Bush replied that every good American should hit the shopping mall ASAP:

> Now, the American people have got to go about their business. We cannot let the terrorists achieve the objective of frightening our nation to the point where we don't—where we don't conduct business, where people don't shop.

Despite his cowboy pose, this Bush is every inch the Shopping President, insisting that we use *more* fossil fuels ("We need an energy bill that encourages consumption," he once blurted out), giving us incentive to purchase *bigger* vehicles (buy a Humvee, get a giant tax deduction), and urging us to go to Disney World and other "destination spots," as a way, supposedly, to thwart the terrorists. No president has done more product placement. At the winter Olympics in 2002, Bush took part in a staged chat with figure skater Sasha Cohen, lately hired by the National Cattleman's Beef Association as their "official youth spokesperson." (Bush had spoken at the association's annual convention earlier that day; the association is a major Bush contributor.) At the behest of hotelier Bill Marriott—who had given Bush/Cheney several hundred thousand dollars—Bush allowed some footage of himself to be incorporated into a TV spot for the Travel Industry Association of America, urging people to book flights and reservations in hotels. (Bush is the first U.S. president to allow his image to be used for commercial purposes.) On December 5, 2003, after a fund-raising speech in Baltimore—where he spoke, again, of "what it means to sacrifice for something greater than ourselves"—Bush stopped off at a Home Depot, ostensibly to speak on the economy, but actually in furtherance of the deal between his regime and that company: a top contributor, and one with high executives recruited from Bush/Cheney's White House.

Bush & Co.'s eat-the-world-now ideology is antithetical to civic virtue. A regime that would slash taxes, cut the economic giants loose to do their thing, and let you drive your Humvee, snowmobile, mountain

bike, or ATV wherever you might feel like it, squandering fuel that has
been purchased with the blood our own soldiers, is hardly virtuous in any
proper civic sense, however chaste its members may purport to be in private. In their philosophy, *your money* is the only thing that matters in this
world. Even—or especially—in time of war, *your* estate, *your* ease, *your*
health, come first: an indication of your blessedness, according to the
theocrats. "Nothing is more important in the face of a war than cut-
ting taxes," said Tom DeLay in early April of 2003. And as the GOP is
all about *your money*, the party's welfare surely matters more than any
lives lost in some battle overseas. "The story of what we've done in the
postwar period is remarkable," said Representative George Nethercutt
(R-WA), after a congressional jaunt to Baghdad. "It is a better and more
important story than losing a couple of soldiers every day." And few yup-
pie navel-gazers could match the presidential Mom for self-absorption.
On the eve of war in March 2003, with the nation fearful at the possibility of mortal casualties, Barbara Bush told Diane Sawyer why she does
not watch the news.

> [W]hy should we hear about body bags, and deaths, and how
> many, what day it's gonna happen, and how many this or what do
> you suppose? Or, I mean, it's, it's not relevant. So, why should I
> waste my beautiful mind on something like that?

To reclaim our republic—a project that will take far more than just
one national election—we must not only publicize such statements, so
that all Americans will know how Bush & Co. really feels about them.
We must also amplify the full and accurate quotation of their words by
calling them, repeatedly, on their ferocious ideology. Bush likes to say
that "we love freedom" and that he especially loves "free speech," and he
and his cohorts routinely claim that they are working for "democracy"
throughout the world. Such pretense is entirely unacceptable; and yet we
tacitly approve it when we let it pass unchallenged. These questions must
be put to them, in public, time and time again: *Do* they "love" American democracy? *Do* they "love" the Constitution? If they do, how do
they reconcile such feeling with their Reconstructionist support? Such

questions, and a lot of others more detailed—about the war, and 9/11, and Dick Cheney's business deals, and Haiti, and Ken Lay, and Bush's military history—must be put to them relentlessly, until we get some reasonable answers.

This struggle will require eternal vigilance, firm discipline and iron solidarity, and an intense awareness of our rights and obligations as free men and women. Thus were we long exhorted by the demagogues of anticommunism, who warned us endlessly against the agents of the Kremlin. Those alarmists were half-right. The price of freedom *is* eternal vigilance, and all the other aspects of a steely civic virtue. It is not some foreign plot that we must guard our liberties against, however, but those seeming patriots forever warning of that alien conspiracy—for it was, finally, they themselves against whom they were always warning us. Obsessed with tracking down and wiping out *bad people*, such hunters are quite blind to the true greatness of this country. For the spirit of American democracy is, finally, not vindictive, cynical, or punitive, but generous and tolerant: inclined to work things out, and let folks be, and try to make the best of it. Democracy does not believe in demons. In an imaginary dialogue with a fierce antirepublican, Madison presents his adversary as concluding hotly: "You have neither the light of faith nor the spirit of obedience. I denounce you to the government as an accomplice of atheism and anarchy." To which the true republican replies, as we too might reply to our accusers: "And I forbear to denounce you to the people, though a blasphemer of their rights and an idolater of tyranny. Liberty disdains to persecute."

Appendix

Barbara Walters' Interview with the Gore Family
ABC-TV's *20/20*, November 15, 2002

The following exchange was not included in the network's broadcast of the interview. Deleted from the evening's program, it was posted on the network's Web site.

WALTERS: I'm not sure that people realize that while you were in the residence of the Vice President [during the Florida recount] there were crowds of people outside screaming at you. What was that all about?

AL GORE: Well, this was the Republican response to what was happening during that 36-day period, and they organized busloads of people that came and stood outside the house all day and all night screaming at the top of their lungs.*

WALTERS: What, "Get out!"?

TIPPER GORE: Things like that, yes, and, and sometimes—things that we don't want to say on your program, and, some people saw that they were buses from "churches," but it was organized. The

---

*Among those out there was George W. Bush's sister, Doro Koch, *Newsweek* reported three years later, on the basis of an interview with Barbara Bush, who found the episode quite droll. " 'That's Doro!' Mrs. Bush hoots when telling about it. 'She felt better' after yelling at the Gores' house for a while, Mrs. Bush says." Melinda Henneberger, "Barbara Swings Away," *Newsweek*, 10/27/03.

one thing that, that they did mainly was reach the bedrooms of our children, and Albert was still in school locally, and trying to study, so we rearranged, you know, they—kids moved to a different part of the house, and I was trying to think of a way that we could kind of laugh about this since obviously it was out of our control, there wasn't anything anybody could do so I got all the boom boxes in the house and—I remember sort of what the government did with Noriega—I thought we'd try that, and I aimed them at, toward, you know, where the crowd—

WALTERS: The crowd?

TIPPER GORE: —and I put nature sounds on and turned it all the way up. And at least the kids laughed.

AL GORE: There were a few, more than a few who supported us and were offended by the organized chanting round the clock who came out on the other street corner during the day to express their support with signs, and—You know, emotions were running high throughout the country and it was just an unprecedented time.

KARENNA GORE: Well, when we were in the Vice President's house during the recount, it was, it was very intense. And one of the things I remember is that there was a—an organized effort by, I don't know whether it was the RNC or it was—it was right-wing groups, it was definitely a Bush-campaign-oriented effort to bus in people to have a sort of siege at the Vice President's house, and, so, they were all lining up there, screaming, and it was kind of an assortment of groups. I mean, some of them were anti-, um, were anti-abortion groups, and some of them were pro-gun groups, and some of them—they all had their different signs. But they were all screaming, "Get out of Cheney's house!" the whole time. And I just remember being there next to my dad, because I went for a run, and I ran back through them, and I was very upset when I came into the house. And my whole attitude was, like, "We've got to fight back harder. And where are our crowds?" And my dad, I'll never forget his response. He said, "We have to do what's best for the country, and it is not good for the country to have this kind of divisiveness." And he was on the phone, really calling off the dogs. There were people who wanted to fan the—the flames of the racial issue and have real unrest. And he was on the phone asking them not to, because of what was best for the country not because of what was best for him politically. And that's really who he is.

WALTERS: Do you remember the crowds outside screaming?

KRISTEN GORE: The crowds that were screaming outside our house, you know, "Get out of Cheney's house!" And other things— of that nature, were really upsetting. It was difficult—It was just very—upsetting that someone would—yell those things at us. It felt—we felt sort of like—trapped in this, you know, little house with all these people yelling mean things. It's no fun. You know, whether you're a child of the person who they're directed at, or any-one else. It—it wasn't a good situation.

WALTERS: Were you scared?

KRISTEN GORE: I was scared that the truth was not going to come out. That's what I was.

Notes

Unless otherwise noted, all citations of President Bush's remarks come from the transcripts published by the Federal News Service.

Preface

Page

xiii "Well, it's an unimaginable honor": Bush with reporters at the Jefferson Memorial, 7/4/01, quoted in *Weekly Compilation of Presidential Documents*, Vol. 37, No. 27, p. 1006 (7/9/01).

xiv "I will use our military": Ken Walsh, "Interview of the President," *U.S.News & World Report*, 12/30/02.

xiv "We want results": Bush at Bush/Cheney fund-raiser in Little Rock, Ark., 11/10/03.

xiv "It'll take time to restore chaos": Bush at White House briefing, 4/13/03.

xiv "One of the problems": Bush in Bentonville, Ark., FDCH Political Transcripts, 11/4/02.

xiv "We need an energy bill": Bush at National Guard base in Trenton, N.J., 9/23/02.

xiv "We're freeing women and children": Bush in Aurora, Mo., 1/14/02.

xiv "The goals for this country": Bush at Capital Area Food Bank, Washington, D.C., 12/19/02.

xiv "We're not into nation-building": Joint press conference with Bush and Japanese Prime Minister Koizumi, White House, 9/25/02.

xiv "The evil ones think": Bush at farm journal conference, Washington, D.C., 11/28/01.

xiv "There are no shades of gray": Bush in Portland, Ore., 1/5/02.

xiv "Bring 'em on": Bush at the White House, 7/2/03.

xv "I'm the commander": Bob Woodward, "A Course of 'Confident Action'; Bush Says Other Countries Will Follow Assertive U.S. in Combating Terror," *Washington Post*, 11/19/02.

xv "There's only one person": *ABC's 20/20 with Barbara Walters*, 12/13/02.

xv "You said we're headed to war": Bush, press conference in Crawford, Tex., 12/31/02.

xv "In 24 hours": "Texas Goes to Washington amid Celebration, Protest," *Philadelphia Inquirer*, 1/20/01.

xvi "That's the great thing about a democracy": Walsh, "Interview of the President," *U.S.News & World Report*, 12/30/02.

xvii "Sometimes that's where you want your opponent": Bush in Bentonville, Ark., FDCH Political Transcripts, 11/4/02.

xvii "momentous truths": James Madison's "Political Reflections," *Aurora General Advertiser*, February 23, 1799, reprinted in Jack N. Rakove, ed., *James Madison: Writings* (New York: Library of America, 1999), p. 606.

xvii "Voice or no voice": Goering expressed his view to prison psychiatrist G. M. Gilbert, who recounts the moment in his *Nuremberg Diary* (New York: Farrar, Straus, 1947), pp. 278–79.

Chapter 1
"The bright constellation which has gone before us"

5 "probably display much presumption": Alexis de Tocqueville, *Democracy in America*, trans. Henry Reeve, ed. Phillips Bradley, 2 vols. (New York: A. A. Knopf, 1945), Vol. 1, p. 318.

8 "The republican is the only form of government": Thomas Jefferson, Reply to Address, 1790, in Andrew A. Lipscomb and Albert Ellery Bergh, eds., *The Writings of Thomas Jefferson*, 20 vols. (Washington, D.C.: Thomas Jefferson Memorial Association, 1904–05), Vol. 8, p. 6.

9 "First the omission of a bill of rights": Jefferson to James Madison, December 20, 1787, in *Thomas Jefferson: Writings* (New York: Library of America, 1984), pp. 915–16.

9 "Equal and exact justice": Jefferson's first Inaugural Address, March 4, 1801, in *Thomas Jefferson: Writings*, pp. 494–95.

11 a million dollars to the anti-Chavez "opposition": Andrew Buncombe, "Secret Documents Show U.S. Paid $1 Million to Overthrow Democracy in Venezuela: U.S. revealed to be secretly funding opponents of Chavez," *Independent* (UK), 3/13/04, http://news.independent.co.uk/world/americas/story.jsp?story=500711.

11 terminated the first democratic presidency: Peter Hallward, "Why they had to crush Aristide," *The Guardian* (UK), 3/2/04; Jeffrey D. Sachs, "Are those dirty U.S. fingerprints on Aristide's ouster?" *Christian Science Monitor*, 3/8/04.

13   "to maintain American military preeminence": Project for the New American Century (PNAC), "Rebuilding America's Defenses: Strategy, Forces and Resources for a New Century," September 2000. A PDF file of the study is available at http://www.newamericancentury.org/publicationsreports.htm.

13   "Every ten years or so": Michael Ledeen quoted in Jonah Goldberg, "Baghdad Delenda Est, Part Two: Get on with It," *National Review*, 4/23/02.

13   "It will be worthy of a free, enlightened": John H. Rhodehamel, ed., *George Washington: Writings* (New York: Library of America, 1997), p. 972.

14   "the world's worst prison": Gordon Thomas, "Guantanamo—The World's Worst Prison," posted on Globe-Intel Web site, 10/13/03 (http://www.etrend.ch/fund grube/win_fundgrube/gt_031015_guantanamo.htm).

14   tortured physically and psychologically: Rosa Prince and Gary Jones, "My Hell in Camp X-Ray," *The Mirror* (UK), 3/12/04.

14   Amnesty International: "Allies under Fire for Terror War," *Toronto Star*, 5/29/03.

14   number of attempted suicides: "Ready to Go to the Island," *Der Spiegel*, 11/24/03.

15   Glenn A. Fine's report: Adam Liptak, "For Jailed Immigrants, a Presumption of Guilt," *New York Times*, 6/3/03.

15   " 'lockdown' for at least 23 hours": "Significant Problems with DOJ Detainees," UPI, 6/2/03.

16   Ashcroft's conduct: Nat Hentoff, "Justice Denied at the Source," *Village Voice*, 6/20/03.

17   "*there never was a people*": James Madison, "Political Reflections," *Aurora General Advertiser*, February 23, 1799, reprinted in Rakove, ed., *Writings*, p. 606.

17   "to prevent the establishment of a standing army"; "form a powerful check": Quoted in William Weir, *A Well-Regulated Militia: The Battle over Gun Control* (North Haven, CT: Archon Books), pp. 164–68.

18   "military assistance to civil authorities": "US NORTHCOM: Who We Are— Mission" (www.northcom.mil/index.cfm?fuseaction=s.who_mission).

18   gross ineptitude: Michael Crowley, "Playing Defense: Bush's Disastrous Homeland Security Department," *The New Republic*, 3/15/04.

19   "100% secret and 0% accountable": Frank Morales, "Homeland Defense: Pentagon Declares War on America," *Global Outlook*, Winter 2003.

19   "If the government is allowed": "Senators Attempt to Close 'Secrecy' Hole," *The Hill*, 7/8/03.

20   the "right to die" law passed in Oregon: "Clash in Court over Oregon's Law on Suicide," *Los Angeles Times*, 5/18/03; "John Ashcroft's Holy War," *Business Week Online*, 4/23/02.

20   Ed Rosenthal: "Medical Marijuana Goes Up against Federal Law," *Los Angeles*

Times, 2/5/03; "Marijuana Grower Sentenced to Day in Prison," *New York Times*, 6/5/03.

21   Guatemalan man: "3 Rulings by 9th Circuit Reverses," *Los Angeles Times*, 11/5/02.

21   Holocaust survivors: "Supreme Court Strikes Down California Law Meant to Help Holocaust Survivors," Associated Press State & Local Wire, 6/24/03.

21   "California's environmental protection laws": "U.S., State Clash over Environment," *Los Angeles Times*, 9/14/03.

21   Bush & Co. engineered regime change there: Greg Palast, "Arnold Unplugged," 10/3/03 (www.gregpalast.com/detail.cfm?artid=283&row=1-25k).

22   Texas must redraw its congressional districts: Jackson Thoreau, "Texas Democrats Learned the Hard Way about Being Nice to Republicans," 8/31/03 (http://houston.indymedia.org/news/2003/08/15306.php); "State Democrats Accuse Bush, Rove of Being Behind Texas Remap Effort," *Bulletin's Frontrunner*, 9/5/03.

22   "to wipe out moderate and white Democrats": "The Soviet Republic of Texas," *Washington Post*, 10/14/03.

22   "Mid-decade redistricting": Joshua Marshall, 5/19/03 (http://talkingpoints memo.com/archives/week_2003_05_18.htm#001492).

23   "[Texas Speaker Tom] Craddick": "DeLay Admits to Role in Hunting for Democrats," *Houston Chronicle*, 5/23/03. See also Glenn Smith, "Homeland Security Department Used to Track Texas Democrats," Common Dreams News Center, 5/14/03 (http://www.commondreams.org/views03/0514-07.htm); "Eyes of Texas, U.S. on Truant Legislators," *Fort Worth Star-Telegram*, 5/14/03.

23   Bill Thomas: "Welcome to the Soviet Style Republican Congress," *BuzzFlash*, 7/19/03 (http://www.buzzflash.com/analysis/03/07/19_soviet.html).

24   "My friends, this is how tyranny begins": "House Vote Erupts into War of Words," *Atlanta Journal-Constitution*, 7/19/03.

24   "I never thought, as a member of Congress": Ibid.

24   "just plain stupid": "Thomas Says He Regrets Calling Capitol Police," *Washington Times*, 7/24/03.

25   Jesse Jackson: "Jesse Jackson's Love Child," *National Enquirer*, 1/18/01. The political motivation for the story was implicit in the color photograph deployed to illustrate the text: "A smiling Jesse Jackson and his mistress Karin Stanford (circled) pose with President Clinton and other Rainbow Coalition staffers on December 3, 1998—five months before Jesse's love child was born."

25   J. H. Hatfield: For background on the Hatfield controversy, see Mark Crispin Miller, "Introduction," and Sander Hicks, "Why I Published *Fortunate Son*," in J. H. Hatfield, *Fortunate Son: George W. Bush and the Making of an American President*, 3rd ed. (New York: Soft Skull Press, 2002), pp. xi–xvi, 369–74. See also the documentary *Horns and Halos: A War of Words* (2003), directed by Suki Hawley and Michael Galinsky (http://www.hornsandhalos.com/).

Hatfield was a complex and troubled character. For a thorough study of his darker aspects, see Marc Schone, "Unfortunate Con," *Oxford American*, Summer 2003.

25 Scott Ritter: "UN's Ritter Faced Sex Rap," *Daily News* (N.Y.), 1/19/03; "Reports Claim Ritter Arrested in Sex Sting; Does ex-weapons inspector pressing impeachment have own legal trouble?" *WorldNet Daily*, 1/19/03 (http://www.worldnet daily.com/news/article.asp?ARTICLE_ID=30570).

25 Harvey John "Jack" McGeorge: "Weapons Inspectors' Experience Questioned," *Washington Post*, 11/28/02.

25 Bill Burkett: E-mail from Lt. Gen Burkett, 4/28/04.

26 Jason Leopold: Leopold's contemporaneous account of his experience—"My Story: Shafted by *The New York Times*"—was posted on the Web site Scoop.nz, 10/9/02. A fuller version will appear in Leopold's forthcoming book, *Fade to Black: Inside the Cutthroat Worlds of Investigative Journalism, Politics and High Finance*. Leopold's revelations about Thomas White were all eventually confirmed as true by the indictment of Enron's Jeffrey Skilling on 2/19/04. The indictment is online at http://news.findlaw.com/hdocs/docs/enron/secskllng21904cmp.pdf.

26 outing of CIA agent Valerie Plame: Joseph C. Wilson IV, "What I Didn't Find in Africa," *New York Times*, 7/6/03; Stuart Taylor Jr., "The White House Leak Scandal: Is a Cover-Up in the Works?" *National Journal*, 10/4/03; Edward Alden, James Harding, and Deborah McGregor, "The Investigation into How the Name of a CIA Operative Became Public Poses a Risk to George W. Bush's Reputation," *Financial Times*, 10/2/03.

27 "If that's the zone": Michael Morrell, quoted in "Stop the Music; Taking to the Streets; View from Denver," *The NewsHour with Jim Lehrer*, PBS, 7/27/00.

28 ACLU filed suit: "Your Right to Say It . . . but Over There," *Chicago Tribune*, 9/28/03.

28 unless, of course, it's in Iran: When Iranian students started agitating for democracy, Bush hailed their gumption. "This is the beginning of people expressing themselves toward a free Iran, which I think is positive," he said on June 16, 2003, and he thus elaborated two days later: "I appreciate those courageous souls who speak out for freedom in Iran. They need to know America stands squarely by their side. And I would urge the Iranian administration to treat them with the utmost of respect."

Four months earlier, when it was his own policies that were the object of mass protest—not just in the United States but all throughout the world—the president did not exactly show "the utmost of respect," but sounded very much like a Shi'ite mullah in Tehran. Asked about those demonstrations, he replied: "Size of protest—it's like deciding, well, I'm going to decide policy based upon a focus group. The role of a leader is to decide policy based upon the security, in this case, the security of the people." 2/18/03.

28 "She was taking a picture": "ACLU Chief, 6 Others Arrested at Protest," *Arizona Republic*, 9/28/02.

28 "fired lead-shot-filled bean bags": "25 Anti-War Protesters Charged; Activist 'disappointed' by legal action in response to April 7 rally," *Alameda Times-Star*, 6/24/03.

28 New York Police Department preemptively arrested: "94 Arrested in Protest on 5th Ave.," *Newsday*, 4/8/03. The treatment of the arrestees was reported independently by several of the protestors themselves.

29 In Miami: Tom Hayden, "Miami Vice," *AlterNet*, 11/21/03 (http://www.alternet .org/story.html?StoryID=17234); Rebecca Solnit, "Fragments of the Future: The FTAA in Miami," *TomDispatch*, 11/24/03 (http://www.nationinstitute.org/ tomdispatch/index.mhtml?pid=1090).

29 "Police violence outside of trade summits": Naomi Klein, "The War on Dissent," *Toronto Globe and Mail*, 11/25/03.

29 "The forces fired indiscriminately": Jeremy Scahill, "The Miami Model: Paramilitaries, Embedded Journalists and Illegal Protests," Common Dreams News Center, 11/25/03 (http://www.commondreams.org/views03/1125-13.htm).

30 "Our goal was to drown you out": Klein, "The War on Dissent."

30 "They were pointing their guns at us": "He Respected the Badge, but 'Not in Miami,' " *Miami Herald*, 11/23/03.

31 action in Miami . . . cost: "City Secures Money to Run Talks," *Miami Herald*, 11/6/03.

31 "As a matter of principle": "F.B.I. Scrutinizes Antiwar Rallies," *New York Times*, 11/23/03.

32 "We must start thinking differently": William Arkin, "Mission Creep Hits Home; American armed forces are assuming major new domestic policing and surveillance roles," *Los Angeles Times*, 11/23/03.

33 "no-fly" list: "Peace Activists Put on No-fly List," *Oakland Tribune*, 10/18/02; Dave Lindorff, "Grounded," *Salon*, 11/15/02 (http://www.salon.com/news/ feature/2002/11/15/no_fly/index_np.html?x).

33 David Nelson, son of Ozzie and Harriet: "David Nelson, Could You Step aside for a Few Moments?" *Sunday Oregonian*, 5/4/03. (Nine months before that story broke, Sean Holstege reported on the post-9/11 air travails of a different David Nelson, a financier from northern California—whose twenty-two-year-old son, also named David, also has a hard time flying. "Some Travelers a Threat to Country in Name Only," *Alameda Times-Star*, 9/5/02.)

34 "To those who scare": John Ashcroft, testimony, House Judiciary Committee hearing on Anti-Terrorism, Federal News Service, 12/6/02.

35 9/11 . . . independent inquest: "White House Drags Its Feet on Testifying at 9/11 Panel," *New York Times*, 9/13/02; "Barriers to 9/11 Inquiry Decried," *Washington Post*, 9/19/02; "Battle over Independent Sept. 11 Probe Keeps Intelligence Authorization in Limbo," *Congressional Quarterly Weekly*, 10/18/02; How a Deal

Creating an Independent Commission on Sept. 11 Came Undone," *New York Times*, 11/2/02; John Prados, "'Slow-Walked and Stonewalled,'" *Bulletin of the Atomic Scientists*, Vol. 59, No. 2, 3/1/03; Eric Boehlert, "Bush's 9/11 coverup?" *Salon*, 6/18/03, http://www.salon.com/news/feature/2003/06/18/911/index_np.html; Eric Boehlert, "Playing politics with the 9/11 commission," *Salon*, 1/26/04, http://www.salon.com/news/feature/2004/01/24/911_commission/index_np.html. Gail Sheehy, "Four 9/11 Moms Battle Bush," *New York Observer*, 8/25/03; Brian Montopoli, "Schlep to Judgment," *Washington Monthly*, 9/1/03.

36 "keep negotiating": "National Journal," *Hotline*, 10/14/02.

36 "the White House is trying": "Announced Agreement on Sept. 11 Commission Falls Apart," *AP*, 10/10/02.

37 Henry Kissinger: "Kissinger Tapped to Lead 9/11 Panel; The president calls for 'an aggressive investigation,'" *Sacramento Bee*, 11/28/02; "Kissinger Steps Down as Chairman of 9/11 Panel, Citing Conflicts," *AP*, 12/13/02.

38 "CIA personnel were not allowed": All quotations in this paragraph come from the Appendix—"Access Limitations Encountered by the Joint Inquiry"—to the congressional report, which is available at http://www.fas.org/irp/congress/2002_rpt/911rept.pdf.

39 Slade Gorton: "Gorton Still Hasn't Received Security Clearance; Delay slows work of Sept. 11 probe," *Seattle Times*, 3/12/02.

40 "The commission feels unanimously": "Panel Turns up Pressure for 9-11 Documents; Defense, Justice singled out; White House says it is cooperating," *Dallas Morning News*, 7/9/03.

40 port security: "Senate turns down Hollings port proposal," *Journal of Commerce Online*, 4/3/03, http://www.joc.com.

40 1 percent and 2 percent of all incoming ships: "Schumer Tells Feds of N.Y.'s Port Perils," *Daily News* (N.Y.), 9/15/03.

41 Chemical Security Act: "An Overlooked Vulnerability?" *Primedia Insight: Access Control and Security Systems*, 10/1/03; "Hydrofluoric Acid at Center of Green Group's Security Study," *Octane Week*, 10/20/03; "Chemical Plant Security: A Tale of Two Senate Bills," National Resources Defense Council, press release, 9/9/03 (http://www.nrdc.org/media/pressreleases/030909.asp).

41 "We need an illuminator": Stephen Cambone, undersecretary of defense for intelligence, "Feds Want All-Seeing Eye in Sky," *Wired News*, 10/17/03.

41 "A lot of people": "For Port Authority Police, Counterterrorism Is Tedious," Newhouse News Service, 4/25/03.

42 train security: According to U.S. Transportation officials, "the Madrid bombings underscored the fact that rail security had lagged woefully behind aviation improvements since the 9/11 attacks." "Bombings Lead U.S. to Raise Security for Trains," *New York Times*, 3/13/04.

42 "Guns and knives are still": "Pre-Board Screening Still Suspect as Weapons Elude Detection," *Airport Security Report*, 10/8/03.

42 uninspected cargo: "Schumer Fires 'Shot' on Security," *New York Sun*, 9/15/03.

44 "On balance, we are not safer": "Two Years Later, Is the U.S. Winning the War on Terrorism?" Cox News Service, 9/3/03.

44 "[T]he United States remains dangerously": Testimony of Jamie Metzl before the House Select Committee on Homeland Security, Federal News Service, 7/17/03. A senior fellow at the Council on Foreign Relations, Metzl was also project director of the Council's Independent Task Force on Emergency Responders.

44 "still lack basic equipment": Ibid.

44 "It is great to": "Mayors Warn of Effect on Security Personnel; Cuts hurt readiness, legislators told," *Boston Globe*, 9/9/03.

45 "President Bush, you are": "Firefighters Blast Bush," *Daily News* (N.Y.), 8/15/03.

45 "It's too bad Mr. Bush": "The Soldiers Bush Didn't Visit on Thanksgiving," *Boston Globe*, 12/11/03.

46 "Thanks for serving as a prop": Richard Leiby, "Babs, Beware the Bogus Bard," *Washington Post*, 10/2/02 (http://www.washingtonpost.com/ac2/wp-dyn/A29583-2002Oct1?language=printer).

47 "A president has got to be": "*Bush at War*; Bob Woodward's new book takes a behind-the-scenes look at the Bush presidency in a time of war," *60 Minutes*, CBS, 11/17/02.

47 "I believe what I believe": "Done with G-8 Summit, Bush Strolls through Rome with First Lady, Then Heads to Vatican City," AP, 7/22/01.

47 "No other foundation can be devised": Jefferson to George Wythe, August 13, 1786, in *Thomas Jefferson: Writings*, p. 859.

48 "The British regularly raised": "Cheney Ignored War Chaos Alert," *Observer*, 11/16/03.

48 "FEMA added, in its own words": "Gov. Davis' 'Giuliani Moment' Came Too Late," *Charleston Gazette* (W.V.), 11/2/03.

49 "I went to tell her that what happened": "Expert Warned That Mad Cow Was Imminent," *New York Times*, 12/25/03.

50 "If there's a kind of a hand-wringing attitude": "*Bush at War*," *60 Minutes*, CBS, 11/17/02.

50 "Conservation may be a sign of personal virtue": "Cheney: Look Hard at Energy Needs," UPI, 4/30/01.

50 "I read the report by the bureaucracy": "Bush Withholds Backing of EPA Report on Warming," *Washington Post*, 6/5/02.

50 "I had the opportunity to go out": Bush to U.S. embassy personnel at Leopold Sedar Senghor International Airport, Dakar, Senegal, 7/8/03. UNESCO maintains an edifying virtual tour of the museum, at http://webworld.unesco.org/goree/en/index.shtml.

Chapter 2
What We Don't Know

57 The Unknown First Amendment: My understanding of the modern misconception of the First Amendment as "a license to offend" owes much to Rochelle Gurstein, *The Repeal of Reticence: A History of America's Cultural and Legal Struggles over Free Speech, Obscenity, Sexual Liberation and Modern Art* (New York: Hill & Wang, 1996).

58 "[T]o the press alone": "Report on the Alien and Sedition Acts" (1799), in *Madison: Writings*, p. 647.

58 "If a nation expects": Jefferson to Col. Charles Yancey, January 6, 1816, in *Writings of Thomas Jefferson*, ed. Albert Ellery Bergh, 20 vols. (Washington-Thomas Jefferson Memorial Association, 1907), XIV, 389.

58n copyright remains in private . . . hands for decades: "The CTEA," writes Chris Sprigman, "extended the term of protection by 20 years for works copyrighted after January 1, 1923. Works copyrighted by individuals since 1978 got "life plus 70" rather than the existing "life plus 50." Works made by or for corporations (referred to as "works made for hire") got 95 years. Works copyrighted before 1978 were shielded for 95 years, regardless of how they were produced. In all, tens of thousands of works that had been poised to enter the public domain were maintained under private ownership until at least 2019." Chris Sprigman, "The Mouse That Ate the Public Domain: Disney, the Copyright Term Extension Act, and Eldred V. Ashcroft," posted at FindLaw's Writ, 3/5/02 (http://writ.news.findlaw.com/commentary/20020305_sprigman.html).

See also Robert S. Boynton, "The Tyranny of Copyright?" *New York Times Magazine*, 1/25/04; Siva Vaidyanathan, *Copyrights and Copywrongs: The Rise of Intellectual Property and How It Threatens Creativity* (New York: New York University Press, 2001); and Lawrence Lessig, *The Future of Ideas: The Fate of the Commons in a Connected World* (New York: Random House, 2001).

59 "go out into the country": John Moyers and Judy Woodruff on "'Misunderestimating' Each Other? Bush II and the Media," a forum held at American University's School of Communication, 9/04/01, and later aired on C-SPAN. Audio source online at http://www.wamu.org/ram/2001/forum.ram; Web source at http://www.wamu.org/auevents/forum0901.html.

61 "to turn your Administraton's attention": Jason Leopold, "Rumsfeld and Wolfowitz lobbied Clinton in '98 to start Iraq war and topple Saddam," *Online Journal*, 2/20/03 (http://www.onlinejournal.com/Special_Reports/022003Leopold/022003leopold.html).

61 "From a marketing point of view": "Quotation of the Day," *New York Times*, 9/7/02.

61 "the threat from Saddam": Tony Blair and Bush, joint appearance at Camp David, FDCH Political Transcripts, 9/7/02.

62 "[i]n the last 14 months": "U.S. Says Hussein Intensifies Quest for A-Bomb Parts," *New York Times*, 9/8/02.

63 "If you start with that": Dick Cheney on *Meet the Press*, NBC, 9/8/02.

64 "We don't want the smoking gun": Condoleezza Rice on *Late Edition*, CNN, 9/08/02.

64 "Imagine a September 11": Donald Rumsfeld on *Face the Nation*, CBS, 9/8/02.

64 "The president will retain": Colin Powell on *Fox News Sunday*, 9/8/02.

64 "A spokeswoman at IAEA": "Bush, Blair Decry Hussein; Iraqi Threat Is Real, They Say," *Washington Post*, 9/8/02.

65 "Kelly, when Prime Minister Blair": *Sunday Morning*, CNN, 9/8/02.

67 "I say it in my speeches": Bush in Crawford, Tex., 8/21/02.

67 "I'm a patient man. And I've got tools": Bush at Kentucky Fair and Exposition Center, Louisville, Ky., 9/5/02.

67 "You said you expected": Bush with Ariel Sharon at the White House, 10/16/02.

68 "Meanwhile, Iraq's main air base": "Blair Steps Up Iraq Rhetoric," *Scotsman*, 9/6/02.

70 "My country seems to be on the verge": "Ex-UN Inspector Addresses Iraqi Parliament, Urges Inspectors' Return," *BBC Monitoring International Reports*, 9/8/02.

71 "Is Scott Ritter disloyal?": Miles O'Brien, Clifford May, and Scott Ritter on *Sunday Morning*, CNN, 9/8/02. All quotations from CNN were taken from the network's own transcripts, available through LexisNexis.

75 "This morning, I'm sure": Catherine Callaway and Eason Jordan, *Sunday Morning*, CNN, 9/8/02.

76 "So what do you make of": Paula Zahn, Richard Shelby, Scott Ritter, and Gary Saymore on CNN, *Sunday Morning*, 9/8/02.

81 "Now, Scott, you say the U.S.": Kyra Phillips and Scott Ritter on *CNN Live Today*, 9/9/02.

85 "Even as the Bush administration": Paula Zahn and Richard Butler on *American Morning with Paula Zahn*, CNN, 9/9/02.

86 "Is he sticking up for Saddam Hussein": John Gibson, David Asman, and Scott Ritter on *The Big Story*, Fox News Network, 9/12/02. All quotations from Fox were taken from the network's own transcripts, available through LexisNexis.

90 "Let me talk to you": Paula Zahn and Scott Ritter on *American Morning with Paula Zahn*, CNN, 9/13/02.

92 "Why did you meet with the Iraqi government?": Arthel Neville, Scott Ritter, and Max Boot on *TalkBack Live*, CNN, 9/13/02.

97 "the path to democracy in Iraq": "Saddam's Fall Could Come Quickly if U.S. Attacked, Opposition Leader Says," *St. Louis Post-Dispatch*, 8/9/02.

98 "massive demonstration of American power": James Woolsey interviewed by Tim Russert on CNBC, 9/14/02.

98 "Once Afghanistan has been dealt with": Max Boot, "The Case for American Empire," *Weekly Standard*, 10/15/01.

99 "possesses and produces chemical and biological weapons": Bush at the Cincinnati Art Museum, Cincinnati, Ohio, 10/7/02.

100 "Case Closed": James S. Robbins, "Case Closed," *National Review,* 10/8/02.

100 "Case Closed": John Podhoretz, "Case Closed—With Facts, the President Soberly Faces down Fear," *New York Post*, 10/8/02.

A year later, Podhoretz, in another column on the nagging subject of Iraq's fictitious WMDs, used the same locution to deny, again, that all those weapons were fictitious. This time the occasion was David Kay's report, released on 10/2/03, that there appeared to be no unconventional weapons in Iraq. Approvingly Podhoretz quoted Andrew Sullivan, who had found a way to represent Kay's disappointing news as vindication of Bush/Cheney's war policy: "As Andrew Sullivan wrote Friday [in his 10/3/03 Web log], 'Translation: Saddam was lying to the U.N. as late as 2002. He was required by the U.N. to fully cooperate. He didn't. The war was justified on those grounds alone. Case closed.' " John Podhoretz, "Size Problem—Key Evidence Found, But Weapons Hunt Must Go On," *New York Post*, 10/6/03.

Some five weeks later, the pro-war propaganda mill invoked the phrase *again* to bring the issue to fake closure: "Case Closed" was the title of a breathless cover story in the *Weekly Standard*, published with a great to-do in mid-November, and duly echoed and reechoed by the tribunes of the right, who claimed triumphantly that it now proved that there *had* been a link between al Qaeda and Saddam Hussein. In an interview with the *Rocky Mountain News*, Cheney called the article the "best source of information" on the subject, and all Bush/Cheney's spinners fell in line—Andrew Sullivan, for instance, livening up his Web log with three different items on the article in just one day (11/17/03). What with such hearty resonance, and the mainstream media's immediate quiescence on the subject, the truth emerged belatedly and weakly: i.e., that the article, by Stephen F. Hayes, was based on a tendentious memo by Cheney aide Douglas J. Feith, who had done nothing more than sift the same old inconclusive batch of intel rumors and "reports," then string together certain of the bits to make it all sound new and plausible.

100 "Well, Connie, this is the most important vote": *Connie Chung Tonight*, CNN, 10/7/02.

102 CNN/*USA Today*/Gallup Poll: "Bush Is Getting Impatient with U.N.'s Debate on Iraq," *USA Today*, 10/24/02.

102 *New York Times*/CBS News Poll: "Public Says Bush Needs to Pay Heed to Weak Economy," *New York Times*, 10/7/02.

103 "I'm Persuaded": Mary McGrory, "I'm Persuaded," *Washington Post*, 2/6/03.

104 "In the final days before": "In US, Support for War Is Rising," *Christian Science Monitor*, 2/5/03.

Chapter 3
The Wrong Man: I

109 "People can read the handwriting": "Americans See Strangers in Their Midst," *New York Times*, 5/14/95.

109 "We don't have a government": "Local Militias Defend Role," *Pittsburgh Post-Gazette*, 4/30/95.

109 "a huge range of people": Allan Holmes, "Raging Rhetoric," *Government Executive*, July 1995.

110 "In this country we cherish": President Bill Clinton in Minneapolis, Association of Community Colleges, Federal News Service, 4/24/95.

111 "a post-Oklahoma *Kristallnacht*": "A Post-Oklahoma *Kristallnacht*," *New American*, Vol. 11, No. 11, 5/29/95.

111 "They must have been dancing a jig": "Talk Radio Not at Fault in Attack, Hosts Say Clinton Comment Stirs Conservative Anger," *Detroit Free Press*, 4/26/95.

111 "inflammatory statements": "President Is Criticized by Oklahoma Senators," *New York Times*, 4/26/95.

112 "trying to label everyone": "Airwaves Crackle with Criticism of Clinton Intimation," *USA Today*, 4/26/95.

112 "closing in . . . on the legitimate speech": Charles Krauthammer, "Talk Radio, Ghoul Politics," *Washington Post*, 4/28/95.

112 "There is a huge difference": "Talk-Radio Talking Indignantly to Itself," *Chicago Tribune*, 4/25/95.

112 "Should Bill Clinton decide": "Talk Show Host Denies Fueling 'Lunatic Fringe,'" *Post and Courier* (Charleston, S.C.), 4/26/95.

112 "The left in this country": "Clinton Denounced 'Reckless' Speech on the Airwaves," *Los Angeles Times*, 4/25/95.

112 "I mean, there is a": Rush Limbaugh, *Rush Limbaugh*, Multimedia Entertainment, Inc., 2/22/95. All quotations from the radio show are available through LexisNexis. On 4/27/95, Limbaugh devoted a long segment of his show to self-defense. He replayed a lengthy excerpt of his February broadcast, including his notorious reference to "the second violent American revolution," asserting that that line was somehow less inflammatory in context. However, the statement was just as provocative in context as it was all by itself, and Limbaugh, in replaying his provocation, even took the opportunity to make it *more* incendiary, by coming up with more examples of the federal government's alleged repressiveness.

113 "They've got a big target on there": "It's Time to Turn Down the Volume of Hatred," *Seattle Times*, 4/25/95.

114 Ruby Ridge: For a thorough and dispassionate account of that traumatic episode, see David A. Neiwert, *In God's Country: The Patriot Movement and the Pacific Northwest* (Pullman, Wash.: Washington State University Press, 1999), pp. 63–67.

114 Waco: See Senator John Danforth, "Final Report to the Deputy Attorney General Concerning the 1993 Confrontation at the Mt. Carmel Complex, Waco, Texas, 11/8/00." (The report was disputed vehemently by the Cato Institute: "Cato Blasts Danforth's Waco Report," UPI, 4/10/01.)

115 "jack-booted government thugs": "Sen. Craig on the NRA, the Constitution and the Media," States News Service, 4/28/95.

116 "Clinton Body Count": See David Neiwert, "Rush, Newspeak, and Fascism: An Exegesis," 8/30/03, available at http://dneiwert.blogspot.com/.

117 "criminals' lobby": "Sloganeering," *Washington Post*, 7/8/81.

117 detention camps: On July 5, 1987, the *Miami Herald* reported that the Reagan/Bush White House had ordered secret plans for mass detentions in the event of violent national protests of a U.S. invasion of Nicaragua, then under consideration as a way to crush the Sandinista government. The plan was to be organized by FEMA, under the supervision of Oliver North. (The plan also surfaced briefly at the Iran/contra hearings in 1987, when Representative Jack Brooks, D-TX, asked to be told more about it. The committee chair, Senator Daniel Inouye, D-HI, aborted the discussion by proclaiming it a matter fit for a closed session.)

According to the *Herald*, the plan was based on a number of presidential directives, handed down in the period 1982–84. As Bush & Co. has now sealed all White House records for the Reagan years, those executive orders must be unavailable. See Ritt Goldstein, "Foundations Are in Place for Martial Law in the US," *Sydney Morning Herald*, 7/27/02.

117 "Bill Clinton has not been called": Anthony Lewis, "Clinton's Sorriest Record," *New York Times*, 10/16/96.

117 "Bill Clinton has the worst civil liberties": Anthony Lewis, "The Clinton Mystery," *New York Times*, 3/4/97.

117 "A single essay cannot do justice": Nadine Strossen, "Speech and Privacy," in Roger Pilon, ed., *The Rule of Law in the Wake of Clinton* (Washington, D.C.: Cato Institute, 2000), p. 69.

118 "the most wire-tap-friendly administration": "First in Damage to Constitutional Liberties," *Washington Post*, 11/16/96.

119 "And Miss Reno, I say to you": "Bombing Alters the Landscape for Gun Lobby," *New York Times*, 4/28/95.

120 "a jackboot liberal": Doug Bandow, "Clinton's Brand of Jackboot Liberalism," Cato Institute Web site, 10/23/97 (http://www.cato.org/dailys/10-23-97.html).

120   "Habeas corpus has little": "Roll Call," *Virginian-Pilot* (Norfolk), 4/22/96.

124   "I brought up one": E-mail from Scott Ritter, 11/9/03.

126   "At 4:30 in the afternoon": Jonathan Schell, "Haircut: A Tale with a Life of Its Own," *Newsday* (N.Y.), 7/18/93.

127   "If you're going to try to impress": "Still Funny and Still a Major Draw, Carson Wows an Awards Luncheon," *New York Times,* 5/25/93.

127   "That's Bill Clinton": Dan Burton quoted in Jill Dougherty, "Bill Clinton Has Bad Hair Day Aboard 'Hair Force One,' " *News,* CNN, 5/20/93.

127   "They are the spoiled brats": "From a Generation of Kultursmog Wanderers," *Washington Times,* 5/30/93.

128   "This haircut business is the most": *Rush Limbaugh,* Multimedia Entertainment, Inc., 5/27/93.

129   "Let me just say something": Al Hunt, Mark Shields, and Margaret Warner on *Capital Gang,* CNN, 5/22/93.

130   "a boner": President Bill Clinton, remarks at a town meeting on *CBS This Morning, Public Papers of the Presidents,* 5/27/93.

131   "lit up the sky": "D.C. Residents Blast Bush over 'Big Bang,' " *Houston Chronicle,* 9/9/01.

131   "Residents on both sides": "Look! Up in the Sky! It's a Late Wake-Up Call from a White House Party," *Washington Post,* 9/7/01.

132   "The federal government may have to take": "D.C. Residents Blast Bush over 'Big Bang,' " *Houston Chronicle,* 9/9/01.

132   "Oh, I was told that it": "Fireworks Bomb in D.C.," *Daily News* (N.Y.), 9/7/01.

132   "Zambelli said he did not question": "Look! Up in the Sky!" *Washington Post,* 9/7/01.

132   "[t]he White House has apologized": Peter Jennings, *World News Tonight,* ABC, 9/6/01.

133   "Clint Eastwood is here": Campbell Brown, *The News With Brian Williams,* MSNBC, 9/5/01.

133   "After Dawn Upshaw sings": *Inside Politics,* CNN, 9/5/01.

133   "She looks wonderful in red": "Foxes taste the glam side of White House," *USA Today,* 9/6/01.

133   "To close the night": "Bush White House Stages First State Dinner," UPI, 9/5/01.

133   "a spicy meal of upscale Tex-Mex cusine": "Spicy Welcome to the White House," *New York Times,* 9/6/01.

133   "Bush thanked his guests": "Guests at 1st State Dinner Feast on Elegance, Politics," *Dallas Morning News,* 9/6/01.

134   "In an evening of traditional social values": "The State Dinner That Ended with a Bang," *Washington Post,* 9/6/01.

135   "round-up": "Senegal rounds up 'bad guys' to protect Bush," *Cape Times,* 7/8/03, available online at http://www.iol.co.za/index.php?set_id=1&click_id=68&art_

id=vn20030708050144329C375378. See also the firsthand account of a Sene-
galese citizen, posted by Joan Herron, a U.S. peace activist, at http://www.sunmt
.org/bushsenegal.html.

135   "We were shut up like sheep": "Cooped-up Locals Angry about Bush Visit,"
      Reuters, 7/8/03, available at http://www.iol.co.za/index.php?click_id=68&art
      _id=qw1057680000828B212&set_id=1.

136   "Armed police backed by bulldozers": Agence France-Presse, "Homes Bulldozed
      to Clear Way for Bush," *Business Day* (South Africa), 7/13/03, available at http://
      www.bday.co.za/bday/content/direct/1,3523,1386802-6078-0,00.html.

137   "Whatever the Party holds to be the truth": George Orwell, *1984*, ed. Bernard
      Crick (Oxford: Clarendon Press, 1984), p. 374.

138   "where everyone else's children": Strobe Talbott, "Clinton and the Draft: A Per-
      sonal Testimony," *Time*, 4/6/92.

139   "I decided to accept the draft": "Text of Clinton's Letter to ROTC Director," AP,
      2/12/92.

140   "purposely deceived me, using": "Clinton Lied, Says ROTC Chief," *Washington
      Times*, 9/17/92.

142   Americans were dying in Vietnam: "U.S. Casualties for February–May 1968 as
      Compiled by the White House Situation Room," available online at http://
      www.richmond.edu/~ebolt/history398/US_Casualties_1968.html. The weekly
      U.S. death rate had been accelerating steadily since January.

142   family connections: "Man Says He OK'd Bush for Guard," AP, 9/27/99; "Barnes
      Called Guard to Help Get Bush In," *Austin American-Statesman*, 9/28/99.

142   "It was sometimes called Air Canada": "Texas Speaker Reportedly Helped Bush
      Get into Guard," *Washington Post*, 9/21/99.

143   deft wisecrack by Michael Moore: In his speech endorsing Wesley Clark's run for
      the Democratic presidential nomination, Moore said, "I want to see that debate:
      the general versus the deserter." Moore's charge made national news weeks later,
      when ABC's Peter Jennings, one of the questioners at the final Democratic debate
      in New Hampshire, called Moore's shot "reckless," and asked Clark why he had
      not disavowed it. Jennings's effort to discredit Moore's remark entirely, thereby
      helping to suppress the facts of Bush's military record, was yet one more example
      of the mainstream media's constant pro-Bush propaganda work. For an account
      of the whole controversy, see Thomas Lang, "Fact Check," *Columbia Journalism
      Review*, "Campaign Desk," 1/26/04, http://www.campaigndesk.org/archives/
      000056.asp.

143   "The other reality in spring of 1968": George W. Bush and Karen Hughes, *A
      Charge to Keep* (New York: Morrow, 1999), p. 50.

144   "I don't think we spent a lot": "In His Own Words: 'I, Like Others, Became Dis-
      illusioned,'" *Washington Post*, 7/28/99.

144   "I don't remember any kind of heaviness": Robert Draper, "Favorite Son," *GQ,*
         September 1998.

144   "Had my unit been called up": "At Height of Vietnam, Graduate Picks Guard,"
         Washington Post, 7/28/99. Two days later, Bush was thus quoted in the *Los Ange-*
         les Times: "I was prepared to do it . . . but no—if I'd wanted to, I guess I would
         have. It was in my control." "To the Manner Born, Bush Finds His Own Way,"
         Los Angeles Times, 7/30/99.

144   reporting nowhere for his days of military service: Reporter Walter Robinson
         broke this important story just six days before Election Day 2000: "Questions
         Remain on Bush's Service as Guard Pilot," *Boston Globe,* 10/31/00.

145   "To my knowledge, he never showed up": "Bush Worked on Senate Campaign
         While in National Guard," AP, 5/23/00.

145   "Questions about Mr. Bush's military service": "Governor Bush's Journey: After
         Yale, Bush Ambled Amiably into His Future," *New York Times,* 7/22/00.

150   "If you looked at the TV picture": "Keepers of Bush Image Lift Stagecraft to New
         Heights," *New York Times,* 5/16/03.

150   "The character of our military": Bush aboard the USS *Abraham Lincoln,* FDCH
         Political Transcripts, 5/1/03.

152   "emerged for the kind of photographs": David Sanger, *New York Times,* 5/2/03.

153   "To me, . . . it is an affront": "Senator Byrd Blasts Bush's Use of Aircraft Carrier
         for Victory Speech," AP, 5/6/03.

153   "shouldn't have to be props": Henry Waxman and Robert Menendez on *Hardball*
         with Chris Matthews, MSNBC, 5/8/03.

156   "Mr. President, if I may": Bush press conference, FDCH Political Transcripts,
         10/28/03.

156   "was suggested by those on the ship": "The Note," *ABCNews.com,* 10/29/03,
         quoting that day's *New York Times.*

157   troops' pay raises: Edward Epstein, "Hazardous Duty Pay Cut: Pentagon Poised
         to Slash Pay of U.S. Troops Serving in Volatile Iraq" (op-ed), *Halifax Daily News*
         (Nova Scotia), 8/20/03; Dave Lindorff, "Dishonorable Discharge; Bush Admin-
         istration Slashes Veteran's Benefits," *In These Times,* 12/22/03.

157   "The two intiatives": Karen Jowers, "An act of 'betrayal,'" *Army Times,* 11/11/03
         (http://www.armytimes.com/story.php?f=1-292925-2386496.php).

157   whole airfare covered: "Leave Program Sends Soldiers Home for Visit," *Ft. Riley*
         Post, 10/3/03 (http://64.233.161.104/search?q=cache:0FhVgjVuit4J:www.riley.
         army.mil/newspaper/Archive/100303%2520Post.pdf+troops+air+fare+Iraq+%22
         gateway+airports%22&hl=en&ie=UTF-8); "Army to Reimburse Troops for Air-
         fare," *Stars and Stripes,* European Edition, 1/12/04 (http://www.military.com/
         NewsContent/0,13319,FL_army_011204,00.html).

158   required to pay for their own meals: "No more meal bills for hospitalized troops,"

CNN.com, 10/1/03 (http://www.nexis.com/research/home?_key=1054339 526&_session=954af1f8-92fb-11d7-aba0-c0a8645eaa77.1.3231792326.107120 .%20.0.0&_state=&wchp=dGLbVlb-lSltW&_md5=b7cc2550c00f44dc1a1ee9e fd9a683d5).

158 Only 40,000 of the troops: "U.S. Soldiers Lack Best Protective Gear," *USA Today*, 12/18/03.

158 "I started out investigating": "Northeast Ohio Community Raises Money to Send Soldiers Body Armor," AP, 10/14/03.

158 "perhaps one in four of those killed": Melinda Liu, John Barry, and Michael Hirsh, "The Human Cost," *Newsweek*, 5/3/04.

159 "The Pentagon reported finding": "Pentagon Finds Discrepancies in Halliburton Food Contract," *NBC Nightly News*, 12/12/03.

159 troops who were "mentally unfit," Mark Benjamin, "Army Sent Mentally Ill Troops to Iraq," UPI, 3/12/04.

159 inordinate number of suicides: "Army's Suicide Rate Has Outside Experts Alarmed," *Baltimore Sun*, 12/30/03; "Iraq Troops Suicide Rate Spikes," CBSNews.com, 1/14/04 (http://www.cbsnews.com/stories/2004/01/14/iraq/print able593160.shtml).

159 numerous sexual assaults: "Female GIs Report Rapes in Iraq War," *Denver Post*, 1/25/04.

159 "Variability in pre-deployment screening": Bill Berkowitz, "The Military's Mounting Mental Health Problems," *AlterNet.org*, 4/30/04 (http://www.alternet. org/story.html?StoryID=18556).

160 "You can get shot": "Troops in Iraq Face Pay Cut," *San Francisco Chronicle*, 8/14/03. The entire text of Syverson's remarks is available online at http://www .mfso.org/Syv21.html.

160 *22,000* casualties: Colonel David Hackworth, "Saddam in the Slammer, so Why Are We on Orange?" posted to Hackworth's Web site, "Soldiers for the Truth," 12/29/03 (http://www.sftt.org).

160 40,000 medical evacuations: Commenting on a story about "medevac missions," Brown summed up: "Since the war began, there have been 3,000 of these flights, 40,000 patients. They haven't lost one yet." *NewsNight with Aaron Brown*, 5/5/04, available online at http://www.antiwar.com/blog/index.php?id=P870.

161 "We're here to give you": CNN, 4/16/03.

161 "They don't see the Iraqi people": "British commanders condemn US military tactics," *The Age* (Australia), 4/12/04 (http://www.theage.com.au/articles/2004/ 04/11/1081621835663.html).

162 "US soldiers driving bulldozers": "US Soldiers Bulldoze Farmers' Crops; Americans Accused of Brutal Punishment Tactics against Iraq," Sunday *Independent* (UK), 10/12/03.

162 screen savers on their computers: "US Soldiers Abused Young Girl at Iraqi Prison," ITV (London), 2/7/04 (http://www.itv.com/news/623337.html).

163 "We had no support": "Abuse of Iraqi POWs by GIs Probed," *60 Minutes II*, CBS, 5/6/04 http://www.cbsnews.com/stories/2004/04/27/60II/main614063 .shtml.

163 "The one thing that motivates": "U.S. Troops Mark 9/11 Anniversary as Payback Time," Reuters, 9/11/03.

163 "There's a picture": Bob Graham, " 'I just pulled the trigger,' " *Evening Standard* (London), 6/19/03.

163 "I'm afraid of going": "Delayed Departure Takes Its Toll on Morale," AP, 7/17/03.

164 those who dare to tell the truth: "Take the case of Drew Plummer from North Carolina who enlisted during his last year in high school, just three months before 9/11.

"Home on leave, he joined his father, Lou, at a 'bring our troops home' vigil. Lou Plummer is a former member of the U.S. 2nd Armored Division whose father, unlike Bush, served his country in Vietnam. Asked for his opinion on Iraq by an Associated Press reporter, Drew Plummer replied, 'I just don't agree with what we're doing right now. I don't think our guys should be dying in Iraq. But I'm not a pacifist. I'll do my part.'

"But free speech has a price for the military in the United States these days. The U.S. Navy charged Drew Plummer with violating Article 134 of the Uniform Code of Military Justice: disloyal statements. At his official hearing, he was asked if he 'sympathizes' with the enemy or was considering 'acts of sabotage.' He was convicted and demoted." Robert Fisk, "Attacked for Telling Some Home Truths," *Independent* (UK), 11/26/03.

164 audience of troops had been preselected: "Stars and Stripes is blowing the whistle on President Bush's Thanksgiving visit to Baghdad, saying the cheering soldiers who met him were pre-screened and others showing up for a turkey dinner were turned away.

"The newspaper, quoting two officials with the Army's 1st Armored Division in an article last week, reported that 'for security reasons,' only those preselected got into the facility during Bush's visit. . . . The soldiers who dined while the president visited were selected by their chain of command, and were notified a short time before the visit."

The paper also published a letter to the editor from Sgt. Loren Russell, who wrote of the heroism of his soldiers and then added: "[I]magine their dismay when they walked 15 minutes to the Bob Hope Dining Facility, only to find that they were turned away from their evening meal because they were in the wrong unit. . . . They understand that President Bush ate there and that upgraded security was required. But why were only certain units turned away?" Dana Milbank, "A Baghdad Thanksgiving's Lingering Aftertaste," *Washington Post*, 12/12/03.

164   to upstage a visit to Iraq by Senator Hillary Clinton: "Bush's visit overshadowed a similar one a day later by Senator Hillary Clinton. A source familiar with the planning of her visit said the administration was informed in late September that she would go." "Rice Defends Bush Trip to Iraq," Agence France-Presse, 11/28/03.

Chapter 4
The Wrong Man: II

168   a piece on Bush's plan: "Back Campaigning, Bush Raises $22 Million," *New York Times*, 5/22/03.

168   on October 31, 2003, an article on Bush & Co.'s tendency: "The Struggle for Iraq Reconstruction; Bush Got $500,000 from Companies That Got Contracts, Study Finds," *New York Times*, 10/31/03.

168   a strong lead editorial: "Campaigning in Wartime," *New York Times*, 11/23/03.

169   "complete, thorough and impartial investigation": "Fiske Named Special Counsel in Clinton Probe," *Chicago Tribune*, 1/20/94.

169   "After a review of all": "Text of Statement by Special Counsel," *Washington Post*, 7/1/94.

170   *Fools for Scandal*: Gene Lyons, *Fools for Scandal: How the Media Invented Whitewater* (New York: Franklin Square Press, 1996).

170   "Who could possibly count that high?": E-mail from Bob Somerby, 2/16/04.

172   "He really was their figurehead": Bill White, interviewed on "The Saudi Connection," *The Fifth Estate*, Canadian Broadcasting Corporation, 10/29/03 (http://www.cbc.ca/fifth/conspiracytheories/saudi.html).

172   wealthy Saudi sheikhs: On the Bush family's long and close relationship with the Saudi elite, see Craig Unger, *House of Bush, House of Saud: The Secret Relationship Between the World's Two Most Powerful Dynasties* (New York: Scribner, 2004).

172   "the Arabs": Bill White, interview on "The Saudi Connection," *The Fifth Estate*, Canadian Broadcasting Corporation, 10/29/03.

173   "two heretofore little-noticed deals": Glenn R. Simpson, "Old-School Bookkeeping—Bush Endorsed Deal with Harvard That Helped Harken Transfer Firm's Debt," *Wall Street Journal*, 10/9/02.

174   "obscure, money-losing company": "The Wackiest Rig in Texas," *Time*, 10/28/91.

174   Charles Hostler: Joe Conason, "Notes on a Native Son," *Harper's Magazine*, February 2000.

174 "On June 22, 1990": Hatfield, *Fortunate Son*, pp. 102–3.

175 *Wall Street Journal* reported that delay: "Bush's Son Misses Deadline for Reporting 'Inside' Sale," *Wall Street Journal*, 4/4/91.

176 "the investigation has been": "Richards Wants Bush to Reveal Documents from SEC Inquiry; GOP challenger denies insider trading with Harken Energy stock," *Dallas Morning News*, 10/11/94.

176 Halliburton: Jeff Gerth and Don van Natta, Jr., "In Tough Times, a Company Finds Profits in Terror War," *New York Times*, 7/13/02. The text is online at http://www.commondreams.org/headlines02/0713-07.htm.

176 "The SEC has already": White House Press Releases, 7/16/02 (http://www.white house.gov/news/releases/2002/07/20020716-5.html).

176 "case was dropped": "Bush Predicts Cheney Will Be Cleared; dodges question on his own business deals," AP, 7/17/02.

176 "The securities commission dropped": "Bush Faces Scrutiny over Disclosing '90 Stock Sale Late," *New York Times*, 7/4/02.

177 "The president was cleared": "Bush Defends Cheney in Halliburton Probe," *Houston Chronicle*, 7/18/02.

177 "Will Democrats Turn Harken": "Will Democrats Turn Harken into Whitewater?" *Salon*, 7/27/02 (http://www.salon.com/politics/feature/2002/07/27/harken/index_np.html).

177 "The SEC cleared Bush": "Board Was Told of Risks before Bush Stock Sale Harken Memo Went to SEC after Probe," *Boston Globe*, 10/30/02.

177 "Bush did not do": "Get Cheney: Democrats Try to Hang the Veep with Halliburton," *National Review*, 8/12/02.

177 "The SEC's decision": "SEC Investigation Puts Cheney in Political Peril," *Washington Times*, 7/16/02.

177 "I think the president": *The NewsHour with Jim Lehrer*, PBS, 7/19/02, transcript available at http://www.pbs.org/newshour/bb/political_wrap/july-dec02/sb_7-19.html.

177 "So those things prompted an investigation": *Talk of the Nation*, NPR, 7/8/02, transcript available at http://www.npr.org/ramfiles/atc/20020708.atc.18.ram.

178 "must in no way be construed": Mark Fineman, "Crisis in Corporate America: Why Investigation of Bush's Stock Sale 'Just Didn't Pan Out,'" *Los Angeles Times*, 7/14/02; "Papers Show Bush Knew of a Crisis as He Sold Stock," *Boston Globe*, 7/13/02.

178 Bob Edwards interviewing a defensive James R. Doty: *Morning Edition*, NPR, 7/12/02 (http://www.npr.org/rundowns/rundown.php?prgId=3&prgDate=12-Jul-2002).

179 "The other members of": Joe Conason, "Notes on a Native Son."

179 "more money than I ever dreamed": Ibid.

181 "largest credibility gap": "Kennedy compares Bush to Richard Nixon," Associated Press, 4/5/04.

181 "Ken Lay is a supporter": "President Calls for Review of Pension Regulations and Corporate Disclosure Rules," White House News Transcript, 1/10/02 (http://www.whitehouse.gov/news/releases/2002/01/20020110-1.html).

182 "difficult situation": Kenneth Lay interview, *Frontline*, PBS, 5/22/01, transcript available at http://www.pbs.org/wgbh/pages/frontline/shows/blackout/interviews/lay.html.

183 "The larger point is": "President Reaffirms Strong Position on Liberia," White House News Transcript, 7/14/03 (http://www.whitehouse.gov/news/releases/2003/07/20030714-3.html).

183 "And Paul, if you'll remember": Representative Mike Pence and Paul Begala, *Crossfire*, CNN, 6/11/03.

183 "And of course": Transcript of Rumsfeld speech to House Armed Services Committee, 9/18/02, available at http://www.cnn.com/TRANSCRIPTS/0209/18/se.01.html.

183 "So there clearly is a role in our world for inspections": Donald Rumsfeld on *The NewsHour with Jim Lehrer*, PBS, 9/18/02, transcript available at http://www.pbs.org/newshour/bb/middle_east/july-dec02/rumsfeld_9-18.html.

184 "Why . . . sending thousands of soldiers": Helen Thomas and Ari Fleischer, transcript of White House Daily Briefing, 10/15/03 (http://usinfo.state.gov/topical/pol/terror/02101512.htm).

184 "You said Iraq threw the inspectors out": Douglas J. Feith and interviewers, Department of Defense transcript, 1/24/03 (http://usembassy.state.gov/tokyo/wwwh20030128a9.html).

184 "He gave up his administration": Ann Coulter and Joe Conason on *Paula Zahn Now*, CNN, 10/10/03, transcript available at http://www.cnn.com/TRANSCRIPTS/0309/10/pzn.00.html.

185 "I just don't think": "THE 2100 CAMPAIGN: 2nd Presidential Debate between Gov. Bush and Vice President Gore Transcript," *New York Times*, 10/12/00.

186 "Rebuilding America's Defenses": PDF available at http://www.newamericancentury.org/RebuildingAmericasDefenses.pdf.

186 "the disparity in sentencing": Bush and Candy Crowley on *Inside Politics*, CNN, 1/18/01, transcript available at http://www.cnn.com/TRANSCRIPTS/0101/18/ip.00.html.

187 "I think if we": "Day II, Morning Session of a Hearing of the Senate Judiciary Committee," Federal News Service, 1/17/01.

187 "I want to escalate": *Larry King Live*, CNN, 2/7/01.

187 "According to McCaffrey, Walters": "Bush's Apparent Choice for Drug Czar Anything but Middle of the Road," *Workplace Substance Abuse Advisor*, 5/17/01.

190 John Kampfner had reported the true story: John Kampfner, "Saving Private Lynch Story 'Flawed,' " BBC News, 5/15/03 (http://news.bbc.co.uk/1/hi/programmes/correspondent/3028585.stm).

190 "I'm no hero": Jessica Lynch and Diane Sawyer on *ABC Primetime*, 11/11/03.

191 done nothing to prevent its happening again: Paul O'Neill tried manfully, along with Alan Greenspan, to toughen up the rules for corporate governance, but Bush & Co. ignored their recommendations. See Ron Suskind, *The Price of Loyalty*, pp. 265–306.

191 "the biggest corporate swindler": Glenn Scherer, Common Dreams News Center, 11/15/03 (http://www.commondreams.org/scriptfiles/views03/1115-08.html).

192 "Clean Skies . . . trades real": "Money Talks: Bush's Environmental Record," Friends of the Earth, no date (http://www.foe.org/camps/leg/bushwatch/envrecord.html).

192 "a near-total overhaul of": "Putting H.R. 1904 in Context," Defenders of Wildlife, 10/20/03 (http://www.defenders.org/forests/forest/102003.html).

192 "Under a system": "White House E-Mail System Becomes Less User-Friendly," *New York Times*, 7/18/03.

193 "Over all, it's a very cumbersome process": Ibid.

193 "enhancement": Ibid.

193 "I just want you to know": "Remarks by the President on Homeownership Department of Housing and Urban Development," White House Transcript, 6/18/02 (http://www.whitehouse.gov/news/releases/2002/06/20020618-1.html).

194 "Clinton the Liar and Deciever [*sic*]": Richard Boyden, "Clinton the Liar and Deciever," 2/2/01 (http://www.netanyahu.org/clinliarandd.html).

194 "lying, Jew-collaborating traitor": "Sinking of the *Wilhelm Gustloff*," *Free Speech*, Vol. 4, No. 3, March 1998.

194 "the pathological liar": Christopher Hitchens called Clinton "a pathological liar" on MSNBC's *Hardball* on 5/14/99, and again on 3/29/00. ("You're cold water on the face of a groggy man," host Chris Matthews gushed at the conclusion of the latter interview.) He said it again on *Fox News Sunday* on 3/7/99. ("I think it's alarming to me that we have an amoral man in the White House," Fox fixture Judith Regan chimed in on her program.) Hitchens repeated the charge on Fox's *The Crier Report* on 4/27/99, Catherine Crier excitedly agreeing with his every point. ("Don't you hate that too, by the way?" Hitchens asked her about one of Clinton's putative falsehoods. "I hate that too," Crier replied.)

  Hitchens's view of Clinton's absolute mendacity, and of the Clintons' many other moral failings, is the subject of the former's book, *No One Left to Lie To: The Values of the Worst Family* (New York: Verso, 2000). For an inquiry into Hitchens's own veracity, see Sidney Blumenthal, *The Clinton Wars* (New York: Farrar, Straus and Giroux, 2003), pp. 600–19, 622–23.

194 "We have a President": William Safire, "Clinton's Compulsion," *New York Times*, 5/24/99.

194 "The guy can't tell the truth!": *The Edge with Paula Zahn*, Fox News Network, 10/9/00.

195 "More than anything": "DECISION 2000: The Presidential Race," *New York Post*, 10/20/00.

195 "There are a lot of people": "Election Presidential Debate: The Voters Respond," CNN, 10/11/00.

195 "fib factor": Jonathan Alter, "Al Gore and the Fib Factor," *Newsweek*, 10/16/00.

195 "Why does Al Gore": "Gore's Worst Enemy? Gore," *Tulsa World* (Okla.), 10/12/00.

195 *Daily Howler*: http://www.dailyhowler.com, passim.

195 Erich Segal: Gene Lyons, "Al Gore down on His Farm," *Arkansas Democrat-Gazette*, 6/23/99.

197 Funeralgate: Roses Prichard, "Funeralgate: Bush Charged with Lying under Oath about Influence-Peddling," democrats.com, 7/10/00 (http://www.democrats .com/view.cfm?id=1292); Michael Isikoff, "The Funeral-Home Flap," *Newsweek*, 8/16/99; Robert Bryce and Anthony York, "Did Bush Lie under Oath in Funeral Home Case?" *Salon*, 8/9/99 (http://www.salon.com/news/feature/1999/08/09/ bush/); Molly Ivins, "Up the Ladder, Down the Tubes," *Ft. Worth Star-Telegram*, 8/12/99; Michael Isikoff, "Funeral Case Targets White House Counsel Gonzales," *Newsweek*, 4/21/01; Tamara Baker, "Some Liars Are More Equal Than Others!" *American Politics Journal*, 12/21/01 (http://www.americanpolitics.com/20011221 Baker.html). For further sources, see the Web page "Dubya and the Gravedigger" at Bushwatch.com (http://www.bushwatch.com/gravedigger.htm), especially Jerry Politex, "Will George Waldo's Bandwagon Turn into a Hearse?"

197 "it was infested with gnats": Isikoff, "Funeral-Home Flap."

197 "I'm going to kill all of you": "Spotlight Turns to Bush Aides in Ongoing Texas Funeral Commission Lawsuit," *Death Care Business Advisor*, 5/30/01.

198 "storm-trooper" tactics: "Funeral Agency Ex-Chief Sues Corporation, State," *Austin American-Statesman*, 3/24/99.

198 "Hey Bobby, are those people": Isikoff, "Funeral-Home Flap."

198 "the meeting ended with Allbaugh": "Fired Bureaucrat Claims Governor's Aide, State Lawmakers Tried to Bury Her Probe of Funeral Giant," AP, 3/23/99. The text of Eliza May's affidavit—"Plaintiff's Response to Request for Disclosure," in *Eliza May vs. Texas Funeral Service, et al.*—is online at http://democrats.com/ images/funeralgate/resp-bushrfd.htm.

199 "Allbaugh . . . simply demanded more information": Prichard, "Funeralgate."

199 "Have you got—you and Bob Waltrip": Ibid.

199 "I have had no conversations": Ibid.

200   "A president cannot operate": Floyd G. Brown, *Slick Willie: Why America Cannot Trust Bill Clinton* (Annapolis, Md.: Annapolis Publishing, 1992), p. 37.

200   "To put it plainly": Charley Reese, "Clinton Exhibits All the Classic Symptoms of the Sociopath He Is," *Orlando Sentinel*, 8/23/98.

200   "They were, in fact": Alan Keyes, remarks given at Alabama Republican Assemblies Luncheon, 4/29/00, transcript available at http://www.renewamerica.us/archives/speeches/00_04_29alral.htm.

201   "Bill Clinton, in some ways": Hugh Sidey on *Larry King Live*, CNN, 2/8/01.

203   "ballots without postmarks": David Barstow and Don Van Natta Jr., "Examining the Vote: How Bush Took Florida: Mining the Overseas Absentee Vote," *New York Times*, 7/15/01.

204   "While the conduct of": Vincent Bugliosi, *The Betrayal of America: How the Supreme Court Undermined the Constitution and Chose Our President* (New York: Thunder's Mouth Press/Nation Books, 2001), p. 115.

205   "It was a transparent": "Suit against Cheney Met with Mixed Reactions," *University Wire*, 11/30/00.

205   "As every Texas homeowner knows": Robert Dennis, "Cheney's Problem with the Constitution," *Tompaine.commonsense*, 8/28/00 (http://www.tompaine.com/feature2.cfm/ID/3566).

206   "The propagandist": Jacques Ellul, *Propaganda: The Formation of Men's Attitudes* (New York: Vintage Books, 1973), p. 58.

207   "This man has outspent me!": Debate between Al Gore and George W. Bush, Boston, Mass., 10/3/00, transcript available at http://www.npr.org/news/national/election2000/debates/001003.transcript3.html.

Chapter 5
They Have Met the Enemy

209   "Mr. Madison, cooperating with Mr. Jefferson": Alexander Hamilton, *Works*, ed. Henry Cabot Lodge, 9 vols. (New York: G. P. Putnam's Sons, 1885–86), Vol. 8, p. 251.

210   "interested, ambitious and intriguing": Ibid., Vol. 7, pp. 288, 266, 271.

211   "a man of profound ambition": Ibid.

211   "insanity": Noah Webster, letter to Alexander Hamilton, September 1800; in Harry Warfel, ed., *The Letters of Noah Webster* (New York: Library Publishers, 1953), pp. 225, 226.

211   "Hamilton must have been looking": Dumas Malone, *Jefferson and the Rights of Man* (Boston: Little, Brown, 1951), p. 455.

211   projectivity: For a basic psychoanalytic history of this concept, which Melanie Klein elaborated brilliantly from certain observations by Sigmund Freud, see James S. Grotstein, *Splitting and Projective Identification* (New York: Jacob Aronson, 1981).

212   "When Hitler wrote his second book": Omer Bartov, "He Meant What He Said," *New Republic,* 2/2/04.

212   students of the tyrant's psyche: The first extensive study of Hitler's projectivity is Robert G. L. Waite's *The Psychopathic God: Adolf Hitler* (repr., New York: Basic Books, 1977). See also the analysis by psychiatrist Fritz Redlich, *Hitler: Diagnosis of a Destructive Prophet* (New York: Oxford University Press, 1999), p. 299ff. Also pertinent is Ron Rosenbaum's *Explaining Hitler: The Search for the Origins of His Evil* (New York: Random House, 1998).

212   "So it was that the villain-image": Robert C. Tucker, *Stalin as Revolutionary. 1879–1929* (New York: Norton, 1973), p. 458.

213   "She once dropped by my house": David Brock, *Blinded by the Right: The Conscience of an Ex-Conservative* (New York: Crown Publishers, 2002), p. 209.

214   "The president's pursuers were a bunch": Susan McDougal, *The Woman Who Wouldn't Talk: Why I Refused to Testify against the Clintons and What I Learned in Jail* (New York: Carroll and Graf, 2003), p. 348.

215   "destructive generation": The phrase comes from the title of David Horowitz's anti-countercultural polemic (cowritten with Peter Collier), *Destructive Generation: Second Thoughts about the Sixties* (New York: Free Press Paperbacks, 1996). It was Karl Rove who, prior to the presidential campaign in 2000, introduced George W. Bush to that book and to Myron Magnet's *The Dream and the Nightmare: The Sixties' Legacy to the Underclass* (New York: W. Morrow, 1993). From both volumes the candidate picked up an ideological rationale for his own animus against the counterculture. See Mark Crispin Miller, *The Bush Dyslexicon: Observations on a National Disorder* (New York: Norton, 2001), p. 49.

216   "Less than a minute before": "War Begins in Iraq," *Dallas Morning News,* 4/20/03.

216   "In response to a student's question": "Scalia Requests Ban on Broadcast Media at Talk; City Club giving justice free-speech award," *Plain Dealer* (Cleveland), 3/19/03.

216   "One of the double voters": David Barstow and Don van Natta Jr., "How Bush Took Florida: Mining the Overseas Absentee Vote," *New York Times,* 7/15/01.

217   "I was lifted": Bush was quoted thus by Lionel Chetwynd, who had interviewed the president at length in researching the script for *DC 9/11,* a propaganda telefilm that Chetwynd made for broadcast in September 2003. "Filmmaker Leans Right, Oval Office Swings Open," *New York Times,* 9/8/03.

217   "To take a guy out": Mike Davis, "Urban warfare: Is Iraq a rehearsal for U.S. hoods?" *San Francisco Bay View,* 4/27/04.

217   "I really want to hurt him": "Spins on the Right; Ann Coulter: Light's All Shining on Her," *Hartford Courant,* 6/25/99.

217 "I know something about Bill and Hillary": "When a Special Prosecutor Comes into Your Life," *Washington Times*, 3/10/94.

218 "We will fuck him": Ron Suskind, "Why Are These Men Laughing?" *Esquire*, 1/1/03.

218 "Bush Derangement Syndrome": Charles Krauthammer, "The Delusional Dean," *Washington Post*, 12/5/03.

219 "better watch out if he comes down": "Helms Warns Clinton: 'He'd Better Have a Bodyguard'," AP Worldstream, 11/22/94.

219 "a scumbag": Scott Shuger, "Big Tools," *Slate*, 4/22/98.

219 "traitor": Joe Frolik, "Fightin' Words," *Plain Dealer* (Cleveland), 2/12/95.

219 "slut": "Issa Calls President a 'Slut'," *Bulletin's Frontrunner*, 4/8/98.

219 lightning just might strike her: "Hillary Could Become Trent's Worst Nightmare," *Sun Herald* (Biloxi, Miss.), 11/16/00.

219 Under his office desk at Fox News Channel: Marshall Sella, "The Red-State Network," *New York Times Magazine*, 6/24/01.

219 "Chelsea is a Clinton": John Derbyshire, "Be Very Afraid," *National Review Online*, 2/15/01 (http://www.nationalreview.com/derbyshire/derbyshire021501.shtml).

220 "huge difference": Rush Limbaugh, see p. 112.

220 "He expressed doubt": "Kennedy Says Case for Iraq War Was Fraud," AP, 9/18/03.

221 "the most mean-spirited and irresponsible": Tom DeLay quoted in "As President Bush Requests $87 Billion for Rebuilding Iraq, Democrats Speak Out against Bush's Record," *NBC Nightly News*, 9/24/03.

221 "wrong": Joe Scarborough, *Scarborough Country*, MSNBC, 9/19/03.

221 "As ad hominem attacks go": Lynn Woolley, "Iraq: The Case for Invasion," *NewsMax.com*, 9/29/03 (http://www.newsmax.com/archives/articles/2003/9/29/121047.shtml).

221 "There are many interesting theories": "POLITICAL NOTEBOOK: NH Newspaper Blasts Dean for Comments on Bush and Sept. 11," AP, 9/9/03.

221 forewarned repeatedly: David Talbot, "See No Evil," *Salon*, 5/16/02, http://www.salon.com/news/feature/2002/05/16/knew/index_np.html.

221 Egyptian president Hosni Mubarak: "Egypt Leader Says He Warned America," AP, 12/7/01.

221 Jordan (and also possibly Morocco's): John K. Cooley, "Other Unheeded Warnings before 9/11?" *Christian Science Monitor*, 5/23/02.

221 forewarned by the Mossad: "Israeli Security Issued Urgent Warning to CIA on Large-Scale Terror Attacks," *Daily Telegraph* (UK), 9/16/01.

222 France had warned the FBI: On 9/14/01, *NewsMax.com* reported that "[t]he FBI apparently ignored warnings from French security sources that a French-Algerian

with an avid interest in flight training was a known extremist linked to Osama bin Laden, France's Europe 1 radio reported today, citing French security sources" (http://www.newsmax.com/archives/articles/2001/9/13/171838.shtml).

222 Russia had warned the United States: "Why was Russia's Intelligence on al Qaeda ignored?" *Jane's*, 10/5/01.

222 Germany confirmed that an Iranian: "German Police Confirm Iranian Detainee Phoned Warnings," *Ananova*, 9/14/01 (http://www.ananova.com/news/story/sm_398414.html?menu). This story came up again—again, abroad—a few years later: "German Trial Hears How Iranian Agent Warned US of Impending al-Qaida Attack," *Guardian* (UK), 9/24/04.

222 "political hate-speech": "Gillespie Says Democratic Field Has Taken Presidential Politics to a New Low," *Bulletin's Frontrunner*, 12/3/03.

223 Trent Lott was booed: For a sharp analysis of how the right used Trent Lott's tribulations as a propaganda weapon, see Al Franken, *Lies and the Lying Liars Who Tell Them: A Fair and Balanced Look at the Right* (New York: Dutton, 2003), pp. 177–205.

223 "I know we could have thousands": "Election Vitriol Subsides; Perry, Sanchez ads focus on positive," *Houston Chronicle*, 11/1/02.

223 Jeffords's photo in the urinal: "Heard on the Hill," *Roll Call*, 6/14/01.

224 "We need to execute people": "MEDIA MONITOR: The Thought Cop," *Hotline*, 2/4/02.

224 "We should invade their countries": Ann Coulter, "This Is War," *National Review Online*, 9/13/01.

224 Pakistani Web site: "Shortly after Coulter's column appeared, it resurfaced on the website of the Mujahideen Lashkar-e-Taiba—one of the largest militant Islamist groups in Pakistan—which works closely with al-Qaida. At the time, the Lashkar-e-Taiba site was decorated with an image that depicted a hairy, monstrous hand with claws in place of fingernails, from which blood dripped on to a burning globe of planet earth. A star of David decorated the wrist of the hairy hand, and behind it stood an American flag. The reproduction of Coulter's column used bold, red letters to highlight the sentence that said to 'invade their countries, kill their leaders and convert them to Christianity'. To make the point even stronger, the webmaster added a comment: 'We told you so. Is anyone listening out there? The noose is already around our necks. The preparation for genocide of ALL Muslims has begun. . . . The media is now doing its groundwork to create more hostility towards Islam and Muslims to the point that no one will oppose this mass murder which is about to take place. Mosques will be shut down, schools will be closed, Muslims will be arrested, and executed. There may even be special awards set up to kill Muslims. Millions and millions will be slaughtered like sheep. Remember these words because it is coming. The only safe refuge you have

is Allah.' " Sheldon Rampton and John Stauber, "Trading on Fear," *Guardian* (UK), 7/12/03.

224 "We have been programmed to think": Melik Kaylan, "Dr. Johnson, Meet Ann Coulter!" *Wall Street Journal,* 8/26/02.

226 "the dirtiest campaign in modern presidential politics": "Clark Comes Aboard Kerry Campaign," *New York Times,* 2/14/04.

226 "Liberals have now become as intemperate": Nicholas D. Kristof, "Hold the Vitriol," *New York Times,* 11/12/03.

227 "Clinton is in love with the erect penis": Ann Coulter on *This Evening with Judith Regan,* Fox News Channel, 2/6/00.

229 William Bennett: "William Bennett a Big Gambler," AP Online, 5/2/03; "William Bennett a Gamblin' Man?" *Times-Union* (Albany, N.Y.), 5/3/02; "Bill's $8M Vice; 'Virtues' author hot for casino slots," *Boston Herald,* 5/3/02; Michael Kinsley, "Bad Bet by Bennett," *Washington Post,* 5/5/03.

229 "Casino gambling": Frank Rich, "Tupac's Revenge on Bennett," *New York Times,* 5/18/03.

230 Rush Limbaugh: The story of Limbaugh's drug addiction broke in the *National Enquirer,* and was then picked up, and elaborated, by a range of other media. See the lead article (untitled) in the *Miami Daily Business Review,* 11/18/03; "Limbaugh Medical Records Seized," *Sun-Sentinel* (Ft. Lauderdale, Fla.), 12/5/03; "Raids on Rush Are Detailed," *Newsday* (N.Y.), 12/5/03; "Limbaugh's Attorney Lambastes Prosecutors," *Sun-Sentinel* (Ft. Lauderdale, Fla.), 1/27/04.

231 "Let's all admit": *Rush Limbaugh,* Multimedia Entertainment, Inc., 10/5/95.

231 "OxyContin® has become the number one": "Statement of Asa Hutchinson, Administrator, Drug Enforcement Administration, before the House Committee on Appropriations Subcommittee on Commerce, Justice, State, and Judiciary," 12/11/01, available on the DEA Web site (http://www.usdoj.gov/dea/pubs/cngrtest/ct121101.html).

The Web site also provides some useful context: "With the abuse of OxyContin on the rise, law enforcement authorities throughout the United States are reporting an increase in the number of burglaries, thefts, and robberies of pharmacies and residences. According to authorities, homes are being robbed and individuals are being targeted for their supplies of OxyContin. In some pharmacy thefts, only OxyContin is stolen.

"Illicit OxyContin distribution is not limited to localized distributors as it also includes polydrug trafficking organizations. In the northeastern United States, a gang operating in southern Maine and New Hampshire obtained controlled substances, primarily OxyContin, using forged, stolen, and altered prescriptions. The drugs were illegally obtained from local pharmacies using cash and insurance cards. Gang members redistributed the drugs throughout areas in the Northeast.

"On December 9, 2001, nine armed individuals wearing masks stole over 30,000 bottles of OxyContin from a pharmaceutical distributor in Mexico City. Each bottle contained 30 tablets of the 20-mg dose.

"In Portland, two armed men broke into an apartment and stole the tenant's legitimate supply of OxyContin. In the town of Millinocket, intruders broke into an elderly couple's home to steal their supply of OxyContin. The intruders fled without the OxyContin after the couple put up a struggle.

"On January 7, 2002, the Cliff House Nursing Home in Winthrop was robbed by 2 armed men who held 6 nurses and 40 patients at gunpoint while demanding all of their OxyContin."

232 "I know the sky probably seems brighter": "Rush Limbaugh Returns from Rehab," AP, 11/18/03.

232 "As early as 1984": Gene Lyons and Joe Conason, *The Hunting of the President: The Ten-Year Campaign to Destroy Bill and Hillary Clinton* (New York: Thomas Dunne Books, 2000), pp. 1–8.

233 "made sexual overtones towards her": "Revealed: Willey Worked at White House," *Drudge Report*, 7/29/97 (http://www.drudgereport.com/72997.txt).

233 Drudge is a longtime regular: Brock, *Blinded by the Right*, pp. 282–83.

233 "ABC News Reporter": Antonia Zerbisias, "TV Man Is (Shock) Gay, and (Horror) Canadian," *Toronto Star*, 7/19/03.

233 "Kids who are members of the Trench Coat Mafia": John Aravosis quoted in "Trench Coat Mafia 'Gay' Angle Critiqued," *Gay Today*, 4/23/99 (http://www.gaytoday.badpuppy.com/garchive/world/042399wo.htm).

234 "a spousal abuse past": Sidney Blumenthal, *The Clinton Wars*, pp. 235–36, 239–56.

234 John Fund: Ibid., pp. 472–73.

234 Fund was hauled in by the NYPD: Cynthia Cotts, "Press Clips: John Fund, Come Clean," *Village Voice*, 3/5/02.

234 Fund had been not only Morgan's lover: Morgan Pillsbury's Web site (www.ruthlesspeople.com) presents a wide array of documentary evidence.

235 "He considers gay marriage": Richard Goldstein, "The Real Andrew Sullivan Scandal," *Village Voice*, 6/26/01.

235 "Everything I've read about her": "Dr. Laura Considers Presidential Run," *NewsMax.com*, 6/3/02, http://www.newsmax.com/archives/articles/2002/6/1/181159.shtml.

235 "After first denying that the photos": "A Nude Dr. Laura to Star Again on clublove.com," *Adult Industry News*, 3/28/00 (http://www.ainews.com/Archives/Story438.phtml).

236 Yolanda Schlessinger: "Mother of 'Dr. Laura' Found Dead; The body of radio host's estranged parent was in her Beverly Hills condo for up to two months," *Los Angeles Times*, 12/21/02; "Long Estranged from Her Daughter, Dr. Laura's Mother

Dies Mysteriously," *People*, 1/13/03; Gerald Plessner, "Dr. Laura Should Join Ranks of Those Who Step Down," *San Gabriel Valley Tribune* (Calif.), 12/25/02.

236 "Oh, you're one of the sodomites!": *The Savage Nation*, MSNBC, 7/5/03.

236 *The Enemy Within*: Michael Savage, *The Enemy Within: Saving America from the Liberal Assault on our Schools, Faith and Military* (Nashville: World Net Daily Books, 2003).

236 "We are now living through the equivalent": "Weimar, Once Again," *News Max.com*, 10/14/99 (http://www.newsmax.com/articles/?a=1999/10/14/43453).

237 "Michael Savage": David Gilson, "Michael Savage's Long, Strange Trip," *Salon*, 3/5/03 (http://www.salon.com/news/feature/2003/03/05/savage/index_np.html).

237 "Eventually, Trueblood": Ibid.

238 "Id-control was the basis": David Frum, *The Right Man: The Surprise Presidency of George W. Bush* (New York: Random House, 2003), p. 57.

238 "I looked the man in the eye": "Putin Urges Bush Not to Act Alone on Missile Shield," *New York Times*, 6/18/01.

238 "I very much enjoyed our time together": Bush with Vladimir Putin in Slovenia, 6/16/01.

239 the elder Bush is just as dedicated to . . . the CIA: See Kevin Phillips, *American Dynasty: Aristocracy, Fortune, and the Politics of Deceit in the House of Bush* (New York: Viking, 2004).

239 "He is a physical fitness person": Bush in Crawford, Tex., 8/25/01.

240 "And it's my honor": Bush with Vladimir Putin at a high school in Crawford, Tex., 11/15/01.

240 "We want to make sure that their ability": Bush with South Korean President Kim Dae-Jung, White House, 3/7/01.

241 "I love freedom": Bush with South Korean President Kim Dae-Jung, Seoul, Korea, 2/20/02.

241 "No question, when he walked": Howard Fineman, "Sniff Some Politics," *Newsweek*, 5/27/02.

242 "I loathe Kim Jong Il": "A Course of 'Confident Action'; Bush says other countries will follow assertive U.S. in combating terror," *Washington Post*, 11/19/02.

243 "I do not need to explain": Ibid.

243 "This is a man who continually lies": Bush at reception for Senate candidate John Cornyn, Houston, Tex., FDCH Political Transcripts, 9/26/02.

243 "These are the actions of a regime": Bush press conference, FDCH Political Transcripts, 3/6/03.

244 "What do you make of the fact": Bush at swearing-in of SEC chairman, Washington, D.C., 2/18/03.

244 "I don't spend a lot of time taking polls": Bush press conference, White House, 11/7/02.

244 "This is a man . . . who has made the United Nations": Bush in Alamagordo, New Mexico, 10/28/02.

245 "Mr. President, looking ahead here": Bush speaking to press pool in Crawford, Tex., 12/31/02.

246 "There's no doubt his hatred": Bush at reception for Senate candidate John Coryn, Houston, Tex., FDCH Political Transcripts, 9/26/02.

246 Iraqi plot to assassinate the elder Bush: Seymour Hersh, "A Case Not Closed," *New Yorker*, 11/1/93; Scott Shane, "FBI Lied to Clinton about Iraqi Assassination Attempt on Bush Sr.," *Baltimore Sun*, 3/2/03.

247 "Four months ago": Peggy Noonan, "Just the Facts," *Wall Street Journal*, 1/27/03.

247 "Cheney, say those who know him": Michael Isikoff, Mark Hosenball, and Evan Thomas, "Cheney's Long Path to War," *Newsweek*, 11/17/03.

247 "After all . . . he stayed in power": Bush press conference, Washington, D.C., 12/15/03.

248 "We are resolved": Bush, delivering remarks at "Teach for America" event, Atlanta, Ga., FDCH Political Transcripts, 1/31/02.

248 "The more we value the ability": Bush speaking on conservation and "forest health," Jackson Suny Fairgrounds Central Point, Ore., 8/22/02.

248 "**Our most important job**": Bush at fund-raiser for Senate candidate Lamar Alexander, Jr., Nashville, Tenn., FDCH Political Transcripts, 9/17/02.

249 "They understand it doesn't matter": Bush at campaign rally, Alamagordo, N.M., 10/28/02.

249 "The second pillar of peace": Bush at Whitehall Palace, London, 11/19/03.

249 "**No, the enemy hit us**": Bush speaking on terrorism insurance, Washington, D.C., 10/3/02.

Chapter 6
The Clear and Present Danger

251 James argues: This speculative profile is worth quoting at some length: "Bush's deep hatred, as well as love, for both his parents explains how he became a reckless rebel with a death wish. He hated his father for putting his whole life in the shade and for emotionally blackmailing him. He hated his mother for physically and mentally badgering him to fulfill her wishes. But the hatred also explains his radical transformation into an authoritarian fundamentalist. By totally identifying with an extreme version of their strict, religion-fuelled beliefs, he jailed his rebellious self. From now on, his unconscious hatred for them was channeled into a fanatical moral crusade to rid the world of evil." Oliver James, "So, George, How Do You Feel about Your Mom and Dad?" *Guardian* (UK), 9/2/03.

251 "Saddam Hussein has gassed his own people": Samantha Power, *"A Problem from Hell": America and the Age of Genocide* (New York: HarperCollins, 2002), pp. 171–245.

252 Zbigniew Brzezinksi: Interview with Brzezinski published in *Le Nouvel Observateur* (Paris), 1/15–21/98. The entire exchange is online at http://www.global research.ca/articles/BRZ110A.html.

253 "The word Christianity": Thomas Paine, "Of the Word 'Religion' and Other Words of Uncertain Signification" (1804), in Norman Cousins, ed., *"In God We Trust": The Religious Beliefs and Ideas of the American Founding Fathers* (New York: Harper & Row, 1958), pp. 171–245.

254 *godless* Constitution: Isaac Kramnick and R. Laurence Moore, *The Godless Constitution: The Case Against Religious Correctness* (New York: W. W. Norton, 1997).

254 "It does me no injury": Thomas Jefferson, *Notes on Virginia* (1782) in *Jefferson: Writings*, p. 285.

254 "Where the preamble declares": Thomas Jefferson, *Autobiography*, in *Thomas Jefferson: Writings*, p. 40.

255 "We were": William Lee Miller, *The First Liberty: America's Foundation in Religious Freedom* (Washington: Georgetown University Press, 2002), p. 3.

255 "1st. Quakers": Kramnick and Moore, *The Godless Constitution*, p. 33.

256 "Can serious": Yale president Timothy Dwight in a Federalist pamphlet, 1800, quoted in James F. Simon, *What Kind of Nation: Thomas Jefferson, John Marshall and the Epic Struggle to Create a United States* (New York: Simon & Schuster, 2003), p. 267.

256 "the just vengeance of insulted heaven": Quoted in John C. Miller, *The Federalist Era, 1789–1801* (New York: Harper, 1960), p. 265, no. 34.

256 "GOD—AND A RELIGIOUS PRESIDENT": Ibid.

256 "The floodgates of calumny": TJ to Uriah McGregory, *Writings of Thomas Jefferson* (1907), X, 171.

257 "I do not know that it": TJ to Benjamin Rush, September 23, 1800, in *Jefferson: Writings*, pp. 1081–82.

258 "To vote for Bill Clinton": Quoted in Frederick Clarkson, *Eternal Hostility: The Struggle Between Theocracy and Democracy* (Monroe, Maine: Common Courage, 1997), p. 7.

259 "Reconstructionism argues": Frederick Carlson, *Eternal Hostility*, p. 78.

260 "The Christian goal for the world": David Chilton, Ibid.

260 "Now man needs regeneration": R. J. Rushdoony, *The Institutes of Biblical Law*, I (Nutley, N.J.: Craig Press, 1973), p. 725.

261 "We live in a deeply": P. Andrew Sandlin, "Christian Culture Today, Not Yesterday or Tomorrow," Chalcedon Foundation, 11/5/01 (http://www.chalcedon.edu/ articles/0111/011105sandlin.shtml).

261 Reconstructionists also condemn those Christians: A. Shupe, "Christian Reconstructionism and the Angry Rhetoric of Neo-Postmillennialism," in T. Robbins and S. Palmer, eds., *Millennium, Messiahs, and Mayhem: Contemporary Apocalyptic Movements* (New York: Routledge, 1997), p. 196.

261 "They feel that the power": Ontario Consultants on Religious Tolerance, "Christian Reconstructionism," no date (http://religioustolerance.org/reconstr.htm).

262 "All who are content": Rushdoony, *The Institutes of Biblical Law*, 2 vols. (Vallecito, Calif.: Ross House Books, 1982), Vol. 2, p. 468.

262 "The Right's quiet": from the Remnant Saints' Intercontinental Congress Web site, on its page linking to the CNP Web site, http://www.rsicc.org/Links/Coun cilforNationalPolicy.

263 Marvin Olasky: Joseph L. Conn, "Compassionate Conservative?: Marvin Olasky and 'Biblical Law' in America," *Church and State*, October 2000 (http://www.au .org/churchstate/cs10008.htm).

263 "[w]hile Scripture": Marvin Olasky, *Fighting for Liberty and Virtue: Political and Cultural Wars in Eighteenth-Century America* (Wheaton, Ill.: Crossway Books, 1995), p. 299, n. 741.

263 Olasky by Karl Rove: James Moore and Wayne Slater, *Bush's Brain: How Karl Rove Made George W. Bush Presidential* (New York: Wiley, 2003), pp. 167, 169, 202, 252.

265 "Well, I—": Brit Hume, interview with President George W. Bush, Fox News Channel, 9/23/03.

265 "a broad cause": Ari Fleischer, White House briefing, 9/18/01.

266 "a very evil and": "Franklin Graham Conducts Services at Pentagon," CNN, 4/18/03 (http://www.cnn.com/2003/ALLPOLITICS/04/18/graham.pentagon/).

266 "They want to coexist": "Pat Robertson Describes Islam as Violent Religion That Wants to Dominate, Destroy," AP, 2/22/02.

266 "I think Muhammad was": "Falwell Calls Islam's Prophet a 'Terrorist' in Television Interview," AP, 10/3/02.

266 "stand with us": Bush addressing troops in Anchorage, Alaska, 2/16/02, FDCH Political Transcripts.

266 "I'm surely not": "You know, he is," Bob Woodward, *Plan of Attack*, pp. 379, 421.

266 God told him to run: Bush has said this to many intimates, including Christian reconstructionist James Robinson; Ed Young, his Houston pastor; and Richard Land, director of the Southern Baptist Convention. Aaron Latham, "How George W. Found God," *George*, September 2000; "The Jesus Factor," *Frontline*, PBS broadcast on April 29, 2004, and available online at http://www.pbs.org/wgbh/ pages/frontline/shows/jesus.

266 God told him to strike al Qaeda . . . occupy Iraq: "**God** told me to strike at al Qaeda and I struck them, and then he instructed me to strike at **Saddam [Hus-**

sein], which I did, and now I am determined to solve the problem in the Middle East. If you help me I will act, and if not, the elections will come and I will have to focus on them." Thus spake Bush to Mahmoud Abbas, Palestinian prime minister, on June 23, 2003. First reported in *Ha'aretz*, the statement went largely unreported in the U.S., although some columnists dealt with it: Al Kamen, "Road Map in the Back Seat?" *Washington Post*, June 27, 2003, online at http://www.washingtonpost.com/ac2/wp-dyn/A37944-2003Jun26?language=printer.

266   "I haven't suffered doubt": Woodward, *Plan of Attack*, 420.

267   "George sees this": Peter Schweitzer and Rochelle Schweitzer, *The Bushes: Portrait of a Dynasty* (New York: Doubleday, 2004), p. 517.

267   "a Christian nation"; "appointed by God"; etc.: William A. Arkin, "The Pentagon Unleashes a Holy Warrior," *Los Angeles Times*, 10/8/03.

268   "Southern Baptists must understand": Mike Creswell, "Southern Baptists Must Do More with Iraq 'Open Door,' " International Mission Board, 12/5/03 (http://www.imb.org/urgent/articledetail.asp?urgentID=57).

268   "The Iraqi people are in a state": "Muslim Groups' Fears over Iraq Missionaries," BBC News (online), 4/29/03 (http://news.bbc.co.uk/2/hi/middle_east/2983433.stm).

269   Jibla Baptist Hospital: "Fired Missionaries Top Baptist News of 2003," *ABP News*, 12/4/03 (http://www.abpnews.com/abpnews/story.cfm?newsId=4006&srch=1).

269   40 "Christian Zionists": " 'Christian Zionists' Resist Bush on Mideast Peace," *Buffalo News*, 8/17/03.

269   "There has been a real lack": Rick Perlstein, "The Jesus Landing Pad," *Village Voice*, 5/18/04.

270   "When the world sees": Greg Bahnsen, "Cross-Examination: The Place of the Jews in Prophecy," *The Counsel of Chalcedon* 14:4 (June 1992), available at http://www.cmfnow.com/articles/pt139.htm.

270   "The war on terror": Tom DeLay, "Be Not afraid: Providential Terms," speech delivered before Israel's Knesset on 7/30/03, text available at *National Review Online* (http://www.nationalreview.com/comment/comment-delay073003.asp).

271   "An advocate": "Bypassing Senate for the Second Time, Bush Seats Judge," *New York Times*, 2/21/04.

271   "the worst abomination": "Democrats Grill Appeals Nominee Pryor," AP, 6/11/03.

272   "prostitution, adultery": "Bush Appoints Opposed Judge," *Miami Herald*, 2/21/04.

272   "If the Supreme Court says": "Sen. Rick Santorum's Comments on Homosexuality in an AP Interview," AP, 4/22/03.

273   "the wife is to subordinate": "Attack on Judicial Nominee Leads Panel to Delay Vote," *New York Times*, 4/11/03. The author (or coauthor, as his wife Susan collaborated on the article) was James Leon Holmes, former president of Arkansas

Right to Life, and Bush's nominee for a position on the Federal District Court in Little Rock.

274 Dr. Joseph Stanford . . . Dr. David Hager . . . the FDA: Susan J. Douglas, "The Real American Taliban," *In These Times*, 3/3/03.

274 a special audience including Lou Sheldon: "For G.O.P., It's a Moment," *New York Times*, 11/6/03.

274 Ashcroft sought to subpoena: "U.S. Lawyers Seek Abortion Records, Stir Privacy Debate," *Chicago Tribune*, 2/12/04.

274 "decency campaign": See the report of the U.S. Senate Committee on Commerce, Science and Transportation, outlining the new FCC Reauthorization Act of 2003, available at http://www.congress.gov; also see Thea Domber, "Media Cares about Money, Not Morality," *University Wire*, 2/27/04.

275 200 TV programs "inappropriate": Dan Moffett, "Censor Scooby-Doo? Words Fail," *Palm Beach Post*, 2/8/04. The full list of the programs concerned is posted on the Web site for the National Association for the Deaf (http://www.nad.org/openhouse/action/alerts/captioningcensorship/list.html).

275 "We are increasingly": R. J. Rushdoony, *The Mythology of Science* (Nutley, N.J.: Craig Press, 1967), pp. 56, 57, 58.

275 "That man is called to dominion": Ruben C. Alvarado, "Environmentalism and Christianity's Ethic of Dominion," *Journal of Christian Reconstruction* 11 (1986–87): 201–15. The pertinent work by Gary North is Appendix A ("From Cosmic Purposelessness to Humanistic Sovereignty") in *The Dominion Covenant: Genesis* (Tyler, Tex.: Institute for Christian Economics, 1982).

Alvarado and North represent the "Wise Use" approach to nature, which wields considerable influence in the Bush administration. "Wise Use" is but one of several evangelical Christian responses to environmentalism. For a thorough survey, see Jim Ball, "The Use of Ecology in the Evangelical Protestant Response to the Ecological Crisis," *Perspectives on Science and Christian Faith* 50 (March 1998):32–40.

276 "God gave us the earth": *Hannity & Colmes*, Fox News Channel, 6/20/01.

277 "My purpose . . . is total integration": "Ahmanson Bankrolls Religious Right's Agenda," *Los Angeles Times*, 10/19/92.

277 Clinton's State Department file: "Prosecutor to Probe Search of Clinton's Passport File," *Los Angeles Times*, 12/18/92; "White House Tied to Passport Case," *Chicago Daily Law Bulletin*, 12/21/92.

277 "a Chinese plan to subvert": "China Had Plans to 'Subvert' Our Election Process, Chairman Says," AP, 7/8/97.

279 "smooth the transition to Christian": Gary North, "Symposium on Social Action," *Journal of Christian Reconstruction*, Vol. 8, no. 1, Summer 1981.

279 Rushdoony . . . of Rahab: R. J. Rushdoony, *Institutes of Biblical Law* (Vallecito, Calif.: Craig Press, 1973), I, p. 566.

279 "Sometimes you have to go above": "Highlights of Hall's Testimony, Hamilton's Statement," *Washington Post,* 5/3/78.

279 "What Ollie North did": Frederick Clarkson, *Eternal Hostility,* p. 123.

280 "We are no longer working": "A Profile in Granite: The Canal Treaties and the New Right," *Washington Post,* 3/3/78.

280 "One booklet on political tactics": "Bush Team Freely Mixes (Christian) Church, State," *Daily Comet* (Boulder, Colo.), 4/26/03.

280 "that lying is necessary": Brock, *Blinded by the Right,* p. 54; David Farris' defense of North: Frederick Clarkson, *Eternal Hostility,* p. 123.

280 "Christo-fascism": David Neiwert, "Rush, Newspeak, and Fascism," posted at Orcinus on 8/30/03 (http://www.cursor.org/stories/fascismintroduction.php).

280 "the only German emigrant": Gerhard Spörl, "The Leo-Conservatives," tr. Christopher Sultan, *Der Spiegel,* 8/4/03. http://www.spiegel.de/spiegel/english/0,1518,259860,00.html.

281 "those who are fit to rule": Drury quoted in Jim Lobe, "Leo Strauss' Philosophy of Deception," AlterNet, 5/19/03, http://www.alternet.org/story.html?StoryID=15935.

281 "the worst possible thing": Ibid.

281 "leads to individualism": Jet Heer, interviewed on "The Brian Lehrer Show," WNYC-FM, 5/22/03, http://www.nyc.org/shows/bl/episodes/05222003.

282 "I think in this case international law": Bush in Britain: War Critics Astonished as US Hawk Admits Invasion Was Illegal," *Guardian* (UK), 11/20/03.

282 "Most leading Reconstructionists": Frederick Clarkson, "Christian Reconstructionism: Theocratic Dominionism Gains Influence," in Chip Berlet, ed., *Eyes Right! Challenging the Right Wing Backlash* (Boston: South End Press, 1995), p. 65.

283 "The key to the John Birch Society's effectiveness": Rushdoony, *Institutes of Biblical Law,* p. 747.

283 "It is now clear we are facing": Report on the Covert Activities of the Central Intelligence Agency, also known as the Doolittle Report, 9/30/54, Appendix A. *The Complete Doolittle Report* (Washington, D.C.: Infantry Journal Press, 1946).

284 "It may become necessary": Stephen Ambrose, *Ike's Spies: Eisenhower and the Espionage Establishment* (Jackson, Miss.: University Press of Mississippi, 1999), p. 188.

284 "had no intention of declaring": H. W. Brands, *The Devil We Knew: Americans and the Cold War* (New York: Oxford University Press, 1993), p. 61.

285 "The Florida elections": Val Finnell, "Slash and Burn Politics," posted in February 2001, on the Web site of the Chalcedon Foundation (http://www.chalcedon.edu).

285 "I find myself thinking of Al Gore": "Mama Bush Raps the Dems," *Daily News* (N.Y.), 10/16/03.

286 "Like it or not": Pat Robertson quoted in *Church & State*, 11/1/00.

287 "At last—some sense": ShopNetDaily.com (http://www.shopnetdaily.com/store/
item.asp?ITEM_ID=1340).

287 "God has a plan for the conquest": R. J. Rushdoony, *God's Plan for Victory: The
Meaning and Post-Millennialism* (Fairfax, Va.: Thoburn Press, 1977), p. 76.

288 "What do you say to the people": "An Interview with David Limbaugh about His
New Book, 'Persecution: How Liberals Are Waging War Against Christianity',"
Right Wing News (http://www.rightwingnews.com/interviews/Limbaugh.php).

289 "No Muslims = No Terrorists": Michelle Goldberg, "Shock Troops for Bush,"
Salon, 2/4/03 (http:www.salon.com/news/feature/2003/02/04/cpac/index_np
.html).

289 "a makeshift carnival game": Ibid.

290 "scorecard" of al Qaeda operatives: "Bush Keeps Terror Photo 'Scorecard'," AP,
2/3/02.

290 "All told, more than 3,000": Bush State of the Union Address, 1/28/03, available
at the White House Web site (http://www.whitehouse.gov/news/releases/2003/
01/20030128=19/html).

291 "We're tracking down terrorists": Bush addressing Department of Homeland
Security employees, Washington, D.C., 2/28/03.

Conclusion

294 "deficits don't matter": Ron Suskind, *Price of Loyalty: George W. Bush, the White
House, and the Education of Paul O'Neill* (New York: Simon and Schulster, 2004),
p. 291.

294 "CO2 is not a pollutant": Andrew Gumbel, "U.S. Says CO2 Is Not a Pollutant,"
Independent on Sunday (London), 8/31/03.

295 "You know . . . I think one of the most defining moments": Bush speaking on
American history and civics, East Literature Magnet School, Nashville, 9/17/02.

295 Todd Beamer . . . final phone call: Lisa Beamer with Ken Abraham, *Let's Roll:
Ordinary People, Extraordinary Courage* (Wheaton, Ill.: Tyndale House, 2002),
pp. 186–87.

296 "Is there no virtue among us?": James Madison, "Speech in the Virginia Ratify-
ing Convention on the Judicial Power," June 20, 1788; reprinted in Rakove,
Madison: Writings, p. 398.

296 "The only principles of public conduct": James Otis, "Against Writs of Assistance," February 24, 1761, available at http://www.constitution.org/bor/otis_
against_writs.htm.

297 "Now, the American people have got": Bush press conference, White House,
10/11/01.

297 "We need an energy bill": Bush at National Guard base, Trenton, New Jersey, 9/23/02.

297 a staged chat with figure skater Sasha Cohen: Alan Balch, "Why Did Bush Sit next to Sasha Cohen at the Olympics? Just Ask, 'Where's the Beef?'" *BuzzFlash*, 2/26/02 (http://www.buzzflash.com/contributors/2002/02/022602_Cohen_Beef.html).

297 TV spot for the Travel Industry Association of America: "Bush's Star Role in TV Travel Ad May Shine On," *Wall Street Journal*, 12/12/01.

297 No president has done more product placement: Bush has even done such placement to enrich not just his campaign but *himself*. On the way home from his pilot act on the flight deck of the *Abraham Lincoln*, he stopped off in Santa Clara, California, for a visit to the headquarters of United Defense Industries (UDI), manufacturer of the Bradley fighting vehicle (then starring in Iraq) and a subsidiary of the Carlyle Group, the giant holding company that, at the time, employed the elder Bush. Repeatedly Bush Junior linked the company to the soldiers in the field, in statements perfect for UDI's annual report and/or promotional videos: "We are proud of everybody who wears the nation's uniform, and we are proud of those who have contributed to the defense of the country, just like the people right here at United Defense have done," Bush said to wild applause. ("You not only help save lives," Bush also said, "but you're an agent for peace.") Such naked shilling for his father's company, and in the afterglow of his triumphant dance aboard the aircraft carrier, amounted to mere cashing in, as Carlyle's fortunes would undoubtedly affect his own eventual inheritance. (Bush at United Defense Industries, Mountain View, CA, 5/3/03; "Bush Lauds Contractor, Presses His Tax Cuts," *Philadelphia Inquirer*, 5/3/03.) The fishiness of Bush's move came up at a May 8, 2003, White House press briefing, where Ari Fleischer laughed it off:

> REPORTER: The president was in Santa Clara last week and he appeared at United Defense, a major defense contractor controlled by the Carlyle Group. The president's father is a paid adviser to the Carlyle Group. So you have a situation where the president is there touting the products of the company that directly benefits, financially, his father. Why isn't that unethical?
>
> FLEISCHER: If the question is, are Bradley fighting vehicles part of what the military does that should be supported, the answer is, of course, yes, regardless of who serves on Carlyle.
>
> REPORTER: But what if the president's father was like the president of United Defense, would that be unethical?
>
> FLEISCHER: What if the president's father was on Social Security and the president wanted to strengthen the Social Security program—[laughter]—so all Americans could have a strong retirement? Connie?

After Fleischer's comments, everyone else moved on. The issue was then mooted when George Bush finally cut his ties to Carlyle in October of 2003.

297 Bush stopped off at a Home Depot: "Home Depot executives, employees and their families have given more than $1.5 million to the GOP since 1999, most of it in 'soft money,' before that practice was outlawed last year. The company's political action committee has also already contributed $31,000 directly to the Bush-Cheney 2004 re-election campaign."

"Buried in two small paragraphs on page 710 of the massive, stalled energy bill is a measure that would lift a tariff on Chinese-made ceiling fans—with Home Depot being the largest retailer of said fans. The measure, inserted during a closed-door conference committee and undebated in either house of Congress, would save Home Depot and other smaller companies about $48 million, at taxpayer expense, of course." Public Citizen elaborated on the tight connection between Home Depot and the White House: "Home Depot CEO Robert Nardelli, who flew up from Atlanta on December 5 to join Mr. Bush, has made at least three trips to the White House since 2001; Home Depot's number-two person, Executive Vice President Francis Blake, left his job as Bush's deputy energy secretary in 2001 to work for Home Depot; and Karen Knutson, wife of Home Depot's top in-house lobbyist Kent Knutson, was a former top aide to Vice President Dick Cheney and deputy director of Cheney's secret energy task force." Public Citizen, "Presidential Mystery Solved: Why Is Bush Stopping at Home Depot?" 12/4/03 (http://www.citizen.org/pressroom/release.cfm?ID=1600).

298 "Nothing is more important": "The Budget Fight Is Now" [editorial], *New York Times*, 4/3/03.

298 "The story of what we've done in the postwar period": "Nethercutt Hails Iraq's Recovery," *Seattle Post-Intelligencer*, 10/12/03. Nethercutt charged that the newspaper had misquoted him; the editors stood by their story. "Nethercutt Alleges P-I Distorted Speech on Iraq," *Seattle Post-Intelligencer*, 10/28/03.

298 "[W]hy should we hear about body bags": Barbara Bush with Diane Sawyer on *Good Morning America*, ABC, 3/18/03.

299 "You have neither the light of faith": James Madison, "Who Are the Best Keepers of the People's Liberties?" *National Gazette*, December 12, 1792; reprinted in Rakove, *Madison: Writings*, p. 534.